BLUE GUIDE

MUSEUMS & GALLERIES OF LONDON

Tabitha Barber
and
Charles Godfrey-Faussett

Somerset Books • London
WW Norton • New York

Blue Guide Museums & Galleries of London
Fourth edition

Published by Blue Guides Limited, a Somerset Books Company
49–51 Causton St, London SW1P 4AT
www.blueguides.com
'Blue Guide' is a registered trademark

ISBN 1–905131–00–3

A CIP catalogue record of this book is available from the British Library.

Published in the United States of America by
WW Norton and Company, Inc
500 Fifth Avenue, New York, NY 10110
USA ISBN 0–393–32729–9

The author and the publisher have made reasonable efforts to ensure the accuracy of all the
information in this book; however, they can accept no responsibility for any loss, injury or
inconvenience sustained by any traveller as a result of information or advice contained in it.

Cover images: Top: Sir Anthony van Dyck: *James Stuart, Duke of Richmond and Lennox* (1636)
Courtesy of English Heritage Photographic Library (Kenwood: The Iveagh Bequest);
Bottom: *The Toilet of Venus* ('The Rokeby Venus'; c. 1647–51) by Diego Velázquez; © The National
Gallery, London; presented by the National Art Collections Fund, 1906
Title page: Detail from the façade of the Natural History Museum
Spine: Geffrye Museum (photo: Hadley Kincade)
All other acknowledgements, photo credits and copyright information are given
on p. 384, which forms part of this copyright page.

About the authors

Tabitha Barber has a degree in History of Art from the Courtauld Institute. She worked for English
Heritage and Historic Royal Palaces before taking up a position at the Tate Gallery in 1992, where
she is curator of 17th- and 18th-century British art, specialising in the period 1650–1730. She
worked on the exhibition *Dynasties: Painting in Tudor and Jacobean England 1530–1630* (Tate Gallery,
1995) and curated an exhibition on Mary Beale (Geffrye Museum, 1999). She is currently working
on the permanent collection catalogue of Tate's Tudor and Stuart collection.

Charles Godfrey-Faussett has lived in London for the last 18 years. A graduate of Oxford
University, he has written general travel guides to Edinburgh, London and England, and contributed
to a number of magazines and newspapers, including *Country Life*, *Heritage Today* and *The Times*.

CONTENTS

INTRODUCTION

by Marina Vaizey

London, the biggest city in the British Isles, and a city since Roman times, is, in the 21st century too, Britain's political and cultural capital, and her richest metropolis. But her past is as important as the present and the future. For several centuries London was also the capital of the world's biggest and most diverse Empire. And for the first half of the 19th century London was not only the world's most populous city but also its biggest mercantile and financial capital. It has been host not only to waves of migration, but also to a spectrum of visitors from every known part of the planet. This long and often successful history is the basis for its hundreds of museums and galleries, its leadership in the art market, and the extraordinarily comprehensive national collections. Quality is outstanding, and variety is paramount: single-subject museums may be just as delightful, several significantly devoted to the outstanding characters of British culture, while the universal museums enshrine in both depth and breadth the history of the world expressed through its objects, both natural and man-made.

And we can start with pre-history. Animatronic dinosaurs, lunging at the visitor with their jaws outstretched, may be admired with a frisson of excitement in the enormous Victorian pile of the Natural History Museum in South Kensington. A few miles away in the East End of London, a series of 19th-century dolls' houses with perfect Victorian interiors are appropriately housed in one of the world's first prefabricated buildings, put up in Kensington, reinstalled in Bethnal Green, and admired more than a century ago by the novelist Henry James as a splendid cabinet of curiosities. Musical instruments from all over Africa are on coherent display in a south London park, in the Horniman Museum, one of London's two Art Nouveau buildings still extant. Boats from the South Seas, hundreds of shrunken heads, scores of Egyptian mummies, and three million prints and drawings including masterpieces by Michelangelo and Leonardo, Rubens and Rembrandt, van Gogh and Picasso are among the millions upon millions of artefacts in the British Museum, which also has the best single collection of Japanese art in Europe. The British Museum also happens to be one of the three universal museums in the world—the others being the Louvre in Paris and the Metropolitan in New York—and the most comprehensive, embracing man's known history from almost the earliest conscious form of art making to the arts of the present day.

But finding your way through the millennia of natural and human history on display in the hundreds of London's museums and galleries is a challenge. The purpose of this publication is to act as a comprehensive and comprehensible guide book, a vade mecum, a companion to help you on your way to the collections which are outstanding on a world scale, as well as those smaller specialist collections which will appeal to particular tastes and interests.

London on the Thames estuary, situated on the southeast of a small island, and a natural port, was founded by the Romans—who always had a good eye for such things. Nearly 2,000 years later, after surviving the great plagues and great fires and great wars that punctuate its history, London has become as famed for its culture as for its past. It is celebrated and condemned in almost equal measure by writers and poets, from Geoffrey Chaucer to Charles Dickens, who perhaps above all others took London as his subject: its fogs, its dustheaps, and its glories. From the diaries of Samuel Pepys to John Betjeman, the poet of suburbia, London has captured the creative imagination. There is practically no great British literary figure untouched by the city. And many a foreigner—Dostoyevsky, Herman Melville, Karl Marx—has also felt its lure. London has nurtured its own artists, and perhaps the greatest of all British artists was born at its heart: Turner, who was born in Covent Garden, and died by the Thames. And artists visited, too: some of the most poetic visual evocations of the Thames and Westminster, as well as the suburbs of London, are by the Impressionists, from Monet to Pissarro.

The praise of London began early: 'Among the noble cities of the world that are celebrated by Fame, the City of London, seat of the Monarchy of England, is one that spreads its fame wider, sends its wealth and wares further, and lifts its head higher than all others.' Thus the monk William Fitzstephen in 1174, in *A Description of the Most Noble City of London*. The poetic Fitzstephen also noted that London's 'mild sky doth soften the hearts of men'. By the 18th century Dr Samuel Johnson famously observed that 'You find no man, at all intellectual, who is willing to leave London. No, Sir, when a man is tired of London, he is tired of life; for there is in London all that life can afford'. At the beginning of the 20th century, in 1904, the politician Joseph Chamberlain was still able to observe, in a public speech to the grandees of the financial centre of the British capital, that London was the clearing-house of the world.

The portable objects of the earth's history follow wealth and power; and it is London's long history combined with its few centuries as capital of the world that has enabled the formation of the collections and their public display. But perhaps above all, the spectrum of museums and galleries echo the command that was the title of a well known Victorian book of knowledge: ENQUIRE WITHIN UPON EVERYTHING. There are several museums and galleries which long antedate the foundation of most modern boundaries of nation states. The British Museum was founded in 1753—well before the United States, Italy, and Germany assumed their modern boundaries; the Dulwich Picture Gallery, the first picture gallery in London open to the public, was founded in 1814. The National Gallery began in 1824. A little late, compared to the Louvre, which was founded in 1793 in the wake of the French Revolution. But the National Gallery was not based on a royal collection opened to the public; London's collections, even when running costs and buildings have been financed by the public purse, have depended almost exclusively on private benefaction.

What is pertinent to the present period of the 21st century are two new aspects for the continued liveliness of London's museums and galleries. One echoes the dicta of the 19th-century polymath Sir Henry Cole (inventor of the adhesive postage stamp and moving spirit behind the Victoria & Albert Museum). Sir Henry felt that visitors to museums should have their body nourished and cared for, as well as their spirit, and to that end determined not only that cafés and restaurants should be provided, but also sanitary facilities as up to date as possible. The Victoria & Albert was also founded as an educational institution, as a museum which housed exemplars of the finest designs the world over, as examples of excellence in order to raise the standards of commercial manufacture in the country that had launched the industrial revolution.

This is echoed in the current concern to widen the remit of museums and galleries, large and small, to provide on the one hand extensive educational opportunities for all ages and backgrounds, and on the other, comfortable places to eat, and also—perhaps even more understandably in our capitalist age—to expand the ubiquitous shop. The shops not only extend the collections by means of reproductions, postcards, videos and books but also of course offer souvenirs pertaining to the works on view, and sometimes original art and craft, not to mention designs, inspired by works in the collection. Thus original prints and multiples connected to individual artist's exhibitions are often commissioned at the Serpentine and the Whitechapel art galleries, while artists design for Tate Britain everything from tea towels to coffee mugs, or provide original prints for sale. In the major galleries shops can be enormous, leading several scholars to liken the rise of the museum to that of the department store, with a variety of departments providing something for everybody. And when the moment comes for the visitor to pause, you can choose between bangers and mash at the Geffrye or the best chocolate brownies in London at the V&A.

The menu, in other words, is not a set menu to be taken in one sitting. It is *à la carte*: just pick and choose what tickles your fancy. *Bon appétit!*

MUSEUMS & GALLERIES

ALEXANDER FLEMING LABORATORY MUSEUM

St Mary's Hospital, Praed Street, Paddington, W2 1NY
Tel: 020-7886 6528
www.st-marys.nhs.uk/about/fleming_museum.htm
Open Mon–Thur 10–1 (other times by appointment)
Admission charge. No disabled access
Tube/Station: Paddington
Shop
Map p. 380, 1B

This small museum includes a reconstruction of the small, cramped laboratory where Alexander Fleming (1881–1955) discovered penicillin on 3rd December 1928. In 1906 Fleming had joined the research department at St Mary's as assistant bacteriologist to Sir Almroth Wright. While working on staphylococci bacteria, Fleming noticed that a mould had grown on some of his culture dishes and that colonies of staphylococci could not survive near it. He correctly surmised that the mould was producing an anti-bacterial chemical. The mould was identified as *penicillium notatum*, which had produced what is now known as penicillin. Fleming published his research in 1929 but it was not until 1938 that it was developed further, by Professor Howard Florey and Dr Ernst Chain of Oxford University, who worked towards purifying the compound. Their work resulted in the commercial manufacture of penicillin in the USA, and the full realisation of its importance to world medicine. Fleming, Florey and Chain were awarded the Nobel Prize for medicine in 1945. Displays and videos tell the story of Fleming and his revolutionary drug.

ALL HALLOWS UNDERCROFT MUSEUM

Byward Street, EC3 5BJ
Tel: 020-7481 2928; www.allhallowsbythetower.org.uk
Open Mon–Fri 11–4, Sat–Sun 11–5 (church is open longer hours)
Free
Tube: Tower Hill
Map p. 383, 2F

This historic church was largely destroyed in the Second World War but the brick tower, the only example of Cromwellian church architecture in London, has survived. It was from here, on 5 September 1666, that Pepys surveyed the destruction of the Great Fire:

London: viewed from the steps of the National Gallery.

'I up to the top of Barkeing steeple, and there saw the saddest sight of desolation that ever I saw. Everywhere great fires. Oyle-cellars and brimstone and other things burning.' The tower is now surmounted by a spire in the manner of Wren by Lord Mottistone of Seely & Paget (1958). Mottistone was also responsible for the rest of the church's post-war reconstruction with, internally, a ribbed perpendicular-style vault of grey concrete. Bomb damage revealed ancient Anglo-Saxon fabric, probably 11th-century. Of particular note is the font cover, an outstandingly beautiful piece of limewood carving by Grinling Gibbons (1682) with cherubs, flowers and delicate ears of wheat. In 1922 All Hallows became the guild church of Toc H, a registered charity which, in the words of its own manifesto, is 'committed to building a fairer society by working with communities to promote friendship and service, confront prejudice and practise reconciliation'. It was founded in the same year by the church's new vicar, 'Tubby' Clayton. In the sanctuary is the tomb of Alderman John Croke (d. 1477) with a casket, a 1923 Arts and Crafts piece by Alec Smithers, containing the Toc H parent Lamp of Maintenance.

The Undercroft museum, entered under the tower, was excavated by Mottistone. There are remains of two tesselated Roman pavements from a 3rd- or 4th-century villa, ashes of Roman London, burned by Boudicca in AD 61, a Roman tombstone and the cosmetic equipment of a Roman lady. Also displayed are fragments of three Saxon crosses, the most important of which, c. 1030–60, is inscribed with the name 'Werhenworth' and has remains of figure carving, including an image of Christ. At the east end is a memorial chapel containing the ashes of members of Toc H and a plain medieval altar table from the Crusader castle of Chastiau Pelerin at Athlit, Palestine.

APSLEY HOUSE
THE WELLINGTON MUSEUM
(English Heritage)

Hyde Park Corner, 149 Piccadilly, W1J 7NT
Tel: 020-7499 5676; www.apsleyhouse.org.uk
Open Tues–Sun 11–5
Admission charge
Tube: Hyde Park Corner (Exit 3)
Shop
Map p. 381, 2D

Surrounded and isolated by busy traffic, Apsley House overlooks Hyde Park Corner, which in the 18th and 19th centuries was the most important entry into London from Kensington and Knightsbridge. Known as 'No. 1 London', as the first house to be encountered after the turnpike, it was the London residence of Arthur Wellesley, 1st Duke of Wellington (1769–1852), the famous 'Iron Duke', victor of Waterloo and Prime Minister from 1828–30. The house has been open to the public since 1853, but in 1947 it and part of its contents were offered to the nation by the 7th Duke. In 1952

Elegant Neoclassicism surrounded by traffic: No. 1 London.

it opened as the Wellington Museum, with a private apartment reserved for the family (still the case today).

The Building

Originally built by Robert Adam in 1771–78 for Lord Apsley, later 2nd Earl Bathurst, Apsley House has undergone several alterations. In 1807 the new owner, the 1st Marquess Wellesley, Wellington's elder brother, commissioned works from James Wyatt; in 1819 Benjamin D. Wyatt remodelled some interiors—chiefly the dining room—for Wellington, who had purchased the house from his brother; and in 1826–30 Wyatt and his brother Philip undertook further lavish improvements. It was in this latter stage that the house was faced with Bath stone, the large Corinthian portico added and the 90-ft Waterloo Gallery constructed, where, from 1830, the magnificent annual Waterloo Banquets took place to mark the anniversary of the great victory. By 1831 the Duke had apparently spent £64,000 on improvements and Wyatt's bill was three times over the original estimate, for which he was 'abused furiously'.

Apsley House is the only historic London mansion to retain the majority of its contents. Guided by inventories, early photographs and watercolour views, trouble has been taken to restore the interiors to how they would have been in Wellington's day. Throughout the house are trophies and decorations, magnificent presentation silver and ceramics, battlepieces, and portraits and sculpture busts of the duke and his illustrious contemporaries. Together they form a remarkable visual record of the Napoleonic period. Even in Wellington's day it was remarked that Apsley House was more a museum than a home.

Tour of the House

The majority of Wellington's magnificent collection of presentation silver and porcelain can be found in the **Plate and China Room** on the ground floor. Chief of the exhibits are the 'Wellington Shield' (c. 1822), designed by Thomas Stothard and made by Benjamin Smith; and the standard candelabra (1816–17), again by Smith, splendid pieces of silver-gilt presented to Wellington by the bankers and merchants of the City. Together with the silver-gilt 'Waterloo Vase' (1824–25), also designed by Stothard, they stood on Wellington's sideboard at the Waterloo Banquets. The principal porcelain services are the the the Sèvres 'Egyptian Service' (1809–12), its astonishing centrepiece based on the Temples of Karnak, Dendera and Philae, commissioned by Napoleon as a divorce present for the Empress Josephine, rejected, and presented to Wellington by Louis XVIII in 1818; and the 'Prussian Service' (Berlin porcelain factory 1816–19), its plates, vases and ice buckets decorated with scenes from the Duke's glorious campaigns, presented by Frederick William III of Prussia. Wall frames contain gold and silver swords and daggers, including Napoleon's court sword, Wellington's own Waterloo sword and the c. 1790 Indian sword of Tipu Sultan (*see p. 333*), a relic of Wellington's military career in India, taken after the siege of Seringapatam. The porcelain collection continues in the basement, where Wellington's death mask and several of his costumes can also be seen, as well as his magnificent collection of orders, decorations and medals, including the Garter, the Golden Fleece and the Danish Order of the Elephant.

Beyond the Inner Hall, Adam's old entrance hall, is the **Staircase**. Remodelled by Wyatt after 1826 and rising the full height of the house, its cast iron stair-rail curves round Canova's astonishing 11-ft 4-in sculpture of a nude Napoleon, holding a small figure of Victory in the palm of his hand. Carved in 1802–06 from a single block of Carrara marble, it was disliked by Napoleon (allegedly because the Victory appeared to be flying away) and stored in the Louvre until 1816, when it was purchased by the British Government and presented to Wellington by the Prince Regent.

Upper floor

The rooms upstairs are the main showpiece apartments, some of which retain their Adam features under the white and gold redecoration favoured by Wyatt, some transformed by Wyatt in 18th-century French taste. The carpeting is a modern reweaving based on a fragment of the original discovered in the attics of the Duke's country house, Stratfield Saye, and some of the wall hangings reproduce the original fabrics. These rooms also contain Wellington's large picture collection. The Duke enjoyed pictures. He purchased at auction (mainly Dutch 17th-century art) and was a generous

Marble statue of Napoleon holding a winged Victory, by Canova (1802–06).

patron of contemporary British artists. Some of the finest pictures, however, are from the Spanish Royal collection. Numbering over 80, including works by Correggio, Murillo, Rubens and Velázquez, they were discovered rolled up in Joseph Bonaparte's captured baggage train following the French defeat at the Battle of Vitoria in 1808. In 1816 they were presented to the Duke by Ferdinand VII of Spain. In some rooms the pictures are hung on Wellington's system of gilded chains in the positions they occupied in Wellington's day.

The **Piccadilly Drawing Room** contains some of the finest 17th-century Dutch pictures in the collection, many from the Spanish Royal collection, including Elsheimer's *Judith and Holofernes* (c. 1601–03), an exquisite small oils-on-copper which once belonged to Rubens, and an important group of works by Teniers the Younger. Also here is a small panel by Juan de Flandes, one of a series of 47 which belonged to Isabella of Castile, Queen of Spain (d. 1504). The most celebrated work, from a British point of view, is David Wilkie's *Chelsea Pensioners reading the Waterloo Despatch*, commissioned by Wellington in 1816 and completed in 1822, for which he paid £1,260. The scene is set in the King's Road, Chelsea, with the Royal Hospital to the left. When exhibited at the Royal Academy it created a massive stir and a protective barrier had to be erected. In the *Portico Drawing Room*, with its Adam 'Cupid and Psyche' chimneypiece, hang portraits of Napoleon and the Empress Josephine, as well as four large copies after Raphael or his followers by Féréol Bonnemaison, the originals having been removed from the Escorial to Paris in 1813 by Joseph Bonaparte. On their return to Spain in 1815 (they are now in the Prado), Wellington arranged to have the pictures restored and copied .

The grand **Waterloo Gallery**, in Louis XVIII style with heavy gilding, was designed by Wyatt to house the majority of the Duke's pictures. It was here, from 1830–52, that the magnificent Waterloo Banquets took place. The east windows have mirrored shutters which, when drawn, transform the room into a supposed Galerie des Glaces: with the lighted candles and richly adorned table, it must have been a sumptuous spectacle. For the walls Wellington apparently insisted on yellow damask, considered by his close friend and confidante Mrs Arbuthnot 'just the very worst colour he can have for pictures'. The 2nd Duke changed the scheme to red. According to the artist William Frith, it was the Duke's 'small weakness' when he had guests to identify the pictures in turn without consulting the catalogue. In his time 130 pictures hung here, but today there are only 70. As well as Dutch 17th-century pieces, by Brueghel and Steen, are Italian works by Guercino, Giulio Romano and Correggio (*The Agony in the Garden*, the Duke's favourite painting, one of the Spanish Royal pictures); several by Velázquez, again Spanish Royal pictures, including the excellent *Waterseller of Seville*; Flemish pieces by van Dyck and Rubens; and Goya's equestrian portrait of Wellington, a large but rather hasty work painted in August–September 1812, the likeness based on the chalk sketch Goya made of the Duke soon after the British army entered Madrid after the Battle of Salamanca. X-rays show that the head is painted over that of another sitter.

In the **Yellow Drawing Room** is Canova's marble bust of a dancer, presented to Wellington by Canova in 1817, and Wilkie's full length *William IV*, presented to

Wellington by the King in 1833. Wyatt's **Striped Drawing Room**, the 'Walhalla', is filled with portraits of British commanders—and adversaries—who fought in the Napoleonic wars, including Lawrence's dashing portrait of Wellington (1815); and Sir William Allan's *Battle of Waterloo* (1815), seen from the French side as it stood at 7.30 pm on 18 June 1815, when Napoleon, on the right, was making his last desperate efforts to turn the allied armies. Wellington found it 'Good—very good; not too much smoke'. The **Dining Room**, created by Wyatt in 1819 and decorated with yellow scagliola pilasters, was where the Waterloo Banquets were held before 1830. On the table is the 26-ft silver parcel gilt centrepiece of the 'Portuguese Service', originally consisting of some 1,000 pieces, presented to Wellington by the Portuguese Council of Regency in 1816. On the walls are full-length portraits of European monarchs, including Wilkie's *George IV*.

In front of the house stands Boehm's equestrian bronze statue of Wellington, with four soldiers at the corners, erected in 1888. In Hyde Park, northwest of the house, is Westmacott's 18-ft bronze *Achilles*, cast from cannon captured at the Battles of Salamanca, Vitoria, Toulouse and Waterloo. It cost £10,000 and was paid for by 'the women of England'. The Wellington Arch (*see p. 343*), on its traffic island, can also be visited (joint tickets with Apsley House possible).

BANK OF ENGLAND MUSEUM

Threadneedle Street, London EC2R 8AH
Tel: 020-7601 5491; www.bankofengland.co.uk/education/museum
Open Mon–Fri 10–5
Free. Limited disabled access
Tube: Bank
Shop
Map p. 383, 2E

The museum charts the rise of the Bank of England from its private, 17th-century origins (founded in 1694 with a staff of 19) to the powerful institution it is today. Nationalised in 1946, it is the central bank of the United Kingdom, is banker to the Government, manages the country's foreign exchange and gold reserves and sets the country's interest rate. The Bank was established on its present site in 1734 but the building was expanded and largely rebuilt by Sir John Soane (*see p. 267*), its appointed architect and surveyor from 1788–1833. Soane's building, which reflected the Bank's growing size and increasingly pivotal position in the City, was his masterpiece. Foreign dignitaries were brought to view its magnificence, and in 1805 Soane conducted Queen Charlotte and her children on what must have been an exhausting two-hour tour. Its demolition and reconstruction by Sir Herbert Baker in 1921–39, albeit along Soane's principles, resulted in a major architectural loss.

Soane wrapped the Bank in a sheer, blind curtain wall, with columns and pilasters at its corners and entrances, and a good sense of this has been retained. The entrance to the museum is on Bartholomew Lane. Off the entrance hall is a reconstruction, by Higgins Gardner 1986–88, of Soane's famous Stock Office, with its flattened dome and top lighting through yellow glazing. It was in this room that the ownership of Bank of England Stock was transferred. Behind the mahogany counter and its wax-work clerks are displays outlining the architectural history of the building. The stat-ue of William III, by Henry Cheere, was commissioned by the Bank in 1732 to mark the opening of its new Threadneedle Street site. Off this room are displays explaining the Bank's early history. Its original 1694 Charter is on view, as is the Minute Book of the first Court of Directors, and correspondence with early shareholders (e.g. Washington and Nelson). In the centre of Baker's impressive 1930s Soane-inspired Rotunda, with caryatids and columns saved from the old building, are imitation gold bars, with one (very heavy) real one, which visitors are invited to handle. Beyond this is a display of the Bank's unique collection of banknotes, along with original designs, issued from the late 17th century onwards, a development from the 17th-century handwritten receipt. The final room explains the work of the Bank today.

BANKSIDE GALLERY

48 Hopton Street, SE1 9JH
Tel: 020-7928 7521; www.banksidegallery.com
Open daily 11–6 during exhibitions
Usually free
Tube: Blackfriars/Southwark
Bookshop
Map p. 383, 3D

A modern, airy building designed by Fitzroy, Robinson and Partners, with fine views of the river and St Paul's Cathedral, and with Tate Modern nearby, Bankside Gallery opened in 1980 and is home to the Royal Watercolour Society (founded 1804) and the Royal Society of Painter-Printmakers (founded 1880). Both have a distinguished histo-ry, the former attracting members such as John Sell Cotman, John Varley, Edward Burne-Jones and John Singer Sargent, the latter Laura Knight, Walter Sickert and Graham Sutherland. The Painter-Printmakers, formerly known as the Royal Society of Painter-Etchers and Engravers, was formed to promote recognition for etchers, engravers and mezzotinters, who at the time were not eligible for membership of the Royal Academy (printmaking being deemed a reproductive, not a creative, process). Selections from the collection of diploma works, given to the Societies by artists on their election to mem-bership, are sometimes on display. The Printmakers have their annual exhibition in May, the Watercolour Society an exhibition every spring and autumn. Otherwise, the gallery has a changing programme of contemporary watercolour and original print exhibitions.

BANQUETING HOUSE
(Historic Royal Palaces)

Whitehall Palace, Whitehall, SW1A 2ER
Tel: 0870 751 5178; www.hrp.org.uk
Open Mon–Sat 10–5 (sometimes closed for official functions)
Admission charge. Partial disabled access
Tube: Westminster/Charing Cross
Small shop
Map p. 382, 3B

The Banqueting House is the most obvious and complete remnant of the old royal Whitehall Palace, which occupied a vast area from St James's Park to the river, and from Charing Cross to Parliament Square, and was the principal residence and seat of government of the Tudor and Stuart monarchy (16th and 17th centuries). The residential part of the palace was almost totally destroyed in a disastrous fire in 1698, but the Banqueting House was saved.

Erected on the site of an old Elizabethan banqueting house, which had been rebuilt in 1606 but destroyed by fire in 1619, the new structure (1619–22) was to be a fitting setting for festive occasions, formal spectacles and grand court ceremonials. A committee was formed to plan the new building, which was designed by the great architect Inigo Jones. Jones's approach to architecture, based on classical Roman models, the mathematical principles of Vitruvius and the pure designs of the Renaissance architect Palladio, was revolutionary in Britain (*see p. 27*). His strict use of the orders, Ionic below and Corinthian above, the alternate triangular and segmental window pediments, and the internal double cube proportions of the main hall, produced a rational, measured and dignified building of tremendous impact. Externally the building has been altered: sash windows were installed in 1713, and in the 19th century it was given a Portland stone façade. Internally, however, it has been restored to how it would have appeared in early Stuart times, a fitting stage for state occasions such as the international marriage negotiations conducted by James I and the reception of foreign ambassadors. The king and court could enter from the north, from the palace's Privy Gallery, where the throne, under its symbolic canopy of state, was erected. For state occasions, when magnificence was required, the walls below the gallery were hung with rich tapestries which blocked the windows. The public was admitted from the south, the entrance approached up a timber staircase (the present entrance and staircase were added by James Wyatt 1808–09—note the sculpture bust of James I by Hubert Le Sueur, commissioned by James's son Charles I in 1639).

The Rubens Ceiling
Peter Paul Rubens, an artist of international fame fêted by the courts of Europe, and whom the Stuart monarchy was eager to engage, seems to have been approached as early as 1621 to paint the great compartmentled ceiling. But, diverted to Paris to deco-

The Apotheosis of James I. Detail from the Rubens ceiling in the Banqueting House (1630–34).

rate the Palais Luxembourg for Catherine de' Medici, it was not until 1629–30, after James I had died and when Rubens was on a diplomatic mission to London as an emissary of the King of Spain, that he was officially commissioned. In London Rubens presented to Charles I his great painting *Peace and War* (National Gallery; *see p. 208*) and was knighted. The nine Banqueting House canvases were painted in Antwerp in 1630–34 and then sent to London where they were installed by 1636 (Rubens was paid £3,000 and never saw the works *in situ*). The theme of the magnificent Baroque scheme, the like of which Britain had never seen, was the glorification of the peaceful rule of James I. Over the centuries the paintings have seen a succession of restoration campaigns, the last taking the opportunity to rearrange the canvases in the order intended by Rubens. Entering from the south, the viewer is immediately struck by the central oval, the *Apotheosis of James I* (*pictured above*), the king borne heavenwards by Religion and Justice, his temporal crown carried by putti while Minerva (wisdom) holds out a wreath of laurel. Flanking this are two friezes of exuberant putti, symbolic of the peace and prosperity of James's reign. Above the throne, visible the right way round to the visitor entering from the south, is the *Benefits of the Government of James I*. Peace and Plenty embrace, Minerva defends the throne against Mars (war), who in turn tramples enemies about to be banished to Hell. On either side are ovals with the *Triumph of Reason over Discord* and *Triumph of Abundance over Avarice*. At the north end, visible to the king seated on his throne, is the *Union of England and Scotland*, James I gesturing towards a child, the new-born union of the two countries, while Britannia holds the joined crowns above his head. To left and right are *Minerva driving Rebellion to Hell* and *Hercules beating down Envy*. Rubens' masterly allegory celebrates James I's wise government and the Stuart adherence to the divine right of kings but also, through its extolling of peace, alludes to the recent Anglo-Spanish peace negotiations.

On the installation of the pictures, the Banqueting House ceased to stage court masques or theatrical spectacles which involved flaming or smoking torches which would have harmed Rubens' works. But with its revolutionary architecture, its painted masterpieces symbolic of the nature of Stuart government and its function as a setting for state occasions, the Banqueting House assumed a potent iconic status. Several architectural designs for a new Whitehall Palace retained the Banqueting House at their heart. Quite deliberately, it was where Charles I was executed (on 30th January 1649), led from the staircase window to the scaffold erected against its walls. Charles II continued to use the Banqueting House for solemn state occasions. It was here that the sovereign touched for the King's Evil, an ancient ceremony performed for those with scrofula, last performed by Queen Anne (mid-18th century); and it was also where the Maundy Thursday ritual of the washing of the feet of the poor, and distribution of money, was performed by the monarch. After the 1698 fire, however, William III had the building converted into the Chapel Royal, a function retained until the 1890s when it became the Royal United Services Institute museum. It is now used for formal royal and state occasions and banquets.

BARBICAN ART GALLERY

Barbican Centre, EC2
Tel: 020-7638 8891; www.barbican.co.uk
Open Mon, Wed, Fri, Sat–Sun 11–8; Tues, Thur 11–6
Admission charge
Tube: Barbican/Moorgate
Restaurants and shops
Map p. 383, 1D

The Barbican Centre is part of a vast residential, commercial and arts complex covering a 35-acre site, including within its boundaries the church of St Giles Cripplegate and medieval stretches of old City wall. It takes its name from an old fortification just outside the City limits, destroyed in the 13th century. The complex was conceived in the 1950s, an optimistic post-war era of social town planning, but building work— to the designs of Chamberlin, Powell & Bon—did not commence until 1963 and was completed only in 1982. As well as residential apartments, the Barbican was to incorporate a theatre for the Royal Shakespeare Company, a concert hall for the London Symphony Orchestra, and an art gallery. In addition, there are conference facilities, a studio theatre (The Pit), a public library and two cinemas.

The Barbican is a complicated and uncompromising building of pre-fabricated concrete on a monolithic scale, its various blocks surrounding a central lake with hanging plants and fountains, the whole connected by terraces and pedestrian walkways. Orientation is notoriously confusing. If approaching the complex from Moorgate, you should follow the yellow painted lines on the ground—a concept similar to using string in the Minotaur's labyrinth. A more fool-proof route is to leave Barbican tube station, cross over Aldersgate and walk up the rather forbidding Beech Street. A right turn towards its end leads round to the Barbican Centre's main Silk Street entrance. An architectural upgrading of the entrances and foyers is underway, the aim to improve navigation. A number of art works are on display in the public spaces, including Roubiliac's bust of Shakespeare.

The Barbican Art Gallery, on level 3, is one of London's major temporary exhibition venues. The space is spread over two floors, the upper overlooking the lower, sometimes filled with one exhibition but more usually two separate ones with a linked theme. The six to seven exhibitions a year concentrate mainly on 20th-century and contemporary art, design, photography and fashion. Changing displays (free) also take place in The Curve, on the ground floor.

BEN URI GALLERY
THE LONDON JEWISH MUSEUM OF ART

108a Boundary Road, St John's Wood, NW8 0RH
Tel: 020-7604 3991; www.benuri.org.uk
Open Mon–Thur 10–5.30, Fri 10–5.30 (summer) or 10–3 (winter),
Sun 12–4. Closed Sat
Tube St John's Wood/Kilburn Park
Map p. 379, 2D

Founded in 1915 by Leon Berson, a young Russian-born Jewish artist, with the aim 'to form a permanent collection of works by Jewish artists that would enrich and ennoble the Jewish population', the Ben Uri Gallery has a collection of around 1,000 works by over 200 British and European Jewish artists, mainly of the 19th and 20th centuries. Gallery space is small, so only selections from the collection can be shown. They include works by Frank Auerbach, Jacob Epstein, Leon Kossoff and R.B. Kitaj; a self-portrait by Max Liebermann, Solomon J. Solomon's *Micha Elman Playing the Violin* (1912), David Bomberg's *At the Window* (1919) and Mark Gertler's *Rabbi and Rabbitzin* (1914). Gertler was the model for one of the characters in D.H. Lawrence's *Women in Love*. Always sensitive, he committed suicide after an unsuccessful exhibition in 1939.

BENJAMIN FRANKLIN HOUSE

36 Craven Street, WC2N 5NF
Tel: 020-7930 9121; www.thersa.org/franklin
At the time of writing, due to open shortly
Tube: Charing Cross
Map p. 382, 3B

This elegant Georgian town house, built in 1730 and now edging the west side of Charing Cross Station, is the only surviving home of Benjamin Franklin, the great American statesman and scientist, and is where he lived almost continuously from 1757–75. The house was owned by the widow Margaret Stevenson, and Franklin rented the principal rooms. It was here that he sat at the windows 'air bathing', learnt to play the harp, guitar and violin, and conducted political negotiations with William Pitt the Elder on the eve of the American Revolution. While in London Franklin forged friendships with many leading intellectuals. He was a member of the Royal Society of Arts, not far from this house, on John Adam Street (*see p. 256*), and continued with his many writings and experiments, including the invention of the lightning conductor (it is also said that he conducted alarming demonstrations of electricity at dinner parties). When the Friends of Benjamin Franklin House took over the building in the 1970s, it was in a state of dangerous disrepair. The house, which retains its original staircase and much of its panelling, has undergone a meticulous restoration, during which a pit with human remains was discovered in the basement—probably connected to the anatomy school run by Franklin's friend William Hewson, Margaret Stevenson's son-in-law. Hewson is said to have died of blood poisoning after cutting himself during a dissection.

BETHLEM ROYAL HOSPITAL ARCHIVES AND MUSEUM

Monks Orchard Road, Beckenham, Kent, BR3 3BX
Tel: 020-8776 4307; www.bethlemheritage.org.uk
Open Mon–Fri 9.30–5
Free
Station: Eden Park (from Charing Cross, Waterloo East or London Bridge)
Map p. 379, 4E

The Bethlem Royal Hospital museum was established in 1970 as part of the combined Bethlem Royal Hospital and Maudsley Hospital, a postgraduate psychiatric teaching hospital. Bethlem is the original 'Bedlam', founded in 1247 as a priory hospital which, by 1377, was caring for 'distracted' patients. The art collection specialises in works by artists who have suffered from mental health problems, many of whom were patients at

Bethlem. The most important and prized items are works by the Victorian artist Richard Dadd, best known for his meticulous and intricate fairy paintings. By 1843 Dadd was suffering periods of delusion and unpredictable violence, which culminated in the premeditated murder of his father in Cobham Park. In 1844 he was admitted to the criminal lunatic department of Bethlem Hospital, then located at St George's Fields, Southwark (the central part of which is now the Imperial War Museum; *see p. 130*). Isolated from the world and never fully to regain his reason, Dadd continued to paint, an occupation which sustained him for the next 40 years until his death in 1886 at Broadmoor Hospital, where he had been transferred in 1864. The museum also has works by Jonathan Martin, the brother of the more famous John Martin, painter of the apocalyptic sublime (*see p. 293*). Jonathan Martin achieved celebrity in 1829 when he set fire to York Minster, after which he was committed to Bethlem for the rest of his life. Also on show are two 17th-century sculptures, *Raving* and *Melancholy Madness*, powerfully realistic nudes which once decorated the entrance gates to Bethlem Hospital's new 1675–76 building in Moorfields. The sculptures are the best and most famous surviving works of the Danish-English sculptor Caius Gabriel Cibber, who worked for a time under Sir Christopher Wren, notably at Hampton Court (*see p. 109*).

BETHNAL GREEN MUSEUM OF CHILDHOOD
(Victoria & Albert Museum)

Cambridge Heath Road, Bethnal Green, E2 9PA
Tel: 020-8980 2415; www.vam.ac.uk/vastatic/nmc
Open daily except Fri 10–5.50
Free
Tube: Bethnal Green
Café and shop
Map p. 379, 2E

The Museum of Childhood, a branch of the V&A, opened in 1872 as the Bethnal Green Museum, satisfying a desire first raised in 1851, in the wake of the Great Exhibition, to establish a museum in the East End to serve a less privileged part of London. The framework of the building is in fact a section of the Iron Building erected in 1857 as part of the South Kensington Museum, as the V&A was then known. The Iron Building was a prefabricated structure consisting of an iron frame clad externally with corrugated metal. It was a problematic building which leaked when it rained, and its three spans were quickly nicknamed the Brompton Boilers. In 1866 it was partially dismantled and re-erected in Bethnal Green, but with an outer façade of red brick designed by J.W. Wild. A series of mosaic panels decorate its two long sides, scenes representing Agriculture (e.g. Ploughing, Harvesting, Sheep Shearing) on one side, Art and Science on the other, all to the designs of Frank Moody. They were made by female students of the South Kensington Museum Mosaic Class under the supervision of Minton's. Inside, the museum reveals its delicate iron framework, its spacious central hall overlooked on either side by upper-level balconies. The mosaic floor was laid by female prisoners. Bethnal Green originally displayed the collection of Animal and Food Products transferred from South Kensington; its focus on childhood and children dates only from the 1920s when its Keeper, Arthur Sabin, encouraged school visits and actively collected material relating to childhood. In 1974 the museum was officially redefined and is now recognised as the National Collection of Childhood.

The Collection

The museum has one of the largest and oldest collections of children's toys, spanning 400 years of childhood. It has over 1,400 dolls, beginning with a fine wooden doll of about 1680. There are toy soldiers, teddy bears and board games including some of the first jigsaw puzzles (giant Snakes and Ladders can be played in the Games Area). Its collection of dolls' houses is internationally famous and includes the Nuremberg dolls' house of about 1673; 'Mrs Bryant's Pleasure', with fine Victorian miniature furniture; and 'Whiteladies', a Modernist house. There is a collection of puppets, both British (notably Punch and Judy) and international (examples from Germany and Central Europe, India, China, Japan etc.) and a collection of toy theatres including an 18th-century Venetian marionette theatre. The recently re-displayed Mezzanine Galleries show the museum's collection of moving toys: a magnificent rocking horse (which can be ridden), train sets, humming tops and gravity-powered cars. Many can be activated by visitors, but those that cannot can be seen in motion at computer terminals.

On the top floor are galleries concentrating on the social history of childhood, embracing topics such as 17th-century childbirth, and growing up throughout the ages. Nursery furniture is on display as well as the museum's excellent collection of children's clothes, which includes the entire wardrobe (c. 1840) of Henrietta Byron.

As well as its permanent collection and activities for children (in addition to those mentioned above, there is a sand pit and dressing-up area), the museum also has a programme of temporary exhibitions focusing on childhood, the history of toys and children's authors such as Beatrix Potter.

BLACK CULTURAL ARCHIVES

378 Coldharbour Lane, Brixton, SW9 8LF
Tel: 020-7738 4591
Exhibitions open Mon–Sat 10.30–6
Tube: Brixton
Map p. 379, 3E

Black Cultural Archives is principally an archive and library (open by appointment), which was established in 1981 as a historical documentation centre for London's black community. Its publication and education programmes and series of exhibitions focus on the history, culture and art of black people in Britain. The ultimate aim is to establish a museum of black history in Britain.

BRAMAH MUSEUM OF TEA AND COFFEE

40 Southwark Street, SE1 1UN
Tel: 020-7403 5650; www.bramahmuseum.co.uk
Open daily 10–6
Admission charge
Tube/Station: London Bridge
Tea room and shop
Map p. 383, 3E

This museum solely dedicated to tea and coffee was founded in 1992 by Edward Bramah, a tea planter in the 1950s and later a tea taster with J. Lyons and Co, before he moved on to China to work with the China National Tea export corporation of Shanghai. He set up Bramah Tea and Coffee in 1966, patenting a filter machine design. He founded the museum based on his reference collection of 1,000 tea and coffee artefacts. The museum traces the commercial and social history of tea and coffee since its introduction to Europe 400 years ago, and explores the roles of the great trading companies, such as the East India Company, which carried rich cargoes from India, Ceylon and China. The original location of the museum was a converted warehouse on Butler's Wharf, where cargoes would have been unloaded. Bramah teas and coffees can be bought in the museum shop and tasted in the tea room. You can call ahead to book a cream tea (with scones and clotted cream) or afternoon tea (with crumpets and cucumber sandwiches).

THE BRITISH LIBRARY

96 Euston Road, King's Cross, NW1 2DB
Tel: 020-7412 7332; www.bl.uk
Open Mon and Weds–Fri 9.30–6; Tues 9.30–8; Sat 9.30–5;
Sun and holidays 11–5
Free
Tube: King's Cross
Café and shop
Map p. 379, 2D

The British Library has only existed as a separate institution since 1973 but its origins are far more historic. As part of the British Museum, founded in 1753, it was housed until 1997 in the main museum building, with magnificent purpose-built reading rooms. In the 1960s, however, it was recognised that the Library had far outgrown its premises and in 1974 the present site in St Pancras was purchased. In 1998, after a catalogue of financial crises, Colin St. John Wilson's new building, originally designed in 1977, was finally opened. The British Library's books (humanities and science); the India Office Library; and the British Institute of Recorded Sound are now united under one roof. At the core of the Library's collections are the three foundation collections of the British Museum, which all contained manuscripts and books: that of Sir Hans Sloane (d. 1753); Sir Robert Cotton (d. 1631); and the Harleian collection of Robert Harley, 1st Earl of Oxford (d. 1724). The Library today is one of the largest and most comprehensive in the world and contains several treasures: two contemporary copies of Magna Carta, 1215; the manuscript of the Anglo-Saxon epic *Beowulf*; the wonderfully illuminated early Northumbrian 'Lindisfarne Gospels', written c. 715–20 in honour of St Cuthbert; William Caxton's two editions of Chaucer's *Canterbury Tales*, 1476 and 1483; the exceptional 'Sforza Hours' from Milan (c. 1490–1520); and the 'Codex Arundel' containing manuscript sheets of Leonardo da Vinci's mathematical notes and diagrams. The Codex was once owned by Thomas Howard, Earl of Arundel, who travelled to Italy with Inigo Jones, introducing the architect to the architecture of the Renaissance and of Classical Antiquity. (*Cont/d overleaf.*)

Thomas, Earl of Arundel and Inigo Jones

The friendship between Inigo Jones and Thomas Howard, Earl of Arundel, began with Jones's court masques, in which Arundel's wife was a keen participant (there is a surviving drawing by Jones of Lady Arundel in the guise of Atalanta, from a masque of 1609). Jones's interest in architecture was already evident, however. Even before he went to Italy he was incorporating classical themes into his work, as is evidenced by surviving designs for remodelling St Pauls, and the new Exchange in the Strand. Henry, the gifted Prince of Wales, who had been Arundel's friend and Jones's patron, died aged eighteen in 1612. This seems to have prompted both men to travel overseas. Arundel had been to Italy before, and had been enthused by what he saw. In 1613 he and Jones accompanied Princess Elizabeth to her marriage in Heidelberg, and then continued to Venice, where they spent time exploring its palazzi. Jones bought an edition of Palladio's *Quattri Libri* as well as a mass of Palladio's original drawings, acquired from Vincenzo Scamozzi, Palladio's pupil. From Venice, the two went to Vicenza where they spent a few days, visiting the Villa Rotonda, and eventually to Rome. Jones filled the margins of his copy of Palladio with notes on what he had seen and the two pored over the surviving ruins, spending hours gazing at antique sculpture and inscriptions. Both were repelled by the growing signs of the Baroque, Jones writing that he preferred his architecture to be austere and ordered. It was a second trip to Venice which fully consolidated Jones's ideas. He was appointed Surveyor of the King's Works in 1615.

The large piazza outside the entrance has, crouching menacingly on one side, Edward Paolozzi's great bronze *Newton*, inspired by William Blake's image of the same. Surrounding the sunken 'amphitheatre' are the eight carved Swedish glacial boulders which make up Antony Gormley's *Planets*. The library's unprepossessing, low exterior of red brick makes the interior a complete surprise: a wonderful white, tall, airy space flooded with light, with broad steps leading up to the reading rooms. In the centre, encased in a tower of bronze and glass reaching up six storeys and with their tooled leather and gold spines visible, are the 60,000 volumes of the King's Library, presented to the British Museum in 1823 by George IV. On the stairs is a tapestry woven after R.B. Kitaj's *If not, not*.

THE BRITISH MUSEUM

Great Russell Street, WC1B 3DG
Tel: 020-7323 8299; www.thebritishmuseum.ac.uk
Exhibitions open daily 10–5.30 (late nights Thur and Fri to 8.30)
Great Court open daily 9–6 (Thur–Sat late nights to 11pm)
Free
Tube: Holborn/Tottenham Court Road/Russell Square
Restaurant, café and shops
Map p. 382, 1B

Founded in 1753, the British Museum is the oldest secular public museum in the world. Its vast collection spans over two million years of the world's cultural history and contains many objects of outstanding international importance. As the mother of other, now independent, national institutions in London (The Natural History Museum and The British Library), the British Museum occupies a position of historical pre-eminence.

History of the Museum

At the core of the collection is that of Sir Hans Sloane (1650–1753), botanist and scientist, President of the Royal College of Physicians and of the Royal Society. His terracotta bust by Rysbrack (1736) is placed to the right of the main entrance. In his will Sloane offered for sale to the Crown, for £20,000, his enormous and renowned collection of 'curiosities': botanical and natural history specimens, coins and medals, shells, paintings, books and manuscripts, the accumulations of a man of the scientific revolution intent on discovering and ordering the products of God's creation. A state lottery raised funds for its purchase together with the important manuscript collection of Robert Harley, Earl of Oxford (1661–1724). Instead of a purpose-built museum these collections, joined by the Cottonian manuscripts which had been left

The Great Court, covered by a glass roof by Sir Norman Foster (2000).

to the nation in 1700, were displayed in Montagu House, a once-splendid post-1686 mansion with highly significant Baroque painted interiors. It was here that early visitors, including the young Mozart in 1765 who composed a motet, 'God is our refuge', dedicated to the museum, came to marvel. Cases of stuffed animals, fish, fossils and minerals, the museum's first Egyptian mummy and classical antiquities were incongruously placed amid late 17th-century grandeur. Watercolours exist of the majestic grand staircase, with Charles de la Fosse's painted mythological scene on the ceiling, rising to meet three giant stuffed giraffes on the landing.

A wave of major acquisitions in the late 18th and early 19th centuries necessitated the provision of new accommodation. In 1772 the great Greek vase collection of Sir William Hamilton (diplomat and archaeologist, and husband of Nelson's lover Emma) was acquired; in 1802 came the first significant haul of Egyptian antiquities, including the Rosetta Stone, followed in 1805 by the Townley Marbles (*see p. 32 below*). Too heavy for the delicate floors of Montagu House, a new adjoining Townley Gallery was built to accommodate these additions. But then, in 1814, came the purchase of the Phigaleian Marbles, swiftly followed in 1816 by the Elgin Marbles, the most significant acquisition in the museum's history (*see pp. 32–33 below*). A temporary structure of brick and wood was erected in the garden to house them, and it was here that the romantic Keats felt a 'dizzy pain' as he gazed upon 'these mighty things'.

The Building

Between 1820 and 1823 Sir Robert Smirke produced plans for a vast new building. Greek-revivalist in style, austere and dignified, it reflected the purity and rationalism of ancient Greece so admired by the English Neoclassicists. It was also a fitting receptacle for the Elgin Marbles, regarded as the very pinnacle of ancient Greek art. The building was conceived as a large quadrangle, with an imposing Ionic colonnaded entrance front and massive portico. It was built wing by wing, parts of Montagu House coming down as the new edifice went up. Construction spanned many years, beginning with the east wing, which on the ground floor housed George III's magnificent library, donated by George IV. The north wing (1833–38) contained mainly books, with mineralogy and geology above. The west wing, constructed for the Egyptian, Greek and Roman antiquities, where they still are today, was built in stages and has undergone several building campaigns, mainly in the early 1850s to accommodate the Assyrian antiquities, excavated from Nimrud and Nineveh, which began to arrive in the 1840s, to the amazement of Victorian London. The colonnaded south front was largely complete by 1847 when the Front Hall, with its Grecian Doric columns and grand staircase with ornamental balustrade and carved vases opened to the public.

Richard Westmacott's frieze of sculptures, *The Progress of Civilisation*, showing man's 'emergence from a rude state' to his embracement of the arts and sciences, was hoisted into place in the pediment above the entrance in 1851. But by then the original ideal of a 'universal' museum containing all branches of learning under one roof was understood to be a physical impossibility. The pictures, the nucleus of the National

Gallery, had already been diverted to Trafalgar Square even before the first floor of the west wing, which was to have housed them, was built. In the 1880s the natural history collections moved to South Kensington, where they became the Natural History Museum, freeing up much space, but it was only in 1998, with the removal of the British Library to St Pancras, that the museum could expand into large areas previously occupied by books. Even so, these spaces, as significant, listed interiors, have restricted use.

Sydney Smirke's inspiring, lofty and echoing **Round Reading Room** (1854–57), built in the centre of his brother Robert Smirke's quadrangle, is only 2ft smaller than the Pantheon in Rome. Under its dome many famous historical and modern-day scholars have worked, but the books are now gone. It retains its layout of reading desks, however, and is now the museum's information centre, where the collections can be viewed online. The quadrangle itself, now the **Great Court** (opened 2000), has been transformed by Norman Foster's vast glass roof which spans the entire space (the size of Hanover Square). From the Great Court access to all sections of the museum is possible. The Reading Room, encased by a shell of shops, a café and, on the first floor, a restaurant, sits in the centre while the façades of Smirke's quadrangle (one portico being a modern construction—controversially, in the wrong kind of stone), hidden from view practically since built, can now be enjoyed. Below the Great Court new display and exhibition galleries have been constructed, the first major additions to the museum's space for many decades.

The Collection

It is not possible to view the museum's vast collections in a single visit, nor to give a comprehensive account of them. Below, beginning with the Enlightenment gallery and then in order of administrative department, is an outline of the museum's highlights.

Enlightenment (Room 1)

In celebration of the British Museum's 250th anniversary, the Enlightenment Gallery opened in 2003 in the restored King's Library, Smirke's magnificent Greek-revival space built to receive George III's library donated to the museum by George IV in 1823. The most imposing Neoclassical interior in London, it is 300ft long and decorated with an austere magnificence, with vast Corinthian columns of Aberdeen granite and a rich yet restrained plasterwork ceiling. This severe grandeur, inspired by the rationalism of ancient Greek civilisation, was a fitting environment to house a library, an encyclopaedia of knowledge which the British Museum itself aimed to be. Following the removal of the King's Library to the new British Library at St Pancras, the space has now been filled with a permanent exhibition looking at the age of the Enlightenment, the era of expanding knowledge, pioneering discovery and rational observation in which the museum was founded. The displays contain objects from all aspects of the museum's collections, making it an ideal introduction to the museum as a whole. The development of methods for ordering and understanding man's burgeoning knowledge of the world is explored, beginning with 18th-century visitors to Montagu House, who encountered objects from all quarters of the globe placed together in the wonderfully titled Department of Natural and Artificial Productions, to the establishment of modern classification systems. The displays include loans from the Natural History Museum of items from Sloane's botanical and zoological collections, including volumes from his *Herbarium* and specimen trays of, for example, seeds, fruits, bark and roots.

Greek & Roman Antiquities (Rooms 11–23, 69–73, 77–85)

The Museum's collection of Greek and Roman antiquities is one of the finest in the world, ranging from the Bronze Age civilisations of the Cyclades and Minoan Crete to the late Roman Empire.

Although classical antiquities were a part of the museum's collection from the start, the first major acquisition was the 1772 purchase of Sir William Hamilton's Greek (then known as Etruscan) vase collection, a large and valuable group mainly from Southern Italy. Over the decades the museum has added to the collection considerably, and it is now one of the most comprehensive in the world. Among the many items of note is the c. 580 BC black-figured **Sophilos bowl and stand**, the first signed Greek vase known (Room 13); and the famous c. 540 BC **amphora by Exekias**, one of the finest draughtsmen of antiquity (also Room 13). The scene on the vase shows a helmeted Achilles killing Penthesilea, whose visor is pushed back to reveal her face in an attitude of vulnerability. In 1805 the Greek vases were joined by another major acquisition, the **Townley Marbles** (Room 84; in the basement), a group of mainly Roman sculptures which Charles Townley began collecting in 1768 when in Rome on the Grand Tour. Interest in Classical sculpture was then at its zenith, fuelled by dealers who excavated sites such as Hadrian's Villa at Tivoli and restorers who worked alongside them. During his lifetime Townley's collection was displayed in his cluttered house in Park Street, Westminster, where it became a celebrated attraction visited by scholars and connoisseurs. Among the highlights was the famous *Discobolus*, actually a Roman copy of a Greek bronze, from Hadrian's villa at Tivoli (displayed on the main stairs); the bust of 'Clytie', Townley's favourite sculpture, which perhaps represents Antonia, daughter of Mark Antony and Octavia, probably recut in the 18th century; and the c. 2nd-century AD graceful pair of greyhounds, again restored in the 18th century.

The Townley collection had an immense impact on 18th-century British taste, but its reputation was eclipsed by the arrival in the 19th century of several examples of Greek sculpture which cemented in people's minds the primacy of ancient Greek art and civilisation over Roman. First to arrive, in 1814, were the **Phigaleian Marbles** (Room 16), in fact slabs from the sculpted frieze of the Temple of Apollo Epikourios at Bassae, in southwest Arcadia, showing Hercules and the Greeks in battle against the Amazons in brutal, fast-moving scenes. The arrival which caused the greatest stir was, however, that of the **Elgin Marbles** (Room 18), acquired in 1816. Removed by Lord

BRITISH MUSEUM
GROUND FLOOR (ROOMS 1–35)

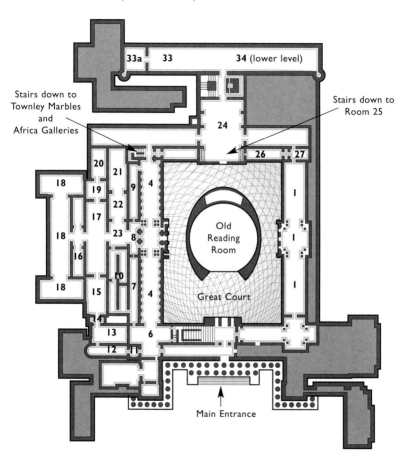

4: Rosetta Stone
6: Nimrud
7: Nineveh
10: Khorsabad gateway figures
13: Early Greek pottery
16: Phigaleian Marbles
17: Nereid Monument

18: Elgin Marbles
21: Mausoleum of Halicarnassus
24: Easter Island statue (may move)
27: Aztec pieces
33: Bodhisattva Tara
33a: Great Stupa reliefs
34: Iznik pottery

Elgin from the 5th-century BC Temple of Athena Parthenos on the Acropolis, Athens, the construction of which was overseen by the great sculptor Pheidias, these sculptures have long been admired as the greatest achievement of Greek art. In the 19th century they became the benchmark against which all art was measured. The 'marbles' include sculptures from the east pediment, originally a rhythmic succession of figurative groups illustrating the birth of Athena; slabs from the sculpted frieze showing the Panathenaic procession held to celebrate the birthday of Athena, carved with amazing skill and finesse; and sculpted panels once placed above the colonnade showing with great vividness the fight between the Lapiths and the Centaurs. Also removed by Elgin was the caryatid from the south porch of the Erechtheion, on the north side of the Acropolis. Although removed with full permission, and with the preservation of the marbles from the careless disregard of the Ottoman authorities in mind, even in the early 19th century Elgin was accused of robbery and plunder (by Byron). Visitors today cannot be unconscious of the arguments for the marbles' repatriation.

In the 1840s and 50s further great examples of Greek sculpture arrived including, in 1844, pieces from the great 4th-century BC **Nereid Monument** (Room 17), the most spectacular of those discovered in Xanthos (in modern Turkey) by Charles Fellows. Its free-standing figures have finely carved swirling folds of drapery. In 1845 slabs from the 4th-century BC **Mausoleum of Halicarnassus** (Room 21), the tomb of Mausolus, King of Caria, and one of the Seven Wonders of the ancient world, arrived at the museum. In 1857 Charles Newton, a museum employee, became Vice-Consul in Mytilene (Lesbos), with the additional brief of collecting antiquities for the museum, and in 1857 he conducted an excavation of the site (at Bodrum, in modern Turkey), where work continued in the 1860s. From the former great white marble stepped pyramidal structure which dominated the town, a vast lion was recovered; two colossal statues, once identified as Mausolus himself and Artemisia his sister-wife; and the head of one of the huge marble chariot horses from the mausoleum's summit. Another of the Seven Wonders, the **Temple of Artemis at Ephesus**, from where St Paul preached to the Ephesians, is represented by a vast sculpted column drum (Room 22) discovered by John Turtle Wood in 1869.

Further rooms in the basement and on the first floor have important collections of smaller artefacts, including ancient jewellery, bronzes, silver and glass. The latter collection includes the well known **Portland Vase** (Room 70). Probably Roman (c. 5–25 AD), it was brought to England by Sir William Hamilton. It is a technical masterpiece of cobalt blue and white cameo glass decorated with a figurative frieze, famously copied by Josiah Wedgwood. In 1845 the vase was smashed into a hundred pieces by a visitor, but successfully repaired.

Ancient Egypt & Sudan (Rooms 4 & 61–66)

The museum's famous Egyptian and Sudanese collection covers the cultures of the Nile Valley from the Neolithic age (c. 10th century BC) through the time of the Pharaohs to Coptic times (12th century AD). As well as massive pieces of Egyptian temple architecture, glorifying the power of kings and the worship of deities, the

BRITISH MUSEUM
UPPER FLOOR (ROOMS 36–73 & 90–94)

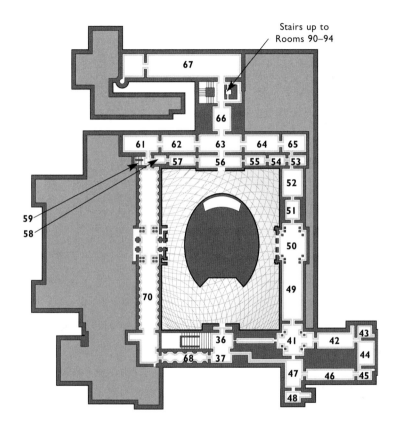

41: Sutton Hoo and Viking-age silver
42: Royal Cup and Lewis Chessmen
44: Horological collections
45: Waddesdon Bequest
46: Medals by Pisanello
49: Roman Britain
50: Snettisham Torc and Lindow Man
52: Oxus Treasure
54: Hittite discoveries

55: Royal Lion Hunt slabs and Flood Tablet
56: Excavations from Ur
57: Phoenician carvings
62: Mummy case of Artemidorus
63: Books of the Dead
65: Rameseum papyrus
67: Moon Jar
68: Money Gallery
70: Portland Vase

museum has an internationally important collection of papyri, funerary goods and household objects illustrative of the daily lives of the region's inhabitants.

Although Sloane's foundation collection had included some Egyptian material, which was supplemented by objects from the Lethieullier collection (including the museum's first mummy), it was not until 1802 that major items, ceded to the British under the terms of the 1801 Treaty of Alexandria, began to arrive. First and foremost among these was the famous **Rosetta Stone** (Room 4), an object of unparalleled importance in the history of Egyptology. Originally discovered by French scholars who accompanied Napoleon's expeditionary force to Egypt, the stone, bearing an inscription in three scripts—hieroglyphic, demotic Egyptian and Greek—held the key to the decipherment of hieroglyphs. The code was finally cracked by the French Egyptologist Jean-François Champollion in 1822, thereby enabling the translation of texts and inscriptions which opened the door to the hitherto mysterious 'lost' civilisation of ancient Egypt.

The first great piece of Egyptian sculpture to arrive was the **bust of Rameses II** (Room 4), 'the Younger Memnon', a colossal seven-ton sculpture (actually only the head) carved from a single block of granite, excavated from the king's vast mortuary temple, the Rameseum, in Thebes. Presented to the museum in 1817 by Henry Salt, British Consul-General in Cairo, and Jean Louis Burckhardt, a Swiss explorer, it had been physically removed from its site by Giovanni Belzoni, a former strongman and hydraulic engineer, whose team had taken 12 days to haul it to the river's edge. Salt and Belzoni continued to excavate in and around Thebes, unearthing great discoveries at the temple of Karnak and the mortuary temple of Amenhotep III, from whence came the colossal **head of Amenhotep III** (18th Dynasty, c. 1350 BC), an excellent piece of sculpture (displayed in the Great Court) showing the king wearing the crown of Lower Egypt. Belzoni's excavations, although officially sanctioned, were not rigorously recorded archaeological digs. By the end of the 19th century, strict antiquities legislation had come into force, and major finds remained in Egypt. It was during this pioneering period, however, that the museum acquired significant pieces of sculpture, mainly as the beneficiary of the Egypt Exploration Fund, led by Flinders Petrie (see p. 234), whose finds from controlled digs were officially distributed. The three remarkable 12th-Dynasty (c. 1850 BC) granite **sculptures of Senwosret III** (on loan at the time of writing), masterpieces of Middle Kingdom art from Deir el-Bahari, Thebes, came from this source. Senwosret's realistic furrowed brow, expressive of the heavy burden of kingship, is far removed from other idealised images of Egyptian kings.

The upstairs galleries house the museum's renowned collection of papyri, mummies, tomb sculpture and funerary objects, acquired mainly under Samuel Birch, the museum's great Egyptologist appointed in 1836, and his successor Ernest Wallis Budge, who was interested in ancient texts and made important purchases from dealers in Egypt. Their scholarly and collecting activities established the museum as a major centre for Egyptology. Highlights include Middle Kingdom papyri (the golden age of Egyptian literature), and the **Rameseum Dramatic Papyrus** (Room 65) acquired in 1929. The mummies and their elaborate cases, including the Roman-

Fowling in the Marshes: fragment of a wall painting from the tomb of Nebamun, Thebes, c. 1350 BC.

period **mummy case of Artemidorus** (Room 62), a young man from Hawara, are displayed alongside X-rays and CAT scans, revealing amulets, scarabs and other sacred objects beneath the wrappings. Other grave goods such as jewellery, canopic jars and mummified animals are on show. The large collection of Books of the Dead, which offered spells to aid the dead in their passage through the underworld, includes the **Book of the Dead of Any** (Room 63), arguably the best illustrated papyrus in existence. The museum's most striking piece of tomb painting is the *Fowling in the Marshes* (*pictured above*) a fragment from the tomb of Nebamun, Thebes (18th Dynasty c. 1350 BC), collected by Salt, showing Nebamun and his wife Hatshepsut in recreation in the afterlife.

Ancient Near East (Rooms 6–10 & 51–59)

The museum's material from the ancient civilisations of the Near East, including art and artefacts from Mesopotamia, Iran, the Levant, Anatolia and Arabia, from the Neolithic period to the arrival of Islam in the 7th century AD, has at its heart one of the finest collections of Assyrian sculpture in the world.

The museum's early collection included sculptures from Persepolis, which were joined, in 1824, by the collection of Claudius James Rich (d. 1820), the East India Company's Representative in Baghdad, who, as well as identifying the site of ancient Babylon in 1811, amassed an important collection of cuneiform scripts and cylinder seals. It was not until the great excavations of Sir Austen Henry Layard (1817–94), however, that eyes were opened to the new, truly magnificent civilisation of the Assyrians. The sculptures arriving in London from the 1840s from Nimrud and Nineveh caused a sensation. They included the **Black Obelisk of Shalmaneser III** (Nimrud 858–24 BC; Room 6) with its carved representation of Jehu paying tribute to the king, a tantalising reference to a Biblical figure; from the Northwest Palace of Ashurnasirpal II a colossal **human-headed winged lion** (883–59 BC; Room 6) which guarded the entrance to the throne room; and carved slabs which lined the walls of the **Palace of Sennacherib** at Nineveh (Room 7). Two further colossal gateway figures, **human-headed winged bulls** (710–05 BC), each weighing 16 tons, arrived in 1849, bought from the French excavations of Sargon II's citadel at Khorsabad (Room 10). Layard's local assistant, Hormuzd Rassam, continued to excavate on behalf of the museum, sending back astonishing discoveries from Ashurbanipal's North Palace at Nineveh, which he unearthed in 1852–54. From this richly decorated palace came the famous Royal Lion Hunt slabs, in particular the **Dying Lion** (Room 55), where the injured and bleeding animal is carved with incredible skill and observation; and thousands of cuneiform tablets from the great Royal Library, the main source for present day knowledge of the literature, culture and lives of these people. The vast collection of cuneiform tablets and the pioneering work of Colonel Rawlinson in deciphering the cuneiform script established the museum as the centre for cuneiform studies. The discovery in 1872 that one of the tablets (the **Flood Tablet**, 7th century BC; Room 55) contained a Babylonian version of the Biblical deluge riveted Victorian minds.

Attracted by its impressive ziggurat, Leonard Woolley's 12-year excavation of the ancient Sumerian town of Ur yielded extraordinarily rich discoveries. From the 'Great Death Pit', which Woolley decided was a royal cemetery, where the dead were accompanied to their graves by as many as 60 attendants each, came the **'Ram in a Thicket'** (2600–2400 BC; Room 56), a sculpture of a goat covered in gold leaf with horns and fleece of lapis lazuli reaching up to nibble leaves from a bush; the **Standard of Ur**, with mosaic figurative decoration of shell, limestone and lapis lazuli, representing the Sumerian army with chariots and spears trampling the enemy, and a procession of goods being borne to a banquet; and the **Royal Game of Ur** (Room 56), an early example of the 'game of twenty squares'. In the 1930s impressive **Phoenician ivory carvings** (Room 57), probably from pieces of furniture, were excavated by Sir Max Mallowan (husband of the detective writer Agatha Christie) at Nimrud.

Other highlights from the collection include important **Hittite discoveries** (Room 54) from Carchemish, on the Turkish-Syrian border, excavated in 1911–14 and 1920 (one of the excavators being T.E. Lawrence); the incredible **Oxus Treasure** (Room 52), a magnificent collection of gold and silver from the 4th–5th centuries BC Achaemenid period, found on the north bank of the River Oxus in 1877–80; and a collection of funerary sculptures, with detailed jewellery, dress and hair, from the great city of Palmyra in the Syrian desert, which arrived at the museum in the 1880s.

Prehistory & Europe (Rooms 36–48 & 49–50)

The department spans a vast expanse of time with objects, including early flint implements, jewellery and funerary offerings, charting the cultural evolution of man from the Palaeolithic and Neolithic stone age eras; through the Bronze and Iron Ages and Celtic Europe; to Roman Britain and the Christian cultures of Medieval, Renaissance and Modern Europe. Collecting in these areas was accidental and sluggish until the mid-19th-century appointment of Sir Augustus Wollaston Franks (d. 1897), whose dedication to British antiquities, and personal gifts to the museum inspired a flow of donations of prehistoric and later objects. Two items of outstanding importance came from Franks: the c. 700 AD Northumbrian 'Franks Casket', with intricate whalebone carving (in the Study Collection); and the incomparable **Royal Gold Cup** (Room 42), decorated in coloured enamels with scenes of the life of St Agnes, given in 1391 to Charles VI of France by the great patron the Duc de Berry.

When other departments found their acquisition of archaeological material restricted by new antiquities legislation, major British finds of incredible importance found their natural home at the British Museum. Archaeological discovery and the ancient law of Treasure Trove, refined by the Treasure Act (1996), have benefited the collection enormously. Buried 'treasure', defined as any object containing 10% silver or gold, over 300 years old and placed in the ground with the intention of retrieval, is administered by the museum. Through this route came the 12th-century **Lewis Chessmen** (Room 42), discovered in 1831 in a stone chamber under a sandbank on the Isle of Lewis, Outer Hebrides; the exceptional **Mildenhall Treasure** (on loan at the time of writing), a hoard of 34 pieces of superb Roman silver tableware of brilliant craftsmanship ploughed up in a field in Suffolk in the 1940s; the great gold **Snettisham Torc** (Room 50), a magnificent 1st-century BC example of early Iron Age British craftsmanship; and the **Water Newton treasure** (Room 49), the earliest known pieces of Christian silver from the Roman Empire, discovered with a metal detector in 1975.

Between 1879 and 1905 a stream of material was given to the museum by Canon Williams Greenwell, all finds from his energetic excavations of prehistoric barrows. One of the greatest archaeological excavations in Britain, however, was the great 7th-century Anglo-Saxon ship burial at **Sutton Hoo**, Suffolk (Room 41), possibly the grave of Raedwald, King of East Anglia. Discovered in 1939 under windswept heathland, the astonishing rich treasure of silver and gold set with garnets, including a perfectly preserved and intricate gold buckle, and a finely crafted but sinister helmet, was given to the museum by the landowner, Mrs Pretty. Important **items from Roman Britain** include the tombstone of Julius Classicianus, Procurator of Britain (Room 49), an exceptionally important historical document discovered in two stages, in 1852 and 1935, when construction work was being carried out near Tower Hill, London; and the 4th-century Hinton Mary mosaic pavement (also Room 49), at its centre the earliest representation of Christ found in Britain, discovered on the site of a Roman villa in Dorset in 1963. In 1984 the extraordinarily well preserved **Lindow Man** (Room 50) was discovered, a 1st-century AD young man of twenty-five who had been bludgeoned, garrotted and then had his throat cut, probably in a Druidic sacrifice.

Later decorative art items include those from the important **Waddesdon Bequest** of 1898 (Room 45), including the 1400–10 'Holy Thorn Reliquary'; an important collection of porcelain; and one of the world's finest horological collections (Room 44), many of the clocks and watches on display gently ticking and striking and chiming the hour (not all at the same time).

Ethnography (Rooms 25 & 26–27)

Sloane's foundation collection contained some ethnographic items but it was not a seriously recognised collecting category until the 1860s. Until then acquisitions were haphazard and accidental. Some material gathered on Captain Cook's voyages of discovery to the South Pacific and northwest coast of America came to the museum, partly through the efforts of Daniel Solander and Joseph Banks (*see p. 127*), who both worked for the museum (Banks was a trustee) and had been part of Cook's retinue of scientific recorders. In 1775 the Otaheite (South Seas) Room opened at Montagu House but, although it was an immensely popular attraction, there was not much dedication to its contents, large parts of which were casually dispersed over the years. The museum still has the great ceremonial cloak of feathers and mother of pearl, probably that presented to Cook in Tahiti in 1774, along with other Polynesian, Maori and American material.

Consisting of objects reflecting the cultures of indigenous peoples throughout the world, the bulk of what makes up the present ethnographic collection came to the museum in the 19th and 20th centuries. Having returned from the Museum of Mankind in 1997, the collection is now displayed in three galleries on the main floor and in the new Africa Galleries below the Great Court. The Wellcome Trust Gallery (Room 24), occupying the old North Library, is where a proposed series of long-term exhibitions will run (currently 'Living and Dying'). It is here, for the moment, that **Hoa Hakananai'a** can be found, the museum's monumental Easter Island statue brought back by the crew of *HMS Topaze* from its surveying expedition of 1868. These great human figures, known as *moai*, part of the island's statue cult, which flourished up until the 17th century, originally stood upright on platforms, surveying the remote island scenery from under their heavy brows.

In 1858 Sir Stamford Raffles' Indonesian collection was presented to the museum, followed in 1865 by that of Henry Christy (whose family textile firm introduced the modern-day towel to the western world, based on a piece of Turkish towelling Christy collected). The greatest treasures from this were the three pieces of **Mixtec-Aztec turquoise mosaic** (Room 27) possibly part of the tribute given by Emperor Moctezuma II to the Spanish conquistador Hernán Cortés in 1519. The museum now has nine of these outstanding ritual and ceremonial objects: masks, animals, a two-headed serpent, carved in wood with the turquoise pieces set in resin. The decorated human skull represents the powerful god Tezcatlipoca.

The **Africa Galleries** (Room 25; basement) include the 12th–14th-century bronze head of a Yoruba ruler, probably Oni, king of Ife on the River Niger, Ife culture being one of the highest achievements of African art; sophisticated brass plaques from Benin, produced for the Oba rulers in the 16th century; and a collection of goldwork collected in 1817 by Thomas Boldwich on a journey to the Asante kingdom (present day Ghana) on behalf of the African Company of Merchants. Asante's great wealth was based on its vast gold deposits: at Kumasi, Boldwich noted the sun glinting off the massy gold ornaments of the people.

Prints & Drawings (Room 90)

On the top floor of the Edward VII block, most easily approached from the museum's north entrance on Montague Place, but also possible via the Great Court, is the national collection of Western prints and drawings, one of the top three collections of its type in the world, with over 50,000 drawings and two million prints. At its heart are the drawings collected by Sloane, including John White's 16th-century views of the Roanoke colony; a group of drawings by the 17th-century artist Wenceslaus Hollar; and, most importantly, volumes of **Dürer's watercolours** and drawings which are among the museum's most important possessions.

Sloane's items were joined in 1769 by William Fawkener's collection of prints and drawings, including important Italian works, and in 1799 by the major bequest to the museum of the collection of the Rev. Clayton Mordaunt Cracherode, a trustee since 1784 and a shy eccentric who had collected, among many other things, important **works by Holbein, Michelangelo, Rembrandt and Rubens**. The department did not exist independently, nor was its collection properly inventoried, which allowed the shady dealer Robert Dighton to thieve from the collection, from 1795, many of the Cracherode items, hiding them beneath his coat or in his pocket, desiring in particu-. lar works by Rembrandt. Dighton was discovered, several items recovered, and in 1808 the department was formally formed and its own keeper appointed in 1836. In the 1820s–60s the department grew enormously, and was further enhanced in 1895 by the arrival of the Malcolm collection of over 1,000 **Old Master drawings** of high quality. Among the highlights of the collection today, as well as the important historical, satirical and topographical prints, the vast collection of portrait mezzotints, and drawings and prints after Italian, German and Netherlandish artists, are the fine collection of Dürer drawings (138 in total) and an almost complete collection of his engravings; over 90 works by Michelangelo, including studies for great commissions such as the Sistine Chapel ceiling; 80 sheets of sketches and drawings by Rembrandt, as well as a collection of his etchings; a large body of excellent works by Rubens; and British watercolours including views made in Rome by Francis Towne, which he bequeathed in 1816, and works by John Sell Cotman. There are also works by Thomas Girtin, a young artist of great promise, recognised as a genius by Turner. He died before he was thirty. Added to this is an important collection of printed material such as trade and visiting cards and playing cards from the collection of Sarah Sophia Banks, sister of the museum's trustee Joseph Banks.

The collection is made available through a programme of temporary exhibitions in a room alongside the Print Room, which is open for research by appointment. Michelangelo's large cartoon in black chalk, *Epifania* (c. 1550–53), and Dürer's vast woodcut *The Triumphal Arch* (1515), one of the largest prints ever produced, are usually on display.

Coins & Medals (Rooms 41, 46, 49, 68)

Since its foundation in 1753 the British Museum has had a fine numismatic collection, which now numbers over a million objects spanning the history of coinage from its beginnings in the 7th century BC to the present day. As well as coins, the museum also has a collection of paper money, from a 14th-century Chinese banknote to the modern euro; and an exceptional collection of commemorative medals dating from the Italian Renaissance to the present. Sloane owned around 20,000 coins and medals, many purchased from the collection of his friend William Courten, and others came from the foundation collections of Sir Robert Cotton. Numerous large numismatic acquisitions were made in the 18th and 19th centuries including those in the large Cracherode bequest of 1799; Richard Payne Knight's collection of over 5,000 items, bequeathed in 1824; and the royal collection of George III in the same year. William Marsden's gift of 1834 was the foundation of the Oriental collection. From the early 19th century it became an aim to have a representative series of British material, greatly aided by the 1859–60 purchase of Edward Hawkins' collection of historic commemorative medals, over 4,500 items, larger by far than the museum's own collection at the time. The medallic collection today begins with excellent cast bronze **medals by Pisanello** (Room 46) designed for the Este and Gonzaga families of Ferrara and Mantua. As well as the British medals there are also important German Renaissance and Netherlandish examples and French medals produced for Louis XIV of France, with highly skilled Baroque allegorical reverses. Over the years the department has also been a Treasure Trove beneficiary (e.g. the Cuerdale Hoard of **Viking-Age silver**, Room 41; and the Hoxne Hoard of **late Roman coins**—Room 49—comprising over 15,000 silver coins and over 500 of gold) and has the responsibility of assessing today's treasure finds of coins. As well as in the **Money Gallery** (Room 68), the collection is displayed through a series of frequently changing exhibitions held in a small space on the first floor, outside the department's fearsome metal security door.

Asia (Rooms 33–34, 67 & 91–94)

The large department covering the material remains of the Asian continent from Neolithic times to the present has as its main focus the cultures of India, Islam, China and Japan and comprises the world's most comprehensive collection of sculpture from the Indian subcontinent; the best collection of Islamic pottery outside the Middle East; an outstanding collection of Chinese antiquities, including paintings, porcelain, lacquer and jade; the most important collection of Korean art in Europe; and, among the Japanese netsuke, samurai swords and ceramics, including tea ceremony ware, the finest collection of Japanese paintings and prints in the West.

Sloane's collection included a number of oriental objects, mainly purchased from the collection of Engelbert Kaempfer, medical officer of the Dutch East India Company in Nagasaki in 1690–92. As with other departments, however, it was not until the mid-19th-century appointment of Franks as Keeper that the museum began to collect in any systematic or dedicated way. Before that, in 1830, the museum had been given by Sir Robert Brownrigg, Governor of Ceylon, one of its most beautiful objects, the gilt-bronze 9th-century Sri Lankan **Bodhisattva Tara** (Room 33), one of the finest examples of Asian figural bronze-casting. In 1836 the 'disgraceful absence' of Indian material was noted, only partly remedied by the 1872 acquisition of the Bridge collection of Indian sculpture. In 1879, however, came the closure and collection dispersal of the India Museum, which had been based at the East India Company headquarters in the City. From here came the 133 1st–3rd-century delicately carved **limestone reliefs from the Great Stupa** (Room 33a), the Buddhist relic-house at Amaravati, Andhra Pradesh, southeast India. The carvings are one of the British Museum's greatest treasures.

In 1888 Franks wrote that the museum 'does not purchase oriental porcelain', but over the years he had been building up his own personal collection, which he donated in 1885. It included many Japanese objects purchased at the 1878 Exposition Universelle in Paris (Japanese material was now flooding into Europe following the opening up of Japan to the West in 1858). Franks' gift was the stimulus for other private donations of oriental material, including Islamic pottery. The museum now has a fine collection of **Persian lustreware** and, most importantly, **Iznik pottery** (both Room 34). The acquisition in 1983 of the Frederick du Cane Godman collection (1834–1919) of Islamic pieces, Godman having been a friend of Franks, transformed the collection.

The most important collection of Chinese artefacts to come to the museum was that of the Hungarian archaeologist and explorer of the Silk Route Sir Aurel Stein. Objects began to arrive from 1900, the most important of which was the group of **artefacts from the Tang period** (618–906 AD): manuscripts, temple banners and paintings on silk and paper, including elaborate Paradise scenes, discovered in the Valley of a Thousand Buddhas, Dunhuang (Study Collection). Strategically placed on the Silk Route, the area had been an important centre for Buddhist pilgrims who hollowed out over 1,000 cave shrines. In 1906, in cave 17, closed since the early 12th century, Stein made his important discovery. In 1903 the museum purchased a major piece of Chinese art, the *Admonitions of the Instructress to the Court Ladies*, a painted scroll illustrating Zhang Hua's political parody attacking the excessive behaviour of the empress. The scroll is a valuable 6th–8th-century copy of the no-longer-extant original by the legendary artist Gu Kaizhi (345–406 AD), of whose work only a few not certainly attributed examples survive. The excellent collection of **Japanese paintings and prints** includes fine pieces from the Kamakura period (1185–1333) and a great collection of Ukiyo-e (prints and paintings of the 'Floating World' school which flourished in the 17th–19th centuries) including the famous *Mount Fuji* woodblock print series by the leading artist of the late Edo period, Katsushika Hokusai (1760–1849).

The Chinese collection was greatly enhanced in the 20th century by the 1935 acquisition of the vast George Eumorfopoulos collection, rich in paintings, ceramics, ivory, lacquer and jade objects. Split between the British Museum and the V&A, private donors helped fund the purchase including Sir Percival David (*see p. 233*). In 1999 the beautiful white porcelain 17th–18th-century Choson dynasty '**Moon Jar**' was purchased for the important Korean collection (Room 67), a magnificent example of pure, austere Confucian taste. It was previously owned by the great British potters Bernard Leach and Lucie Rie.

BRITISH OPTICAL ASSOCIATION MUSEUM

42 Craven Street, WC2N 5NG
Tel: 020-7766 4353; www.college-optometrists.org/college/museum
Open Mon–Fri 9.30–5 (phone ahead)
Free. Limited disabled access
Tube: Charing Cross
Map p. 382, 3B

This small museum (founded 1901) within the College of Optometrists' building has a fascinating collection of optical-related items: over 2,000 pairs of spectacles dating from the 17th century onwards; eye glasses; pince-nez; lorgnettes; and monocles. There is also a collection of fans with spy glasses in the handles, instruments used by opticians and a collection of glass eyes. Dr Johnson's spectacles can be seen, as can C.P. Snow's, Dr Crippen's and a pair of 17th-century green-tinted ones, similar to those described by Samuel Pepys in his diary. Pepys was afraid that he was losing his sight, and reported some benefit to his eyes from the wearing of green-tinted lenses. Among the paintings is a portrait of the famous American statesman and scientist Benjamin Franklin, wearing silver folding nose spectacles. Franklin lived a few doors down, at no. 36 (*see p. 23*). He is usually credited with the invention of bifocals. As well as the museum, a pre-booked tour of the College Meeting Rooms is possible, which includes the Council Chamber and anteroom, the Panelled Room and the Print Room. The latter's walls are covered with a dense hang of prints showing scientists, historical optical instruments, and famous people wearing spectacles. Such a display was the wish of J.H. Sutcliffe, Secretary of the British Optical Association from 1895. The museum is open every weekday but pre-booking is essential as the college is a working building and the Meeting Rooms will sometimes be in use.

BRUNEI GALLERY SOAS

Thornhaugh Street, Russell Square, WC1H 0XG
Tel: 020-7898 4915; www.soas.ac.uk/gallery
Open Mon-Fri 10.30–5
Free

Tube: Russell Square/Goodge Street
Shop
Map p. 382, 1A

Opened in 1995 with a generous benefaction from the Sultan of Brunei, the Brunei Gallery, administered by the School of Oriental and African Studies (SOAS)—part of the University of London—has a programme of historical and contemporary exhibitions on subjects and from regions with which the school is concerned, namely Africa and Asia. Past exhibitions include Chinese textiles; art of the Ottoman Empire and contemporary Syrian art. The building (Nicholas Hare Architects), off Thornhaugh St on the northwest corner of Russell Square, opposite the entrance to SOAS, has three floors linked by a glass staircase and a Japanese Roof Garden, redesigned in 2001.

BRUNEL ENGINE HOUSE

Railway Avenue, Rotherhithe, SE16 4LF
Tel: 020-7231 3840; www.brunelenginehouse.org.uk
Open Thur–Sun 1–5
Admission charge. Partial disabled access
Tube: Rotherhithe
Café and shop
Map p. 379, 3E

This small museum, close to Rotherhithe Station, is set up in the engine house used by the great civil engineer Marc Isambard Brunel (1769–1849) and his son Isambard Kingdom Brunel (1806–59) when they were building the Thames Tunnel (1825–43), which linked Rotherhithe with Wapping. The tunnel, a monumental feat of engineering hailed in its day as the Eighth Wonder of the World, was the world's first under-river thoroughfare. The two tubes, one intended for pedestrians, the other for road traffic, are 406m (1,506ft) long and cost £468,249 to build amid financial crises, devastating accidents (flood and fire), several fatalities and dangerous and uncomfortable working conditions. Two previous attempts to tunnel the Thames had failed, but Marc Brunel's invention of the tunnelling shield (patented 1818) was able to overcome the river's liquefied sediment. The tunnel opened to pedestrians in 1843 and in 1869 reopened as a railway. It is still in use today by the East London Line, part of the London Underground network.

The simple red brick building with its elegant chimney, a roofless ruin in 1975, housed the engines which pumped water from the tunnel. It now features a small exhibition explaining the history and significance of the tunnel, including an image of a great banquet which took place in it on 10th November 1827.

BUCKINGHAM PALACE

BUCKINGHAM PALACE: MALL FAÇADE

Ticket office at Canada Gate, Green Park, W1 (open 9–4)
Tickets Tel: 020-7766 7300; 020-7766 7324 for disabled visitors
www.royalcollection.org.uk
Tours from late July to early October each year—dates and details vary
Admission charge
Tube: Victoria/St James's Park
Shop
Map p. 381, 2E

Buckingham Palace, impressively situated at the west end of the Mall, is the official
residence of the British monarch (when the Queen is in residence the Royal Standard
flies from the top of the flagpole on the palace roof). It is the Mall façade, from the
balcony of which the Queen waves on great public occasions, that is best known to
the world. A picturesque view of it, framed by trees, can be had from the bridge over
the lake in nearby St James's Park. The façade in fact dates only from 1913 and was
designed by Sir Aston Webb, who was also responsible for the spacious circus in front
of the palace with its radiating avenues and the Victoria Memorial at its centre. The
Memorial, executed by Sir Thomas Brock in 1911, shows Queen Victoria seated on
the east side with groups representing Truth, Motherhood and Justice on the others
and is crowned by a gilded bronze figure of Victory. On the wide palace forecourt,
behind the ornamental railings, the Changing of the Guard ceremony takes place
(*11.30am, daily April–end June, otherwise alternate days, weather permitting*). The new
guard, accompanied by a band with pipes and drums, marches from the nearby
Wellington Barracks to relieve the old guard assembled on the forecourt. When the
officers of the old and new guards advance and touch left hands, symbolising the
handing over of the keys, the guard is 'changed'.

The Building

Buckingham Palace was originally Buckingham House, a private mansion built by John Sheffield, 1st Duke of Buckingham in 1702–05. In 1762 the house was purchased by George III and it became the chief residence of Queen Charlotte, who had it enlarged and altered by Sir William Chambers. It was for George IV that the building was transformed into a palace; on his accession the new king signalled his intention to vacate his magnificent home, Carlton House, and to rebuild Buckingham House on a grand and regal scale. Parliament voted £250,000 for the project, John Nash was the chosen architect, and building work began in 1825. On the king's death in 1830, with the palace still unfinished and costs having spiralled to £600,000, Nash was dismissed and Edward Blore, considered a safe pair of hands, was appointed in his place. Blore removed Nash's insubstantial and much criticised dome, added an attic storey, and in 1846–50 created the east wing across the forecourt, now hidden behind Webb's 1913 refacing. The new wing necessitated the removal of Nash's Marble Arch, designed as a ceremonial gateway to the palace: in 1850–51 it was relocated to its present site, on the edge of Hyde Park at the junction of Park Lane and Oxford Street.

The palace was first opened to the public in 1993 to help fund the restoration of the then fire-damaged Windsor Castle, and has remained open to visitors in the summer ever since. For obvious reasons, not all areas of the palace are accessible but the tour takes in the main State Rooms, the majority of them opulently conceived by Nash in the 1820s and completed by Blore. Nash's inventive interiors, with their gilded plaster ceilings, heavily decorated coves, wall hangings in richly coloured silks and use of expensive materials (Carrara marble; gilt bronze) offered the unsurpassed grandeur sought by George IV. Many of the rooms were partially designed around the king's magnificent collection of pictures, furniture and porcelain from Carlton House, several items from which, together with other items from the Royal Collection—a private collection unrivalled in its size, scope and importance—still furnish them.

Tour of the Palace

Visitors enter the palace via the Ambassador's Entrance on Buckingham Gate, which leads to the **Courtyard** behind the east wing. Here, Nash's building, in warm Bath stone, with Blore's alterations, is revealed. The sculptural theme is British sea power: in the pediment *Britannia Acclaimed by Neptune*, designed by Flaxman (*see p. 312*) and executed by E.H. Baily in 1828; and inside Nash's two-storey columned portico J.E. Carew's *The Progress of Navigation*. The friezes in the attic storey, *The Death of Nelson* and *The Meeting of Blücher and Wellington*, both by Westmacott, were added by Blore and were originally intended for the Marble Arch.

The portico entrance leads into the **Grand Hall**, actually relatively low-ceilinged, with mahogany hall furniture from Carlton House and Brighton Pavilion. From here, visitors approach the magnificent **Grand Staircase**, one straight flight leading to a landing and branching into two to the upper floor. The stairs are of Carrara marble, the intricate balustrade, supplied by Samuel Parker 1828–30 for £3,900, of gilt bronze. Parker also made the gilt metal mounts for the mirror-plated doors which

occur throughout the State Rooms. The small but ornate **Guard Room**, with an apsed end, Carrara marble columns and rich plaster ceiling in white and gold, contains full-length sculptures of Queen Victoria—the first monarch to occupy the palace—and her consort Prince Albert.

The **Green Drawing Room** serves as an anteroom to the Throne Room and occupies the site of Queen Charlotte's Saloon, designed by Chambers. The deeply coved and bracketed ceiling, set off by the green silk hangings, is Nash's. The room contains items from George IV's priceless collection of Sèvres porcelain, the finest in the world, much of which was purchased from the French Royal Collection, sold during the French Revolution. The **Throne Room** itself, with red silk wall hangings and another rich ceiling, the cove of which is decorated with heraldic shields and garter stars, was intended for investitures and ceremonial receptions. The throne (the chairs were made for the Queen's Coronation Ceremony of 1953) is divided from the rest of the room by a proscenium with two winged Victories holding garlands, modelled by Francis Bernasconi, the chief plasterer employed at the palace. The classical sculptural frieze, designed by Stothard, has a medieval theme: the Wars of the Roses.

The **Picture Gallery**, 155ft long, was designed by Nash for George IV's outstanding collection of Dutch and Flemish art but was much altered, and tempered, in 1914. Nash's hammerbeam design for the roof was replaced by the present arrangement, more practical for lighting the pictures. Some of the greatest works from the Royal Collection usually hang here, including van Dyck's equestrian portrait *Charles I with Monsieur de St-Antoine* (1633); van Dyck's 'greate peece', *Charles I and Henrietta Maria with their Two Eldest Children* (1632); and Rubens' *Landscape with St George and the Dragon*.

The **East Gallery** is the first of the rooms in the new block added by Queen Victoria in 1853–55 to designs by James Pennethorne, which added a magnificent new Ballroom, the previous one having been considered too small. The interior decoration was overseen by the Prince Consort although it is now much altered. Of the pictures usually on show, the most important is the familiar Franz Xaver Winterhalter's *Family of Queen Victoria* (1846). Further rooms lead to the actual **Ballroom**, 37.5m (123ft) long, where present-day investitures and other official receptions take place. The **State Dining Room** has a heavy and elaborate ceiling by Blore, with three saucer-domed compartments and large roundels in the cove. The series of full-length Hanoverian royal portraits was hung here by Queen Victoria. The room is used for official luncheons and dinners. Examples from George IV's magnificent silver-gilt service by Rundell, Bridge & Rundell are on show. The **Blue Drawing Room** was formerly the Ballroom. It is a magnificent, pure Nash interior, one of the finest in the Palace, with wide, flaring ceiling coves and coupled columns painted in imitation onyx. The delicate plasterwork reliefs show the apotheoses of Shakespeare, Spenser and Milton. The gilt sofas and armchairs are from Carlton House and the 'Table of the Grand Commanders', commissioned by Napoleon in 1806–12, with a

The Throne Room at Buckingham Palace.

top of hard-paste Sèvres porcelain with the head of Alexander the Great in the centre, was presented to George IV by Louis XVIII.

The **Music Room** is the most beautiful interior in the palace. Completed by Nash in 1831 and not much altered, it has a coffered domed ceiling and occupies the bow window, the central feature of Nash's west front, with views over the palace's private gardens. The large plate glass windows were an innovation of the 1820s. Between the windows and mirrors are lapis lazuli scagliola columns. The parquet floor is by Seddon and the magnificent early 19th-century cut glass and gilt bronze chandeliers are from Carlton House. The **White Drawing Room**, with its innovative convex ceiling and white and gold damask wall hangings, has Siena scagliola pilasters with capitals incorporating the garter star. The Minister's Stairs, redecorated in white and gold by Edward VII, as was much of the Palace, leads to the **Marble Hall**, George IV's sculpture gallery which runs underneath the Picture Gallery. It is dominated by Canova's *Mars and Venus*, commissioned by George IV for Carlton House.

From here, via the Bow Room, visitors pass out to the **Gardens**, landscaped by Nash and W.T. Aiton of Kew Gardens, and including an ornamental lake, fed by the Serpentine. It is on these spacious lawns that the Queen's public garden parties take place. Nash's garden façade itself, a hidden and less familiar view of the palace, is worth a backward glance. Above the central bow is Westmacott's *Fame Displaying Britain's Triumphs*. The 'King Alfred' frieze, designed by Flaxman, is also by Westmacott. Visitors exit this peaceful seclusion onto the heavy traffic of Buckingham Palace Road, where the Royal Mews (*see p. 253*) and the Queen's Gallery (*see p. 237*) can also be visited.

John Nash (1752–1835)

'His style lacks grandeur, and great monotony is produced by his persistent use of stucco.' Thus the *Dictionary of National Biography* dismisses John Nash, the millwright's son who became one of the most distinctive of all British architects, whose grand, aspirational creations add character to much of London. There is more behind the portentous façades than meets the eye. Nash was a brilliant engineer and gifted town planner. He was chosen by the Prince Regent as architect of an ambitious project: developing a tract of former farmland into a graceful 'garden city', with a ceremonial avenue linking it with the prince's residence at Carlton House. Regent's Park, the layout of Trafalgar Square, and the graceful sweep of Regent Street (though altered since) are all legacies of this splendid scheme. When George became king, he retained Nash to transform Buckingham House into a palace of a splendour to rival Napoleon's Paris. Napoleon, by his own account, approved of what he saw, remarking that Nash had made London appear 'for the first time like a royal residence, no longer a sprawling city for shopkeepers'. Though Nash longed for a knighthood, he never received one. Wellington, the prime minister, refused to grant it so long as Buckingham Palace remained unfinished. And Nash never completed it.

BURGH HOUSE
THE HAMPSTEAD MUSEUM

Burgh House, New End Square, Hampstead, NW3 1LT
Tel: 020-7431 0144; www.burghhouse.org.uk
Open Wed–Sun 12–5 (Sat by appointment only); bank holidays 2–5
Free. Toilet for disabled visitors
Tube: Hampstead
Buttery open Wed–Sun 11–5.30; bank holidays 1–5.30
Map p. 379, 2D

A handsome Grade I listed Queen Anne house built in 1704, Burgh House is set behind attractive wrought iron gates in the heart of old Hampstead village, overlooking Well Walk. Over the centuries it has been occupied by a succession of interesting professionals, including, from 1720, Dr William Gibbons, physician of the Hampstead Wells Spa, much frequented in the 18th century for the supposed medicinal properties of its foul-tasting chalybeate waters; from 1822 the Rev. Allston Burgh, vicar of St Lawrence Jewry, from whom the house takes its name; in 1906–24 the eminent art historian and specialist on portrait miniatures, Dr George Williamson; and in 1933–37 Rudyard Kipling's daughter, Elsie Bambridge. The house, which retains many of its original internal features including its carved staircase, is now run by the Burgh House Trust and was opened as a museum and community arts centre in 1979. Local art exhibitions take place on the ground floor while the first floor is occupied by the Hampstead Museum of local history. Displays explain the history of Hampstead and its famous inhabitants, including the artist John Constable—who made his famous cloud studies on Hampstead Heath—and the Victorian watercolourist Helen Allingham (d. 1888), items relating to her life and work having been bequeathed to the museum in 1989. The museum also possesses an Isokon Long Chair, designed by the Hungarian-born architect Marcel Breuer (a director of the Bauhaus and later partner of Walter Gropius in America) for the 'Isobar' at the Isokon flats, Lawn Road, in 1936. Its clean, bent plywood design was the most famous item marketed by Isokon, the modern design firm established in the early 1930s. The Buttery serves lunch and tea—on its pleasant garden terrace in summer, and at other times in the basement.

CABINET WAR ROOMS & CHURCHILL MUSEUM
(Imperial War Museum)

Clive Steps, King Charles Street, SW1A 2AQ
Tel: 020-7930 6961; cwr.iwm.org.uk
Open Oct–March 10–6; April–Sept 9.30–6, last admissions 5.15
Closed 24th Dec–6th Jan
Admission charge

Tube: Westminster
Café and shop
Map p. 382, 3A

The Cabinet War Rooms occupy the basement of the vast New Government Offices, built in 1899–1915, which span an area between Horse Guards Road to the west and Parliament Street to the east. An airless subterranean warren over two floors, the rooms are 10ft underground with reinforced concrete above. Constructed between June 1938 and August 1939 (completed a week before Britain's declaration of war), they were the operations headquarters from which, secure from air raids, Britain's Second World War effort was directed: here, Churchill, the War Cabinet, the Chiefs of Staff and their advisors planned British strategy. The rooms remain almost exactly as they were at the height of the war, with tin hats and gas masks still on their pegs. The books, maps and wall charts in the Map Room occupy the same positions as they did when the room was closed down on 16 August 1947. The Cabinet Room, used for War Cabinet meetings, remains uncannily intact, with Churchill's chair, blotters and 'utility' pencils, as does Churchill's bedroom and office, from where he made his stirring wartime radio broadcasts. The Transatlantic Telephone Room was where Churchill discussed crucial strategy with President Roosevelt.

In 2003 a suite of nine further rooms was opened—faithfully restored and reconstructed from wartime photographs—which had been used by Churchill's wife and his private office staff, and which also included his private dining room. In February 2005, to mark the 40th anniversary of Churchill's death, the Churchill Museum opened. At its heart is an interactive 'lifeline', surrounded by sections on, for instance, Churchill as War Leader and as a Cold War statesman.

CAMDEN ARTS CENTRE

Arkwright Road, NW3 6DG
Tel: 020-7472 5500; www.camdenartscentre.org
Open 10–6, late opening Wed until 9
Free
Tube: Finchley Road/Hampstead
Café and shop
Map p. 379, 2D

Camden Arts Centre is a well known exhibition venue for modern and contemporary visual art. Its active exhibition programme includes painting, sculpture, film, video, design and graphic art and features the work of established and influential artists as well as lesser known names, mainly British and Continental European. The building, a late 19th-century Grade II listed former public library, has recently been refurbished, but many of the architecturally clean, modernised galleries retain their large, handsome windows and parquet floors. Artist residencies and educational courses and events go hand-in-hand with exhibitions. The centre has a bookshop, a reading room, a café and an architect-designed garden.

CARLYLE'S HOUSE
(National Trust)

24 Cheyne Row, Chelsea, SW3 5HL
Tel: 020-7352 7087; www.nationaltrust.org.uk
Open Apr–Oct Wed–Fri 2–5, Sat–Sun 11–5
Admission charge. No disabled access
Tube: Sloane Square, then bus 11, 19, 22. Bus 239 from Victoria
Map p. 380, 4C

Off Cheyne Walk in this sedate corner of old Chelsea is the 1708 Queen Anne ter-raced house which was the home of the great historian, essayist and social thinker Thomas Carlyle (1795–1881), 'the sage of Chelsea'. Carlyle and his wife Jane (1801–66), known for her beauty, intelligence and wit, moved here from Scotland in 1834; the couple remained here until their deaths. The house is substantially unchanged and, though their highly-charged relationship was often tempestuous, an atmosphere of quiet and dignified simplicity remains. It was here that Carlyle, a difficult, irritable and habitually melancholy man, wrote his epic works: *The French Revolution* (1837); the influential *On Heroes, Hero Worship and the Heroic in History* (1841), in which he outlined his theories on the importance of powerful and conviction-led individuals; and biographies of his personal heroes, *Oliver Cromwell* (1845) and *Frederick the Great* (1858–65). The freehold of the house was purchased by public subscription in May 1895, and a trust formed to administer it. In 1936 it passed to the National Trust. The rooms contain much of the original furnishings, including portraits, photographs, books, manuscripts and many other personal relics. Carlyle's statue (1882) by Sir Joseph Edgar Boehm is nearby, in the gardens on the Embankment.

The Sitting Room, or Parlour, is furnished much as it appears in Robert Tait's paint-ing, *A Chelsea Interior* (c. 1857), which hangs in the room. Mrs Carlyle was much irri-tated that Tait had made her dog Nero look the size of a sheep; she also commented on the 'wrong perspective' and 'frightful table-cover'. Among the photographs and por-traits is Boehm's plaster maquette for his seated statue of Carlyle. The Back Dining Room, the rear of the room, contains James Archer's 1869 portrait of Carlyle and one of Frederick the Great of Prussia, whose biography Carlyle had recently completed when his wife bought it in 1866, the day before she died (suddenly, of an attack brought on by the shock of Nero escaping from the carriage at Hyde Park Corner). Chico the canary lived in the birdcage. Downstairs, the kitchen is little altered. Here Carlyle would smoke in the company of Tennyson, and it was also where Mrs Carlyle's domestic servant (she was a difficult woman to work for and got through several) slept. Up the stairs, passing portraits (another of Frederick the Great; one of Cromwell) and photographs of Carlyle by the pioneer Victorian photographer Julia Margaret Cameron, is the Library, or Drawing Room, where Carlyle wrote *The French Revolution* and his wife entertained such figures as Dickens, Browning, Thackeray, Darwin and Ruskin. Carlyle died here on 5th February 1881. In Mrs Carlyle's Bedroom is a chest of drawers with Carlyle's dressing-gown, waistcoats and smoking cap. The Attic Study was built for Carlyle by the firm of Cubitt in 1853 as a sound-proof retreat from noise which distracted him from his work. Unfortunately the room actually had the effect of amplifying sounds from the nearby Thames, but nevertheless Carlyle used it for 12 years, until his biography of Frederick the Great was complete. In the room are books and personal items, including some of his famous 'notekins' to his wife. The garden, with its walnut and cherry trees and lilac bushes, is much as it would have been in Carlyle's day. Mrs Carlyle's dog Nero is buried about 5ft from the southeast corner of the garden.

THE CHARLES DICKENS MUSEUM

48 Doughty Street, WC1N 2LX
Tel: 020-7405 2127; www.dickensmuseum.com
Open Mon–Sat 10–5; Sun 11–5
Admission charge. Limited disabled access
Tube: Russell Square
Shop
Map p. 382, 1B

The novelist Charles Dickens (1812–70), his wife Catherine and their infant son Charles, came to live at this late 18th-century house in March 1837, and stayed until the end of 1839. Here, two daughters, Mary and Kate, were added to the family, and Dickens established his fame as a writer with the publication of *Pickwick Papers*, *Oliver Twist* and *Nicholas Nickleby*. The house, saved from demolition by the Dickens Fellowship in 1922, is a place of pilgrimage, and holds an enormous collection of Dickens memorabilia, including portraits of the novelist, his family and friends, personal relics, for example his snuff-box and cigar-cutter, autograph letters and manuscripts, and a comprehensive Dickens library. The clutter of a literary shrine does not entirely destroy the atmosphere of the family house it once was.

The Dining Room on the ground floor was where Dickens held the dinner parties in which he delighted. It contains a Spanish mahogany sideboard, which Dickens bought in 1839, and the grandfather clock which belonged to Moses Pickwick, a coach proprietor of Bath, whose name Dickens took for his famous character. Throughout the house are items of furniture from Gad's Hill Place, Rochester, Dickens' last home, including the Hall clock and, on the first floor, in the Study, the desk which he used at the end of his life. It was in this room that *Pickwick Papers* was completed and *Oliver Twist* and *Nicholas Nickleby* written, and the table is the one at which he was writing *The Mystery of Edwin Drood* the day before he died. The museum also has Millais' drawing of Dickens on his deathbed, Dickens' china monkey (which accompanied him wherever he went), the Goldbeater's Arm sign from 2 Manette Street, Soho, mentioned in *A Tale of Two Cities*, and the velvet-covered reading desk designed by Dickens and used by him for his public readings on his extensive tours of England and America.

The Drawing Room is decorated and arranged as it would have been in Dickens' day, and on the second floor is the bedroom of his beloved sister-in-law, Mary Hogarth, who died here on 7th May 1837, aged seventeen. The basement contains the still room, wash house and wine cellar and also the Library of Dickens' work which also shows a video of Dickens' life and career.

THE CHARTERED INSURANCE INSTITUTE MUSEUM

20 Aldermanbury, EC2V 7HY
Tel: 020-7417 4417; www.24hourmuseum.org.uk
Open by appointment only, Mon–Fri 9–5. Closed bank holidays
Free
Tube: Bank/Moorgate/St Paul's
Map p. 383, 1E

This small one-room museum on the 2nd floor of the Chartered Insurance Institute is dedicated to the early history of firefighting and the birth of accident insurance. The room is decorated with murals by C. Walter Hodges illustrating the themes of fire, marine and life insurance and displays early firefighting equipment, including hand-drawn fire-engines, fireman's helmets, leather buckets, axes etc. There is a large collection of fire-marks of the early fire brigades, which were operated by insurance companies and would only fight fires in properties which bore the company's mark.

CHELSEA PHYSIC GARDEN

66 Royal Hospital Road, Chelsea, SW3 4HS. (Access from the gate on Swan Walk)
Tel: 020-7352 5646; www.chelseaphysicgarden.co.uk
Open Apr–Oct Wed 12–5, Sun 2–6
Admission charge. Disabled entrance at 66 Royal Hospital Road
Bus: 239 from Victoria
Café and shop
Map p. 380, 4C

Established in 1673 and first known as the Apothecaries' Garden, Chelsea Physic Garden first functioned as a training ground for apprentices of the Worshipful Society of Apothecaries, involved in the cultivation of plants for medicinal use. The ornamental gates on the Embankment once led directly to the river, where the Company's barge was housed. In 1681 the garden boasted the first heated greenhouse in England, known as the 'stove', which attracted the attention of eminent botanists and scientists such as Sir Hans Sloane and John Ray, both keenly interested in the cultivation of rare 'exotics'. In 1685 John Evelyn visited Chelsea and noted the 'the tree bearing the Jesuit's bark', the source of the expensive anti-malarial quinine. It was also in the 1680s that four cedars of Lebanon were planted, the first in England (the last one died in 1904). One of the trees produced its first cone in 1725, and seeds were distributed widely around the estates of Britain, and also to America. The garden was part of the Manor of Chelsea, which had been purchased by Sloane in 1712. In 1722 Sloane transferred the freehold to the Apothecaries in virtual perpetuity, for an annual rent of £5, for use as a Physic Garden where 'the power and glory of God in the works of creation' could be studied. The statue of Sloane, placed at the centre of the garden where its four lawn walks meet, is a copy of that commissioned from Michael Rysbrack in 1733–37, the original having been removed to the British Museum to protect it from further erosion.

Under the care of Philip Miller (1691–1771), appointed by Sloane in 1722, Chelsea became one of the best-known botanic gardens in Europe. In 1732 cotton seed was sent from Chelsea to the new settlement of Georgia and in 1736 the great Linnaeus visited the garden to study and collect plants. Many of the species introduced to Britain over the centuries and associated with Chelsea still thrive in the garden today, including magnificent magnolias named after Sloane's professor, Pierre Magnol.

Hidden behind its tall brick walls, the garden is a secret paradise, but also a museum of living plants, arranged according to species and purpose. As well as the Systematic Order Beds, there is a Herb Garden, a woodland area, a fern house, a Garden of World Medicine and a Pharmaceutical Garden, where Deadly Nightshade (*Atropa bella-donna*) grows, with its round, black glossy fruits known as devil's cherries. The garden is still used for research: the Natural History Museum's Botany Department, for example, propagates tomatoes here for taxonomic research. Near the garden's main buildings is the first rock garden in England. Built in 1773, it is made up of white Portland stones, some with ornamental moulding, from parts of the Tower of London then being demolished, and black basaltic lava from Iceland, donated by Sir Joseph Banks (*see p. 127*). Later in the 18th century it was further ornamented with shells and corals brought back from Tahiti as ships' ballast by Captain Cook. A giant clam shell remains.

Today, Chelsea is a beautiful and tranquil place to spend a summer Sunday afternoon, when excellent home-made teas are served on the terrace overlooking the well cared-for lawns and ornamental but historic beds.

CHISWICK HOUSE
(English Heritage)

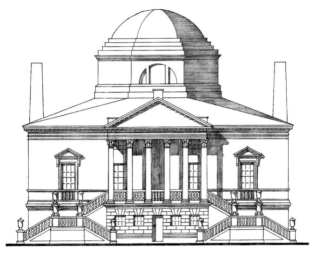

CHISWICK HOUSE

Burlington Lane, Chiswick W4 2RD
Tel: 020-8995 0508; www.english-heritage.org.uk/visits
Open April–end Oct Wed–Fri, Sun and bank holidays 10–5;
Sat 10–2. Nov–March by appointment
Admission charge. Ground floor disabled access;
phone first for access to main floor
Station: Chiswick (from Clapham Junction)
Shop. Café nearby in park
Map p. 378, 3C

Chiswick House is the greatest architectural statement of Richard Boyle, 3rd Earl of
Burlington (1694–1753), the early 18th-century 'Apollo of the Arts' and the chief promoter of Palladianism. Heavily influenced by the architecture of ancient Rome and
that of Palladio, which he had witnessed on his tours of Italy (returning from the second trip in 1719), as well as the architecture of the great Inigo Jones, Burlington conceived Chiswick as an embodiment of his architectural ideals. The jewel-like villa,
with ornate interiors and Jonesian ceilings painted by Burlington's protégé William
Kent, was originally attached to the estate's Jacobean mansion and was used as a temple of the arts, an intellectual retreat where Burlington displayed his fine pictures and
sculptures and entertained friends, including the poet Alexander Pope. On

Burlington's death the estate passed via his daughter to Lord Hartington, later 4th Duke of Devonshire, and in 1788, under the 5th Duke, the Jacobean house was demolished and wings added to the villa north and south. Throughout the 18th and 19th centuries the house was a centre of English social life. In 1809 Charles James Fox died here and Edward VII, as Prince of Wales, spent time here, as did the Tsars of Russia. The Chiswick estate remained with the Dukes of Devonshire until 1929. In 1956–57 the Ministry of Works restored the villa, demolished the wings which were obscuring Burlington's design, but retained the Link Building which had attached the villa to the old Jacobean house. Burlington's pictures and much of the furniture designed for the house by Kent have either been dispersed or are in the Devonshire collection at Chatsworth. Several loans from the latter, however, and the odd chance purchase of important pieces original to the house, give a sense of the villa as it was in its 1730s heyday.

The approach to the house is from the gateway on Burlington Lane, which opens on to a courtyard enclosed by a box hedge. Burlington's extraordinary creation, built in 1727–29, is directly ahead. Palladio's Villa Rotonda is usually cited as the main inspirational source, but in fact the villa is Burlington's own unique interpretation of several. The central octagonal dome is flanked by four chimney stacks in the shape of obelisks, while an elaborate double staircase rises to the first floor entrance, under a Corinthian portico of great richness, the carving crisp and pure. At the foot of the staircase, to either side, are statues by J.M. Rysbrack (c. 1730) of Burlington's architectural heroes, Palladio and Inigo Jones.

The Interior

Visitors enter at ground level through the doors under the staircase. The symmetrical room layout, around the central octagon, or **Lower Tribune**, echoes the arrangement on the upper floor, but these basement rooms are of a deliberate austerity, rich grandeur retained for the principal rooms above. Burlington's private rooms and library were down here, but now the rooms are given over to an architectural introduction to the house and gardens. The **Library** occupied three rooms, through which access is gained to the lower floor of the Link Building and, beyond it, the **Summer Parlour** with its fine ceiling. Below the Lower Tribune is the octagonal wine cellar. A concealed spiral staircase leads up to the main floor.

A sequence of nine rooms of a studied, intellectual magnificence is arranged around the octagonal domed Tribune, or **Saloon**, with light flooding in from its Diocletian windows, its walls punctuated by four pedimented doorways, based on Jones designs. Classical busts sit on gilded brackets and above them hang large pictures from Burlington's collection at Burlington House, Piccadilly, but which were brought to Chiswick in 1733 (*see Royal Academy, p. 244*). They include *Charles I and his Family*, after van Dyck; *Liberality and Modesty*, after Veronese; *Louis XIII* and *Anne of Austria*, by Poussin's master Ferdinand Elle; and Kneller's *The Moroccan Ambassador* (1684), an equestrian portrait of Mohammed Ohadu, famous for his displays of horsemanship in Hyde Park. The **Gallery** runs the full length of the garden front and is one of the most

A suburban retreat recreating the villas of northern Italy: the gardens at Chiswick House.

important rooms in the house. A tripartite space with a rectangular, apsed centre, with flanking circular and octagonal cabinets, it is a rigorously controlled architectural enfilade. The actual dimensions are small but an effect of grandeur is achieved through the skilfully judged proportions and the richly carved and ornamented surfaces, decorated in white and gold. The ceiling painting is a copy of Veronese's *Defence of Smyrna*, attributed to Sebastiano Ricci, who also decorated Burlington House (now the Royal Academy; *see p. 244*). The surrounding ceiling panels, within compartments with ornamentation derived from Jones, are by Kent. The magnificent carved and gilded marble-topped tables, designed by Kent, were made for the house in 1730 and returned in 1996. The **Red Velvet Room** was originally filled with paintings. Another rich compartmented ceiling, again based on Jones, has Kent's *Mercury Presiding over the Arts* in the centre, surrounded by signs of the zodiac. The marble chimneypieces are based on Jones designs and the ornate, gilded overmantels contain paintings by Ricci: *Bacchus and Ariadne* and *Venus and Cupid*. The **Blue Velvet Room** has an elaborate ceiling design with console brackets with Kent's *Architecture* in the centre. The carved and gilded pedimented doorways are surmounted by portraits, held by putti, including *Inigo Jones* by William Dobson and *Pope* by Kent. The **Red Closet** beyond it showed prized, smaller scale pictures.

The Gardens

Burlington and Kent's interior, a fusion of classical, 16th-century Italian and 17th-century Jonesian taste, was augmented by a similarly carefully designed garden. The garden had been evolving from 1716 onwards, but in the early 1730s Kent was brought in to complete for Burlington a Roman suburban retreat. Many of the features can still be seen, including the broad avenue lined with urns and sphinxes, culminating in a semi-circular exedra, originally of myrtle but now of yew, framing busts of Caesar, Pompey and Cicero. Radiating paths once terminated in garden buildings of which the Rustic House still survives. The bridge over the Canal was built by James Wyatt in 1788. At the Canal's south end is the recently restored **Cascade**, two triple arched storeys of rough masonry down which water flows. To the southwest extremity of the estate is a tall obelisk, and elsewhere a turfed amphitheatre with a small Ionic temple with an obelisk and a sheet of water in front of it.

The gardens at Chiswick are important in marking a departure from the intricate, formal designs of the Baroque age and the introduction of a more natural landscape, with semi-contrived wildernesses and expansive vistas. They are in a neglected state, however, and vandalism has been a significant problem (e.g. the beheading of a sphinx). The grounds are the responsibility of the local borough council (English Heritage manages the house only), but the two authorities have united in a campaign of restoration, with work due to begin towards the end of 2005.

North of the house is the **Inigo Jones Gateway**, brought to Chiswick from Beaufort House, Chelsea in 1736, a gift of Sir Hans Sloane and the subject of a poem by Pope:

> *Passenger: O Gate! how cam'st thou here?*
> *Gate: I was brought from Chelsea last year,*
> *Battered with wind and weather;*
> *Inigo Jones put me together,*
> *Sir Hans Sloane let me alone,*
> *Burlington brought me hither.*

THE CLOCKMAKERS MUSEUM

The Clock Room, Guildhall Library, Aldermanbury, EC2P 2EJ
Tel: 020-7332 1868; www.clockmakers.org
Open Mon–Sat 9.30–4.30
Free
Tube: Bank
Map p. 383, 2E

This interesting one-room museum, just inside the entrance to the Guildhall Library, to the left, houses the collection of the Worshipful Company of Clockmakers, a livery company established in 1631. At that date, clock- and watchmaking in the City of

London was predominant in the area around Guildhall. On display are around 600 clocks, watches and marine chronometers dating from the 15th century to the present day, including the work of leading British and many foreign makers, among them Thomas Tompion and John Harrison. There are also portraits of clockmakers, manuscripts and other items relating to the history of the craft. Many of the exhibits represent important technological advances in watch- and clockmaking, but there are also exquisitely designed and decorated cases, masterpieces of applied art in enamels, gold repoussé, pin-work and other techniques. Watch keys, fobs and chatelaines are on show as well as a silver skull watch, said to have belonged to Mary Queen of Scots, and the wristwatch worn by Sir Edmund Hillary on his successful ascent of Everest in 1953. The room is filled with the gentle sound of ticking. NB: The museum is sometimes closed for short periods to allow for the adjustment, re-setting and winding of timepieces.

CONTEMPORARY APPLIED ARTS

2 Percy Street, W1T 1DD
Tel: 020-7436 2344; www.caa.org.uk
Open Mon–Sat 10.30–5.30
Free
Tube: Goodge Street/Tottenham Court Road
Map p. 382, 1A

Founded in 1948 as the Crafts Centre of Great Britain, its aim to support and promote excellent craftwork, Contemporary Applied Arts is the showcase of an association of around 200 professional makers. There is a constant retail display of members' work including jewellery, metalwork, ceramics, woodwork, textiles, glass and bookbinding, but there are also special exhibitions which focus on innovations in the crafts. It is usually home to the annual exhibition of artists shortlisted for the Jerwood Applied Arts prize (*see Jerwood Space, p. 134*).

CRAFTS COUNCIL GALLERY

44a Pentonville Road, Islington, N1 9BY
Tel: 020-7278 7700; www.craftscouncil.org.uk
Open Tues–Sat 11–5.45; Sun 2–5.45
Free
Tube: Angel
Café and shop
Map p. 379, 2E

Established in 1971, the Crafts Council is the national organisation for the promotion of fine contemporary craftsmanship in all media. As well as a programme of British and international modern and contemporary craft exhibitions, there is an annually changing exhibition featuring items from the permanent collection. Begun in 1972, the Crafts Council possesses over 1,500 craft objects, mainly pottery, including important pieces by the British potters Bernard Leach and Lucie Rie. The shop sells contemporary craft pieces including jewellery, ceramics, glass and woodwork, and makers can be researched in the reference library and on the National Register of Makers, a visual database. The Crafts Council runs a second shop within the main shop of the V&A.

CUMING MUSEUM

155–157 Walworth Road, Walworth, SE17 1RS
Tel: 020-7525 2163; www.southwark.gov.uk
Open Tues–Sat 10–5
Free. No disabled access
Tube: Elephant and Castle
Map p. 379, 3E

Located on the first floor of Newington Public Library, this small local museum is based on the collection of Richard Cuming (1777–1870) and his son Henry Syer Cuming (1817–1902), who between them amassed an eclectic range of nearly 100,000 objects encompassing natural history, ethnography, local archaeology and social history. Henry Cuming left the collection to the local borough, together with a sum of money for the employment of a curator, and the museum was opened in 1906 by Lord Rothschild. There is a small but interesting collection of ancient Egyptian artefacts, mainly bought at auction in the 1830s by Richard Cuming from the collection of Henry Salt, whose excavated finds greatly enhanced the Egyptian collections of the British Museum and the Louvre. Cuming also purchased at auction many items from Captain Cook's voyages of discovery to the South Pacific, Australia, New Zealand and the Americas, as well as coins, geological specimens, textiles and prints. Henry Cuming's main interest was local history. He was Vice-President of the British Archaeological Association and collected items relating to the Roman, medieval and post-medieval archaeology of the Southwark area. Social history items include theatre bills, rail tickets and good luck charms, the latter collection being augmented in 1916 by that of Edward Lovett, who was interested in the history of superstition and in 1878 had founded the Folklore Society. The museum today continues to collect material relevant to the past and recent history of Southwark and its local communities.

CUTTY SARK

King William Walk, Greenwich, SE10 9HT
Tel: 020-8858 3445; www.cuttysark.org.uk
Open daily 10–5
Admission charge. Disabled access to tween deck
Station: Cutty Sark on DLR
Shop
Map p. 379, 3F

The *Cutty Sark* is the most famous and fastest of the great tea clippers, which raced each other annually to bring back the lucrative new-season China tea crop from the Far East. Now the only tea clipper to survive, she was built by the firm Scott & Linton at their shipyard at Dumbarton, on the Clyde, and launched in 1869. Her name comes from the short shirt of Paisley linen worn by the witch Nannie in Robert Burns' poem 'Tam O'Shanter', who serves as the ship's figurehead, grasping the tail of Tam's grey mare in her hand. Elegant and sleek, with a great expanse of sail, the *Cutty Sark* cost £16,150, is 280ft long, weighs 938 tons and had a maximum crew of 28. At her fastest she covered 368 miles in a day. She worked in the China tea trade between 1870 and 1877, then carried coal from Shanghai to Sydney, wool between Melbourne and New York and, from 1885–95, wool between Australia and London. In 1924 she was restored as a tea clipper by Captain Dowman, and on his death was presented to

The *Cutty Sark*, in dry dock at Greenwich.

the Thames Nautical Training College. Exhibited at Greenwich in 1951 as part of the Festival of Britain, she has been in dry dock there ever since, but recent survey work has revealed serious corrosion of her ironwork and an extensive programme of restoration is necessary, funds permitting.

DALÍ UNIVERSE

County Hall Gallery, Riverside Building, County Hall, SE1 7PB
Tel: 0870 744 7485; www.countyhallgallery.com
Open daily 10–6.30 (last entry 5.30)
Admission charge
Tube: Westminster
Map p. 382, 3B

Dalí Universe is a theatrically staged exhibition dedicated to the great Surrealist. With black walls and spotlit exhibits, it was put together by Beniamino Levi, a Milanese art dealer who first met Dalí in the 1960s. Levi became a friend of Dalí, whose love of performance and showmanship is reflected in the exhibition's presentation. The majority of the exhibits are sculptures, including a reproduction of the famous 1930s *Buste de Femme Rétrospectif* and multiple production pieces such as *Profile of Time*, one of Dalí's famous dripping watch creations. There are also prints, including the well known illustrations to, for example, the Bible and Dante's *Divine Comedy*. Other reproductions include the Mae West 'Lips' sofa, a design classic created by Edward James with Dalí in 1936–38. Also on show is the large canvas commissioned by Alfred Hitchcock for his 1945 film *Spellbound*. Dalí Universe is a popular venue for corporate entertaining and is also something of a brand: similar Dalí experiences are available in Paris and Vienna.

DANSON HOUSE

Danson Park, Bexleyheath, DA6 8HL
Tel: 020-8303 6699; www.dansonhouse.com
Open Easter–Oct Wed, Thur, Sun and bank holidays 11–5
Admission charge
Station: Bexleyheath (from London Bridge or Charing Cross), then a 10-minute walk
Map p. 379, beyond 3F

Danson House is an important mid-18th-century Palladian villa, recently rescued from dereliction. Set in a municipal park in suburban southeast London, it was designed from 1763–67 by Robert Taylor, architect of the Bank of England, for Sir John Boyd, a director of the East India Company and heir to West Indian sugar plantations. The last private owner was Mr Alfred Bean, a railway entrepreneur, who sold it to Bexley Borough Council in 1921. It was taken on a long lease from the Council by English Heritage in 1995.

The architect William Chambers was involved in designing the interior, notably the marble fireplaces. In a dramatic twist to the story of the restoration of the house, the fireplaces were discovered awaiting shipment abroad, after being stolen from the semi-derelict building. They were replaced in the correct rooms thanks to a series of seven detailed mid-19th-century watercolours of the interior, done by Sarah Jane Johnson, daughter of the second owner. These paintings contributed substantially to the accuracy of the ten-year English Heritage restoration project (architects Purcell Miller Tritton). The house is now managed by the The Bexley Heritage Trust, which is undertaking the complete restoration of the service areas, kitchen, attic storey and grounds, to the original plans of the 18th-century landscape designer Nathaniel Richmond.

The restored rooms include the Dining Room, where two large gilded mirrors decorated with griffins have been recessed into the walls at each end; the Library, with verdigris wall decoration and, in pride of place, a rare late 18th-century chamber organ made by George England of Sheffield; the Octagonal Salon, where the starburst plaster ceiling has been repaired and re-gilded and—the highlight of a tour—the Grand Dining Room, complete with 19 panels painted by the French artist Charles Pavillon in 1766. Carefully restored to their original position and appearance after decades of neglect, they depict festive scenes from mythology, including the fable of Pomona and her ageing lover Vertumnus. They were commissioned by John Boyd to celebrate his recent marriage to the much younger Catherine Chapone.

DENNIS SEVERS HOUSE

18 Folgate St, E1
Tel: 020-7247 4013; www.dennissevershouse.co.uk
Open 1st and 3rd Sun of each month 2–5;
Mon following the 1st and 3rd Sun 12–2;
Also open on Mon evenings for candlelight viewings (booking essential)
Telephone for additional Dec and early Jan openings,
when the house is dressed for Christmas
Admission charge
Tube: Liverpool Street
Map p. 383, 1F

18 Folgate Street, a 1724 Georgian terrace house in the heart of historic Spitalfields, was created by Dennis Severs, an American designer and eccentric enthusiast for times past, who lived in the house with no electricity and few concessions to the modern world until his death in 1999. With period decoration and furnishings, many bought from local markets, the rooms are presented at different historical periods as they would have

appeared when inhabited by successive generations of the fictional Jervis family. Historically, Spitalfields was an area dominated by Huguenot silk weavers (*see box below*) and this was the Jervis family trade when they first occupied the house in the early 18th century. Visitors progress through the centuries from the Kitchen and Front Parlour, to the late 18th-century prosperity of the elegant Drawing Room and to the collapse of the silk industry and the cold, damp poverty of the Victorian attics. An evening candlelight tour is the most atmospheric. To best savour the series of *tableaux vivants*, visitors are asked to maintain silence (and can be asked to leave if they do not). Sounds and smells hint at the family near at hand. Floorboards creak, clocks tick, a bird flutters in its cage, carriages bowl past on the cobbled street outside, candles flicker and warm fires crackle and hiss. Throughout the house the emphasis is on evocation of atmosphere and mood rather than pinpoint historical accuracy, and a visit is an unforgettable experience.

The Huguenot Contribution

Throughout the 16th and 17th centuries large numbers of Huguenot (French Calvinist) refugees found a safe haven in England, exiles from religious persecution. Many came to escape the French Wars of Religion and the 1572 Massacre of St Bartholomew, and numbers peaked sharply following the 1685 Revocation of the Edict of Nantes, which removed Protestant freedom of worship. Huguenot communities were established in East Anglia, Kent, and along the south coast, as well as London, which was the main draw. By 1700 Spitalfields, Leicester Fields and Soho had become distinct Huguenot areas. Spitalfields, being beyond the jurisdiction of the Weavers' Company in the City, became increasingly identified with the silk industry.

Many Huguenots were prosperous international merchants who were able to escape with their goods intact. Their investments in London banking and insurance houses (several Huguenots were foundation subscribers to the Bank of England) contributed substantially to the capital's wealth, whilst marriage alliances created powerful trading and financial dynasties. A great many more Huguenots were skilled craftsmen, whose expertise and innovatory techniques had a profound impact on London's luxury trades. An early key figure was Daniel Marot, a pupil of Louis XIV's *maître ornemaniste*, who was in England in the 1690s, working for William and Mary at Hampton Court. His interior designs, with grotesque ornament, mirrors, lacquer work, massed displays of porcelain and elaborate upholstery, provided rich sources for contemporary craftspeople. Important carvers and gilders included the Pelletier family, who provided furniture for Kensington Palace and Hampton Court, and a leading upholsterer was Francis Lapiere, based, with others, in Pall Mall. Many of London's leading 18th-century goldsmiths, such as Paul Crespin, Paul de Lamerie and the Rococo master Nicholas Sprimont, were second-generation Huguenots, while native masters such as George Wickes and Thomas Heming were Huguenot-trained.

DESIGN MUSEUM

28 Shad Thames, Butlers Wharf, SE1 2YD
Tel: 0870 833 9955; www.designmuseum.org
Open daily 10–5.45
Admission charge
Tube/Station: London Bridge/Tower Hill
Restaurant, café and shop
Map p. 383, 3F

Founded by Sir Terence Conran in 1989, the Design Museum occupies a building in the Butler's Wharf redevelopment on the South Bank, east of Tower Bridge. Part of the historic area of warehouses and wharves stretching down to Docklands, Butler's Wharf was originally used for the importing of tea, spices and fruit and, later, rubber. Regenerated by Conran & Partners it is now a residential and commercial area with restaurants, bars, shops and galleries. The museum itself occupies a bright, white-rendered converted 1950s warehouse, provided by the Conran Foundation rent-free. The museum's founding purpose was to celebrate and promote modern and contemporary design, principally functional industrial design. The permanent collection focuses on product design, from cars to tableware, telephones and televisions, washing machines, furniture, including Rennie Mackintosh, and office equipment. There is also a programme of temporary exhibitions. The museum has come under recent criticism for its current emphasis on style and interior design (with exhibitions on, for example, the 50s flower arranger Constance Spry) rather than the more serious subject, the role of design in engineering and technology. As well as a café and shop, the Blueprint Café, a Conran restaurant, is on the first floor with impressive views over the Thames to the Tower of London, the City and the Swiss Re building (the 'Gherkin'), and to Canary Wharf.

DR JOHNSON'S HOUSE

17 Gough Square, (off Fleet Street), EC4A 3DE
Tel: 020-7353 3745; www.drjh.dircon.co.uk
Open May–Sept Mon–Sat 11–5.30; Oct–April Mon–Sat 11–5
Closed bank holidays
Admission charge. No disabled access
Tube: Blackfriars/Chancery Lane
Shop
Map p. 382, 2C

Dr Johnson's House lies tucked behind Fleet Street, approached via a number of passages, Hind Court, St Dunstan's Court or Johnson's Court, narrow alleyways which are part of London's pre-1666 Great Fire street pattern. They open into Gough Square with its granite paving and, in the evening, atmospheric gas lighting. The house occupies the square's west end and is its principal remaining old building. A handsome c. 1700 house of red brick, with a later 18th-century doorcase, it was where the great lexicographer Dr Samuel Johnson (1709–84) lived from 1748–59. The house has had a mixed history since Johnson's occupation. In the 19th century it was a hotel, a print shop and a storehouse, but was restored by Cecil Harmsworth and opened as a museum in 1912. The small-scale house immediately adjoining is the curator's residence.

Originally from Lichfield in Staffordshire, Johnson moved to London with his friend the actor David Garrick. A struggling journalist when he first occupied the house, he produced *The Rambler* here and wrote his novel *Rasselas*. It was also while he was living here that he was commissioned to write the celebrated Dictionary. Published in two volumes in 1755, it went through four editions in Johnson's lifetime and instantly became the standard authority. A congenial man with a wide circle of intellectual friends, including at this point in his life the artist Sir Joshua Reynolds and Charles Burney, Johnson nevertheless was not a wealthy man. He lived simply at Gough Square with his wife, Elizabeth Porter, 20 years his senior, until her death in 1752, and later his Jamaican servant, Francis Barber, joined him.

The interior

The house is by no means an ostentatious one. Only one room deep with no windows on the back wall, it has a central staircase and simply panelled rooms. The Dining Room and Parlour are on the ground floor. The stairs lead to a landing with hinged walls, allowing the staircase to be blocked off and one large room created. Off the landing is the Withdrawing Room and Miss Williams's Room, the authoress Anna Williams being a friend of Mrs Johnson and companion to Dr Johnson after his wife's death. The museum's portrait of her, once owned by Johnson's great friend and biographer James Boswell, was painted by Reynolds' sister Frances. Johnson's bedroom was on the next floor and at the top of the house is the garret, where the Dictionary was written and where, at long tables, six clerks took down Johnson's succinct and often witty definitions. Throughout the rooms are period furnishings and objects, several of them personal to Johnson or to his close friends. They include Reynolds' china caddy, dish and saucer for tea (1775), Boswell's drinking mug and coffee cup, a self-portrait by Reynolds, a pencil drawing of Mrs Thrale (by John Jackson, 1810) and an oak chest which belonged to Garrick, in which he is said to have kept his theatrical costumes. Johnson's own walking stick is on show as is his piece of 'healing gold', a medal he received when as a young child he was touched for the King's Evil by Queen Anne. Other exhibits include numerous engravings of Johnson and his friends, letters, manuscripts and Eyre Crowe's painting *Dr Johnson Doing Penance in the Market Place of Uttoxeter*. A first edition of the Dictionary is in the Dining Room.

Facing the house, at the east end of the square, is a modern sculpture of Dr Johnson's cat, Hodge, sitting with oysters by his side, which Johnson regularly bought for him.

Just beyond the square, in Wine Office Court, is the Cheshire Cheese inn, a frequent haunt of Johnson's and still evocative of his era.

DULWICH PICTURE GALLERY

DULWICH PICTURE GALLERY: EAST FRONT

Gallery Road, Dulwich, SE21 7AD
Tel: 020-8693 5254; www.dulwichpicturegallery.org.uk
Open Tues–Fri 10–5, Sat–Sun and bank holidays 11–5
Admission charge
Station: North Dulwich (from London Bridge)/West Dulwich (from Victoria)
Café and shop
Map p. 379, 3E

Designed by the great architect Sir John Soane in 1811–13, Dulwich Picture Gallery is the oldest public art gallery in the country. Purpose-built for the display of pictures, it houses a significant collection of Old Master paintings, the majority of which were bequeathed in 1811 by Sir Francis Bourgeois, including many originally destined for the King of Poland. Dulwich opened its doors to the public in 1817 (seven years before the National Gallery), and in June of that year its first annual dinner took place. Over 30 guests, including many Royal Academicians, feasted on turtle soup and venison accompanied by madeira, claret, port, sherry and champagne. Visitors to the gallery had to purchase tickets in advance from one of a number of shops in central London. Today, Soane's great building, its east façade recently reconstructed to better accord with Soane's original intention (galleries had been added along the front c. 1910), sits in spacious grounds in a gracious area of old Dulwich which retains much of the 'delightful country' feel remarked on by Bourgeois. The new cloister-like wing, with café (Rick Mather 2000), which wraps itself round the east and north edges of the grounds, against the building of old Dulwich College (relocated nearby in the late 19th century) is low-built and glass-fronted so as not to detract from Soane.

History of the Collection
Now an independent charitable trust, until 1994 Dulwich was part of Alleyn's College

of God's Gift (which included the school, Dulwich College), a 17th-century educational and charitable foundation established in 1619 by the Elizabethan actor and theatre manager Edward Alleyn (1566–1626). Alleyn, manager of the Rose and Fortune Theatres, rivals to the Globe, as well as of London's bear-baiting, bequeathed to his college his collection of pictures, which included a set of English monarchs beginning with William the Conqueror, and a set of Sibyls. Of historical rather than aesthetic importance, these are rarely displayed. They were joined in 1686 by about 80 from the collection of the actor William Cartwright which, with their surviving inventory, stand as an important record of the collecting tastes of a moderately wealthy, neither rich nor noble, 17th-century Londoner. Among the portraits are important works by John Greenhill; the only contemporary likeness of the actor Richard Burbage; and good quality seapieces by Laureys de Castro.

Sir Francis Bourgeois' bequest in 1811 of over 350 Old Master pictures, many of great distinction, transformed the College collection. Bourgeois (1756–1811), an artist of moderate ability (several examples of his work are in the collection), was the protégé of the ambitious art dealer Noel Desenfans (1744–1807), with whom he collaborated. Between 1790 and 1795 Desenfans was collecting on behalf of Stanislaw II Augustus, King of Poland, who wished to establish a National Gallery of Poland; but with the partition of that country and the forced abdication of the king in 1795 Desenfans was left with the pictures on his hands. On Desenfans's death in 1807 the remarkable collection, which included works from great collections auctioned as a result of the French Revolution and Napoleonic Wars, passed to Bourgeois.

Highlights of the Collection

The pictures at Dulwich include about 56 of those intended for Poland (others were sold at auction in 1802), and those Bourgeois continued to collect. Highlights of the French works include works by Claude and his circle; Charles Le Brun's *Massacre of the Innocents*, previously owned by Louis XIV's Keeper of the Royal Treasury and then the Duc d'Orléans; Poussin's *Nurture of Jupiter* and *The Triumph of David*, showing David parading the head of Goliath through Jerusalem; and Watteau's *Plaisir du Bal*, which the artist Constable, on a visit to Dulwich, found 'so mellow, so tender, so soft, so delicious'. The collection has a particularly strong collection of Dutch and Flemish pictures: several works by Cuyp, Pynacker, Ruisdael and Teniers the Younger, Dou's *A Woman Playing a Clavichord*, possibly that in the de Bye collection, Leiden, in 1665; Aert de Gelder's *Jacob's Dream*, with its huge sky and angel appearing in a dazzling, bright light, formerly owned by Le Brun; Rembrandt's well known *A Girl at a Window*, signed and dated 1645, probably owned by the influential French art critic Roger de Piles; several works by Rubens, including *Venus, Mars and Cupid*, also from the Orléans collection; and Wouwermans' *Halt of a Hunting Party*, another Orléans picture. Italian pictures include works by Guercino; Sebastiano Ricci's *Resurrection*, an oil sketch for the painted apse in the chapel of the Royal Hospital, Chelsea; Veronese's *Saint Jerome and a Donor*; and Guido Reni's *Saint Sebastian*, a version of the work in the Prado, Madrid (but with a reduced loin cloth), which was a highly celebrated pic-

Rembrandt: *A Girl at a Window* (1645).

ture at Dulwich in the 19th century. Another popular work, and much copied, was Murillo's *Flower Girl*, probably modelled by the artist's daughter Francisca, later a nun.

The British pictures came largely from Charles Fairfax Murray, who bequeathed them between 1911 and 1919 in order to boost the gallery's British School representation. The bequest included van Dyck's extraordinary *Venetia Stanley, Lady Digby, on her Death-bed*, painted in 1633 two days after she died in her sleep; Lely's *Nymphs by a Fountain* (before 1640) and the beautiful *Young Boy as a Shepherd*, possibly once owned by the English 17th-century portraitist Mary Beale. These works joined the early Alleyn and Cartwright British pictures; the Linley portraits, including Gainsborough's excellent full-length *The Linley Sisters*, bequeathed by William Linley in 1831; and Sir Joshua Reynolds' great *Mrs Siddons as the Tragic Muse*, a replica of the one now at the Huntington Art Gallery, San Marino, which Desenfans ordered from Reynolds in 1789.

The Building

Soane's task was to design a new gallery for the pictures which was also to incorporate a mausoleum for the tombs of Bourgeois and Desenfans and later Desenfans' wife (d. 1813), all of whom had been Soane's friends. This dual purpose, and association between death and art, excited Soane, and Dulwich became his 'favourite subject'.

Nicolas Poussin: *The Nurture of Jupiter* (1636–37).

Due to lack of funds, the actual building (which cost less than £10,000) is stark and austere with little embellishment: though celebrated today, it was not truly Soane's wish. The main galleries, a succession of plain interlinked spaces, had toplighting in the form of large lanterns, influential for later gallery design in Britain; and the mausoleum was centrally placed on the west side, flanked by almshouses (a key function of Alleyn's college), now converted to galleries. The contrast between the 'dull, religious light' of the mausoleum, filtered through amber glass, and the daylight clarity of the gallery, was deliberate. Internally the gallery has been restored as far as possible to its original early 19th-century appearance, including the smoky dark red of its walls.

The main galleries at the Dulwich Picture Gallery, top-lit by Soane's octagonal lanterns.

ELTHAM PALACE

(English Heritage)

Court Yard, off Court Road, Eltham SE9 5QE
Tel: 020-8294 2548; www.elthampalace.org.uk
Open April–Oct Mon–Wed and Sun 10–5; Nov–March 10–4
Closed 24 Dec–1 Feb
Admission charge
Station: Eltham (from Charing Cross), then bus 126, 161
Café and shop
Map p. 379, 3F

The manor of Eltham was one of the oldest estates belonging to the Crown and by the 14th century one of the largest and most frequented of the English Royal Palaces. Originally a moated manor house, it was a favourite Christmas residence of English sovereigns from Henry III to Henry VIII. Chaucer was clerk of the works to Richard II here, and here Henry IV entertained the Byzantine emperor Manuel II Palaeologus. After Agincourt Henry V stayed at Eltham before his triumphal entry into London. The Great Hall, the most evident feature of the medieval palace which remains today, was constructed by Edward IV in 1475–80. Henry VIII was the last monarch to spend much time at Eltham, and after the Civil War both the palace and its grounds were given over to agricultural use. The Great Hall was used as a barn and romantic views of it as such were made by several artists, including Turner.

The Courtaulds and Eltham

In 1933 the site was purchased by the wealthy couple Stephen and Virginia Courtauld, who conceived a spectacular and luxurious house. Designed by Seely & Paget, the aim was to construct a glamorous and modern home while retaining as much as possible of the medieval palace. The result is an extraordinarily eclectic mix, the 1930s house incorporating the Great Hall and other palace walls, and the gardens, the medieval moat, and the exposed foundations of various royal lodgings. Externally the house is inspired by Wren's Hampton Court, but inside a succession of stylish rooms was created by leading 1930s interior designers. A programme of restoration was completed by English Heritage in 1999.

Stephen Courtauld never joined the family textile firm, which manufactured rayon, but his inherited shares generated immense wealth. In 1923 he married Virginia Peirano, of Italian-Hungarian parentage. Both were interested in the arts (Stephen's brother, Samuel, was founder of the Courtauld Institute Galleries, *see p. 275*) and in modern design, and Eltham was conceived as a showcase for their art collection. The interiors were created by a team of artistic advisers, personal friends of the Courtaulds, including Winifred Knights and her husband Tom Monnington, the Swedish interior designer Rolf Engströmer (head of the Swedish company Jefta) and the Italian decorator Peter Malacrida. Malacrida, then working for the company White Allom, had been a neighbour of the Courtaulds in Grosvenor Square. The house was a stage for extravagant weekend parties, the quality of its materials and craftsmanship matched by the luxury of the innovative 1930s technological features: an internal telephone system, concealed ceiling lights, underfloor heating, speakers which broadcast music throughout the ground floor, and a centralised vacuum cleaner with sockets in each room.

Tour of the House

The entrance to the house, over the medieval bridge across the moat, is through a curved colonnade flanked by two tall staircase turrets. H. Carlton Attwood's relief carving *Hospitality* directly above the door welcomes visitors. The **Entrance Hall** is triangular in shape, with light flooding in from Engströmer's shallow domed ceiling, of concrete

The Entrance Hall of Eltham Palace, with Rolf Engströmer's famous shallow domed ceiling.

with pierced glazing. The walls are lined with Australian blackbean veneer with inset marquetry scenes incorporating Florentine and Venetian architecture, and landmark buildings in Stockholm. Large figures, a Roman centurion and a Viking, flank the entrance door. The central rug, with geometric patterns, is a reproduction of the original by Marion Dorn (V&A) and the furniture placed on it, under the dome, replicates Engströmer's 1930s blackbean and walnut originals, upholstered in cream.

To the left is the **Dining Room**, a bold Art Deco interior designed by Malacrida. The walls and ceiling are of maple flexwood, the ceiling having a central rectangular recess finished with aluminium leaf which shimmers in the lighting concealed around its perimeter. The ceiling also conceals the central heating. The fireplace contains a very early instance of an electric imitation log fire which is flanked by curved, ribbed aluminium panels, the whole surrounded by an Art Deco design in black marble with a Greek key design. The latter also appears on the ebonised doors and cupboards, which also have large applied lacquer designs of animals and birds.

The **Drawing Room**, to the right of the entrance hall, was also designed by Malacrida, in Florentine Renaissance style. Originally it would have had sumptuous soft furnishings in silk damask and velvet, with Turkish rugs on the floor. The false beams, with Hungarian folk art decoration, conceal lighting for the Renaissance pictures which once hung here, the most important being Veronese's *Astronomer and Patriarch*, now in the National Gallery, Zimbabwe (the Courtaulds emigrated to Southern Rhodesia in 1951).

The corridor off the hall leads to Virginia Courtauld's **Boudoir**, designed by Malacrida with a coved and mirrored ceiling with concealed lighting and a large sofa with attached side tables and shelves. The **Library** next door was originally hung with the Courtaulds' collection of watercolours, including works by Turner now at the Courtauld Institute Galleries. Edward IV's medieval **Great Hall** is at the end of the corridor. The Courtaulds conceived it as a music room and held great parties here. The impressive and lofty hammerbeam roof, with its carved tracery, was restored but the Minstrel's Gallery, the carved screen and the stained glass are imaginative medieval-style creations. Instead of tapestries, the walls were hung with decorative rayon hangings.

From the entrance hall, the West Stairs lead up to **Stephen Courtauld's Suite**, designed by Seely. The bedroom has walls of aspen veneer and expensive hand block printed Kew Gardens wallpaper. **Virginia Courtauld's Bedroom**, by Malacrida, is approached through a circular lobby with a sliding door and niches for vases of flowers. The bedroom itself, with a circular ceiling with concealed lighting and heating, has walls of maple flexwood with inlaid marquetry. The bathroom is luxuriously appointed, with walls lined with onyx and a bath set in a gold mosaic niche with, above the gold-plated taps, a classical sculpture of Psyche.

Returning to the landing visitors can see **Mah-Jongg's Quarters**, designed for the Courtaulds' pet ring-tailed lemur, bought at Harrods in 1923. 'Jongy' enjoyed central heating, a bamboo forest mural and a bamboo ladder leading down to the Flower Room. He accompanied his owners everywhere and had his own small deckchair for foreign cruises. Among the guest bedrooms is the **Venetian Suite**, which incorporates 1780s Venetian panelling into Malacrida's design of mirrored walls painted with elaborate arabesques.

The Grounds

The gardens retain their 1930s layout and include important remains of the medieval palace and its moat, particularly in the area of the Turning Circle and Squash Court. The South Garden retains its luxuriant 1930s herbaceous border and the sunken Rose Garden has at its centre a tranquil pool planted with water lilies. There is a rock garden with a gentle water cascade, and a wisteria-covered pergola made from Ionic columns salvaged from the Bank of England after its reconstruction in 1921 (*see p. 17*).

ESTORICK COLLECTION OF MODERN ITALIAN ART

39a Canonbury Square, Islington, N1 2AN
Tel: 020-7704 9522; www.estorickcollection.com
Open Wed–Sat 11–6, Sun 12–5
Admission charge. Disabled access to galleries 1–4 only
Tube: Highbury and Islington
Café and shop
Map p. 379, 2D

The Estorick Collection, which opened in 1998, is the best collection of Futurist art outside Italy. It was formed by the American-born sociologist and writer Eric Estorick and his wife Salome Dessau (d. 1989), who married in 1947 and began to collect Futurist works on their honeymoon in Switzerland and on their return to England via Milan. Further trips to Italy in the 50s shaped the collection, which they began to exhibit from 1954, including a show at the Tate Gallery in 1956. By this time Estorick had become an art dealer, and in 1960 founded the Grosvenor Gallery. Before his death in 1993 he set up the Eric and Salome Estorick Foundation, to which the Estorick collection of Italian works was donated, and in 1994 the Georgian house at 39a Canonbury Square was purchased for their display. Futurism, which embraced the modern world and new technology and which called for a cultural rejuvenation of Italy, was launched in 1909 when Filippo Marinetti published its manifesto in *Le Figaro*. The Foundation has an excellent collection of works by Futurism's early pioneers, a group of artists in Milan which included Umberto Boccioni, Carlo Carrà, Luigi Russolo, Giacomo Balla and Gino Severini. Their subjects were urban and frequently political, emphasising the rapidity of change in modern life by their focus on the dynamism, speed and power of machines. The collection also contains works by other well-known Italian modern artists, mainly figurative art and sculpture dating from 1890–1950, including a series of drawings by Modigliani, his portrait of Dr François Brabander, and early works by de Chirico.

FAN MUSEUM

12 Crooms Hill, Greenwich, SE10 8ER
Tel: 020-8305 1441; www.fan-museum.org
Open (Museum) Tues–Sat 11–5, Sun 12–5 (Orangery for afternoon tea) Tues and Sun from 3pm
Admission charge
Station: Greenwich (from Charing Cross); DLR to Cutty Sark
Afternoon teas, Tues and Sun only. Shop
Map p. 379, 3F

This small museum, which occupies two 1721 Georgian town houses, is dedicated to the history of the fan and fan making. It was the brainchild of Hélène Alexander, whose own collection forms the heart of the museum's over 3,500 items. The collection ranges from the 11th century to the present day and includes fans from all over the world, from India, China and Japan as well as Europe. There is a fine representation of 17th-century French fans from the court of Louis XIV, elaborately painted on vellum, as well as intricate lace fans, a large collection of 18th- and 19th-century European fans, a c. 1889 fan painted by the British artist Walter Sickert, and other rare examples. The collection is shown through a series of exhibitions (three a year) which highlight the ceremonial, social and fashionable use of fans as well as different craftsmanship techniques. The mural-decorated orangery, which is open for afternoon tea, overlooks a Japanese-style garden with a fan-shaped parterre and small pond.

FASHION AND TEXTILE MUSEUM

83 Bermondsey Street, SE1 3XF
Tel: 020-7403 0222; www.ftmlondon.org
Open Tues–Sun 10–4.45
Tube/Station: London Bridge
Map p. 383, 3F

Founded in 2003 by fashion designer Zandra Rhodes, this small museum of contemporary fashion and textiles mounts two or three special exhibitions each year. The designer has cited the success of her 1999 San Diego exhibition 'Fashion Is' as germane to the museum's inspiration as a forum for the display, study and practice of contemporary garment design. Focusing on British and international design from 1950 to the present, the museum's permanent collection (viewable by appointment) comprises some 3,000 original articles of clothing donated by Zandra Rhodes, along with many of her working drawings, sketchbooks and show videos. The museum building was purpose-built by the Mexican architect Ricardo Legorreta, his first commission in London. With a bright orange façade and cheerful pink interior, it provides one large, high room with a catwalk ramp to the balcony gallery above, a vibrant setting to explore the changing forms and faces of cutting-edge haberdashery.

FENTON HOUSE
(National Trust)

Windmill Hill, Hampstead, NW3 6RT
Tel: 020-7435 3471; www.nationaltrust.org.uk/fentonhouse
Open April–Oct Wed–Fri 2–5, Sat–Sun 11–5; March Sat–Sun 2–5
Admission charge. Some disabled access
Tube: Hampstead
Map p. 379, 2D

This handsome red brick William and Mary house, one of the best late 17th-century houses to survive in London, stands at the very top of Hampstead in one of the most attractive parts of the 'village'. From 1936 until her death in 1952, it was the home of Lady Binning, who bequeathed it to the National Trust. Lady Binning was the beneficiary of George Salting (1835–1909), a celebrated 19th-century connoisseur-collector. Though the finest items from his collection are now in national museums, something of his eclectic taste can still be felt here; the array of Chinese blue and white porcelain is especially striking. Also on display here is the important Benton Fletcher Collection of early musical instruments, given to the Trust in 1937, thus narrowly avoiding destruction in the wartime bombing of Old Devonshire House, Bloomsbury, where it had previously been housed. Music students often play the instruments, and it is a memorable experience to visit this airy house and beautiful garden, and to hear from a distant room the evocative sound of a harpsichord or spinet.

Little is known for certain about the early history of the house. It stands on manorial land which between 1682 and 1690 passed through the hands of four different lords, the last of them only six years of age. It was probably built by William Eades, the son of a master bricklayer, apparently without the help of an architect. In the early 18th century it was bought by Joshua Gee, a Quaker linen merchant who went into partnership with George Washington's father, importing pig-iron from Maryland. Gee was also the acclaimed author of *The Trade and Navigation of Great-Britain Considered* (1729); his initials and those of his wife, Anna Osgood, are worked into the handsome wrought iron gates at the south entrance from Holly Hill. By 1786 the place was called Clock House. Six years later it was bought by Philip Fenton, son of a coal merchant from Yorkshire, whose family owned it until 1834. During their time here, the Regency loggia between the wings on the east side, which now forms the main entrance to the house, was added. Otherwise the house appears externally much as first built.

Tour of the House

The **Hall**, with original 17th-century panelling, contains an oval portrait of Philip Fenton's son James. There is also the right-hand part of a diptych by Adriaen Isenbrandt, *A Donor with St Christopher*, part of Salting's collection. Thirteen paintings by Sir William Nicholson (best known for his woodcut portrait of Queen Victoria) are on loan to the house from Ramsden Hall, Essex. Two can be seen here.

The **Dining Room** occupies the whole of the south front, originally two separate rooms, one of them a morning room. Refurbished—as was much of the house—in 1973–74 by John Fowler, the man whose taste, together with that of Sybil Colefax, shaped what we now think of as the 'English country house style', the room now displays the rest of the Nicholson paintings. These include the *Jewelled Bandalore* (1905), showing a sombre woman in a feathered hat dangling an 18th-century forerunner of the yo-yo, and *Hawking* (1902), which shows the artist's more famous son Ben (who later married Barbara Hepworth) as a young boy, dressed in a kilt with accompanying greyhound. Another portrait, *Nancy in Profile* (1912), depicts Nicholson's daughter, who after a brief marriage to the poet Robert Graves went on to make a name for herself in textile design. Other paintings are characteristically muted still lifes and his forceful *South Down Landscape Sunset 1912*. Winston Churchill cited Nicholson as the formative influence on his own painting. Also in this room is the largest harpsichord in the collection, a Shudi and Broadwood of 1770. Burkat Shudi, a Swiss emigré who enjoyed the patronage of both the Prince of Wales and Handel, took on John Broadwood as his apprentice in Soho in 1761.

The **Porcelain Room** (which also provides a good view of the garden) contains some of the finest figures produced by English and continental factories in the 18th century. The former are displayed in the left-hand alcove: porcelain from Bow, Chelsea and Derby, a rare Longton Hall figure of a harlequin (c. 1755) and a remarkable Bristol set of the 'Rustic Seasons' (c. 1773–74). In the right-hand alcove early Meissen figures by master-modeller J.J. Kändler, including harlequins designed to decorate the table at the Dresden court of Augustus the Strong (*see p. 159*), can be compared with a Scaramouche modelled by F.A. Bustelli for the Bavarian Nymphenburg manufactory, and other pieces by J.C. Ludwig von Lücke for Höchst, near Frankfurt (c. 1752). On the walls hang bird and flower paintings by Samuel Dixon (d. 1769), his so-called '*basso relievos*', which use an unusual method of applying gouache to embossed paper. They appear in their original black and gold frames.

The **Oriental Room**, formerly Lady Binning's library and little altered since her time, takes its name from the collection of Song- and Ming-dynasty porcelain displayed here, mostly in a mahogany glazed cabinet in Chinese Chippendale style. On the mantelpiece stand translucent blanc-de-Chine Dehua joss-stick holders in the shape of Dogs of Fo, from the Kangxi period (1662–1722). An alcove closet contains a curious collection of Qing dynasty (1644–1911) snuff bottles in porcelain, glass and hard stones.

Upper Floors

The **Rockingham Room** takes its name from the china now displayed here. Rockingham ware was produced on Lord Rockingham's estate near Manchester between the mid-18th and mid-19th centuries. By the fireplace hangs an early print of Dürer's *The Sea Monster* (c. 1525). The harpsichord in this room is a Shudi single-manual (i.e. an instrument with a single keyboard) of 1761 that once belonged to the pianist Fanny Davies, a pupil of Clara Schumann. In the small closet is the oldest instrument in the collection, an Italian virginal of 1540, signed Marcus Siculus, with stencilled decoration, the keyboard boxwood with ebony accidentals.

Next door is the **Blue Porcelain Room**, formerly Lady Binning's bedroom. The Chinese blue and white porcelain is of the Kangxi period (late 17th–early 18th centuries), of the type later successfully copied by the Delft factories. The double-manual harpsichord of 1777 by Jacob and Abraham Kirckman, Shudi's main rivals, features a 'nag's head swell', a curved lever used for opening part of the lid. It was developed after the invention of the piano—which could create crescendos and diminuendos—in order to make the harpsichord suitable for the new musical scores, which called for changes of dynamics.

The main room on this floor is the **Drawing Room**. Though also redecorated by Fowler, it is more of a piece than some of the other rooms, the satinwood Sheraton-style furniture and display cabinets having been specially commissioned by Lady Binning. In the alcove to the right of the fireplace is a landscape drawing by Jan Brueghel; between the windows an Elizabethan sweet purse embroidered with silver, gold and pearls. Either side of the chimney breast are alcoves displaying outstanding examples of Worcester porcelain. The hexagonal pink-scale vase and cover, with unusual decoration of birds and chinoiserie figures, is the most important English piece in the house. A pair of tea bowls depicts scenes from *Aesop's Fables*. Meissen porcelain on display here includes an early grotesque teapot and cover modelled by J.J. Irminger and a fine pair of parrots on ormolu bases. Also here is a very important pair of Frankenthal court dancers, sometimes called 'Louis XV and Madame de Pompadour', in the guise of Acis and Galatea.

Across the landing, the **Green Room**, formerly a bedroom and dressing room, has been redecorated by interior designer David Mlinaric. There are Staffordshire figures on the mantelpiece. A Dutch cabinet displays a pair of ceramic hares from the Plymouth factory (c. 1768) and two Bow dogs of a type known as the 'Dismal Hounds' (c. 1758). In the closet alcove hangs *Psyche, a Persian Cat* (1787) and *A Terrier*, both by Francis Sartorius.

Leading up to the attic from the landing, the **Service Staircase** is hung with a series of engravings by Houbraken and Vertue made for Thomas Birch's *The Heads of Illustrious Persons of Great Britain* (1743). At the top hangs G.F. Watts' *Neptune's Horses* (1888–92), inspired by the waves at Sliema in Malta. On the attic landing stands a French or Italian late 16th-century buffet, carved with representations of the river god Tiber and the infants Romulus and Remus. On it stands a Rhenish bellarmine wine-jar: the mask of the bearded man on this and all other 'bellarmines' represents Cardinal Roberto Bellarmine (1542–1621), opponent of Protestantism and of the divine right of kings.

The **Attic Rooms** (those on the southeast and southwest side give superb long-distance views towards the landmarks of central London) display the rest of the Benton Fletcher collection. In the southeast room is a single-manual harpsichord by Jacob Kirckman from 1752, rare in having only two sets of strings, as well as an 18th-century hurdy-gurdy and small 19th-century archlute. In the southwest room is a German clavichord, a painted Venetian virginals, and a single-manual harpsichord made by Thomas Culliford in 1783.

In the northwest room is a double-manual harpsichord by the Kirckmans from 1762, a 1925 Arnold Dolmetsch clavichord, and a spinet rescued by Fletcher from a leaking outhouse in Wales. In the north room the Hatley virginals (1664) can be seen (and like many of the other instruments, sometimes also heard). With traditional flower and fruit decoration, it is one of only ten English virginals to survive from before the Great Fire of London, and the earliest English instrument in the collection. Also in this room is a 1774 Broadwood square piano. In the northeast room stands a grand piano (1763–78), at one time attributed to Americus Backers, the inventor of the revolutionary escapement which came to be known as the 'English grand action'. Though the piano is now known not to be by Backers, it is still of a very early date. There is also a Broadwood piano from 1805, of the type given to Beethoven a decade or so later.

FIREPOWER!
THE ROYAL ARTILLERY MUSEUM

The Royal Arsenal, Woolwich, SE18 6ST
Tel: 020-8855 7755; www.firepower.org.uk
Open April–Oct Wed–Sun and bank holidays 10.30–5; Nov–March
Fri–Sun and bank holidays 10.30–5
Admission charge
Station: Woolwich Arsenal (from Charing Cross)
Café and shop
Map p. 379, 3F

The museum of artillery was founded in 1776 by Lt Gen. Sir William Congreve as a teaching collection, known as the Royal Military Repository. His son, Col. Sir William Congreve, succeeded his father as Superintendent of the Military Machines at Woolwich, and managed to have the collection installed in the Rotunda (viewable by appointment), a strikingly original building by John Nash (1820). Modelled around the huge tent designed for the meeting of the allied sovereigns at Carlton House Gardens in 1814, and built to celebrate Wellington's victory at Waterloo the next year, the Rotunda remained the museum's home until early 2001, when the museum moved into the buildings of the Royal Ordnance Factory at the Royal Arsenal. The Royal Artillery Regiment was founded here in 1741.

The approach to the museum passes an impressive variety of 18th-century buildings, including the Royal Brass Foundry (1717) and Verbruggen's House (1772). The latter was purpose-built by The Ordnance Board for Jan Verbruggen, Master Founder, his two daughters and son Peter. During the Second World War it housed the Ordnance Committee and also the Ordnance Board. Dial Square, with its imposing archway designed by Vanbrugh and Hawksmoor c. 1717–20, one of the earliest of their collaborations to survive, was also the birthplace of Arsenal Football Club, which started life in 1886 as the Dial Square Football Club, a team composed of workers in the gun machining factory. The modern Firepower! museum is housed further down No. 1 Street, the Royal Arsenal's processional avenue down to the river, in the former Paper Cartridge Factory: early 19th-century buildings where the majority of workers would have been women.

The Museum

The displays are introduced by a 15-minute presentation called Field of Fire, an audio-visual display in a large, darkened auditorium that gives visitors a loud and vivid impression of gunners and gunnery in action. The **History Gallery**, on the balcony level overlooking the main hall, describes the development of artillery pieces from the trebuchet through cannons and mortars to the Maxim machine gun. In 1240 gunpowder was rediscovered by the English monk Roger Bacon, possibly while working with texts captured from the Arab world. He concealed his dangerous secret in code—nevertheless, an explosive combination of saltpetre, nitrate, sulphur and charcoal was in use by the end of the same century. Bacon's exact formula remained undeciphered until the 20th century, when Lt Col. Hime broke the code.

Some of the earliest guns in the collection are displayed here: a pair of Chinese *t'ungs*, small short-range pellet-firing weapons, one of them dated 1409, and the Bodiam Mortar. This early siege weapon, dating from the 15th or 16th century, was unearthed in the moat of Bodiam Castle, Sussex. The oldest English piece in the collection, it was designed to fire incendiary bombs or showers of small stones. A falconet from the English Civil War, one of the lightest pieces of field artillery in use in the 17th century, is mounted on its original carriage. Nearby, the three-pounder Galloper gun, from 1756, was designed to be pulled by one horse. The story continues with a six-pounder from 1796, typical of those used in the Peninsular War, and replaced by the nine-pounders used at the Battle of Waterloo, up to an early British Maxim machine gun. Made in London in 1895, it is the kind that was sold to the Boer Republic in 1899–1902.

A unique survivor on display here is the Gatling gun, dated 1865, manufactured by Colt. Both weapons make an appropriate introduction to the exhibition on the First World War, recounting the key role played by the Royal Artillery in that terrible war of attrition.

On the ground floor, the **Gunnery Hall** is home to a formidable collection of retired artillery pieces: a rare World War Two British 18-pounder Mark II, donated by the Jordanian Army, of the type used in France by the British Expeditionary Force in 1940; a Maxim Sokolov machine gun M1910, used by the Russian army against Japan; anti-tank and self-propelled guns; a Thunderbird missile launcher Mark 6, 1960, the first guided anti-aircraft missile system used by the Royal Artillery; and a Rapier anti-aircraft missile system from 1985, used in the Falklands and the Gulf.

Across No. 1 Street, the **East Wing Gallery** houses a collection of trophy guns, including a superb French 12-pounder presented to Queen Victoria by the Emperor Louis Napoleon. The **Cold War Gallery** tells the story of the regiment from 1945 to the present day, using an impressive collection of tanks, armoured cars and self-propelled guns.

FLORENCE NIGHTINGALE MUSEUM

St Thomas's Hospital, 2 Lambeth Palace Road, SE1 7EH
Tel: 020-7620 0374; www.florence-nightingale.co.uk
Open Mon–Fri 10–5, Sat–Sun and bank holidays 10–4.30
Admission charge
Tube: Waterloo and Westminster
Shop
Map p. 382, 4B

Hidden away beneath the modern blocks of St Thomas's Hospital, this small museum describes the life and work of Florence Nightingale (1820–1910) and preserves a memorial collection of 'Nightingalia', formerly the pride of the Matrons of St Thomas's. The museum opened here in 1989, on the site of the pioneering nursing school that Nightingale founded in 1860. As the 'lady with the lamp' who cared for the sick and wounded in the Crimea (1854–56), she became a reluctant legend in her own lifetime. The marble bust which heads the display was one of the very few portraits of herself that she ever allowed to be taken from life, and then only because it had been commissioned by the soldiers who had been her patients. Nightingale's careful control of her own image also played an important role in securing the political influence that would enable her to contribute to a complete transformation in the status of nursing, eventually providing many women with a new means of achieving economic independence.

Nightingale's own considerable fortune was provided by the will of her great-uncle Peter, a prominent Whig and supporter of Parliamentary reform. Born during her parents' three-year honeymoon, she was christened Florence after her birthplace. Her sister, older by one year, was called Parthenope, the Greek name for Naples. To each other, they became Pop and Flo. Some sketches by her sister of the young Nightingale and their family home are shown here. Unusually, their father William educated the girls himself, elucidating the finer points of mathematics, algebra, Euclid, philosophy and statistics. This last proved particularly useful to Nightingale's improvements in hospital administration. She would eventually be the first female honoured with membership of the Society of Statisticians.

Florence Nightingale regarded her career as a vocation. Aged seventeen, while walking in the garden at home, she experienced a calling from God, and a further adumbration of her purpose in life came during a visit to Kaiserswerth on the Rhine, a Lutheran institution for the help of the poor, founded in 1825. Her decision to become a nurse appalled her family, at a time when the secular side of the profession was best characterised by the likes of Sarah Gamp in Dickens' *Martin Chuzzlewit*. When the horrors of the Crimea were reported in the *Times*, Nightingale gathered together a disparate team of 38 ladies in four days, all prepared to endure the terrible voyage out to the military hospital at Scutari. Three times as many men were dying from disease as from wounds received in battle. Her first order upon arrival was for 200 scrubbing brushes. Nightingale also called upon the services of the ex-chef of the Reform Club, Alexis Soyer, transforming her patients' diet. Her celebrity upon her return is demonstrated here by a variety of contemporary china figurines cast in her image; her mission by new designs for hospital wards, the foundation of the nursing school and development plans for district nursing and midwifery. Some of the furniture and a harpsichord from her house at 10 South St, Mayfair, from where she orchestrated her campaigns, can be seen. Also displayed are her black bodice and matching skirt from 1859. In that year she self-published *Suggestions for Thought to the Searchers after Truth*, still in print today. Frequently unwell herself throughout her long life, she remained unmarried and died at her home in 1910, surrounded by a colony of cats. The exhibition concludes with her pet Little Owl called Athena, rescued from the Parthenon and kept in her pocket, now stuffed and mounted in a glass case. It died, much to her distress, the day before she set out for the Crimea.

FORTY HALL

Forty Hill, Enfield, Middlesex, EN2 9HA
Tel: 020-8363 8196; www.enfield.gov.uk/fortyhall
Open Wed–Sun 11–4
Free
Train: Turkey Street (from Liverpool Street) then a 20-min walk
Bus: 191, W10 to Forty Hill roundabout
Café, open Oct–March 11–4.30
Map p. 379, beyond 1E

This notable Caroline mansion of red brick was built 1629–32 for Sir Nicholas Rainton, a wealthy haberdasher, Lord Mayor of London and President of St Bartholomew's Hospital. The architect is not known, although a case has been made for Edward Carter, Chief Clerk of the King's Works, colleague and successor of Inigo Jones as Surveyor-General. The hipped roof is of particular interest, being advanced for its time and an important early example of this popular style. On Rainton's death in 1646, the estate passed through several owners, being purchased by Major Henry Bowles, MP for Enfield, in 1895. Internal alterations were carried out around this time. In 1951 Forty Hall was sold to Enfield Council by Derek Parker Bowles.

Surrounded by attractive informal gardens, which include one of the most ancient cedars of Lebanon in the country and an avenue of limes planted in the 18th century, the house still appears externally much as it did when built. In the grounds some few remains have been found of Elsyng Palace, a Tudor royal manor and hunting lodge, where in 1547, in the presence of Princess Elizabeth, Edward VI received the news of the death of his father Henry VIII and of his consequent accession.

The Entrance Hall has good Rococo plasterwork of c. 1787, with medallions representing the Seasons. The fine carved panelling on the early 17th-century Hall Screen is an outstanding survival from the original house. The Dining Room and Drawing Room retain their original fireplaces, panelling and plaster ceilings with bold strapwork decoration. In the Rainton Room is a fine portrait of the original owner of the house, ascribed to the great Civil War-era portraitist William Dobson. Of the four rooms on the first floor, two keep their original elaborate plaster ceilings (one of them dated 1629). One of the rooms contains a Childhood Gallery displaying local toys, clothes and cribs from the 19th century to the 1940s. Temporary exhibitions are also mounted here.

FOUNDLING MUSEUM

40 Brunswick Square, WC1N 1AZ
Tel: 020-7841 3600; www.foundlingmuseum.org.uk
Open Tues–Sat 10–6; Sun and bank holidays 12–6
Admission charge
Tube: Russell Square/King's Cross
Café and shop
Map p. 382, 1B

The Foundling Museum is a remarkable institution which records the foundation, history and continuing work of the Foundling Hospital, a charitable home for illegitimate children established in 1739 by Captain Thomas Coram (1668–1751). A humble Dorset man, Coram was a master mariner who had arrived back from the American colonies to be appalled by the plight of the abandoned, orphaned and destitute children on the streets of London. In 1739, after 17 years of relentless campaigning among the titled, wealthy and influential, Coram persuaded George II to grant a Royal Charter to open 'A Hospital for the Maintenance and Education of Exposed and Deserted Young Children'. An entirely secular organisation, the first of its kind, it was funded through private donations and subscription.

History of the Hospital

The Hospital opened in 1741, in temporary premises in Hatton Garden. On its first day it was open for the receipt of children until full, 18 boys and 12 girls being accepted. All Foundling children were baptised on admission. The first child was named Thomas Coram, and the first girl Eunice Coram, after Captain Coram's wife, who had died in 1740.

In 1742 the foundation stone of the Hospital's permanent buildings was laid in Lamb's Conduit Fields, present-day Coram Fields. Consisting of three wings around a courtyard—the west wing for boys, the Governor's Court Room and a Picture Gallery, the east wing for girls, and a central chapel—the Hospital was designed by Theodore Jacobsen, an amateur architect and one of the Hospital's governors. The chapel was begun in 1747. In 1749 Handel, who became a Hospital governor, conducted a concert there to raise funds for its completion, for which he composed the *Foundling Hospital Anthem*. Fundraising musical concerts became a feature of the Hospital's calendar, with Handel conducting annual performances of the *Messiah*. A terracotta bust of him by Roubiliac is in the collection.

Further social fundraising events included ticket sales for Ladies' Breakfasts, and opportunities to visit the Hospital, admire its buildings, inspect the children and view its art collection. The latter was an important component of the Hospital. The ornate

Hogarth's portrait of Captain Thomas Coram (1740), showing the master mariner with a globe at his feet and the seal of the Hospital's Royal Charter in his right hand.

Governor's Court Room and Picture Gallery contained fine paintings and works of art by leading contemporary British artists, principally Hogarth and his circle, presented to the Hospital from 1746, many of which remain in the museum today. In return for their philanthropy, the Hospital offered to artists a means by which to promote the talents of the native school through public exhibition of their work (the Foundling offered the first public exhibition space in the country). A number of artists were elected governors, and these formed a separate committee which met annually, 'to consider of what further Ornaments may be added to the Hospital'.

Coram, a bluff and forthright man, was ousted from the Board of Governors soon after the Hospital's foundation. He made frequent visits to the Hospital however, was godfather to over 20 Foundlings, and was buried under the altar of the chapel. In 1926 the Governors decided to move the Hospital to the cleaner air of the country, first to Redhill, then to Berkhamsted. The original building was sadly demolished, but several of the finer rooms were carefully salvaged and re-erected within the Hospital's new headquarters at 40 Brunswick Square, completed in 1938. Opposite the new building the Hospital's old site, Coram Fields, became a playground for children. In 1953 the Hospital ceased to operate as a school for abandoned children, and the policy of placing children in foster homes was adopted in its place. The charity was renamed the Thomas Coram Foundation; in 1999 it became Coram Family, its headquarters in the building adjoining the museum. The museum and its collections became a separate museum trust in 1998, and after an extensive renovation programme opened as the Foundling Museum in 2004.

The Building and its Exhibits

On the ground floor is the exhibition **Coram's Children**, which explains the origins and history of the Foundling Hospital, and the social conditions of 18th-century London. The Hospital originally had official appointment days for receiving children, with desperate queues forming outside the gates with more children than could possibly be accommodated. A ballot method was introduced instead. On reception days mothers drew a ball from a bag, its colour deciding the fate of their child. Careful records were made of each child admitted, as well as identifying keepsakes which could be used to reclaim children. Several of these touching Foundling tokens are on show: metal tags with names, ribbons, buttons, lockets and even a hazelnut shell. Handel's annotated musical score for the *Foundling Hospital Anthem*, based on Psalm 41, 'Blessed is he that Considereth the Poor' is displayed, as is a modern scale model of the original Hospital building and original admissions registers. The **Committee Room** was where mothers were interviewed before being submitted for the ballot process. Pictures include 19th-century scenes with charitable themes and Hogarth's great *March to Finchley*, the scene set in the Tottenham Court Road in the winter of 1745, where a band of guardsmen is moving off to Finchley before marching north against Bonnie Prince Charlie's rebels. The King's Head tavern has been commandeered by the notorious brothel-keeper Mother Douglas. Hogarth sold the picture by lottery; 167 of the unsold 2,000 tickets were donated to the Hospital, which won the picture. Set into panelling above the chimneypiece is George Lambert's *Landscape with Figures*, his Hospital presentation picture. The **Staircase** is the original 18th-century boys' wing oak staircase, originally fitted with a rail and spikes to stop the boys sliding down. Hung on it are paintings with sentimental and moral subjects; portraits of governors; and Benjamin West's *Christ Presenting a Little Child*, the Hospital chapel altarpiece. On the first floor landing is Andrea Casali's *Adoration of the Magi*, the 1750 altarpiece which West's replaced in 1801.

The **Picture Gallery** was the principal 18th-century visitor attraction. Here important full-length portraits of governors and other Hospital figures hang, principally Hogarth's *Captain Thomas Coram* (1740), a masterpiece of British art, which Hogarth presented to the Hospital. Coram is shown seated on a dais, with columns behind, holding the seal of the Hospital's Royal Charter: the composition is redolent of traditional Baroque pomp, and yet Coram appears wigless and ruddy-cheeked, a direct realism contrary to expected polite decorum. Other portraits include Ramsay's *Dr Richard Mead*, the internationally famous physician, scholar and collector, and Hospital governor, with a statue of Hygieia, goddess of health, in the background; Hudson's *Theodore Jacobsen*, shown holding architectural plans and elevations of the Hospital; and *George II* by Shackleton. In the **Foyer** are seapieces (many Foundlings followed naval careers) including a monochrome preparatory sketch for Copley's enormous *Siege of Gibraltar* (Guildhall Art Gallery; *see p. 100*).

The **Court Room**, where the Board of Governors met and where select social entertaining took place, was the most elaborately decorated room in the 18th-century building, carefully reconstructed in 1937. The spectacular Rococo plasterwork was the free gift of the plasterer William Wilton, the marble chimneypiece, by John Devall, was donated by him in 1747, and its marble relief overmantel, *Charity*, is by Rysbrack. The four large biblical paintings are *Hagar and Ishmael* by Highmore; *The Little Children Brought before Christ* by James Wills; *The Finding of the Infant Moses in the Bulrushes* by Hayman; and *Moses Brought before Pharoah's Daughter* by Hogarth, all of them appropriate themes for a charity caring for abandoned children. The landscape roundels between them, set into plasterwork surrounds, were installed in 1751 and show views of London charitable foundations by leading British landscape artists: the *Foundling Hospital* is by Richard Wilson and the *Charterhouse* by the 21 year-old Thomas Gainsborough.

The **Gerald Coke Handel Collection** on the second floor is a scholarly resource with manuscript musical scores and a library. Next door visitors can sit in leather winged armchairs with built-in audio systems which play a selection of Handel's music (but disappointingly not the *Foundling Anthem*).

FREUD MUSEUM

20 Maresfield Gardens, Hampstead, NW3 5SX
Tel: 020-7435 2002; www.freud.org.uk

Open Wed–Sun 12–5
Admission charge
Tube: Finchley Road
Shop
Map p. 379, 2D

In June 1938 Sigmund Freud (1856–1939), the father of psychoanalysis, was forced by Nazi oppression to leave his native Vienna. An anglophile, with a son already living in St John's Wood, he bought this relatively modern (1920s) house on a quiet tree-lined street of Victorian red-brick mansions in an area popular with Jewish refugees. After his death from cancer of the jaw in September 1939, his wife Martha and daughter Anna continued to occupy the house, keeping it much as it had been left by Freud. On Anna's death in 1982, it was decided to open the house as a museum, which welcomed its first visitors in 1986.

Ground floor

In a sense, Freud himself was the first curator of the museum. In preparation for his arrival, the contents of his Viennese home were rearranged here as accurately as possible by his faithful housekeeper. The main room on the ground floor was his working library, where he completed *Moses and Monotheism*, began his *Outline of Psychoanalysis*, and continued to see patients until two months before his death. Along with the famous couch, given to him in fact before his development of the 'talking cure', while he was still a research neurologist, the centrepiece of the room is his desk and chair. The latter was purpose-built for Freud's peculiar reading posture—he liked to study books with one knee slung over a chair arm—by architect friend Felix Augenfeld, with arms designed to double as leg rests. His large desk supports a massed array of Greek, Egyptian, Asian and Chinese statuettes and figurines. These form part of his extensive and important private collection of antiquities, carefully positioned in glass cabinets and in every available space around the room. They include Egyptian gods, goddesses and mummy masks, Bodhisattvas and Chinese buddhas (one a rare walking penitent), as well as Greek and Roman sculpture. (There are no explanatory labels because of the need to maintain the display exactly as it was known to the great man.) A small statue of Athena was the mascot of the family's emigration to England, sent ahead for safe-keeping to Princess Marie Bonaparte in Paris before they left Vienna. While many of the sculptures are exceptional pieces in themselves, what makes them doubly interesting is their meaning for Freud: as Marina Warner says in the preface to the museum guide, they represent the 'tools of thought'.

On a table at the foot of the couch, itself covered by a Qashqa'i carpet, is the Freud *azmalyk*, one of only 12 in existence, a five-sided Turkoman rug woven by the nomadic Tekke tribe to cover the leading camel in a wedding procession. Many of these Oriental furnishings were obtained by Freud's brother-in-law. The other room on the ground floor contains Anna Freud's collection of 19th-century Austrian peasant furniture, the most complete of its kind outside Austria: stout wooden bridal chests, wardrobes and cupboards decorated with exuberant floral patterns. Beyond is the gift shop in the loggia, transformed into a conservatory by architect son Ernst Freud, father of Clement and Lucien.

Upper floor

Up the wide staircase from the hall, filled with natural light in a way that put Freud in mind of a palace, the stairwell is hung with screenprints specially commissioned for the museum by Patrick Caulfield, Cornelia Parker, Claes Oldenburg and other contemporary artists. Pride of place on the landing goes to a portrait sketch of Freud made from life by Salvador Dalí in 1938. Nearby, two paintings by the Wolfman (Russian aristocrat Sergei Pankejeff) depict the dream that gave the artist his name, showing wolves perched on the branches of a leafless tree. In celebration of the centenary of the publication of *The Interpretation of Dreams* (1999), 'interventions' in the form of printed excerpts have been positioned at significant points around the house, encouraging visitors to explore some of the major themes of Freud's work.

Of the three rooms open to visitors on the first floor, the largest is given over to Anna Freud and her own pioneering work in child psychoanalysis. She started the renowned Hampstead Child Therapy courses in 1947, opening a clinic in Maresfield Gardens five years later, now called the Anna Freud Centre. Standing in the corner is her loom, which she herself found to be of great therapeutic value. The other rooms are given over to temporary exhibitions relevant to the Freuds, and two 20-minute videos on a loop: one concerning the history of the house followed by a rare recording of Freud's own declaration of purpose, and the other an intriguing collection of home videos from the Freuds' days in Vienna, narrated by Anna. The museum still contributes to the advancement of the cause of psychoanalysis through conferences and archival research.

FULHAM PALACE

Bishop's Avenue, SW6 6EA
Tel: 020-7736 3223
Open Sat–Sun 2–5
Free
Tube: Putney Bridge
Map p. 378, 3C

NB: Under development at the time of writing.
Close to the river and Bishop's Park, the site of Fulham Palace remained in the possession of the Bishopric of London from the early 8th century until 1973. The picturesque red-brick Tudor quadrangle that can now be seen on the approach to the museum is the earliest part of the building to survive, although much restored in the 19th century, around the time that the adjoining chapel was designed by William Butterfield in 1866. The museum is situated in the former Bishop's dining room, in a late 18th-century

building, and traces the history of the Bishops of London and Fulham Palace itself with a small collection of pictures, stained glass and archaeological finds.

The monastic botanical gardens founded here were developed in the 17th century by Bishop Compton, who introduced many rare species, some never before grown in Europe. Botanic beds, a herb garden and wisteria walk in the walled kitchen garden can still be seen.

GEFFRYE MUSEUM

Kingsland Road, Shoreditch, E2 8EA
Tel: 020-7739 9893; www.geffrye-museum.org.uk
Open Tues–Sat 10–5, Sun and bank holidays 12–5. Historic almshouses open first Sat of the month 11–4, timed tickets on the hour. Gardens open April–end Oct. Closed Mon unless bank holiday
Free
Tube: Liverpool Street, then bus 149 or 242; Old Street, then bus 243
Café and shop
Map p. 379, 2E

This small museum in Shoreditch is a welcome, friendly oasis in the somewhat grim environment of the Kingsland Road, which lies mid-way between the old villages of

Haggerston and Hoxton (the latter now a hub of the contemporary art scene). Set behind iron railings are the gardens, tall trees and low-lying early 18th-century buildings of the Geffrye almshouses, converted to a museum in 1914. A museum of the English domestic interior, explained through a succession of period room recreations, the Geffrye is one of London's hidden treasures.

The Almshouses

The old almshouses were the charitable foundation of Sir Robert Geffrye (1613–1704), a merchant with interests in India and the Far East, a Master of the Ironmongers' Company, a member of the City's governing body, the Court of

Central elevation of the old almshouses, with the statue of Robert Geffrye above the door.

Aldermen, and Lord Mayor of London in 1685. In his will he left in trust, to be administered by the Ironmongers' Company, a sum of money for the establishment of almshouses for the poor. In 1712 a plot of land was purchased on the Kingsland Road, then an area of market gardens and plant nurseries, and a simple but dignified building was constructed, the design following typical almshouses of the period. Externally, the building is little altered. In the centre is the former Great Room, its door flanked by round-headed windows with a clock turret above the pediment. The statue of Sir Robert Geffrye in the niche above the door is a copy after the 1723 original by John van Nost the Elder (now at the new almshouses in Hook, Hampshire; *see below*). The pensioners, 43 of them when the almshouses opened, who each

Marble monument to Sir Robert Geffrye and his wife, in the chapel.

received £6 per year, lived in suites of rooms to either side, grouped in series of four around successive staircases. Each pensioner had one room, where they would eat, sleep and live, with a fireplace and two windows overlooking the front gardens, with a small closet off it. One of the **historic almshouses** has been restored (*see opening times above*), one room sparsely furnished to reflect 18th-century living, the other the more comfortable conditions of the late 19th century.

With the decline of the local area, in 1911 the almshouses moved to Mottingham, Kent, and in 1974 to Hook, Hampshire. A campaign to save the historic Kingsland Road building resulted in its purchase by the London County Council. Envisaged as the first of a series of museums focusing on local London crafts, the Geffrye at first displayed woodwork and furniture, historic as well as contemporary, as inspiration and encouragement for the local furniture industry. It now displays a chronological succession of period rooms, furnished and decorated to reflect the domestic living arrangements, and the changing tastes and fashions, of the urban middle classes through the ages. The old Great Room, converted to a **chapel** in 1716, has been restored and contains a fine marble monument to Geffrye and his wife, by Saunders, removed from Geffrye's local parish church of St Dionis Backchurch on its demolition in 1881 (their remains were reburied in a small graveyard entered via a gate in the northwest corner of the front garden). In 1998 a modern extension (to the rear of the building and invisible from the Kingsland Road) opened, allowing expansion of the 20th-century period displays; a temporary exhibition gallery (the Geffrye has a growing reputation for excellent shows); a Design Centre for contemporary design and craft; and a restaurant. A particularly good time to visit the museum is in December, when the period rooms are dressed for Christmas in the traditions of the times.

The Museum

The enfilade of period rooms begins with the **Elizabethan and Jacobean Room**, set up as the parlour of a wealthy London merchant c. 1600, with fine linenfold carved oak panelling, an expensive Flemish 'verdure', or landscape, tapestry, carved oak furniture and rush matting on the floor. A portrait of an unknown lady by Cornelius Johnson, in a fine carved but slightly later frame, hangs on the wall. The **Stuart Room**, 1660–85, has panelling removed from the Master's Parlour of the Pewterers' Hall in the City, demolished in the 1930s, and a cast of its plaster ceiling. The expensive cabinet, veneered in ebony with engraved flowers, was made in Paris in 1652 and was owned by the famous diarist and antiquarian John Evelyn. Evelyn was one of the founder members of the Royal Society, established to promote scientific enquiry, and the objects in the room (exotic shells; an armadillo etc) reflect this new mid-17th-century interest in natural science. Hanging on the wall is a family portrait by Mary Beale, England's first professional female artist, showing herself, her husband (a London civil servant) and her eldest son, Bartholomew. The elegant **Queen Anne Room**, 1685–1714, has furnishings reflective of the increase in foreign and luxury trade: a china cabinet with blue and white Chinese export porcelain and English delftware; tall-backed chairs, some upholstered, one with a caned seat; good examples of walnut furniture such as the fine 'cushion' frame mirror, with inlaid marquetry; and a japanned table in imitation of Chinese lacquerwork. The **Georgian Room**, 1720–60, represents a gentleman's study in a genteel townhouse, with pine panelling, a handsome mahogany serpentine ladder-back chair, a good quality English mahogany bureau and bookcase, an ebonised bracket clock (c. 1735) by Robert Higgs of London, and an elegant tripod table. The painting above the fireplace is of the silversmith George Moser and his wife, by C. M. Tuscher. Another portrait, by Arthur Devis, shows Elizabeth Hemyng in a dress of Spitalfields silk. The stylish **Late Georgian Drawing Room**, 1760–1800, was where guests would be entertained for tea and polite conversation. The room and its furnishings reflect the advance of Neoclassical taste. The mahogany chairs are in the style of Hepplewhite, and a tea-caddy stands on the satinwood table. The **Regency Room**, 1811–20, has stencilled wallpaper; a reproduction of a period fitted Kidderminster carpet; sofa and chairs upholstered in coordinated blue; and a girandole mirror with an elaborately carved and gilded frame. The mahogany writing table is believed to have belonged to Jane Austen's brother, Edward Austen Knight, of Godmersham Park in Kent. The **Victorian Room**,

The Regency Room.

1840–70, has gas lighting and a coal fire, a deep upholstered armchair, a busy floral carpet and a three-tiered 'whatnot' for displaying ornaments, reflective of the Victorian

drive towards comfort. The **Aesthetic Room**, 1875–90, is decorated according to the purist tastes of writers and artists such as Oscar Wilde, Rossetti and Burne-Jones. The two ebonised beech chairs (1877) are by E.W. Godwin, and the wallpaper is after a design by Christopher Dresser. The armchair, with its original Utrecht Velvet upholstery, was designed by Philip Webb for Morris, Marshall, Faulkner and Company. The **Edwardian Room**, 1901–10, represents a typical suburban drawing room c. 1910, still the best reception room in the house, but also used for family activities, this one reflecting the influence of the Arts and Crafts movement. Ornaments are simply displayed on the tall wooden overmantel; the carpet was hand-knotted in Ireland c. 1910; and the ash corner cupboard (c. 1900) was designed by Ernest Gimson. The 1930s **Flat** represents new convenient living. The simple living/dining room, with balcony access, has clean lines and bold designs; an electric fire set in a surround of green marble with stripes of slate; and upholstery and curtain fabric designed by Marian Pepler. The **Mid-Century Room**, 1955–65, is a living/dining room in a modern town house. The white, modernist interior with wood-block floor has lightweight unit furniture; a coffee table; and a television. The 1990s room represents a fashionable minimalist loft apartment, with white walls, wooden floor and spare furnishing. The sofa is from Heal's and the brightly coloured leather 'Balzac' armchair designed by Matthew Hilton.

The Geffrye's **Gardens**, at the rear of the building, have recently been redeveloped. The Herb Garden is planted with species for medicinal or culinary use, and with plants that were used for dyes. The Period Gardens evoke successive historic planting styles, from the formality of the 17th-century knot garden to Edwardian herbaceous borders.

GRANT MUSEUM OF ZOOLOGY & COMPARATIVE ANATOMY

Darwin Building, University College London, Gower Street WC1E 6BT
Tel: 020-7679 2647; www.grant.museum.ucl.ac.uk
Open Mon–Fri 1–5 (and other times by appointment)
Free. For disabled access phone first
Tube: Warren St/Euston Square
Map p. 382, 1A

On the site of Charles Darwin's home from 1838–42, the Grant museum occupies one room in the basement of University College's Department of Biological Sciences. It displays a massed array of animal skeletons and soft-tissue specimens preserved in formalin, and began life as the teaching collection of Robert Grant (1793–1874), the first professor of Comparative Anatomy and Zoology in Britain, at the new University of London founded in 1827. Probably the first person to teach evolutionary zoology in a British university, Grant influenced the thinking of the young Darwin, but later in life refused to accept the advances in his field and died in penniless obscurity.

Over the years the museum has absorbed other university collections and now preserves some 32,000 different specimens, a small but comprehensive selection of which is displayed here in Victorian glass cabinets. On the left of the entrance a small exhibition tells the history of the museum and displays some of Grant's original collection, including the baculum or penis-bone of a walrus and the dried urino-genitary tract of a duck-billed platypus. Another case contains several rare and superbly delicate glass models of jellyfish, gastropods, sea anemones and cephalopods. They were made in the late 19th century by the Czech father-and-son team, Leopold and Rudolf Blaschka, who went on to supply Harvard's Botanical Museum with more than 4,000 meticulous glass replicas of flowers. To the right, the museum's prize exhibits are the skeletal remains of various extinct species: some Dodo bones, and one of only seven complete quagga skeletons known to exist. A type of South African zebra, the quagga had been hunted to extinction by the 1870s for its unusual skin. Also here is the skeleton of a thylacine or Tasmanian wolf, a large marsupial carnivore largely exterminated by sheep- and chicken-farmers. A law protecting the species was passed, too late, in 1936, the year that the last-known thylacine died in captivity.

Retaining the shape and layout of a small Victorian teaching museum, the taxonomical arrangement of some of the specimens has been elucidated with modern labelling. The skeleton of the hedgehog-like—though spineless—Madagascan terek, for example, is enlivened by the information that it has more nipples than any other mammal and is capable of feeding 32 young from its 29 teats. Others are formidable sculptural presences in themselves: the twisting skeleton of an anaconda; several massive elephant skulls; a giant tortoise's shell; the skeletons of an Indian rhino and a dugong or sea cow.

GUARDS MUSEUM

Wellington Barracks, Birdcage Walk, SW1
Tel: 020-7414 3428
Open daily 10–4 (sometimes closed January)
Admission charge
Tube: St James's Park
Shop
Map p. 382, 4A

The museum of the five regiments of Foot, Grenadier, Coldstream, Scots, Irish, and Welsh Guards occupies a series of purpose-built subterranean rooms in the Chapel Square complex of Wellington Barracks. The five regiments named above furnish the troops that can usually be seen on parade, here and in front of Buckingham Palace, at the Changing of the Guard (*see p. 46*). Along with the cavalry regiments, the Blues and Royals and Queen's Life Guards, they form the Household Division. This very well-kept museum opened in 1988 and displays a thoroughly annotated collection of uniforms, medals, silverware, weapons, colours, trophies and memorabilia.

At the entrance, a small mannequin wears the tailored uniform of HRH Prince Arthur of Connaught, aged five in 1838, followed by a useful lesson in regimental identification by button spacing, forage cap bands, bearskin plumes and collar tabs. A formidable array of Victoria Cross medals is also presented. Some were among the first ever to be awarded, for the saving of the colours at the Battle of Alma at the start of the Crimean War.

The exhibition then tells the glorious—and occasionally unfortunate—history of the regiments from their establishment in the 17th century up to the present day. An impressive portrait by Sir Peter Lely depicts General George Monck (1608–70), 1st Duke of Albermarle and the first Colonel-in-Chief of the Coldstream Guards, formed under him in 1650 from part of Lord Fairfax's New Model Army fighting the Commonwealth cause in Scotland. A Dunbar medal from that year, with the head of Oliver Cromwell on one side and Parliament in session on the reverse, was the first medal to be awarded selectively to the army, for their victory against the Scots. Also exhibited here is General Monck's gold enamelled snuffbox containing a piece of an elm tree planted by Princess Elizabeth (later Queen Elizabeth I) while a prisoner of her half-sister Mary Tudor. Next to General Monck, who later marched rapidly south with his regiment to help restore Charles II to the throne, is a display on Thomas, Lord Wentworth, who had exiled himself to Bruges with 400 men loyal to the future King Charles II. In 1656, he became the first Colonel of the Royal Regiment of Guards, later called the Grenadier Guards, the most senior of the five foot regiments. The Coldstreams' reaction can be gauged from their motto: 'Second to no one'. The oldest of the regiments is in fact the Scots Guards, formed in 1642. Another portrait, attributed to the circle of Marcellus Laroon, shows the three Keppel family children acting in a private theatrical performance, possibly of Farquhar's *The Recruiting Officer*, wearing early uniforms of the Coldstream guards.

Displays then relate the role played by the regiments at the Battle of Blenheim, in the War of American Independence, at Waterloo (featuring the major's colour carried by the 2nd battalion of the First Foot Guards) and in the Crimean War, among other conflicts, and tell of the formation of the Irish and Welsh Guards in 1900 and 1915. Highlights include the bearskin cap worn by the 'grand old Duke of York' (George III's second son Frederick), and the head of Jacob the Goose, who attached himself to a battalion of Coldstream Guards sent to defend a sentry post in Canada, and gave the alarm when the rebels attacked. An honoured regimental mascot, he was eventually run over by a van at the Portman Barracks in 1846.

Particularly fine are the full-dress 19th-century uniforms of the Dukes of Cambridge, presenting an extraordinary array of sash badges, breast stars, garters and medals from different nations around the world. Among these the collar, badge and breast star of the Order of the Annunziata, the Italian equivalent of the Order of the Garter, remain a mystery, there being no mention in the Order's meticulous records of any Duke of Cambridge. The Order of Shafakat was a women's Order: the sash badge displayed here was possibly awarded mischievously by the Turkish Sultan to the 2nd Duke's beautiful wife, the actress Louise Fairbrother, who because of her lowly origins was never created Duchess of Cambridge, but was known instead as 'Mrs FitzGeorge'. More recent memorabilia include a pair of *chaplis*, sandals hand-made in Egypt for the late Michael Crichton Stuart, serving in the Long Range Desert Patrol Group that undertook hazardous reconnaissance behind enemy lines in North Africa. On a similar theme are 'the boots that walked a thousand kilometres' on the feet of a captain of the Guards making his escape from a POW camp in northern Italy.

GUILDHALL ART GALLERY

Guildhall Yard, EC2P 2EJ
Tel: 020-7332 3700; www.guildhall-art-gallery.org.uk
Open Mon–Sat 10–5, Sun 12–4
Admission charge
Tube: Moorgate/Bank
Small shop
Map p. 383, 2E

Opened in 1999 in a new building designed by Richard Gilbert Scott (with D.Y. Associates) on the east side of Guildhall Yard, the Guildhall Art Gallery displays around 250 pictures at any one time from the Corporation of London's collection of over 4,000 works. The administrative body of the City of London, the Corporation has its headquarters at Guildhall, on the north side of Guildhall Yard, the ancient civic heart of the City. Guildhall itself dates from 1411–30 (although a civic hall has been on the site since at least the late 13th century), but has been altered over succeeding centuries. A separate art gallery for the Corporation's growing collection was opened in 1886 but destroyed in an air raid in May 1941. A temporary gallery was used for exhibiting a selection of pictures until 1987, when it was demolished and work on a new, permanent building began—although the astonishing discovery of London's Roman amphitheatre on the site delayed progress. The remains of the amphitheatre have been preserved and entry to them is included on the gallery's admission ticket (*see below*).

The **New Gallery** has display spaces spread over two floors, smaller rooms on the ground floor, visible from an open balcony gallery on the floor above, ruthlessly covered with a busy carpet. The interesting and varied collection includes works which have been commissioned and collected by the Corporation since the 16th century. Among the portraits are monarchs and eminent City officeholders, such as John Michael Wright's full-length portraits of two of the Fire Judges appointed to assess property claims following the disastrous Great Fire of 1666. Sir James Thornhill's painted canvases, *An Allegory of London* and four *Cardinal Virtues*, 1725–27, were formerly set into the ceiling of the new Council Chamber at Guildhall, demolished in 1908. Topographical views of London include Jan Griffier the Younger's *The Thames during the Great Frost*; Samuel Scott's *Entrance to the Fleet River*; and views of the City's landmarks such as St Paul's Cathedral and Smithfield market. Works celebrating national victories and events include John Singleton Copley's enormous *Siege of Gibraltar*, commissioned by the Corporation in 1783 and completed in 1791. One of the largest pictures in the country, it originally hung in the Common Council Chamber at Guildhall, was moved to the new art gallery on its opening in 1886, and in 1941 was rolled up and evacuated for safe storage outside London. A particular requirement of the new 1980s building was a wall large enough to accommodate it. It hangs on the double height wall between the ground and first floors, visible from both. Ceremonial subjects include William Logsdail's *Ninth of November*, depicting the Lord Mayor's Show of 1887.

Other works have been presented or bequeathed to the collection, including Sir Peter Lely's *Sir Edward Hales*, an early group portrait by Charles II's Principal Painter. Many 18th-century portraits and other works came to the collection in the 1790s from that of Alderman John Boydell, engraver, printseller and publisher, and founder of the Shakespeare Gallery in Pall Mall. Sir Thomas Lawrence's portrait of the actor John Philip Kemble shows him in the role of Coriolanus. Further works include Constable's full-size sketch for *Salisbury Cathedral from the Meadows*, and many fine Victorian pictures, in which the collection is particularly rich. Well known Pre-Raphaelite works include Millais' *My First Sermon, My Second Sermon* and *The Woodman's Daughter*; Holman Hunt's *The Eve of St Agnes*; and Rossetti's *La Ghirlandata*. Other notable works are Landseer's *The First Leap*; Tissot's popular *Too Early*, 1873; and Sir John Lavery's dashing portrait of his American society wife, Hazel, *The Silver Swan*, presented by Lady Cunard in 1923.

The darkened, spot-lit **Amphitheatre Chamber** is on the Lower Ground Floor. The scant remains of the stone walls of the eastern entrance to the arena are visible, as well as some sections of the drains. The theatre was first constructed around AD 70, with a timber superstructure, and was capable of seating some 6,000 spectators at a time when the population of *Londinium* would have been only around four times that number. Elliptical in shape, more than 100 yards long and 90 yards wide, it would have been used mainly for animal fights and public executions, rarely for expensive gladiatorial contests. In the 2nd century it was improved with stone, and abandoned at some time in the 4th century. Information panels evoke the atmosphere of the ring in full cry.

GUNNERSBURY PARK

Gunnersbury Park, Pope's Lane, W3 8LQ
Tel: 020-8992 1612
Open April–Oct Mon–Fri 10–5, Sat–Sun 1–6; Nov–Mar daily 1–4
Tube: Acton Town
Free. Partial disabled access
Shop
Map p. 378, 3C

Opened in 1929 as the local museum for the London boroughs of Ealing and Hounslow, Gunnersbury Park Museum occupies the Large Mansion, a 19th-century house built on the Gunnersbury estate in 1802 by Alexander Copland (c. 1774–1834), a partner of the architect Henry Holland. The house replaced the old 17th-century villa built by John Webb for Sir John Maynard, which in the 18th century was occupied by Princess Amelia, third daughter of George III. She is said to have entertained lavishly, with firework parties in the beautiful grounds, which in the early 18th century had been landscaped by William Kent. On Copland's death the estate was purchased by Nathan Mayer Rothschild, who commissioned Sydney Smirke to enlarge the house. In the early 19th century the original 17th-century Gunnersbury estate had been split into two. The early 19th-century Small Mansion occupies the second half, which was purchased in 1828 by Thomas Farmer, who enlarged it and commissioned several garden buildings. In 1889 his descendants sold the estate to the Rothschild family, thus reuniting the two halves. The Rothschilds used the Small Mansion as their guest annexe, and it is now an Arts Centre. Following the death of Leopold de Rothschild in 1917, the estate was gradually dispersed, but in March 1925 186 acres of land and the two houses were purchased by the local borough, and opened to the public the following year.

The **museum in the Large Mansion** has a large and varied collection illustrative of local history and the lives and professions of the people of the area: Victorian and Edwardian costume and costume accessories; an early 19th-century Stanhope iron printing press, used by the Chiswick Press; and objects relating to the Acton laundry businesses. Displays are in the grand State Rooms: the once opulently furnished c. 1900 Drawing Room, with its glittering chandeliers, is now occupied by the transport collection with horse-drawn carriages and traps.

The **grounds** now incorporate sports fields, but many of the old garden buildings remain: the early 18th-century Temple by the Round Pond, built for Princess Amelia; Sydney Smirke's 1900 Orangery; fragments of the mid-19th-century 'Gothick' ruins in the grounds of the Small Mansion, built to screen the Rothschilds' stables; and the Folly Tower, built by the Rothschilds as a boathouse on the Potomac Lake, an ornamental fishing pond.

HAM HOUSE
(National Trust)

Ham, Richmond, TW10 7RS
Tel: 020-8940 1950; www.nationaltrust.org.uk/places/hamhouse
Open (House) mid March–end Oct Mon–Wed, Sat–Sun 1–5; (Garden) all year Mon–Wed, Sat–Sun 11–6
Admission charge. Partial disabled access. Phone first for help
Station: none close, bus 67, 371 from Richmond or Kingston
Restaurant and shop
Map p. 378, 4B

Ham House is a remarkable 17th-century survival, having remained almost untouched since the 1670s. It preserves much of its original interior decoration and furniture (early inventories indicate how it was arranged) as well as its garden layout. The original 1610 Jacobean house, built by Sir Thomas Vavasour, Knight Marshal to James I, was remodelled first by William Murray, 1st Earl of Dysart in 1637–39, and more substantially by Elizabeth, his daughter, and her second husband, John Maitland, Duke of Lauderdale, from 1672. Both periods of rebuilding and redecoration were according to the latest fashions, with no expense spared. The remarkable survivals from both these schemes make Ham a key house for the study and appreciation of grand 17th-century interior decoration.

Ham in its Heyday

Dysart, a childhood friend of Charles I and one of his inner circle at Whitehall, was a distinguished connoisseur. At Ham he employed leading artists and craftsmen to create interiors which reflected current court fashion. The Grand Staircase, elements of the first floor Grand Dining Room, and the first floor Green Closet and Long Gallery retain their 1630s plasterwork and painted decoration, carried out by the court artists Francis Cleyn and Matthew Goodricke. Ham was inherited by Dysart's daughter Elizabeth, who in 1672 married the Earl, soon Duke, of Lauderdale, a member of Charles II's Cabal ministry, Secretary of State for Scotland and renowned for his grand living. Bishop Burnet acknowledged the Duchess's beauty (an excellent early portrait at the house, by Sir Peter Lely, shows her in her youth), as well as the intelligence and learning of her and her husband, but he criticised her 'ravenous covetousness' and his craving for luxury. Their work at Ham, which saw the creation of a sequence of new apartments along the south front, built by William Samuel, was certainly lavish. A new, centrally placed ground floor dining room was created, to either side of which they each had separate suites of rooms. The new State Bedchamber, the principal room in the house, was positioned above the dining room, on which the design of the garden, viewed from the window, with its elaborate parterre and Wilderness beyond, was axially centred. Throughout the rooms were expensive hangings, paintings and furniture provided by court craftsmen, leading artists or imported from abroad. Ham is particularly important for the astonishing survival in some rooms of the original damask wall hangings, faded but still in place after 300 years, and also for the survival *in situ* of the specially commissioned painted overdoors and overmantels. Set into panelling are landscapes and seascapes by Abraham Begeyn, Dirck van Bergen, Thomas and Jan Wyck and Willem van de Velde the Younger; classical landscapes by Hendrick Danckerts and 'Vergazoon'; and bird pieces by the important English artist Francis Barlow, the first native-born painter of birds and animals. Inset pictures of this type were at the forefront of fashion, and many of those at Ham are signed and dated.

With the beautiful marquetry or japanned 17th-century furniture, the rich plasterwork, with detail picked out in gold, the once vibrant wall hangings, painted ceilings by Cleyn, and by the Baroque decorative painter Antonio Verrio (who also decorated Hampton Court), and the pictures, silverwork and porcelain, Ham must have presented a sumptuous spectacle. To the diarist John Evelyn the house was 'furnished like a Great Prince's'. The Lauderdales' extravagances, however, did not ensure Ham a secure financial future. After the Duchess of Lauderdale's death in 1698 the estate passed to Lionel Tollemache, 3rd Earl of Dysart, her son by her first marriage. In 1770 Horace Walpole, whose niece had married the 4th Earl, visited Ham and found it in a 'state of pomp and tatters'. In 1879 Augustus Hare thought it a 'Sleeping Beauty' house, its former splendour now forlorn and dusty. The house was given to the National Trust in 1949 by Sir Lionel Tollemache Bt and Mr Cecil Tollemache.

Tour of the House

Externally the house is comparatively plain, of brick with stone dressings, with a hipped roof. The forecourt has side walls with niches containing classical busts, and the wrought iron gates date from 1671. The entrance façade has a recessed five-bay centre with, between the ground and first floors, oval niches for busts. The modest central doorway has attached Tuscan columns and a metope frieze; the initials of Sir Thomas Vavasour, with the date 1610 and 'Vivat Rex', are carved on the door.

Ground floor

The **Great Hall** occupies the site of the old Jacobean hall. The two extraordinary sculptural figures flanking the overmantel are said to be William Murray, 1st Earl of Dysart, and his wife as Mars and Minerva, by Francesco Fanelli, sculptor at the court of Charles I. The octagonal balustraded balcony above was created c. 1690. The **Marble Dining Room** is the central room of the south front apartments created by the Lauderdales. The carved oak panelling with 'bunches of leaves about ye dores' is the work of John Bullimore, for which he was paid in 1672/3. The 18th-century parquetry floor replaces the marble original, as does the 18th-century gilt leather on the walls. The original leather was richly decorated with cherubs, fruit and flowers. The **Duke's Dressing Room**, to the right, was the antechamber to the adjoining Bedchamber. It has fine floral marquetry cabinets, of various woods and ivory, and originally had six caned armchairs. The **Duchess's Bedchamber**, actually intended as the Duke's but appropriated by his wife by 1675, has a great carved and gilded frame surrounding the bed alcove and a ceiling painting attributed to Verrio, who stimulated the fashion for Baroque mural decoration in Britain. The silver chimney furniture (a feature of several rooms) is a mark of the Lauderdales' ostentation. The bed is a copy based on an inventory of 1679. The **Duke's Closet** is a small, richly decorated room for private retirement. The ceiling, with figures representing Music, is also by Verrio.

To the left of the Dining Room is the Duchess's suite. The **Withdrawing Room** has 1670s lacquer furniture. The **Yellow Bedchamber**, named after its damask hangings, was originally the Duchess's but became the Duke's. After his death it became known as the Volury Room, from the French *volerie*, because of the birdcages constructed outside the bay windows. The cabinet has a very elaborate architectural interior, with red tortoiseshell and gilded decoration, probably made in Antwerp in the 1630s. The Duchess's private closets are adjacent. The **White Closet** is decorated in the most advanced taste, with a corner chimneypiece and a coved ceiling, with *Wisdom presiding over the Liberal Arts*, again by Verrio, in the centre. The **Private Closet** has japanned furniture and another Verrio ceiling, *Fortitude with Time, Death and Eternity*. The **Chapel** has furniture and carved decoration by Henry Harlow, 1673–74, and the original altar table and cloth are rare survivals.

Netherlanders in Britain

A distinct feature of the artistic community in England in the 16th and 17th centuries was the presence of foreign artists and craftsmen, of which the majority were Netherlandish. England had enjoyed profitable commercial and artistic links with Flanders since the Middle Ages and the wealthy and prosperous city of Antwerp was a base for English bankers and merchants, particularly those in the cloth trade. Netherlandish artists and craftsmen, who provided a level of skill which to some extent native artists lacked, were encouraged to settle in England and to work for the court and for private patrons. Guillim Scrots, formerly court painter to the Habsburg court at Brussels, worked for Henry VIII and Edward VI, while Hans Eworth, from Antwerp, was painter to Mary I. Religious and political events in the Low Countries provided added reasons for Netherlanders to emigrate. Large numbers of Protestant refugees arrived from those parts of the Low Countries under Habsburg rule. The etcher and painter Marcus Gheeraerts the Elder fled to London from Bruges in 1568 and his son, Marcus Gheeraerts the Younger, was to become the leading artist under Elizabeth I. John de Critz, whose sister married Gheeraerts the Elder, arrived from Antwerp and headed an artistic dynasty active in England for several generations. Legislation designed to protect native workers restricted the activities of 'alien' artists and craftsmen, who could only set up workshops if they assumed English citizenship. Many therefore lived in parishes beyond the jurisdiction of the City guilds. St Anne, Blackfriars was a particular haven for artists and miniaturists, as well as a circle of Antwerp refugees. Later, the parish was home to Anthony van Dyck.

The focus of London's Netherlandish community was the Dutch Church, Austin Friars (which still exists today). Not all Netherlandish artists and craftsmen were religious refugees, however. London offered career opportunities for artists such as Daniel Mytens and van Dyck, as well as for specialists in genres other than portraiture. The renewed cultural programme of the royal court following the Restoration of Charles II in 1660 attracted skilled artists and craftsmen, and Dutch and Flemish artists were at the forefront of the development of British marine and landscape painting (eg the van de Veldes, and Jan Siberechts respectively).

Upper floor

The early 17th-century **Great Staircase** dates from the Dysart era, c. 1637–38. The fine balustrade, of panels carved with trophies of arms, by Thomas Carter, was 'veined' to imitate walnut and picked out in gold by Matthew Goodricke. Upstairs, the **Yellow Satin Room** has a very fine marquetry looking-glass and table decorated with elaborate scrollwork. The **Round Room**—the gallery around the Hall—is what remains of the 1630s Dining Room. Formerly a sumptuous room decorated a 'fair blue', the Inigo Jones-style compartmented ceiling remains. Guests would retire to the **North Drawing Room**, which retains its magnificent 1630s decoration, including a fine plasterwork ceiling and frieze (1637, by Kinsman), and carved Mannerist panelling. The marble chimneypiece, flanked by great twisted columns, with cherubs climbing up floral garlands on either side of the overmantel, was probably moved from the 1630s Dining Room. It was possibly designed by Francis Cleyn. The columns with their cherubs among vines are taken from one of Raphael's 'Acts of the Apostles' cartoons, *The Healing of the Lame Man* (V&A, *see p. 324*), then owned by Charles I and which would have been familiar to Cleyn through his work at the Mortlake Tapestry Works (*see p. 116*). The **Green Closet** is an important rarity, an early 17th-century cabinet which has survived with the majority of its original contents. Created for the Earl of Dysart in 1637–39 for the display of his small-scale pictures and portrait miniatures, the design was probably overseen by Cleyn. The room offers a tantalising glimpse of the rich court style of Inigo Jones, under whom Cleyn worked on the royal palaces. It was fully restored in the 1990s. The ceiling and cove is by Cleyn (tempera on paper, with paintings of putti based on Polidoro Caldara) but in the 1670s the Lauderdales undertook changes, introducing the fringed green damask and the green sarsenet curtains, hung on a gilt rod, which protect the miniatures. They also introduced the elaborate furniture, including the table with high-quality silver mounts and Japanese lacquer. Among the miniatures and other objects are *Elizabeth I* by Hilliard; family miniatures of the Tollemache family, by Hoskins and Dixon; and a large cabinet miniature of Catherine Bruce, Countess of Dysart, by Hoskins; small oil paintings, placed here by 1679; and a lock of hair cut from the head of Robert Devereux, Earl of Essex, favourite of Elizabeth I, on the day of his execution. The **Long Gallery** was remodelled in 1639, with panelling with Ionic pilasters, their fluting picked out in gold. Its chief glory is the magnificent set of over 23 quarter-length portraits in superb contemporary carved gilt frames of auricular style (so called because the swirls resemble the human ear), supplied by the court frame carver John Norris in 1672–75, with an important group by Lely, including the *Duchess of Lauderdale with a black Servant*, and John Michael Wright's *Colonel John Russell* (1659).

The **Library** once contained many rare books. The **Antechamber to the Queen's Bedchamber**, on the south front, was added by the Lauderdales, with its grained panelling and carved swags of fruit and flowers. The 1680s wall hangings, now faded, were once blue and are framed by panels of blue velvet with appliqué embroidery. They are a remarkable survival. The **Queen's Bedchamber** was prepared for a visit by Catherine of Braganza, queen of Charles II. The bed stood on a raised platform, behind a balustrade. The carved swags over the chimneypiece are by Bullimore. The **Queen's Closet** is the most richly decorated room in the house. The plasterwork ceiling has marbled flat surfaces, with details of the relief picked out in gold, and a central painting by Verrio, *The Rape of Ganymede*. The wainscoting is richly carved and the chimneypiece is surrounded by panels of scagliola, a material made from selenite but made to look like marble. Probably imported from northern Italy, this is perhaps the earliest examples of this type of decoration in England. The crimson and gold silk wall hangings, bordered by green, are original and another amazing survival.

HAMPTON COURT PALACE
(Historic Royal Palaces)

East Molesey, Surrey, KT8 9AU
Tel: 0870 752 7777; www.hrp.org.uk
Open April–Oct Mon–Sun 10–6; Nov–March Mon–Sun 10–4.30. Tickets are for the historic palace and gardens, or garden only or maze only. Joint tickets with other Historic Royal Palace properties possible. Visitors can book tours with historic costumed guides
Admission charge
Station: Hampton Court
Cafés and shop
Map p. 378, 4B

Hampton Court Palace, sprawling and magnificent on the north bank of the Thames, is from a distance a fantasy of Tudor turrets and twisted chimney stacks. Formerly the extravagant home of Cardinal Wolsey, it was requisitioned by Henry VIII in 1528, on Wolsey's failure to support the king's desire for a divorce from Katherine of Aragon. It was here that Henry VIII was betrothed to his third wife, Jane Seymour and here, a year later, that Jane died giving birth to Edward VI. Shakespeare may have acted in his own *Measure for Measure* in the Great Hall. Hampton Court was a favoured royal residence of the later Tudors and early Stuarts, a pleasure palace with tennis courts, bowling alleys, a tilt yard and parks stocked with deer and other game. From 1645 Charles I was imprisoned at the palace and, following his execution, it became Oliver Cromwell's country residence. From 1689 Hampton Court was transformed for William III and Mary II by Sir Christopher Wren into a modern Baroque palace, its size and splendour in conscious competition with Louis XIV's Versailles. Suites of King's and Queen's State Apartments were created, outstanding ornamental gardens, with topiary and fountains, and a maze which is still one of the palace's best-known features. The court last visited Hampton in 1737. The State Apartments were opened to the public in the 19th century, shortly after the accession of Queen Victoria, while other parts of the palace were awarded as 'grace and favour' apartments to pensioners of the Crown and others. It was in one of these that, in 1986, a fire broke out, which caused catastrophic damage to some of the King's Apartments. A meticulous restoration campaign has been undertaken, and the refurbished rooms now offer a true sense of the exuberant and rich interiors of the time of William III.

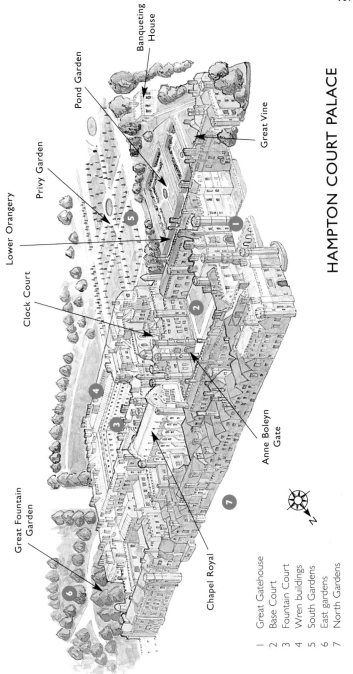

HAMPTON COURT PALACE

Banqueting House

Pond Garden

Privy Garden

Lower Orangery

Clock Court

Great Vine

Anne Boleyn Gate

Chapel Royal

Great Fountain Garden

1 Great Gatehouse
2 Base Court
3 Fountain Court
4 Wren buildings
5 South Gardens
6 East gardens
7 North Gardens

The Tudor Palace

The first buildings at Hampton belonged to the Knights Hospitaller of St John of Jerusalem, who acquired the manor in 1236 and used it as a grange. By the 15th century the great barn had been replaced by residential buildings, used by the Abbots of the Order of St John as a rural retreat. In 1494 Sir Giles Daubenay, Henry VII's Lord Chancellor, purchased an 80-year lease on the property and transformed the country manor into a major courtier house. It was in 1514–15 that Hampton Court's important association with royalty and political and national life began, with Sir Thomas Wolsey's acquisition of a 90-year lease. Henry VIII's Lord Chancellor, appointed Cardinal by Pope Leo X in 1515, Wolsey transformed Hampton Court into a complex of buildings of international importance. As well as a private residence, he envisaged the palace as a show house for entertaining the king and his court, and as a fitting residence to receive foreign dignitaries. Built by architects and master craftsmen associated with the country's most important late Gothic buildings, Hampton Court also had innovative features and Renaissance embellishments not seen in England before. Its succession of courtyards and elaborate, turreted gateways provided accommodation for the court; lavish apartments for the king (which remained the principal State Apartments of the monarch until the reign of William and Mary); a chapel; and a long gallery, erected in 1515–16, glazed on either side. Gardens were laid out, and a moat and ponds for fish constructed, the latter providing freshwater shrimps and carp. These major alterations were undertaken in two principal phases: in 1515–22, the last date being that of the visit to Hampton Court of the Holy Roman Emperor, Charles V (nephew of Katherine of Aragon); and a second phase, until 1527, when Wolsey received the huge entourage of the French court. The palace was furnished with costly magnificence, reflecting Wolsey's status as international statesman. Tapestries, a commodity of the wealthy elite, were purchased abroad for staggering sums in 1520, with the Emperor's visit in mind, while Wolsey's own apartments were hung with cloth of gold.

In September 1528 Henry ordered Wolsey to vacate the palace for the duration of the visit of the papal delegation, in London to discuss the King's divorce. From that time on Henry assumed ownership of Hampton Court, which was completed during his reign. Alterations and additions were made to Wolsey's buildings, including the construction of new kitchens, a Council Chamber and the Great Hall, and practical improvements were undertaken, such as the construction of the Great House of Ease (communal lavatories).

The Exterior

The main entrance to the palace is from the main road, through Trophy Gate, built for William III. At its far end is the west front of the palace, built by Wolsey and completed and altered by Henry VIII. The central **Great Gatehouse** ❶, of mellow brick with limestone dressings, was originally two storeys higher but nevertheless preserves an excellent sense of the imposing silhouette it would have presented to visitors. The fine moated bridge, built by Henry VIII, is guarded by the King's Beasts. On the turrets to either side are terracotta roundels by the Florentine sculptor Giovanni da

Maiano, two of eight imported and set in place in 1521 (others appear in the succeeding courtyards). Henry VIII's arms were inserted in 1530. Visitors pass through to **Base Court** ❷, originally cobbled but which remains much as Wolsey built it. Straight ahead is the **Anne Boleyn Gate**, built by Wolsey, but so-called because the fan-vaulted ceiling was added after Anne became queen in 1533. It bears her badge of a falcon and the intertwined initials H and A. Its small 18th-century bell-tower contains an original bell of the Knights Hospitallers.

Clock Court was the principal court of Wolsey's palace, now much altered. The original west range has Wolsey's arms, supported by cherubs and surmounted by his cardinal's hat, in terracotta, above the gate. Henry VIII's Astronomical Clock, probably designed by Nicholas Kratzer and made in 1540 by Nicholas Oursian, Devisor of the King's Horologies, its dial altered, shows the hour, month and day, the number of days passed since the beginning of the year, the houses of the zodiac and the phases of the moon. The east side, constructed in Tudor style, was remodelled by William Kent in 1732 for George II. It replaces the magnificent apartments constructed by Wolsey for Henry VIII, which were used by monarchs until the reign of William and Mary, their former great feature being tall glazed windows which in their day would have amazed and astonished. The colonnaded south side was constructed by Wren as an entrance to William III's new State Apartments. On the north is the buttressed mass of Henry VIII's new Great Hall.

Continuing through to **Fountain Court** ❸, visitors find all trace of the Tudor palace removed, supplanted by the arched cloisters and Baroque façades of Wren's new courtyard. It replaces Henry VIII's Fountain Court, so named in 1536. The tall first-floor windows are those of the State Apartments, above which were the lodgings of important courtiers and officeholders. On the south side carved wreaths surround 12 (much faded) paintings by the French Baroque decorative artist Louis Laguerre, the *Labours of Hercules*, part of the heroic iconography glorifying William III that appears throughout the late Stuart palace.

An exit on the east side leads to the gardens and Wren's imposing **east and south fronts** ❹, among the most important examples of Baroque architecture in the country. Eager to avoid the smog of London and the damp of Whitehall Palace (William III suffered from chronic asthma), William and Mary ordered Wren to 'beautify' Hampton Court in March 1689. Wren transformed it into a modern Baroque palace, architecturally influenced by Continental precedents. In May 1689 demolition of portions of the Tudor palace began, and by July the foundations of the new apartments were being dug. The frantic pace of work led to partial collapse of the south front, and work resumed at a more orderly rate. The east front is architecturally the more elaborate, with a great central pediment filled with a sculptural relief, *Hercules Triumphing over Envy* (further allusion to William's might), by Caius Gabriel Cibber, supported by giant Corinthian columns. The south front, which contains the King's Apartments, with views over the elaborate Privy Garden, has over the central window a carved trophy of arms with a Latin inscription, 'Gulielmus et Maria Rex et Regina Fecerunt', glorifying William and Mary's building project.

The Tudor Interiors

Henry VIII's State Apartments

The apartments of Henry VIII which survived the demolition and renovation campaigns of successive centuries are approached via Clock Court, up the staircase in Anne Boleyn's Gate. They lead to the **Great Hall**, the largest room in the palace, begun by the king in 1532. As well as being a traditional component of a high-status building, the Hall provided a magnificent entrance to the State Apartments. The remarkable hammerbeam roof, one of the finest in existence—but which serves no practical function—was designed by the King's Master Carpenter, James Nedeham, and is richly decorated with carved pendants, the royal arms and heraldic badges. The exceptional Flemish 'Story of Abraham' tapestries, woven in Brussels in the 1540s by Wilhelm Pannemaker, with silver and gold thread, were among the most expensive tapestries commissioned by Henry VIII.

Beyond Horn Court (where old Tudor antlers were stored at the time of William III) is the **Great Watching Chamber**, the first of Henry VIII's sequence of State Apartments, and the only one to survive. A door at the far end would have led to the Presence Chamber and the rest of the state rooms. It was a room at the heart of court life, where senior courtiers would have dined and where the Yeomen of the Guard were stationed, controlling access to the king in the Apartments beyond. Although altered, it is the only state room of Henry VIII's, from any palace, to survive in anything approaching its original appearance, and is thus of immense historical significance. The decorated ceiling is original, as are the 16th-century tapestries, but the deep heraldic frieze has been whitewashed.

The Pages' Chamber was where courtiers waited before being presented to the king. The **Haunted Gallery** is named after the shrieking ghost of Catherine Howard said to inhabit it. Catherine, Henry VIII's fifth wife, was held at Hampton Court, in her lodgings, before her execution on charges of adultery. Sixteenth-century Flemish tapestries, probably owned by Elizabeth I, show scenes from Virgil's *Aeneid*. Important Tudor pictures from the Royal Collection hang here (the selection can change), including the *Family of Henry VIII*, showing the king enthroned, flanked by Jane Seymour and his only son, the future Edward VI, with, to the sides, his daughters Mary and Elizabeth; and the famous *Field of the Cloth of Gold* and *The Embarkation of Henry VIII*, showing the English fleet preparing to leave for Calais.

The **Chapel Royal** was built by Wolsey and is still in use (services on Sunday). Its most magnificent adornment is the astonishing fan-vaulted ceiling, carved and decorated with gilded pendants, installed by Henry VIII in 1535–36. The high altar, with its oak reredos by Grinling Gibbons and painted angels by Sir James Thornhill, was installed by Queen Anne, who also altered the upper Royal Pew, where the monarch would attend services. Its painted ceiling is also by Thornhill.

The Wolsey Rooms

Entered via the colonnade in Clock Court and down Stone Hall, the Wolsey Rooms occupy the site of Wolsey's private apartments, built in the 1520s. Refitted in the 18th and 19th centuries, they nevertheless retain some original Tudor features: linenfold panelling, plain early 16th-century fireplaces and a ribbed ceiling with early Renaissance decorative motifs. Important pictures displayed here (the choice is liable to change) include a fantastical lady in a Persian headdress surrounded by Elizabethan symbolism, by Marcus Gheeraerts the Younger; *George Villiers, 1st Duke of Buckingham* (1628) by Gerrit van Honthorst; and Leonard Knyff's large bird's-eye panorama of Hampton Court, c. 1703.

Tudor Kitchens
Access to the Tudor kitchens is from Clock Court, through the basement of the Great Hall and out into Master Carpenter's Court. The kitchens fed Henry VIII's court of 1,200 people, who dined in the Great Hall and the Great Watching Chamber, and were administered by the Board of the Greencloth which met above Seymour Gate, which can be seen from Lord Chamberlain's Court. The Boiling House was the Tudor butchery, where great cauldrons of stock and stew were also prepared. Fish Court houses various kitchen departments, such as the spicery, the pastry house and the fish larder. The Great Kitchens, a vast, cavernous space with huge hearths and spits, is divided into three spaces, the third being the oldest, part of Wolsey's kitchens built c. 1514. Dishes were elaborately dressed and garnished in the Dressers, then passed out to the Serving Place to be taken to diners via the North Cloister. The Cellars were where quantities of beer, ale and wine for the court were stored. The vaulted Great Wine Cellar contains great oak barrels hooped with willow.

Interiors of the Late Stuart Palace
The transformation of Hampton Court from an old-fashioned shrine to the Tudor monarchy into a great Baroque palace which challenged the supremacy of Louis XIV was undertaken for William and Mary from 1689 by a team of great architects and designers: Sir Christopher Wren; Nicholas Hawksmoor; the virtuoso carver Grinling Gibbons; William Talman; and the leading Baroque decorative artist Antonio Verrio. Queen Mary had keenly overseen progress at the palace until her premature death, of smallpox, in 1694, when work virtually ceased until late 1697 when William, his European wars over, took a renewed, personal interest. In January 1698, after fire had virtually destroyed the chief Royal residence, Whitehall Palace, Wren submitted an estimate for the completion of the interiors, but the cheaper William Talman was chosen. Tapestries from the Royal Collection were used throughout the rooms, as well as pictures, mainly royal portraits which deliberately emphasised the Dutch William's association with the Stuart dynasty. The Master of the Great Wardrobe, Ralph, Baron, later Earl, later 1st Duke, of Montagu, took charge of the furnishings. Former Ambassador in Paris, he promoted French Huguenot artists and craftsmen. Throughout the State Apartments is elaborate upholstery, expensive carved giltwood furniture supplied by Jean Pelletier and exceptional mirrors by Gerrit Jensen, cabinet-maker and glass seller in ordinary to the King. The court removed to Hampton Court

for the first time in April 1700 and thereafter it was William's habit to spend spring and early summer and autumn at the palace, until his death following a riding accident in the park here in 1702.

According to convention, the King and Queen had their own suites of rooms, reached by separate grand staircases. Access to the apartments was governed by strict court protocol. While most visitors to court could mount the Great Stairs and linger in the Guard Room, further progression was strictly governed by rank. The closer one got to the private apartments of the monarch, the more exclusive the room, and the richer its furnishing and ornamentation. The King's Private Apartments, where only the most favoured were admitted, were the most lavish of all. All the State Apartments at Hampton Court illustrate these conventions to rich and grand effect. Many of the furnishings are original to the rooms, which underwent a six-year restoration following the fire in 1986.

The King's Apartments

The entrance to the King's Apartments is under the colonnade in Clock Court. The spectacular **King's Staircase** was decorated by Verrio in 1700–02. An overwhelmingly Baroque space, it was supposed to awe visitors as they approached the State Rooms above. The walls and ceiling illustrate scenes from the *Satire of the Caesars*, written by Emperor Julian the Apostate. Alexander's triumph over the Caesars is paralleled with William's over the Roman Catholic James II, and celebrates the king as Protestant champion of Europe. *The Banquet of the Gods* is on the ceiling; on the east wall *Hercules and Romulus pressing the rival claims of Alexander the Great and the Twelve Caesars to be invited to the Heavenly Banquet of the Saturnalia*, and on the south wall *Mercury suggesting to Julian the subject of the 'Satire of the Caesars'*. The fine wrought iron balustrade is by Jean Tijou. The **King's Guard Chamber** was where the Yeomen of the Guard controlled access to the king, letting past into the State Rooms only peers, officeholders, privy councillors or gentlemen of good quality and fashion. The oak panelling is decorated with more than 3,000 pieces of arms, arranged in patterns by John Harris, Master Gunner of Windsor Castle, for William III.

The **King's Presence Chamber** was used for formal ceremonial occasions such as the reception of ambassadors. Facing the entrance is the king's throne. Made for William III in 1700, its tall crimson canopy bears his arms and the national emblems. Courtiers would bow three times in its direction even when unoccupied. Opposite it is Sir Godfrey Kneller's enormous *William III on Horseback*, a prominent, heroic image of the king, painted in 1701 and framed *in situ* by the king's framer, John Norris. The tapestries, *The Labours of Hercules* and *The Triumph of Bacchus*, were hung here for William III in 1700 but originally belonged to Henry VIII. The **King's Eating Room** was where the king dined in public, a ceremony not undertaken by William frequently. Placed between the windows are tables, modern reproductions of the originals, flanked by carved giltwood candlestands by Jean Pelletier and surmounted by mirrors by Gerrit Jensen. Similar ensembles appear in the succeeding rooms. Above the chimneypiece is a portrait of Christian IV of Denmark, brother of James I's queen,

Anne of Denmark, set within a majestic overmantel of carved limewood by Grinling Gibbons: brilliantly realised drops of leaves and flowers, with a cresting of arching wheat and palm fronds. The 'Acts of the Apostles' tapestries are of 17th-century Brussels manufacture.

The **King's Privy Chamber**, to which only gentlemen of good rank were admitted, was the most important ceremonial room in the palace. It was here that the king received foreign ambassadors at their first, official, entrance and where other court functions, such as the performance of Birthday Odes, took place. The room was badly damaged in the 1986 fire. Most of the contents were rescued before the ceiling collapsed, but the canopied throne and great rock crystal chandelier, now restored, were buried in rubble. The tapestries are part of Henry VIII's *Story of Abraham* series intended for the Great Hall. This important room occupies the central place along the south front enfilade, and the Privy Garden visible from the window is centrally aligned to it. The richly carved overmantel is by Gibbons, with sections painstakingly re-carved.

Only court officeholders, privy councillors and Secretaries of State were admitted to the **King's Withdrawing Room**, a more intimate size than the preceding room, where social gatherings would take place and cards would be played. The elaborate silver sconces are reproduced from originals at Windsor Castle, and the tapestries are from the 'Acts of the Apostles' series. The carved overmantel is a masterpiece of carving by Gibbons, with leaves and fruit hanging in dense ropes, with complex gatherings of fruit and flowers, crisply carved. This was the last room that visitors could access from the King's Staircase. The **King's Great Bedchamber** next door, one step further into the sanctum, admitted privileged courtiers only, by way of the King's Back Stairs. This magnificent space was a ceremonial room where the king was dressed in front of courtiers, who were kept at a distance behind a rail. The gilded furniture and mirrors, by Gerrit Jensen, are the finest in the apartments, including one 13-ft high, incorporating, in strips of blue glass, the king's monogram and crest. The great state bed, with plumed finials, soars towards the richly painted ceiling by Verrio, which appropriately shows *Endymion in the arms of Morpheus*, Greek god of dreams and sleep, with episodes from the story of Diana in the cove. Below is a remarkable carved frieze by Gibbons, of scrolling acanthus, songbirds, blossoms, fruit and ears of wheat. The **King's Little Bedchamber** was where the monarch actually slept. The bed and hangings, of silk and silver lace, are reproductions, based on surviving bills and warrants. Displayed on the chimneypiece are rare pieces of oriental porcelain from Mary II's collection. The Verrio ceiling, an excellent piece of painting unusually well preserved, shows Mars and Venus, with cupids, billing doves and orange trees in the cove. The **King's Closet** was his private study, where he would receive Ministers and Secretaries of State. The overmantel painting, *Birds in a Landscape*, is by Jacob Bogdani, who worked for Mary II.

The Back Stairs lead to the **King's Private Apartments** on the ground floor. Although the East Closet formed part of the king's private apartments, it was also used by William's favourite, the Earl of Albemarle, who had extensive lodgings at the palace. Most of the paintings are from William's collection, as are those in the Middle

Closet. The long and airy Orangery has a series of sculpture busts of philosophers by Hubert Le Sueur (Praxiteles Le Sueur, as he liked to sign himself), and the palace's original Privy Garden statuary (copies are in the garden). The King's Private Drawing Room and Private Dining Room were where William entertained unofficially, the latter hung with Sir Godfrey Kneller's important *Hampton Court Beauties*, a series of full-length portraits of the principal court ladies, commissioned by Queen Mary.

The Queen's Apartments
The apartments are entered via Clock Court, through George II's gateway. Intended for Mary II, who died in 1694 before the completion of the palace, some of the Queen's Apartments were used by William III but the rest remained empty. In 1715–18 they were set up for the use of the Prince and Princess of Wales, later George II and Queen Caroline, and on George II's accession to the throne the Queen's State and private apartments were redecorated and refurbished for Caroline. The **Queen's Staircase**, originally panelled and whitewashed, was painted by William Kent in 1734 to create a more lavish entrance. The grisaille decorations are on canvas applied to the wall, not plaster. The vast allegorical oil painting, *Mercury presenting the Liberal Arts to Apollo and Diana*, by Gerrit van Honthorst, 1628, shows Charles I and Henrietta Maria as Jupiter and Juno with the Duke of Buckingham as Apollo. The **Queen's Guard Chamber** is where the Yeomen of the Guard were stationed to control access to the Queen. They appear on the extraordinary chimneypiece, possibly made by Gibbons, the design sometimes attributed to Sir John Vanbrugh, who was also responsible for the room's architecture. The sober **Queen's Presence Chamber** was also designed by Vanbrugh, who was employed at the palace early in the reign of George I.

The **Public Dining Room**, originally a music or dancing room, was used by George II and Queen Caroline when they dined in the presence of the court. The **Queen's Audience Chamber** was the principal room in the suite used for the reception of important visitors. It retains Queen Caroline's crimson throne canopy. The **Queen's Drawing Room** is the central room on Wren's east façade. Aligned with the long canal, dug for Charles II, the view from the window shows the avenue of yews and other trees stretching into the distance. The queen's 'drawing rooms' took place here, where ladies of the court gossiped and played cards. The painted ceiling and walls, the latter in imitation of tapestries, were executed by Verrio and a team of assistants from 1703. Commissioned by Queen Anne, who succeeded William III, the theme is royal naval power. Anne's husband, Prince George of Denmark, features prominently, as Lord High Admiral. Prince George was fond of Hampton Court and these apartments were set up for his use. This was Verrio's last commission—he was by this time an ageing man with poor eyesight—and the work has, with justification, been much criticised, although it is much restored, George II having covered it up with wallpaper.

The **Queen's State Bedchamber** has its original bed, made for George and Caroline when Prince and Princess of Wales in 1715, and an excellent painted ceiling by Sir James Thornhill, *Leucothoe restraining Apollo from entering his Chariot*, with oval portraits of members of the Royal family in the cove. The **Queen's Gallery** was used by William

III who displayed here Mantegna's *Triumphs of Caesar* (*see p. 117 below*). The 18th-century Brussels tapestries, episodes from the story of Alexander the Great, were hung here by George I. The excellent chimneypiece by John Nost, with putti either side of an oval mirror, was moved from the King's Great Bedchamber. The **Queen's Closet** is hung with needlework panels made for Mary II, in the style of the French Huguenot Baroque designer Daniel Marot, who worked for the Queen when he was briefly in England. Here also are blue and white Delft tulip vases, made for William and Mary in the 1690s. The use of porcelain was a characterising motif of Marot's interior designs.

The Georgian Rooms

The Georgian Rooms are approached from Clock Court, through George II's gateway, up the small staircase on the left. The rooms comprise the apartments occupied by George II and Queen Caroline—who last visited the palace with the court in 1737—and the new apartments on the east side of Clock Court created in 1732 by William Kent for their second son, William Augustus, Duke of Cumberland. The **Cumberland Suite** was built on the site of Henry VIII's abandoned State Apartments. The Duke's Presence Chamber, hung with Georgian royal portraits, has a 'Jacobethan' ceiling and painted and gilded panelling, while the Duke's Bedchamber has an elaborate Palladian bed niche flanked by Ionic columns, painted white. The **Wolsey Closet** is a 19th-century assembly of salvaged Tudor fragments which evokes a 1530s royal closet. The densely elaborate gilded Renaissance ceiling is part Tudor leather mâché, the rest 19th-century imitation. The paintings were probably commissioned by Henry VIII, but have been cut down to fit this space.

The **Communication Gallery** was built for William III in the 1690s. It displays Sir Peter Lely's exceptional *Windsor Beauties*, a set of pictures of court ladies commissioned by Anne Hyde, first wife of James II, in the early 1660s. Notable figures such as Charles II's mistress Barbara Villiers, Duchess of Cleveland, and Frances Stuart, Duchess of Richmond are included. The important **Cartoon Gallery** was built by Wren as William III's private picture gallery. It was soon altered specifically to take Raphael's 'Acts of the Apostles' cartoons, the exceptional Italian Renaissance works commissioned by Pope Leo X in 1516 as patterns for tapestries for the Sistine Chapel (*see box overleaf and also Ham House, p. 105*). William III ordered their restoration, by Parry Walton and Henry Cooke, and installation at Hampton Court in 1697. The pictures seen here are 17th-century copies (the originals were loaned to the V&A by Queen Victoria in 1865, where they remain; *see p. 324*). The Cartoon Gallery was used for the weekly meetings of William III's Privy Council.

The **Queen's Private Apartments** were built by Wren for Mary II. They are presented today as occupied by Queen Caroline in the 1730s. The Queen's Private Drawing Room is hung with rare 18th-century crimson flock wallpaper and has a large 17th-century Isfahan carpet. Her Private Bedchamber is hung with Mortlake tapestries of c. 1685 depicting the 1672 Battle of Solebay. The great state bed, not original to Hampton Court, formerly belonged to the 2nd Viscount Townshend, George II's Secretary of State. Above the chimneypiece, set within a dense roundel of carved flowers by Gibbons, is a portrait of Caroline by Joseph Highmore. The Queen's Dressing Room and Bathroom preserve a silver-gilt toilet service made c. 1695 by Daniel Garnier, and engraved in 1740. Beyond the Private Dining Room and Sideboard Room is the Queen's Private Oratory, with a lofty carved and moulded dome, where Caroline would hear sermons and services before her Chaplain.

The Mortlake Tapestry Works and the 'Acts of the Apostles'

Shortly after Giovanni de' Medici, son of Lorenzo the Magnificent, became Pope Leo X, he commissioned ten cartoons from Raphael, depicting the Acts of the Apostles, for tapestries for the Sistine Chapel. The cartoons were woven in Flanders in the workshops of Pieter van Aelst. Charles I purchased the cartoons in 1623, and had tapestries made up from them at Mortlake: lavish and costly items that made copious use of metallic thread. The Mortlake manufactory had been set up by Royal Charter four years previously. It had 18 looms, an artist's studio, and employed over 50 Netherlandish weavers. Among them was Louis Dermoulen, who specialised in heads, and Pieter de Craigt, who sepcialised in flesh parts. Mortlake's golden era began in the 1620s, under the directorship of Francis Cleyn, who was chief designer there until his death in 1657. He was appointed on the strength of the new working cartoons which he produced from the Raphael series. Raphael's own cartoons were restored later in the century by order of William III. Monumental examples of High Renaissance art in England, they were held up as exemplars of artistic excellence. Sir James Thornhill studied them when working on the dome of St Paul's, and in 1729 he was granted a Royal Warrant to make copies. He hoped to make them more accessible to art students, and as such a focus for academic instruction. These great works of art—the gestures of the figures and their composition—made an impact on English art for generations.

The Palace Gardens

Henry VIII laid out elaborate ornamental gardens which comprised a privy garden to the south; a public garden to the east, with parkland beyond; pleasure gardens to the north; and to the west the great Tiltyard, for jousting and tournaments. The gardens today, however, reflect their Baroque transformation under William and Mary, who laid out the great avenues of trees to the east—such a defining feature of the present Hampton Court—as well as the Privy Garden's elaborate parterre to the south and the Wilderness to the north.

South Gardens ❺

The **Privy Garden**, the King's private garden, was completed for William III in 1702, its magnificent symmetry of design seen to best effect from the windows of the King's Apartments. Recent restoration has re-established the great ornamental parterre, with its box and gravel arabesques, carefully placed clipped evergreens, its fountain basin at the centre, and elegant statuary. The Earl of Portland was William's Superintendent of the Royal Gardens, the nurseryman George London his deputy, William Talman the Comptroller, and the Dutch gardener Hendrick Quellingburgh maintained them. When work resumed on the gardens in 1697, following the respite after Mary's death, Henry Wise joined the team. The great screens at the bottom of the garden, by the Thames, of wrought iron with elaborate gilded panels, are by Jean Tijou, originally made for the east front Fountain Garden. The Knot Garden, with box hedging, gives an impression of the Tudor gardens, and the **Pond Garden** was where Henry VIII's freshwater ponds were, which provided fish for the kitchens.

The **Lower Orangery** originally held Mary II's botanical specimens, but today houses Andrea Mantegna's magnificent *Triumphs of Caesar* (c. 1486–94), exceptional Italian Renaissance works made for the Gonzaga court at Mantua, purchased by Charles I in 1629 with other works from the Gonzaga collection. William hung them in the Queen's Gallery, where their triumphal allegory reflected the King's military prowess. The **Great Vine**, in its purpose-built glasshouse, is from a cutting of the Black Hamburg vine at Valentine's Park, Essex. Planted by 'Capability' Brown in 1768, it is the oldest vine in the world and is tended by a resident keeper. On the east facing wall of the Vine Keeper's house is the Great Wisteria, only a couple of decades younger than the vine.

The elegant **Banqueting House** is on the south side, on the edge of the Thames. A pleasure pavilion built for William III, it was probably designed by Talman. Its three rooms are richly decorated, with Gibbons carving and Verrio decorative work. The Painted Room has a mythological ceiling and walls, the latter incorporated within a unifying decorative framework of illusionistic carved cartouches, decorative swags of flowers, panels of grotesquework and mirrors with gilded frames.

East Gardens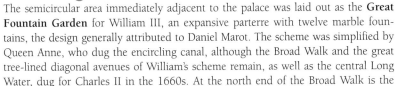

The semicircular area immediately adjacent to the palace was laid out as the **Great Fountain Garden** for William III, an expansive parterre with twelve marble fountains, the design generally attributed to Daniel Marot. The scheme was simplified by Queen Anne, who dug the encircling canal, although the Broad Walk and the great tree-lined diagonal avenues of William's scheme remain, as well as the central Long Water, dug for Charles II in the 1660s. At the north end of the Broad Walk is the **Royal Tennis Court**, built in the 1620s and still in use today.

North Gardens

The Northern Gardens occupy the site of the Wilderness, in place by 1686 but to which William III made alterations, a plantation of hollies and bay trees with winding paths and openings in elaborate, symmetrical patterns, a great yew tree at its centre. The feature which remains today is the world-famous **Maze**, the oldest planted maze in the country, although its hedges have been renewed over the centuries. Originally hornbeam, it was entirely replaced with yew in the 1960s, although there is a current plan to reintroduce the former. Introduced in 2005 was an audio installation: lost visitors will hear fragmented music, distant laughter and the rustle of silks.

HANDEL HOUSE MUSEUM

25 Brook Street, Mayfair, W1K 4HB (entrance at back)
Tel: 020-7495 1685; www.handelhouse.org
Open Tues, Wed, Fri, Sat 10–6; Thur 10–8; Sun 12–6
Admission charge
Tube: Bond Street
Shop
Map p. 381, 1E

From 1723, when he was appointed Composer to the Chapel Royal, until his death here in 1759, George Frideric Handel (1685–1759) lived and worked at this medium-sized Mayfair townhouse. Born in Halle, Saxony, Handel came to London in 1710, having been *Kapellmeister* to the Elector of Hanover, later King George I. What attracted him was the opportunity to stage Italian operas. In the next year his *Rinaldo*, at the Haymarket, proved a huge success. Naturalised a British citizen by Act of Parliament in 1727, he composed *Zadok the Priest* for the coronation of George II later in the same year. The anthem has been sung at all subsequent coronations. Concentrating increasingly on the composition of English oratorios, Handel's work often drew parallels between British history and the Old Testament: they were patriotic pieces extolling by association the glories of the new Hanoverian dynasty. The most popular remains the *Messiah* (1741), of which regular Christmas charity performances in aid of the Foundling Hospital (*see p. 86*) were given after 1750. After 1751, unsuccessful operations on his cataracts left Handel completely blind. Until that time, he was exceptionally prolific, composing some 50 operas and over 20 oratorios, as well as cantatas, concerti and instrumental pieces—the majority of them while he was living in the rooms that can be seen here.

The House

The Handel House Trust was founded in 1991 to honour and perpetuate the composer's memory, and to promote the understanding and performance of his music. Ten years later, the Handel House Museum opened to the public, four rooms on the first and second floors having been restored to a likeness of their appearance during Handel's occupancy. He was the first tenant of the house, which was part of the development of Lower Brook Street between 1717 and 1726.

A visit begins on the second floor, with a short video introduction, before proceeding into the first of the period rooms, possibly the composer's dressing room. The wall panelling has been recreated in standard Georgian grey, hung with portraits either socially or culturally relevant to Handel, some on loan from national collections: there is one of Alexander Pope, who contributed libretti, another of the famous eccentric 'musical small-coal man' Thomas Britton, an itinerant coal vendor who held cramped but prestigious musical evenings every Thursday above his Clerkenwell coalshed.

The next room, at the front of the house, was Handel's bedroom, now complete with an original 18th-century full tester bed, dressed in replica crimson harateen, a type of ribbed worsted fashionable at the time. The bed, as with all the museum's furnishings, is of a type mentioned in the inventory of the house taken on Handel's death (in this room) in 1759. On the panelled walls, among other pieces from the era, is a print of Francesco Bernardi, the famed castrato better known by his stage name Senesino.

The most obvious original interior feature of the house to survive can be seen next: the dog-leg staircase and balustrade banisters. The balusters are inverted to Baroque effect, possibly at Handel's own request, while the ornamental carved tread ends, definitely of Handel's time, revert to a simpler design for the flights up to the servant's quarters above.

On the first floor are the two main rooms that Handel used for entertaining and composition. In the first front room stands a double-manual harpsichord, a copy of the composer's Coleman Ruckers specially commissioned from Bruce Kennedy in 1998 and regularly practised upon by music students during museum opening hours. From here Handel ran his opera company, giving the first rehearsal of his opera *Alcina*, for example, in 1735. His dining habits in these rooms were the subject of the following anecdote, reported by Charles Burney in 1785: 'During the repast, Handel cried out 'Oh—I have de taught' ... the company begged he would retire and write them down, with which request he so frequently complied that, at last, one of the most suspicious had the ill-bred curiosity to peep through the key-hole into the adjoining room, where he perceived that 'dese taughts' were only bestowed on a fresh hamper of Burgundy'. Nevertheless, it was in this adjoining room, rather dark, at the back of the house, that Handel is believed to have composed all his works from the opera *Giulio Cesare* (1723) to his final oratorio *Jephtha* (1752). A fine portrait by Thomas Hudson of Charles Jennens, the librettist of *Messiah*, hangs on the wall.

From here there is access to no. 23 Brook St (incidentally where Jimi Hendrix stayed for about 18 months in 1968–69. He is honoured here with an exhibition of photographs taken during his time in the top flat; *flat not open to the public*). The Byrne Collection here consists of several hundred pieces of material relating to Handel, including letters, prints, portraits and manuscripts, such as the score for a Handel fugue arranged in Mozart's hand in the early 1780s.

HAYWARD GALLERY

Belvedere Road, SE1 8XZ
Tel: 020-7921 0813; www.hayward.org.uk
Open during exhibitions daily 10–6, late evening openings Tues and
Wed until 8pm, Fri until 9pm
Admission charge
Tube: Waterloo/Embankment
Café and shop
Map p. 382, 3C

The Hayward is one of London's most important temporary exhibition spaces, featuring fine art shows of all periods but focusing particularly on the work of 20th-century and contemporary artists, sculptors and photographers. The gallery forms part of the South Bank Centre cultural complex, which includes the Royal Festival Hall, Poetry Library, Queen Elizabeth Hall and Purcell Room, occupying a tract of land on the south bank of the river, near Waterloo station. This was the site of the 1951 Festival of Britain, a national celebration to lift post-war spirits, which promoted British art, design and industry. The Festival's London centrepiece was the South Bank, the new Royal Festival Hall at its heart, with pavilions and walkways constructed around it, including the slender Skylon reaching into the sky, lit internally at night. After the dismantling of the exhibition's temporary structures, the site was developed by the Greater London Council's Department of Architecture, led by Geoffrey Horsefall. The long promenade along the Thames was retained from the Festival, behind which sit a series of concert halls, the Hayward Gallery and the National Film Theatre, accessed by concrete walkways and stairwells with confusing shifts of level.

The Hayward itself (named after the London County Council's former leader, Sir Isaac Hayward) is a purpose-built exhibition space dating from the 1960s. An uncompromising Brutalist building of grey, wood-pressed concrete, it is a series of joined cubes with jutting strata, its interior levels linked by concrete ramps, topped externally by the Neon Tower, designed by Philip Vaughan and Roger Dainton in 1970 and erected in 1972. Made up of coloured fluorescent tubes which are activated by the strength and direction of the wind, it has become a familiar part of the London evening and night-time landscape. From the South Bank there are excellent vistas over the river to the 'Gherkin' and St Paul's Cathedral. The Hayward's architecture is loathed and admired in equal measure. Particularly dismal on a grey, rainy day, a scheme to improve the environment is underway, of which the Hayward's 2003 glass-fronted foyer extension is a part, which includes a pavilion jointly designed by the New York artist Dan Graham and the architectural office Haworth Tomkins.

The Hayward's excellent programme of temporary exhibitions is eclectic and varied. Since its very first show, a Matisse retrospective in 1968, it has built up a distinguished record of contemporary art and photography exhibitions, as well as group, themed and international shows. In recent years it has staged monographic exhibitions on Howard Hodgkin, Francis Bacon and Henri Cartier Bresson; a contemporary African art show, *Africa Remix*; and an exhibition to celebrate the National Art Collections Fund, displaying star items saved for the nation. In addition the Hayward stages the annual British Show, which promotes the work of the most significant emerging British artists; manages a programme of national touring exhibitions; and administers the large Arts Council Collection of over 7,500 British works, a loan collection begun in 1949 to which contemporary work is continually added.

HMS BELFAST
(Imperial War Museum)

Morgan's Lane, Tooley Street, SE1 2JH
Tel: 020-7940 6300; hmsbelfast.iwm.org.uk
Open March–Oct daily 10–6; Nov–Feb daily 10–5
Admission charge. Partial disabled access
Café and shop
Tube: London Bridge
Map p. 383, 3F

The last surviving big gun World War Two armoured warship in Europe, *HMS Belfast* was saved from the scrapheap and opened to the public on Trafalgar Day (21st October) 1971. She provides a compelling insight into the nature of war at sea. An 'Edinburgh' class large light cruiser, she was designed during the mid-1930s in response to the threat posed by Japanese 'Mogami' class cruisers. Built by Harland and Wolff of Belfast, the vessel was launched by Mrs Neville Chamberlain on St Patrick's Day, 17 March, 1938.

On the outbreak of war in September of the following year, *HMS Belfast* formed part of the maritime blockade of Germany operating out of the Home Fleet's main base at Scapa Flow in the Orkney Islands. Badly damaged by a magnetic mine, she was com-

HMS Belfast at high tide on the river near London Bridge.

pletely refitted, eventually rejoining active service in 1943 on Arctic convoy duty. As the flagship of the Tenth Cruiser Squadron, she successfully provided close-range heavy cover for several convoys of the kind that supplied the Soviet Union with some four million tons of supplies during the course of the war, including 5,000 tanks and 7,000 aircraft. In the Battle of North Cape in December 1943, she engaged and contributed to the sinking of the German battle cruiser *Scharnhorst*. Only 36 men survived from that ship's complement of almost 2,000. On 6 June 1944, *HMS Belfast* was one of the first ships to open fire on German positions in Normandy in support of the D-Day landings, a role that she continued to play until 8 July, amid heavy fighting for the city of Caen.

After 1945, the ship was occupied in peace-keeping duties in the Far East, helping to evacuate survivors of Japanese prisoner-of-war camps and Chinese civilian internment centres. From 1950–52, *HMS Belfast* spent at least 404 days on active patrol in support of UN forces during the Korean War. In August 1963, after circumnavigating the globe via the Pacific Ocean and Panama Canal, she returned to Portsmouth to be reclassified as a Harbour Accommodation Ship. 'Reduced to Disposal' in 1971, she was rescued from the ship-breakers by an independent trust chaired by one of her former captains, Rear-Admiral Sir Morgan Morgan-Giles, and opened to visitors 'not as an exercise in nostalgia, but as an act of faith for the youth of the future'. The ship was purchased for one pound by the Imperial War Museum in 1978.

Appropriately enough, the ship is now anchored to the Thames riverbed at the former 'breakfast wharf', where tons of tea were once unloaded into Frederick J. Horniman's warehouses (*see p. 124*): it was this type of trade that cruisers were originally designed to protect. Visitors board at the Quarterdeck, the 'Officer Country' towards the stern of Royal Naval vessels. The ship has been divided into eight different 'zones' in an attempt to facilitate orientation around a confusion of different decks, hatchways, ladders and rooms. Above decks, highlights include scoping Tower Bridge and the Tower of London through the gun direction sights; the 6-inch Mark XXIII Triple Gun Turrets, now trained on Scratchwood Services on the M1; the 40mm Bofors guns; Admiral's Bridge and Compass Platform, with the Operations Room behind enhanced by sound effects, 'state boards' and uniformed mannequins recreating the scene during the Battle of North Cape. Below decks, visitors can explore the ship's living quarters, mess-decks, galley, chapel, magazine, communications room and—perhaps most impressive of all—the bewildering, claustrophobic array of gleaming pipes, valves and passageways in the boiler and engine rooms (zone eight). Exhibitions in zone five tell the story of *HMS Belfast* in war and peace, and describe life at sea for officers and men.

HOGARTH'S HOUSE

Hogarth Lane, Great West Road, Chiswick, W4 2QN
Tel: 020-8994 6757; www.information-britain.co.uk

Open Tues–Fri 1–5 (closes at 4pm in winter); Sat, Sun 1–6 (closes at 5pm in winter)
Free. Wheelchair access by prior arrangement to ground floor only
Tube: Turnham Green. Bus: 190
Shop
Map p. 378, 3C

This modest Queen Anne house, fragile and small on the edge of the Great West Road with its relentless roar of traffic—a brutal piece of planning which ripped through historic Chiswick—is Hogarth's House, the 'little country box by the Thames' that the great artist used as a summer retreat from 1749–64. Chiswick was then an elegant rural village, the home of fishermen and watermen, but also of more substantial figures such as Lord Burlington, whose support of Italianate art was a favourite subject of Hogarth's needling wit. Burlington's posturing Palladian villa was close by (Chiswick House; *see* p. 57). Hogarth's small house was simple and unassuming in comparison. Once surrounded by fields, its rooms comprised a downstairs parlour and stone-flagged kitchen; a best parlour upstairs, with a hanging bay window; two main bedrooms; and servants' quarters above. The stables with a painting studio above it have since disappeared. A high wall surrounds the house, isolating it from the hectic world outside, and most windows overlook its garden. Here Hogarth had a humble grave for his pet bullfinch, Dick, (buried in 1760, aged 11) and a mulberry tree, which was struck by lightning in his day, but still survives. A public appeal to buy the property in 1900 failed but a local benefactor, Lt Col. Robert Shipway, stepped in and in 1902 Hogarth's House opened to the public. In 1940 it was seriously damaged by bombing but was restored, and in 1997 underwent a major refurbishment, funded by the Heritage Lottery Fund, in celebration of Hogarth's 300th anniversary.

Little is known of Hogarth's life at Chiswick. He is known to have taken a little cheese for breakfast; to have been absent-minded at meals; and to have received local neighbours and friends from town. Today, the rooms are modestly furnished in the style of the period. A small exhibition looks at Hogarth's life, circle and work and throughout the house is a selection of his engravings, his 'modern moral histories', which satirised contemporary society. The kitchen is now a gallery, with engravings of *The Harlot's Progress*, *An Election*, and *Marriage à la Mode* (original paintings at the National Gallery). *The Man of Taste* mocks Lord Burlington and his favourite decorative painter, William Kent (who, through Burlington's promotion of him, won commissions from Hogarth's father-in-law, Sir James Thornhill). In the parlour, where Hogarth had engravings of Thornhill's celebrated 'St Paul's' cycle, are *Beer Street* and *Gin Lane*. Hogarth himself appears over the mantelpiece in the Best Parlour upstairs.

Nearby, at the bottom of Church Lane on the river, in a pretty and tranquil portion of old Chiswick, is the **parish church of St Nicholas**. Hogarth is buried in the attractive graveyard, his handsome but much weathered tomb designed by his friend, the actor David Garrick, a palette and brushes carved on one side.

HORNIMAN MUSEUM

100 London Road, Forest Hill, SE23 3PQ
Tel: 020-8699 1872; www.horniman.ac.uk
Open daily 10.30–5.30
Free.
Station: Forest Hill (from London Bridge). Bus: 176, 185, 312, P4
Map p. 379, 4E

During the 1860s and 70s, while working for the famous firm of tea merchants founded by his father, Frederick J. Horniman travelled extensively. His passion also lay in collecting; much of his hoard was bought at auction in London, and here it remains, in deepest Forest Hill, illustrating the arts, crafts and religions of the world at large. The museum first opened in Horniman's own home, Surrey House, in 1888. This soon proved inadequate, and was demolished to make way for the present Art Nouveau building, described by Pevsner as 'one of the boldest public buildings of its date in Britain'. The architect was C. Harrison Townsend (1897), who also designed the Whitechapel Art Gallery (*see p. 348*). In 1901, five years before his death, Horniman gave the museum to the people of London in perpetuity.

The Exterior

The façade is dominated by a landmark clocktower of eclectic design, and also by Robert Anning Bell's large mosaic panel (10ft by 32ft) symbolising the course of human life: Humanity in the 'House of Circumstance' is flanked by gates representing Birth and Death and tended by figures representing the Arts, Poetry, Music, Endurance, Love, Hope, Charity, Wisdom and Resignation. Beneath is a plaque bearing the brave and inspiring inscription: 'This building and its contents ... are dedicated to the public for ever as a free museum for their recreation, instruction and enjoyment'.

Since extensive redevelopment of the museum in 2002, the main entrance is now on the northwest side, reached from the gardens that were also part of Horniman's generous gift. They give wide views over London, and also contain a bandstand (1912), and children's zoo. Left of the main entrance, the glasshouse conservatory (1894) was moved here from Horniman's house in Croydon.

The Museum

On the ground floor on the left, the **Natural History Gallery** has retained its Victorian design, a barrel-vaulted ceiling arching over a formidable array of stuffed animals and birds in glass cases. Dominating the centre of the room, the most popular exhibit—especially with children—is the stuffed walrus, one of the original creatures on display when the museum first opened. It came from Hudson Bay, Canada, and was mounted by taxidermists around 1870. Other cases contain a reconstructed badger set, the classification of primates, featuring the skeletons of orangutans, gorillas and chimpanzees, and a stuffed ostrich. Yet more chart the evolution of the horse, and of the elephant, and contain stuffed birds including game birds, gulls, geese, ducks and hawks, notably a Golden Eagle, Harpy Eagle, and White Tailed Sea Eagle. Next door is the **River Journey** in the aquarium, where visitors can walk upstairs from mouth (sea) to source (mountain).

On the same floor, to the right, the **African Worlds Gallery** presents a selection from the estimated 22,000 African objects that make up almost a third of the museum's ethnographic collections. Particularly important early items come from Egypt, Benin and Ethiopia. From the 1950s the museum focused on acquiring examples of the material culture of specific peoples, especially the Sua of Zaire, the Hadza of Tanzania, the San of Botswana, the Tuareg of Algeria and Samburu of Kenya. More recently curators have concentrated on developing collections illustrating contemporary masquerade: good examples come from the Dogon of Mali and the Bundouku region of the Côte d'Ivoire. Displays are usually arranged by theme rather than by geography or chronology. Examples of current themes are altars from Benin and Brazil, and a brightly coloured Haitian voodoo altar or *pe* with dressed dolls' heads, skulls and Madonnas; masks such as the bird's head battledress, an Igbo Omabe mask from Nigeria, named after the 'dead fathers' of the Igbo and worn to protect the people and their crops; a Yoruba *epa* mask, now a symbol of the Nigerian nationalist movement Eliti Parapo; and the flamboyant headgear of the Midnight Robber's costume in the Trinidad Carnival.

The Horniman has one of the most important ethnographic collections in the United Kingdom.

The **Centenary Gallery** displays some of the multifarious objects that have been brought to the museum since its foundation and considers why they might have been chosen. The 'Gift of the Horniman Family' explores the founder's main enthusiasms: colourful, exotic and educational objects. One such is a grisly metal contraption called the Torture Chair, with a dubious provenance once ascribed to Cell 23 of the dungeons of the Spanish Inquisition, now believed to be a 19th-century fake incorporating a genuine garotte. Others include 19th-century mangle boards from Norway, a Merman from Japan, and part of Horniman's original collection of over 16,000 butterflies, beetles and insects, as well as rare birds in bell jars. 'Illustrating Evolution' explores the work of the first London County Council curators such as Alfred Cort Haddon, a founder of modern anthropology, who wanted the museum to 'illustrate the evolution of culture', demonstrating the now discredited idea that non-western societies were not 'advanced' in evolutionary terms.

The **Music Gallery** displays are drawn from the museum's collection of some 8,000 musical artefacts from all periods and cultures. The theme of the central showcase is 'The Rhythm of Life': it shows instruments associated with celebrations of rites of passage: weddings, funerals, graduation concerts and inititation ceremonies. 'Listening to Order' shows the technological evolution of European brass and woodwind instruments from the 18th century to the present day, based on more than 300 historic instruments given to the museum in 1947 by Adam Carse, Professor of Harmony and Counterpoint at the Royal Academy of Music, in memory of his son who died in the Second World War. The display is complemented by the three ingenious interactive 'listening tables', where these instruments and many others are described and can be heard in action.

HUNTERIAN MUSEUM

Royal College of Surgeons, 35–43 Lincoln's Inn Fields, WC2A 3PE
Tel: 020-7869 6560; www.rcseng.ac.uk
Open Tues–Sat 10–5
Free
Tube: Holborn
Shop
Map p. 382, 2B

On the first floor of the Royal College of Surgeons' grand Neoclassical home in Lincoln's Inn Fields, the Hunterian Museum re-opened in 2005 after a £3.5million refurbishment. Of the original building, designed by George Dance the Younger in 1813, only the portico survives, with the addition of an extra column after Charles Barry's complete re-modelling of 1832. Five different galleries now display the College's extensive collections of pathology and comparative anatomy specimens, as well as paintings, prints and drawings, and artefacts relating to the development of surgical practice since the 18th century.

William Hunter (1718–83) was one of the first to profit from the dissolution of the Barber-Surgeons, and recruited his younger brother John (1728–93) to help with his work. John Hunter, who built up the museum's core collection, developed theories on the relationship between the body's structure and function, illustrating his lectures with examples from some of his 15,000 different specimens. He is now considered to be one of the founding father's of 'scientific surgery'. (*Cont/d overleaf.*)

Sir Joseph Banks (1743–1820) *and Dr Daniel Solander* (1736–82)

Natural History owes much to the friendship between Joseph Banks, son of a Lincolnshire landowner, and Daniel Solander, the son of a Swedish Lutheran pastor. Even as a boy Banks was intensely interested in nature, and especially plants. Solander was a pupil of Linnaeus, sent by his master to England to promote the Linnaean system of classification to botanists there. In 1768 both men accompanied Captain Cook to Tahiti and the South Seas on the *Endeavour*. There they made important collections of specimens hitherto unknown in Europe, their zeal getting them through the rigours of sea travel and the diet of verminous ship's biscuit. The maggots, Banks commented, tasted 'as strong as mustard', and he claimed to have seen 'hundreds, nay thousands, shaken out of a single biscuit'. So important were their collections, that after their return Linnaeus suggested naming the newly discovered country (Australia) Banksia. The proposal was not accepted, but a family of Australian plants, the genus *Banksia*, does bear the name. Botany Bay is also named after Banks and Solander's activities. While Captain Cook had only seen desolation in that uncharted sound, and voted to name it Stingray Harbour, the two naturalists were captivated by its plant life, and the name Botany Bay is the one that stuck. So taken was Banks with the place, in fact, that when the government began looking for somewhere to establish a penal colony, Banks nominated Botany Bay as the ideal contender. Solander gives his name to the 'Solander box', a type of acid-free, soft board container which he devised to transport botanical specimens and keep them from spoiling. Such boxes are still used for storage of books, prints and papers today.

On their return to England, Solander was made keeper of the British Museum, where he catalogued the natural history collections, many of the items bequeathed by himself and Banks. Banks was a trustee of the Museum, and overseer of the Royal Botanic Gardens at Kew. When Cook invited them to join him on his next voyage, on the *Resolution*, Banks felt unequal to the privations and elected not to accompany him. Solander stood by his friend and chose to remain behind too. The two men went to Iceland, with Solander acting as Banks's secretary, and where they also made important discoveries. Both men became fellows of the Royal Society, and Banks was its president after 1778.

Tour of the Museum

The **Introductory Gallery** displays some of the museum's original artefacts and illustrates the history of the College from its origins in the Barber-Surgeon companies of the 16th century. The four Evelyn Tables presented here are some of the oldest surviving anatomical preparations in Europe. Bought as a curiosity in Italy by the diarist John Evelyn in 1646, these dissections of nerves, veins and arteries pasted onto wooden boards were once important teaching aids. A painted plaster bust by Louis François Roubiliac depicts William Cheselden (1706–85), one of the first anatomy teachers, who published the *Anatomy of the Human Body* in 1713.

In the middle of the room, from floor to ceiling, the **Crystal Gallery** presents a dazzling display of the remaining portion of John Hunter's specimen collection. Around two-thirds of the museum's collection were destroyed by enemy action on 10th May 1941. Eight state-of-the-art showcases now display over 3,500 specimens preserved in jars of alcohol, or of a more modern formaldehyde-based solution. Specimens injected with dyes were also often pickled in turpentine. As well as providing an important insight into 18th-century science, the gallery also provides challenging subject matter for students of drawing. The skeleton of Charles Byrne (1761–83), the 'Irish Giant', who stood 7ft 7in tall, can be seen at the far end.

The one-room **Art Gallery** displays the College's striking collection of 18th-century portraits, prints and drawings. It begins with a *Portrait of Omai* by William Hodges. Omai was brought over from Huahine, near Tahiti, in 1744 by Lt Tobias Furneaux, on *HMS Adventure*, and placed in the care of Sir Joseph Banks and Daniel Solander (*see p. 127 above*). He was presented to George III, and toured around the country in 1776. Also by Hodges are portraits of the Cherokee Indians Richard Justice and Moses Price. They visited London in 1791 accompanying William Augustus Bowles, self-styled commander-in-chief of the Cherokee nation. Next to them hangs *Portrait of a Malay Woman* by Robert Home. Home was John Hunter's brother-in-law, who trained under Angelica Kauffman and moved out to India after 1788. Other portraits depict people afflicted with achondroplasia (dwarfism), including the famous small person Count Joseph Boruwiski (1739–1837). He charged curious people a fee to visit him at home, married and had several children of average height. The marble bust of King George III by Francis Chantrey (1781–1841) was commissioned in 1813 to commemorate the Royal Charter granted in 1800.

Perhaps the most celebrated painting in the Hunterian collection is *Rhinoceros* by the famous horse-portraitist George Stubbs. It is a meticulous depiction of an Indian rhino that had recently been brought back to London. Also by Stubbs are *Yak* (1791), an animal brought back alive by Warren Hastings, the first British Governor-General of India, later impeached and acquitted. The yak was kept at his estate at Dalesford in Gloucestershire, where the original portrait sill hangs. This version was commissioned in 1791. Other works by Stubbs include his portrait of an albino baboon which was known as the 'child of the sun', and some of his sketchings for an atlas on midwifery by John Burton. Equally remarkable are the animal paintings by Jacques-Laurent Agasse (1769–1849), who trained in the studio of David in Paris, under the patronage of Lord Rivers. They include an ibex, a white mule, white antelope and a quagga. Also here is a pencil portrait (1793) of John Hunter by George Dance the Younger, the architect of the first college building and founder member of the Royal Academy. John Hunter published his first book *The Natural History of the Human Teeth* in 1771. It was illustrated by Jan van Riemsdyk, some of whose original sketches can be seen here, along with a plaster-cast copy of the death mask of Sir Isaac Newton by John Michael Rysbrack.

The **Museum after Hunter** gallery profiles the work of curators since Hunter, taking in the development of comparative osteology and odontological collections and the effects of the bombing during the Blitz, which reduced the College's collection of 75,000 specimens by over half. Upstairs, at balcony level, the **Science of Surgery** is an exhibition looking at the development of surgery as a profession, with its increasingly specialised fields, and displays items from the Lister Collection such as Lister's examination couch, original antiseptic spray, microscopes and experiment flasks. Displays trace the influence of anaesthetics and antisepsis, up to the development of keyhole surgery, with the chance for visitors to try their hand at the Minimal Access Training Unit.

ICA
INSTITUTE OF CONTEMPORARY ARTS

The Mall, SW1Y 5AH
Tel: 020-7930 3647; www.ica.org.uk
Open Mon 12–10.30pm, Tues–Sat 12–1am, Sun 12–11pm. Gallery open daily 12–7.30 during exhibitions
Admission charge for some of the spaces
Tube: Charing Cross
Café and bookshop
Map p. 382, 3A

Founded in 1947, the Institute of Contemporary Arts (ICA) is a centre for contemporary art in all media, with a programme of exhibitions, a new media centre, which promotes Internet art, a programme of world cinema screenings as well as frequent talks and symposia. When conceptual art was new, the ICA was a famous venue for cutting edge, anti-establishment events and exhibitions, as well as a centre of theory and debate. While some charge it with having become too much of a social drinking club with a cinema attached, the ICA is still at the forefront of the promotion of contemporary culture, and stages the annual Becks Futures contemporary art prize. Based in a handsome house in a Nash terrace overlooking the Mall (its home since 1968), white and minimalist inside, the ICA is also known for its organic restaurant and its bar, open until 1am most weekdays. Entry to the ICA requires day membership (only £1.50 for the day, £2.50 during an exhibition).

IMPERIAL WAR MUSEUM

Lambeth Road, SE1 6HZ
Tel: 020-7416 5000; www.iwm.org.uk
Open daily 10–6
Free
Tube: Lambeth North
Café and shop
Map p. 382, 4C

The museum illustrates and records the experience of war, with particular attention paid to the role played by Britain and the Commonwealth, since the start of the First World War in August 1914. The varied collections tell the story of military and civilian, Allied and enemy, tactical, strategic, social and political aspects of warfare by land, sea and air, employing an extraordinary array of memorabilia, fine art, film, sound archives, background information, interactive audio-visuals, models and reconstructions. In the late 1980s, the museum pioneered the 'visitor-oriented' curatorial approach, widely imitated since by other London museums and galleries.

The decision to found the museum was taken by the Cabinet during the First World War, in March 1917, in order to record experience of that conflict. Originally called the National War Museum, interest from the Dominion governments prompted the title Imperial War Museum. In 1936 the museum moved to its present premises, in a building which had been completed in 1815 for the Bethlem Royal Hospital for the insane. Inmates had included the York Minster arsonist Jonathan Martin (*see p. 24*), the architect Augustus Pugin (who designed the Houses of Parliament and St George's Roman Catholic Cathedral just across the Lambeth Road), and also Charlie Chaplin's mother. The two massive side wings of the building were demolished when the hospital moved out to Beckenham in 1930. The museum occupies the surviving central building, with a grand front portico beneath a lantern cupola added in 1846 by Sydney Smirke, architect of the British Museum's round Reading Room. Around it is a park containing a small Tibetan Peace Garden opened by the Dalai Lama in 1999. In front squat an enormous pair of 15-inch British Naval guns, the last survivors of their type, and a free-standing section of the Berlin Wall painted with a face screaming the words 'Change your Life' by the graffiti artist Indiano.

Ground Floor

The museum interior was completely re-modelled by Arup Associates in the late 1980s. Rising through the full height of the building is the Large Exhibits Gallery, an airy setting for the most important weapons and vehicles in the collection: guns, tanks, aircraft, bombs and rockets, each labelled with a general description of their type, technical specifications and provenance. One of the first large pieces to join the collection was the 60-pound field gun that took part in operations that led to the capture of Kut-el-Amara and eventually the fall of Baghdad on 11 March 1917. Another is the German mobile mast periscope, here extended to its maximum height of 80ft providing a view over the tree tops in the park, an unusual First World War method of observation, along with the one-man pod designed to be suspended below a zeppelin hidden in the clouds. Other artillery pieces of the era include the 13-pounder gun of East Battery, Royal Horse Artillery, which fired the first British shell of the land war, and also the four-inch QF Mark IV naval gun from the destroyer *HMS Lance*, which fired the first British shot of the war. The museum's collection of tanks—a British invention—begins with a Mark V no 19 'Devil' of 1918, of the kind that helped to break the deadlock of trench warfare. Second World War tanks ranged around the room include a Churchill, American M4 Sherman, Russian T-34 and a German Jagdpanther tank destroyer. A German V2 rocket, 47ft tall, dominates the space, the first long-range ballistic missile, a *Vergeltungswaffen* (reprisal weapon) that hit Britain to devastating effect almost a thousand times between 1944 and the end of the war. A drill version of the Polaris A3 missile, the first submarine-based ballistic missile and the UK's independent nuclear deterrent from 1968–96, can be compared with a 'Little Boy' atomic bomb casing of the type dropped on Hiroshima in 1945. Aircraft suspended from the roof are a First World War Sopwith Camel 2F1, a Supermarine Spitfire Mark 1A that saw action in the Battle of Britain, an American P-51 Mustang, a German Focke Wulf 190 and Heinkel 162. Naval exhibits include *Tamzine*, the smallest surviving fishing boat to have taken part in the evacuation of Dunkirk in 1940, and a German Biber one-man submarine found sinking off Dover in 1944. The crewman had died from carbon monoxide poisoning after failing to close off the engine exhaust.

Lower Ground Floor

The core of the museum is a subterranean maze of themed displays divided into the First World War and Second World War. Here the museum's three main categories of collection—objects, official material, and personal experience material—are arranged amid busy illustrations of their context. The First World War themes include 'Recruitment in Britain 1914–1915' dominated by the famous Kitchener poster 'Wants You'; 'Western Front' featuring a Maxim machine gun from 1902 of the type that forced the opposing armies into trench warfare; 'War at Sea' describing the indecisive Battle of Jutland in 1916, the British Naval Blockade and the escalation of German submarine attacks that brought the United States into the conflict; and 'The Home Front', where women's involvement in the war effort prompted radical social change. 'The Trench Experience' is a walk-through re-creation using sound, lighting and olfactory effects to suggest a front line trench and dugout on the Somme.

The Second World War includes displays on the 'Phoney War' of 1939–40, before the invasion of France, then 'Blitzkreig' illustrating that strategy with archive footage and a German motorcycle machine gun, followed by 'Battle of Britain' and the forestalling of Nazi invasion plans codenamed 'Operation Sealion'. 'Home Front 1940–45' describes the Blitz, rationing, refugees and the arrival of thousands of American servicemen: 'oversexed, overpaid and over here', according to one contemporary account. Other themes are the 'Mediterranean and Middle East 1940-45', 'Eastern Front 1941–45' and 'Europe under the Nazis' (covered in more detail in the Holocaust Exhibition on the Third floor, *see p. 134 below*), along with 'Bomber Offensive', 'War in the Far East 1941–45' and 'North West Europe 1944–45'. 'The Blitz Experience' is a guided walk-through reconstruction of an air-raid shelter and bomb-damaged street on one of the 57 consecutive nights that the city was hit between September 1940 and spring 1941.

Also on this floor, 'Conflicts since 1945' goes into the history of the Cold War with a series of small exhibitions on the conflicts in Korea, China and Vietnam, the Far East, Middle East, Cyprus, and the Suez Crisis, the Falklands and the Gulf, along with Terrorism and Peacekeeping. Next door is 'Monty: Master of the Battlefield', a memorial exhibition dedicated to Field Marshal Viscount Montgomery of Alamein (1887–1976). The son of a clergyman and abstemious cadet at Sandhurst, his midlife was marred by the death of his wife Betty from an insect bite in 1937. He went on to rally the morale of the 8th Army in the North African desert, turning round Britain's fortunes in November 1942 by defeating Rommel at El Alamein and masterminding the assault on the Normandy beaches, codenamed 'Overlord', in 1944.

Accessible from both Ground and Lower Floors, the 'Children's War' is a major exhibition marking the 60th anniversary of the end of the Second World War with a look at the conflict through the eyes of young British evacuees—city children sent to the countryside for safety—as well as children who stayed on in towns and cities during the Blitz. Along with a wealth of personal recollections of their experiences, the heart of the walk-through exhibition is a thorough, full-scale reconstruction of a four-up, four-down 1940s house, complete with eiderdowns on steel-frame beds, coal scuttle and clothes mangle.

First Floor

Overlooking the Large Exhibits Gallery are more large exhibits, most of which relate to aerial warfare, including the fuselage of a Handley Page Halifax bomber, a Chevrolet truck used by the Long Range Desert Group, the eyes of the infant SAS, and an Argentinian anti-aircraft gun captured during the Falklands War in 1982. Also on this level is the Victoria and George Cross Gallery, where some of the medals awarded respectively for outstanding feats of gallantry in action and civilian acts of courage or bomb disposal are displayed beneath portrait photographs and life stories of their recipients. One such is Sub-Lieutenant John Herbert Babington GC, who in 1940 defused an unexploded bomb that had brought much of Chatham dockyard to a standstill.

Second Floor

Also overlooking the Large Exhibits Gallery, are two suites of art galleries. The museum holds some 4,000 works of art commissioned during the First World War initially as an exercise in pictorial propaganda and later as a record and memorial of the conflict. They include work by Wyndham Lewis, Paul Nash, C.R.W. Nevinson,

Stanley Spencer and Sir William Orpen. John Singer Sargent's monumental painting *Gassed* (1919) is permanently on display. A large number of works were also commissioned during the Second World War by the War Artists' Advisory Committee under Kenneth Clark, then director of the National Gallery. Artists included John Piper, Henry Moore and Graham Sutherland. The Committee gave particular emphasis to life and work in wartime Britain, as in Stanley Spencer's series of large paintings *Shipbuilding on the Clyde*, and after 1942 also to foreign subjects. Sculptures in the museum's collection include a series of portrait busts by Jacob Epstein and maquettes for war memorials by Charles Sargent Jagger. In 1972 the museum established its own Artistic Records Committee to record British forces in war and peace. (*Cont/d overleaf.*)

London Museums and Galleries in the Second World War
Shortly before the outbreak of the Second World War, on 23rd August 1939, the government ordered the evacuation of all major London collections. The British Museum moved the Elgin Marbles into a disused Tube tunnel at the Aldwych. Unable to remove Stanley Spencer's large-scale *The Resurrection, Cookham* (1924–27), the Tate protected the painting on site behind a purpose-built brick wall. Within 11 days most of the National Gallery's paintings had been moved by rail and road to north Wales. Initially many were housed at Penrhyn Castle, where the owner's drunken behaviour gave the gallery staff serious misgivings about the collection's safety. Other institutions also relied on country houses—the V&A sent some of their collection to Montacute House in Somerset, the Wallace Collection to Hellens in Herefordshire—until the fall of France brought the Luftwaffe within range of these more remote areas and suggestions arose in the press that home-owners were keen to store artefacts in order to dodge army billets and avoid working-class evacuees. In September 1940, five large chambers in the Manod slate quarries near Blaenau Ffestiniog, north Wales, were identified by the National Gallery as a suitable bomb-proof repository for their pictures. Specially adapted within a year for temperature and humidity control, the storage rooms here also provided a sterling opportunity to catalogue and conserve the collection. Meanwhile, throughout the war, the almost empty National Gallery in London staged enormously popular lunchtime concerts for charity. Organised by the great concert pianist Dame Myra Hess, the first of more than 1,500 consecutive recitals was given on 10th October 1939. Another very popular morale-boosting initiative began in early 1942, in response to a letter to *The Times* from the sculptor Charles Wheeler, when the first 'Picture of the Month', Rembrandt's portrait of Margaretha de Geer (1661), was displayed in the gallery. Forty-three pictures were transported to and from Manod on a three-week cycle for the duration of the war. In his capacity as chair of the War Artists' Advisory Committee, Kenneth Clark also arranged for a continuous series of exhibitions by official British war artists.

Third Floor

The Holocaust Exhibition is a major project which opened to considerable acclaim in June 2000 after four years of research and preparation. At its heart are personal recollections of the industrial-scale murder of Jews and others organised and perpetrated in Nazi-occupied Europe during the Second World War. Not recommended for children under 14 years of age, profoundly disturbing images of the mass disposal of corpses and an annotated bleached-white scale model of Auschwitz are introduced by simple displays placing the genocide in its historical context. Objects exhibited range from a typewriter used to draw up deportation orders to a button found in one of the death pits.

Fourth Floor

'Crimes against humanity' (not recommended for children under 16) is based around a specially commissioned 30-minute film illustrating and interpreting more recent genocide and ethnic atrocities around the world. Interactive monitors mounted in plain white desks provide details of a grim succession of appalling mass race- and hate-crimes from 1945 to the present day.

JERWOOD SPACE

171 Union Street, SE1 0LN
Tel: 020-7654 0171; www.jerwoodspace.co.uk
Open daily 10–6
Free
Tube: Southwark
Café and restaurant
Map p. 383, 3D

The Jerwood Space, which opened in 1998 in Southwark, behind Tate Modern, is the visual face of the Jerwood Foundation which, through the Jerwood Charity, funds a variety of cultural and visual arts projects. As well as providing space for dance and theatre companies and rehearsal studios, the complex includes the Jerwood Gallery, which has a changing programme of contemporary exhibitions. It is also the exhibition space of the Jerwood Foundation's annual arts awards: the Jerwood Painting Prize; the Jerwood Artists Platform, which gives a selected emerging artist their first one-person show; the Jerwood Drawing Prize; and the Jerwood Sculpture Prize, the winner being awarded a commission for the Jerwood Sculpture Park at Ragley Hall. (The Jerwood Applied Arts Prize exhibition takes place at the Crafts Council Gallery; *see p. 62*). The café and restaurant in the Glasshouse is a stylish, minimalist place to have lunch.

JEWEL TOWER
(English Heritage)

New Palace Yard, SW1
Tel: 020-7222 2219; www.english-heritage.org.uk
Open April–Oct daily 10–5; Nov–March daily 10–4
Admission charge (guided tours only)
Tube: Westminster
Shop
Map p. 382, 4B

The most accessible surviving part of the medieval Palace of Westminster, the small, L-shaped, three-storey Jewel Tower was once Edward III's personal strong room, protected by a moat and known as the King's Privy Wardrobe. Built in 1365–66, it was designed by the master mason Henry de Yevele to replace the main Privy Wardrobe in the Tower of London, at that time taken up with storing military equipment for the war against France. All that remains of the private royal palace, it dates from a similar period to parts of Westminster Abbey, as well as to the Westminster Hall, chapel and cloisters that are now within the Houses of Parliament. Until 1547 the tower continued to be used by the monarch as safe storage, although by Henry VIII's day it was known as 'the old jewel house' and contained less precious items of clothing and soft furnishings. Occupied for a period by Sir Richard Shelley, last Grand Prior of the Order of the Hospital of St John of Jerusalem (*see p. 193*), from 1621 until 1864 the building became the repository of the official records of parliament. From 1869, the thick stone walls and relatively constant temperature of the tower's rooms made them a suitable home for the 'standards' of weight and measurement used by the Board of Trade, a function they performed until 1931.

On the ground floor, now mainly taken up by the shop, the vaulted ceiling with grotesque carved bosses is largely original. Late 11th-century carved corbels and capitals from the original Westminster Hall can also be seen here—the first 'story-telling' capitals in England—one showing a soldier attacking a town. Also here is the 'Westminster Sword', a remarkably well preserved Rhineland sword from around AD 800, unearthed in Victoria Tower Gardens in 1948. On the first floor, up the narrow, winding stone staircase, is a small exhibition entitled 'Parliamentary Government: what does this mean?' describing the three elements of parliament—House of Commons, House of Lords, The Queen and Parliament—and recounting the history of the institution. The second floor displays the working standards of the Board of Trade, in use until 1962. Here is the place to discover how 4 gills = 1 pint, 2 pints = 1 quart, 4 quarts = 1 gallon, 2 gallons = 1 peck, 4 pecks = 1 bushel, and 36 bushels = 1 chaldron. The 'standard pint' of George IV can be seen, along with some 18th-century pottery discovered in the vicinity of the tower: stamped wine bottles from the Sun, Royal Oak and Lamb Taverns.

JEWISH MUSEUM

129–131 Albert Street, Camden Town, NW1 7NB
Tel: 020-7284 1997; www.jewishmuseum.org.uk
Open Mon–Thur 10–4, Sun 10–5
Admission charge
Tube: Camden Town
Shop; pre-booked catering available
Map p. 379, 2D

Theatre poster for London's longest-running Yiddish play (1943–44).

Founded in 1932, the museum traces the history of the Jewish community in Britain from 1066 up to the present day and displays an outstanding collection of rare and beautiful Judaica. The collection is the only one of its type in Britain, particularly strong in items with an English provenance. The works of Jewish ceremonial art are among the finest in the world.

Ground floor

The history of Jews in Britain is told through a combination of wall-mounted information panels and significant artefacts. It begins with William the Conqueror's invitation to the Jews of Rouen to settle in London, and charts the community's subsequent persecution under Edward I and final expulsion in 1290. The Jewish religion continued to be practised secretly for the next three centuries, later especially by refugees from the Portuguese Inquisition, until Oliver Cromwell responded favourably to a petition from Rabbi Menasseh ben Israel from Amsterdam to readmit Jews to England. In 1656, they were given permission 'to meet privately in their houses for prayer' and to lease a cemetery near Mile End in east London. In the early 18th century, the synagogue in Bevis Marks was built. A silver salver from 1702 and two cups from 1745 and 1777 that formed part of an annual gift to the Lord Mayor by the Spanish and Portuguese Congregation can be seen. For several years up to 1795, the Jewish boxer Daniel Mendoza was champion of England and a popular hero: *vide* the ceramic jug depicting his bout with Richard Humphreys in 1788. A push-button illuminated map reveals the distribution of Jews in Britain down the ages.

First floor
The Arthur Rubens gallery displays the museum's collection of Judaica. Ceremonial objects, many of exceptional quality, are supported by descriptions of their roles in the major Jewish festivals and rituals. The highlight is a large, richly painted and decorated 16th-century Venetian synagogue ark, acquired unexpectedly at an auction sale from Chillingham Castle, in Northumberland, where it had been used as a wardrobe in a servant's bedroom. Here it is presented flanked by a pair of the museum's more recent acquisitions: fine brass synagogue gas lamps discovered by chance in Falmouth, Cornwall. Other highlights are silver Torah (scrolls of the Law) ornaments from the Great Synagogue in Duke's Place, City of London, destroyed during the Blitz; silver jewelled pointers; a Torah crown bearing an engraver's error, the patriarchs David and Solomon holding each other's symbol, temple and harp; and the earliest item in the collection, a gold Byzantine votive plaque from the first century, inscribed in Greek and Hebrew.

There is another Jewish Museum, in the **Sternberg Centre** (*80, East End Road, Finchley, N3; open Mon–Thur 10.30–5, Sun 10.30–4.30; Tel: 020-8349 1143*), aimed mainly at school parties, which covers the history of the Jews in London. There are displays on daily life in the East End, reconstructed tailors' shops, and a Holocaust Education Gallery.

KEATS HOUSE

Wentworth Place, Keats Grove, Hampstead, NW3 2RR
Tel: 020-7435 2062; www.cityoflondon.gov.uk
Open Tues–Sun and bank holidays 1–5
Admission charge. Disabled access to ground floor only
Tube: Hampstead
Shop
Map p. 379, 2D

In one of the leafiest parts of Hampstead, this charming small Regency house contains a remarkable collection of relics of the Romantic poet John Keats (1795–1821), who lived here for two of his five creative years. It was here that he wrote his 'Ode to a Nightingale', under a plum tree in the garden, and several other of his best-known works including 'The Eve of St Agnes' and 'La Belle Dame Sans Merci'. Keats House is a place of pilgrimage for the poet's admirers where, in the words of the Poet Laureate, Andrew Motion, 'Keats still seems alive'.

History of the House

The house dates from 1814–16 and was originally built as a pair of semi-detached cottages known collectively as Wentworth Place. Charles Wentworth Dilke, a civil servant, and his family occupied the west house and Charles Armitage Brown, a bachelor, the east. In 1817 Keats was introduced to Dilke and Brown by the poet Leigh Hunt, and in December 1818, after the death of his brother Tom from tuberculosis, he came to live here with Brown. Here he remained until September 1820 when, much weakened by tuberculosis himself, he was advised recovery in a warmer climate and left for Italy. In 1819 Dilke quit his part of the house, letting it to a Mrs Brawne, a widow with three children. Her eldest daughter Fanny, then eighteen, was introduced to Keats by Dilke and they were engaged in the autumn of that year. The marriage never took place; Keats died in Rome in 1821. In 1838–39 the two houses were bought by Eliza Chester, a retired actress, and converted into one. She also added the large drawing room on the east side. In 1920–21 the house was rescued from imminent destruction by international public subscription; it opened as a museum for the first time in 1925. A much needed, mainly structural, conservation programme began in 1999, the exterior work being completed in 2003, the interior redecoration due for completion soon. (*NB: Periods of closure may be necessary so visitors should telephone in advance of a visit, as well as for details of the regular programme of poetry and literary events.*)

Tour of the House

The house retains many of its original features, such as fireplaces and shutters, and throughout its rooms are books, manuscripts, letters, prints, paintings, furniture and other artefacts relating to Keats and his circle of friends. Downstairs are the living rooms of Dilke, and then of Mrs Brawne and her family, where Keats first met Fanny. Also at ground level is the **Sitting Room** probably used by Brown and Keats, where the latter lay on a 'sopha-bed' during his illness of February and March 1820, nursed devotedly by Brown. Items in the house relating to Brown include portraits of his parents and his bust by Andrew Wilson, sculpted in Florence in 1828. Keats' Sitting Room has its original bookcases. Behind the books in one of them Keats carelessly placed the manuscript of the 'Ode to a Nightingale', whence it was rescued by Brown. A copy by Edmund Dyer of Joseph Severn's *Keats at Wentworth Place*, painted in Rome from details supplied by Brown, shows the poet reading in this room. Upstairs is **Keats' Bedroom**, where he first spat blood and realised he was mortally ill with consumption, as well as Brown's Bedroom and a special display on Fanny Brawne. The museum possesses the almandine engagement ring given to her by Keats, a brooch in the form of a lyre with strings made from Keats' hair, his love letters to her, and an 1833 miniature of her.

Keats listening to the Nightingale on Hampstead Heath (c. 1845) by Joseph Severn.

Other Keats memorabilia include letters, literary manuscripts, books from his library, portraits of his friends, his inkstand and portable writing desk, editions of his works and his copy of Shakespeare with the manuscript of 'Bright star, would I were steadfast as thou art'—the sonnet he wrote to Fanny—written in it. Also in the house is *Keats Listening to the Nightingale on Hampstead Heath* (c. 1845) by Joseph Severn, the friend who nursed Keats through his last illness in Rome. The garden layout is much as it was in Keats' day, with an ancient mulberry tree and a new plum tree planted on the spot of the one under which Keats sat to write.

KENSINGTON PALACE
(Historic Royal Palaces)

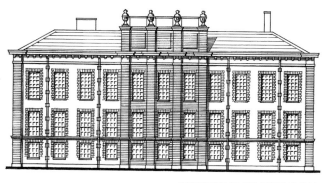

KENSINGTON PALACE: SOUTH FRONT

Kensington Gardens, W8 4PX
Tel: 0870 751 5170; www.hrp.org.uk
Open March–Oct daily 10–6; Nov–Feb daily 10–5
Admission charge. Partial disabled access
Tube: High Street Kensington
Refreshments in Orangery. Shop
Map p. 380, 2A

Although no longer an official residence of the monarch, Kensington Palace is a build-ing of great architectural and historical significance. Formerly Nottingham House, a Jacobean mansion owned by Daniel Finch, Earl of Nottingham, it was purchased by the Crown in 1689 for £20,000 and underwent a rapid architectural transformation under the supervision of Sir Christopher Wren, with Nicholas Hawksmoor as Clerk of the Works. William III and Mary II's new home was to be a winter retreat from the damp of Whitehall, a more suitable environment for the king, who suffered from asthma. It was always regarded as a private residence rather than a palace, and referred to as Kensington House. Between 1689 and 1691 Kensington was enlarged to encompass suites of apartments for the king and queen, the latter lavishly furnished with displays of oriental porcelain (*see Queen's Apartments below*); a suitably grand King's Staircase, the main approach to William's apartments; a chapel; a Council Chamber (it was here that government business was conducted in winter); and also accommodation for senior courtiers and household officers (despite Kensington's domestic character, when William and Mary were in residence, around 600 courtiers were too). Mary died at Kensington, of smallpox, in 1694, and it was to Kensington that William was carried following his riding accident at Hampton Court, which proved mortal. His successor, Queen Anne, spent much time at Kensington, apparently hating the 'stinking & close' air around St James's Palace which, following the Whitehall Palace fire of 1698, had become the seat of government and administration. It was to Kensington that Anne retired during her extensive periods of painful illness; it was here that she nursed her husband, Prince George of Denmark, whose death in 1708 'flung her into an unspeakable grief'; and it was also here that Anne herself died in 1714. Following the accession of George I, in 1718, an extensive new building programme saw the remodelling of the King's apartments and their redecoration by William Kent. The apartments remain today as important early Hanoverian survivals.

Although Kensington had been one of the principal residences of the early Hanoverians, after the death of George II in 1760 it ceased to be a seat of the reigning monarch. Family members continued to use the palace, however. The lower floors were remodelled for Edward, Duke of Kent (1767–1820), the fourth son of George III, and it was here that his daughter, the future Queen Victoria, was born. In 1832 Sir Jeffry Wyatville converted rooms adjoining the King's Gallery for her use, where she received the news of her accession. Throughout the 19th century Kensington continued to house members of the royal family (including Victoria's daughter Princess Louise, and the Duke and Duchess of Teck), but the architecturally important State Apartments were used as storerooms. In 1898–99 they were restored and opened to the public, and in 1911–14 were occupied by the London Museum (which returned to Kensington, to the lower floors, in 1950–76; *see Museum of London*) and the court dress collection. Most recently Kensington was famous as the home of Diana, Princess of Wales, who occupied apartments here from 1981 until her death in 1997, when the palace witnessed extraordinary scenes, the grounds in front of the main gates completely hidden under a sea of flowers and cellophane.

Visiting the Palace

The palace is approached from either Kensington Road or Bayswater Road. From Kensington Road the short walk through Kensington Gardens takes you first to the main south front of the palace, added by William III in 1695: a handsome design in red brick, the four central Portland vases on the roofline were carved by Caius Gabriel Cibber. The rather diminutive bronze statue of William III, by Heinrich Baucke, was presented by

Kaiser Wilhelm II in 1907. The visitor entrance is via a path which leads first to the east front, part of George I's building campaign of 1718–21, past the tranquil sunken garden of 1908–09, behind its enclosing hedge, to the west block. The visitor route is somewhat confusing, making it difficult to retain a complete sense of a Baroque palace, with its suites of King's and Queen's Apartments with their orderly progression of state rooms. Visitors see first the Royal Ceremonial Dress Collection (which it is possible to omit), are then directed up a back staircase to the 18th-century dress collection which leads out, finally, to the palace proper, at the top of George I's King's Staircase.

Royal Ceremonial Dress Collection

This is on the ground floor, to the left of the entrance hall, in rooms occupied by the London Museum until 1976. They now display the history of royal, court and ceremonial dress from the 18th century to the present day. A series of tableaux, with waxwork figures, tells the story of the wearing and making of court finery, including dresses worn by members of the royal family, ceremonial dress worn by officers and courtiers, and by debutantes for their presentation at court. Edwardian ladies with elaborate ostrich headdresses are shown preparing for an evening Drawing Room at Buckingham Palace, assisted by their maids; an interior of a gentlemen's tailor displays official court uniforms; intricate lace and embroidery is on show in a seamstress's shop; the 20th-century rise of the couturier is illustrated through a selection of outfits worn by the present Queen over the decades, designed by Sir Norman Hartnell and Sir Hardy Amies; and Coronation robes—for instance Queen Mary's, wife of King George V, worn in 1911—are on show. A special display is devoted to the outfits worn by Diana, Princess of Wales, including elegant day and evening wear by Catherine Walker.

The King's Apartments

Narrow stairs, formerly the private back stairs leading to the King's Apartments, take visitors up to what was once William III's private bedchamber but which now displays 18th-century court dress, including an astonishingly wide side-hooped silk brocade mantua, its breadth showing off the fine embroidery. The main sequence of rooms which make up the King's Apartments begins with the **King's Staircase**, today seen from the landing only. The site of William III's earlier staircase (the fine wrought iron balustrade by Jean Tijou dates from 1696), the current painted decoration was carried out by William Kent in 1725–27 for George I. The figures crowding against the *trompe l'oeil* balustrade, as if welcoming the king as he mounts the stairs, represent figures from the king's court, including his Polish page, his two Turkish Grooms of the Chamber, Mustapha and Mehmet, and 'Peter the Wild Boy', found living in the woods near Hanover and brought to England as a curiosity to be tamed. Kent himself appears on the ceiling. Kent's decoration can be seen throughout the rooms remodelled for George I, all of it undertaken between 1722 and 1727, some of it mural painting in its true sense, on plaster, but some, such as the staircase, painted on canvas. The **Presence Chamber**, used for formal receptions, has Italian 'grotesque' decoration on the ceiling, with Apollo in his chariot in the centre. The carved Grinling Gibbons overmantel was moved from William III's King's Gallery; its cupids, one cheerful, the other mournful, are apparently reflective of the death of Mary II in 1694. George I's architectural remodelling of Kensington, begun in 1718, involved the creation of new rooms, in the new Palladian taste, on the site of the surviving core of old Nottingham House. Little remains of their original furnishings but the **Privy Chamber**, used for more intimate and select audiences, retains its Kent ceiling, which shows Mars and Minerva resting on clouds, with symbols of the arts and sciences. The 1623–24 Mortlake tapestries were made for Charles I when Prince of Wales, and the statue of a Moor, by John van Nost the Elder, was probably made for William III and has been at Kensington since 1710.

The **Cupola Room** was one of the most important of the new rooms for George I. Lavishly decorated, it was the principal state apartment and a showcase for Kent, whose work at Kensington began here. Ionic pilasters with gilded fluting alternate with marble niches containing gilded lead statues of Roman deities. The bas-relief above the fireplace, by Rysbrack, depicts a Roman marriage. The blue and gold feigned coffering on the ceiling, giving an illusion of height, with the Garter Star in the centre, in fact follows an earlier design by the great Baroque artist Sir James Thornhill. As the king's official history painter, Thornhill should have been awarded the Kensington commission, but Whig political faction, along with the promotion of the new Palladianism, saw Kent triumph despite his indifferent talent (instead of stark Roman grandeur, the early 18th-century art commentator George Vertue found the Cupola Room 'a terrible glaring show', and the ceilings in the other rooms 'poor stuff'). The clock in the centre of the room, by Charles Clay and John Pyke (completed 1743), was acquired by Augusta, Princess of Wales. Surmounted by Atlas and Hercules, with painted sides by Jacopo Amigoni, it originally played tunes by Corelli, Handel and Geminiani. The **King's Drawing Room** was where the weekly court Drawing Rooms took place. Richly decorated with fine pictures from the Royal Collection hung against crimson damask, it originally had furniture designed by Kent, who also designed the fireplace and painted the ceiling (with *Jupiter and Semele* at its centre).

In an odd interruption of chronology, visitors see next the rooms occupied by the young Princess Victoria and her mother the Duchess of Kent in the early 19th century. **Princess Victoria's Bedroom** was where she was woken on 20th June 1837 with news of her accession to the throne. The rooms were redecorated in the 1930s by Queen Mary to evoke their appearance when occupied by the princess. The **King's Gallery** is a magnificent return to the early 18th century. Ninety-six feet long, it occupies the site of William III's gallery and retains its 1690s carved cornice as well as the important wind-dial above the fireplace, made by Robert Morden for William in 1694. Points of the compass circle the map of the seas around Great Britain and a pointer, attached to the wind-vane on the roof, indicates the direction of the prevailing wind. Although not a great artist, Kent was a talented designer, and the entire decorative scheme, of white and gold woodwork and crimson wall hangings and curtains, is his. The doorcases were redesigned by him, as was the fireplace and overmantel.

The rich ceiling, by Kent and his assistant Francisco de Valentia, has scenes from the story of Ulysses, surrounded by feigned decorative plasterwork against a gold mosaic. The picture hang was also devised by Kent, who designed many of the frames. During the reigns of George I and II some of the most important works from the Royal Collection were hung at Kensington. Included here are important Tintorettos and originally, at either end, were the king's two most important van Dycks, *Charles I and Henrietta Maria with their Two Eldest Children*, and *Charles I with M de St-Antoine* (the latter is a version; both originals are now at Buckingham Palace; *see p. 49*).

The Queen's Apartments

Visitors should now double back to the beginning of the sequence of the Queen's Apartments, built for Queen Mary II in the early 1690s and the part of the palace which best retains its late 17th-century atmosphere. Originally the suite comprised nine rooms, accessed by their own grand staircase. **Queen Mary's Drawing Room**, completed in 1692, was badly damaged by bombing in 1940 but part of the finely carved cornice survives. **Queen Mary's Bedchamber**, an intimate room, has its original elm floorboards. From inventories it is known that Mary's bed was hung with velvet lined with gold satin, with green and silver passementerie. The current hangings seem to have come from a bed belonging to James II or his queen Mary of Modena, whose cyphers they bear. **Queen Mary's Drawing Room** is furnished with a 17th-century table and high-backed chairs, and hung with cabinet-sized pictures from the Royal Collection, including fruit and flower pieces by the Hungarian-born Jacob Bogdani, one of Queen Anne's favourite artists. The portrait above the fireplace, by John Riley and John Baptist Closterman, is of Katherine Elliot, nurse of James II and later Dresser and Woman of the Bedchamber to Mary of Modena. The **Closet**, hung with Indian damask with a blue and gold embroidered couch with a tented canopy in the time of Queen Mary, contains portraits of Queen Anne in profile by Kneller, and George of Denmark by Michael Dahl, the latter being the Queen's favourite image of her husband. She demanded to have it with her at St James's Palace after his death in 1708. It was in this room that Anne and her once-favourite, Sarah, Duchess of Marlborough, had their last, bitter quarrel in 1710.

Queen Mary's Gallery was the richest and most grandly furnished of the Queen's rooms. Her taste for oriental porcelain, which was displayed throughout her apartments, was given free rein here. It was massed in symmetrical, towering displays on lacquer cabinets placed between the windows, as well as above the doors and chimneypieces. The latter displays were set against looking glasses with elaborate carved surrounds, supplied by the royal cabinet maker Gerrit Jensen and by Grinling Gibbons. Displays of this nature were fashionable at the courts of Europe, and Mary was one of the chief promoters of the vogue in England. The richness of the room, with its expensive curtains (scarlet taffeta in winter and white flowered damask in summer), and embroidered wall hangings, its porcelain and lacquerwork, would have been most apparent by candlelight. The **Queen's Staircase**, a plain and handsome space, was designed by Wren and retains some of its original sash windows.

The Gardens

The late 17th-century gardens at Kensington were once very elaborate, but have long since disappeared. On an axis with the south front was a 12-acre garden with a parterre and wilderness and a central walk, laid out by George London in 1689–91. Queen Anne, who loved gardening, engaged Henry Wise to develop a larger wilderness to the north, with intersecting walks, terraces and topiary. Her most lasting achievement in the garden was the **Orangery**, designed by Hawksmoor and altered by Sir John Vanbrugh, which housed plants in the winter and was used for entertainments in the summer. It is now an elegant and airy tearoom with, at either end, two magnificent carved vases by Cibber and Edward Pierce, originally from the gardens at Hampton Court but now placed here, safe from further weathering. In 1728 Queen Caroline, queen of George II, had an octagonal basin constructed to the west of the palace, on land claimed from Hyde Park. It remains today as the Round Pond, and beyond it the Serpentine was formed.

KENWOOD HOUSE (THE IVEAGH BEQUEST)
(English Heritage)

Hampstead Lane, NW3 7JR
Tel: 020-8348 1286; www.english-heritage.org.uk
Open end March–end Oct daily 11–5; Nov–end March daily 11–4
Free. Disabled access ground floor only
Tube/Station: none. Take bus 210 from Golders Green or Highgate
Restaurant and shop
Map p. 379, 2D

Kenwood, an elegant mansion set on a ridge of land with a magnificent prospect over Hampstead Heath towards London, is one of the principal properties of English Heritage. The former house of c. 1700 was remodelled and redecorated in 1764–79 by the Adam brothers, Robert and James, for William Murray, 1st Earl of Mansfield, Lord Chief Justice, who lived here from 1754. The resulting elegant and imposing villa is a major piece of 18th-century Neoclassical architecture and interior decoration, which the Adam brothers regarded as one of their major commissions. Their designs for Kenwood, including furniture, are preserved at the Soane Museum, and were published in their 1774 *Works in Architecture*. The most magnificent of the new ground floor reception rooms created for Mansfield is without doubt the Library, or 'Great Room', regarded by many as Robert Adam's finest achievement.

The Adam brothers' alterations included the building of a third storey and a new wing, on the east side, to house the Library. Externally, the entire house was encased in white stucco and on the south front embellished with pilasters and panels of ornamental detail, carried out by the skilled plasterer Joseph Rose in 'Liardet', an oil cement. Entrance is via the north side portico, an Adam addition, but the flanking wings were added by George Saunders after 1793 for the 2nd Earl of Mansfield, for a Dining Room to the east, and a Music Room to the west. The 1st Earl began the landscaping of the park, which was continued by the 2nd Earl aided by the great landscape gardener Humphrey Repton, who was probably responsible for the ornamental flowerbeds of the west garden and the looped foliage passage near the front of the house. The grounds today are a beautiful combination of lawns, a lake, winding rhododendron walks among woodland (recorded here by 1806), an avenue of limes (a favourite resort of the poet Pope), the whole surrounded by Hampstead Heath. Dr Johnson's summer house from Thrale Place was brought here in 1968.

Kenwood today has none of its original contents, save for a few Adam pieces of furniture which have fortuitously returned following the house contents sale of 1922. It is, however, home to the Iveagh Bequest, a major collection of paintings left to the nation in 1927, along with the house, by Edward Cecil Guinness, 1st Earl of Iveagh. He had purchased Kenwood from the Mansfield family in 1925, who had ceased to use it. In 1922 the Kenwood Preservation Committee purchased 100 acres of the park, and in 1925 Lord Iveagh purchased the house and a further 80 acres, which were about to be sold as building plots. His bequest to the nation thus saved the house, which has been open to the public since 1928.

Tour of the House

The **Hall** was the last major room designed by Robert Adam for Kenwood (James Adam seems to have had an initial involvement at Kenwood, but the work is largely Robert's), in 1773. Originally it had Adam-designed Hall furniture (the two Neoclassical stools are after 1768 Adam designs for the Earl of Shelburne), but the ceiling survives, with its central painting, *Bacchus and Ceres*, by Antonio Zucchi. To the left is the next space of Adam's new reception suite, the **Grand Staircase**, relatively modest with a wrought iron balustrade, with anthemion (honeysuckle) motifs of cast brass. Visitors would pass through to the **Antechamber** beyond, a handsome vestibule preparatory to the visual climax of the Library. Designed by James Adam in 1764, it has Ionic columns, niches for sculpture and a grand Venetian window facing south, with views over the picturesque landscape. The **Library** itself, or 'Great Room', is an impressive Neoclassical space and one of the finest Adam rooms in the country. A double cube, with apsidal ends, it was completed in 1770. The original vast pier glasses and carved curtain cornices remain *in situ*. The coved ceiling, the room's crowning glory, has ornament inspired in part by the Mausoleum of the Palace of Diocletian at Split on the Dalmatian coast. The intricate gilded stucco work is by Rose, offset by a background of white, pale pink and blue. The paintings, with *Hercules between Glory and the Passions* in the centre, is by Zucchi, painted on paper applied directly to the plaster. Two screens of Corinthian columns divide the apses from the main body of the room and either side of the chimneypiece are mirrored and highly

The Guitar Player (1672) by Jan Vermeer.

decorated recesses (modern restorations) offering, in Adam's words, 'a singular and beautiful effect'. The original silvered plate glass was provided by Thomas Chippendale.

Retracing one's steps and turning left from the Grand Staircase, one enters the east wing addition of the 1790s, which provided a **Dining Room Lobby**, with a lofty coffered ceiling, and the **Dining Room**, with appropriate Bacchic decoration (Bacchus himself appears on the chimneypiece, and the leopards—his companion animals—on the frieze below the ceiling). Returning to the Antechamber and turning right, one enters the original core of the house. Lord Mansfield had his private apartments here, beginning with the **Breakfast Room**, which was originally two rooms, Mansfield's Drawing Room and Parlour. The dividing wall was removed in 1815 but Adam's chimneypiece remains.

From the **Orangery**, which was filled with exotic plants and trees in the 1780s, one can exit to the grounds, or turn left into the west wing extension. The **Green Room** has Ionic columns carrying entablatures, inspired by Adam's Library, and leads into the second most important reception room in the house, the **Music Room**. Originally it had terracotta coloured panels with scrollwork containing cupids and musical instruments by Julius Caesar Ibbetson. The main room on the upper floor is the **Upper Hall**, above the entrance Hall. It has a magnificent Adam chinoiserie chimneypiece, completed in 1773, with mermen and flying griffins carved and gilded by Sefferin Nelson, and Chinese painted marble tiles. These upper rooms are occasionally used for loan exhibitions.

The Iveagh Bequest

Lord Iveagh, Chairman of Guinness Breweries—and on his death in 1927 reputedly the second richest man in the country—amassed an extraordinary collection of pictures between 1887 and 1891, purchased through the Bond Street dealer Agnew's. Reflecting a taste typical of connoisseurs of the late 19th and early 20th centuries, the collection is particularly rich in British portraiture of the second half of the 18th century, and 17th-century Dutch and Flemish works. The pictures are now displayed throughout Kenwood's historic interiors. They include some world-famous masterpieces, such as Rembrandt's *Self Portrait* of c. 1663, and Vermeer's *Guitar Player*, probably a very late work and known to have been in the collection of his widow in 1676. Hals's *Pieter van der Broecke* (1633) wears a gold chain valued at 1,200 guilders, a reward for 17 years' service in the Dutch East India Company. Seventeenth-century works painted in Britain include de Jongh's early topographical view of Old London Bridge (1630s) and van Dyck's *Henrietta of Lorraine* (1634), a noble full-length which belonged to Charles I. The succession of late 18th-century British works, by Gainsborough, Reynolds, Romney, Hoppner and others, is extraordinary. Gainsborough's *Mary, Countess Howe* (c.1763–64), one of Kenwood's treasures, dates

Henrietta of Lorraine (1634) by Sir Anthony van Dyck.

Going to Market (c. 1770) by Thomas Gainsborough, one of several fine works of his in the Iveagh Bequest at Kenwood.

from the artist's Bath period and is one of his loveliest portraits. His important *Greyhounds coursing a Fox* is a very late, sketch-like work. The lyrical conversation piece *Going to Market* is a charming mid-period landscape. There are many portraits by Reynolds, including the celebrated beauty Mrs Musters as Hebe, and Kitty Fisher as Cleopatra; Kitty Fisher was a notorious courtesan who died young, apparently of lead poisoning from cosmetics. There are two Romneys of Lady Hamilton, wife of Sir William Hamilton and mistress of Nelson, and Romney's favourite muse. *Lady Hamilton at the Spinning Wheel* shows her demure, in the guise of a simple country girl. The celebrated comedienne Mrs Jordan appears as Viola in *Twelfth Night*, painted by Hoppner. Turner's 'Iveagh Sea-Piece', 1802, is one of the earliest of his important marine paintings.

The Suffolk Collection
The Suffolk Collection of pictures, formed by the Howard family, Earls of Suffolk, at Charlton Park, Wiltshire, was originally donated to Ranger's House (see p. 242) by Mrs Greville Howard but, following rearrangements there, was relatively recently trans-

ferred to Kenwood. The most outstanding items are the full-length portraits by William Larkin (d. 1619) which make up the 'Berkshire Marriage Set', a group of family portraits possibly commissioned to commemorate the 1614 marriage of Elizabeth Cecil to Thomas Howard, later Earl of Berkshire. They are notable for their brilliant colouring, painstaking delineation of the richly elaborate costumes, the swagged curtains in the background and the oriental carpets on which the sitters stand.

Lord Iveagh and Kenwood

Edward Cecil Guinness (1847–1927), 1st Earl Iveagh, first began collecting paintings in earnest in 1887, the year after he had floated the family brewing company on the stock exchange. He had bought the company from his elder brother, the first Baron Ardilaun. Over the next four years Iveagh bought more than 200 paintings. All but one of his more than 60-strong bequest to the nation at Kenwood were purchased through Agnew's, allegedly because he had been spurned one after-lunch visit by another dealer on Bond Street. He attached considerable importance to the provenance of his paintings, showing a marked preference for those formerly in the possession of aristocrats and connoisseurs. Prodigiously wealthy, the brothers are mentioned in James Joyce's *Ulysses*, when Leopold Bloom reflects in the 'Lotus Eaters' episode on the price of a pint of Guinness: 'Lord Iveagh once cashed a seven-figure cheque for a million in the bank of Ireland. Shows you the money to be made out of porter. Still the other brother Lord Ardilaun has to change his shirt four times a day, they say.'

When Iveagh purchased Kenwood, shortly before his death, he was deliberately looking for a suitable home for his art collection. The house came close to being another branch of the National Gallery. Four consecutive directors of the gallery were on the board of trustees after the house opened its doors to the public in 1928, and the first hang of the paintings, after their transfer from Grosvenor Place, was guided by Sir Charles Holmes, then director of the National Gallery and the first to catalogue the bequest. Iveagh already had links with the gallery, having supported the purchase of Titian's *Portrait of a Man* and Holbein's *Ambassadors*, among other paintings.

A generous philanthropist, in 1890 Iveagh established the Guinness Trust to help the destitute and homeless, pioneering affordable housing schemes in the East End, Chelsea and Walworth. He also donated a new set of bells to St Patrick's Cathedral, Dublin, and to the village church of his estate in Elveden, Suffolk, in memory of his wife and cousin Adelaide Maria Guinness.

Their three sons added colour, some of it sad, to the family name: Rupert founded the *Guinness Book of Records*; Walter was assassinated by a Jewish terrorist group in Cairo in 1944; and Arthur's three daughters were known as the 'Golden Guinness Girls'. The death of one of their sons at the wheel of his Lotus sports car in 1966 inspired the first lines of the Beatles' song *A Day in the Life*.

KEW BRIDGE STEAM MUSEUM

Green Dragon Lane, Brentford, TW8 0EN
Tel: 020-8568 4757; www.kbsm.org
Open daily 11–5. Best to visit at weekends or bank holidays, when the
engines are in action
Admission charge. Partial disabled access
Station: Kew Bridge (from Waterloo)
Café and shop
Map p. 378, 3C

The Kew Bridge Engines Trust was founded in 1973 with the aim of restoring to steam
the beam engines of the Grand Junction Water Works at Kew Pumping Station, built
in 1837 to provide a steady water supply for west London. Now the greatest collection of working large beam engines in the world, they, along with their listed buildings, convey a powerful impression of high Victorian technological achievement. The
extensive site of this working museum, largely maintained by volunteer enthusiasts,
also contains displays on the history of London's water supply, a comprehensive
collection of rotative steam, diesel and gas engines, and a short, narrow-gauge railway.

Tour of the Museum

Visitors first enter the **Water for Life Gallery**, passing short examples of different
types of water-pipe down the centuries, from hand-bored elm trunks to cast iron
Victorian mains, strong enough to support the pressures achieved by the new steam
pumps. The height of one wall is hung with a variety of domestic appliances, antique
and modern, that rely upon the water supply: from mops, buckets and tin tubs to
lavatories, baths, washing machines, water heaters and boilers. A walk-through section of the giant modern-day Thames Water Ring Main follows, introducing displays
on the history of London's sewers, tales of Victorian flushers and toshers, and the pioneering work in hygiene of John Snow, who forestalled the worst of the cholera epi-
demics by proving that they were water-borne and installing a clean water pump in
Broad St, Soho, in 1849. The technological development of the water supply is also
illustrated with a selection of antique stop-cocks, supply pipes and sluice valves.

The **Steam Hall** occupies the original boiler house of the pumping station (note the
wrought iron rafters and absence of roof insulation), now home to the museum's collection of lovingly restored rotative steam engines. Remarkable works of engineering
craftsmanship, their rhythmic sound in action is also memorable. The Pulsometer
pump is an early 20th-century design based on the first practical steam pump patented by Thomas Savery in 1698. The Waddon Engine, the largest in the collection, with
a 21- by 42-inch bore and 3-ft stroke, built in 1910, was operational at Croydon's
Waddon waterworks until as recently as 1983. The Easton and Amos Engine is a rotative beam engine from 1863 of a type used in small rural locations. Especially beautiful, with a name to match, is another rotative beam engine, the Dancer's End Engine,

that once pumped well water on Lord Rothschild's estate near Tring. Also built in the 1860s, with a distinctive red livery, this kind of engine was favoured by the Lancashire and Yorkshire textile mills and this one may have been specially adapted to pump water. The powerful Hathorn Davey Triple Expansion Engine, built in 1910, is considered to represent a mid-point of the progression from beam to internal combustion engine. The compact, powerful and relatively inexpensive Robey Engine was the popular steam predecessor of modern industrial electric motors. The one here was used to drive hoists at the Truman's brewery in Stepney until 1972.

Adjoining the Steam Hall are the **East and West Engine Rooms**, flanking the Neoclassical front lobby of the original pumping station where a large elm junction pipe, in use from 1610–1810 and unearthed in Coventry in 1933, is displayed along with a model of the tool used to bore such pipes. The West Engine Room was built for the massive Maudslay Engine in 1837, the first mighty beam engine steam pump to be installed at Kew, much restored and repaired since then. In the East Engine Room is the Boulton and Watt 'West Cornish' Engine, the oldest of the Cornish engines in the museum, built in 1820 and the first to be restored by the museum in the 1970s. With a 64-inch cylinder bore and 8-ft stroke, it was capable of delivering 130 gallons on each stroke. The cast iron frame is a free version of the Tuscan order.

A passage leads from the Steam Hall to the museum's main event: the largest surviving beam engines in the world. The two huge **Cornish beam engines**, named the 90-inch and 100-inch after their cylinder bores, were built in Cornwall and shipped to Kew by sea, the house then being built around them. Once both were installed in 1869, this was probably the single greatest concentration of mechanical power on the planet. Both engines are supported on cast iron Doric columns, a motif repeated elsewhere in the design. The beams are over 30ft long, weigh around 32 tonnes and were made in a single casting. The 90-inch, also known as the 'Grand Junction', was built in 1846 and can be seen in action at weekends, filling the engine house with a rushing, roaring sound. The 100-inch was in use until 1944 when it was replaced by diesel and electric pumps, but kept on standby until 1958. It was capable of pumping ten million gallons of water a day, 717 gallons being delivered at each stroke. Between them, these two superb engines supplied much of west London with water for three-quarters of a century.

KEW PALACE
(Historic Royal Palaces)

Royal Botanic Gardens, Kew, Surrey, TW9 3AB
Tel: 0870 751 5175; www.hrp.org.uk/webcode/kew_home.asp
Open April–Sept daily 10–6
Admission charge
Tube: Kew Gardens
Map p. 378, 3C

Kew Palace is a fine example of the 'artisan mannerist' style popular in the early 17th century, and worthy of comparison with Forty Hall (*see p. 85*). A royal residence from the early 18th century, it is all that remains of George II and III's palace at Kew. Formerly known as the Dutch House, it was built in 1631 for the Flemish merchant Samuel Fortrey. By the mid-18th century this fine three-storey block with its rubbed brickwork and Dutch gables was being used as an annexe to the royal residence known as The White House or Kew House, built in the 1730s by Frederick, Prince of Wales. As such it was the childhood home of George III, later the nursery for his own children and his retreat during the onset of his nervous disorder, porphyria. This was a role that the house played increasingly after the partial demolition of the White House in 1802. King George's beloved wife Queen Charlotte spent the last six months of her life here in 1818, a year in which the palace also saw the marriages of two of their sons, the Dukes of Clarence and Kent. The latter married Princess Victoria of Saxe-Coburg and their daughter later became Queen Victoria, who opened the palace to the public in 1899.

Since 1996 the palace has been undergoing an extensive programme of restoration and re-presentation, still in progress at time of writing. The façade has been re-covered with its distinctive red brick-dust limewash over the Flemish bond brickwork. Inside, the wallpaper has been recreated from remaining fragments and the 18th-century brass door locks, engraved with the crest of Frederick, Prince of Wales, have been preserved. The re-presentation project focuses on the late 18th and early 19th centuries, when the house was most frequently in use by George III, Queen Charlotte and their children. Added attractions promised are a wax life cast of George III made by Madame Tussaud, a waistcoat specially adapted for him, and the shirt he wore during his illness, an image made famous in the film *The Madness of King George III*. Also on display is a remarkable 'baby house' or dolls' house made both for and by the daughters of George III in 1780, complete with tiny Hepplewhite furniture and bright green wallpaper.

KINGSTON MUSEUM

Wheatfield Way, Kingston upon Thames, KT1 2PS
Tel: 020-8546 5386; www.kingston.gov.uk/museum
Open daily 10–5 except Wed and Sun
Free
Station: Kingston (from Waterloo)
Shop
Map p. 378, 4C

Kingston was for a long time the first bridgeable point on the river Thames above London Bridge. It was also the birthplace of the pioneer photographer and cinematographer Eadweard Muybridge (1830–1904), who left a collection of his possessions to the borough in his will. This is displayed here, in what is in fact a small local history museum with an important collection of Anglo-Saxon and Bronze Age arte-facts. Those are housed in the ground floor galleries, and include bronze rapiers and axes discovered locally, as well as an unusually well preserved nine-foot Anglo-Saxon logboat carved from the trunk of a single oak. Even so, the museum's main claim to fame undoubtedly remains the collection of items associated with Muybridge, displayed in one small gallery on a mezzanine level.

Edward James Muggeridge was born in Kingston in 1830. He changed his name first to Muygridge and then to Muybridge, adopting the spelling of his first name from the name of Eadweard the Elder on Kingston's coronation stone, unveiled in 1850. Hoping to find a market for his topographical photographs, he left Britain for America, where he earned himself a reputation with his Yosemite landscapes and made a living as official photographer of the building of the Pacific Railway. In 1872, Muybridge was asked to photograph the racehorse Occident, which belonged to a former governor of California, in order to prove that all four of the horse's feet left the ground at once when at a trot. His famous experiments conducted at Palo Alto farm and racetrack, using an ingenious system of trip wires, proved that indeed they did. In 1873 he photographed the final conflict between the US Army and the Modoc Indians, the year before he shot dead the man whom he suspected of fathering his son Floredo. Brought to trial for murder, he was acquitted thanks to a brilliant defence by his lawyer.

Continuing his experiments with the phenomenon known to the Victorians as Persistence of Vision, Muybridge worked on developing simple zoetropes. A pair of the kind that he used are shown: revolving slotted drums showing an ostrich running and a man jumping up and down; along with a phenakistiscope, one of the earliest moving picture projection devices. The real breakthrough, though, came with his invention of the zoöpraxiscope. His second machine, from 1879, along with a 16-inch glass disc from his first model, can be seen here. He described it as 'the first apparatus ever used for synthetically demonstrating movement analytically photographed from life', and toured the projector to considerable acclaim in Paris in 1881 and London the next year. During 1884, at the University of Pennsylvania, Philadelphia, Muybridge took over 20,000 photographs of people, animals and birds in movement for *Animal Locomotion*, published in 1887, complete with 781 folio-sized plates that continue to be of great use to draughtsmen and designers. One of only nine surviving examples of his 17ft-long *Panaroma of San Francisco*, taken from Hopkins' residence in 1878, is also held here, and a reproduction displayed.

LEIGHTON HOUSE

12 Holland Park Road, Kensington, W14 8LZ
Tel: 020-7602 3316; www.rbkc.gov.uk/leightonhousemuseum
Open daily 11–5.30 except Tues
Admission charge

Tube: High Street Kensington/Olympia
Shop
Map p. 379, 3D

With this purpose-built studio house, Frederic, Lord Leighton of Stretton (1830–96), High Victorian painter *par excellence*, and the first British artist to be given a peerage, created for himself an exotic 'Palace of Art' where he lived and worked for the last 30 years of his life. Returning to England in 1864 at the age of thirty-four, after spending much of his youth abroad, and newly elected an Associate of the Royal Academy, Leighton planned the construction of his London home in collaboration with his architect friend George Aitchison. Together they developed a house where he could severally work, entertain guests (his circle included Clara Schumann, William Gladstone and George Eliot), and also retire. On his death, the contents of the house were sold at auction, the building itself being saved for posterity through the efforts of Leighton's close neighbour and biographer, Mrs Emilie Russell Barrington, who was instrumental in establishing the house as a museum, presenting several of Leighton's works to it, and organising a popular series of fundraising concerts. In 1926, the house was donated to the Royal Borough of Kensington. After suffering bomb damage during the Second World War, it re-opened in 1951 as the children's section of the Kensington Borough Library. By the early 1980s a programme of repair and restoration had begun with the aim of recreating the distinctive character of the place during Leighton's lifetime.

Ground floor

The **Inner Hall**, with a black and white mosaic floor, is decorated with the pervasive blue tiles by William de Morgan that give much of the ground floor its special character, interspersed with 16th-century tiles from Damascus. Beyond is the **Hall of Narcissus**, so named after a statue that once stood here, and now home to showcases containing examples of de Morgan's work. To the left is the **Library**, with some of its original fittings and books as well as one of the few Old Master paintings from Leighton's original collection still in the museum: *Marcantonio Bragadin Worshipping the Trinity* (1571), from the school of Tintoretto. Another can be found upstairs on the first floor landing: Jacopo Tintoretto's *Portrait of an Elderly Gentleman*, recently returned to hang in its original location. This was the first of Leighton's collection of 27 Old Masters (20 of them from 16th-century Venice). Along with the works of his contemporaries that can be seen here, these two paintings go some way towards illustrating the main influence on Leighton's own art, of which the house contains many notable examples. One relatively recent acquisition, hung in the **Dining Room**, is Leighton's *Portrait of Professor Giovanni Costa* (1878). Costa, a passionate supporter of Italian independence, was an artist and close friend from Leighton's early years in Rome, when he enjoyed the company of the Brownings and was talent-spotted by Thackeray. The only portrait by Leighton of a fellow artist, it bears comparison with the museum's most important acquisition in half a century (acquired in 2004), the *Portrait of Frederic, Lord Leighton* (1871) by his close friend and neighbour George Frederic Watts (*see p. 220*). Watts was suspicious of the Royal Academy's power and influence; it is a token of his esteem for Leighton—who became president of the Academy in the late 1870s—that he resigned from it tactfully only after Leighton's death. Also in the dining room can be seen *Private View at the Royal Academy* by William Powell Frith (1819–1909), a large oil depicting the opening of the Summer Exhibition in 1881. A record of personalities associated with late-Victorian Aestheticism, it includes portraits of Leighton, John Everett Millais and Oscar Wilde, who wears a large lily in his buttonhole. Powell Frith, who specialised in large-scale Victorian crowd scenes, achieved instant fame in 1854 when Queen Victoria bought his *Ramsgate Sands*. The next year Leighton himself received royal approval when the Queen bought his *Cimabue's 'Madonna' carried in Procession through the streets of Florence*. Next door, right of the Hall, is the **Drawing Room**, which has been returned to an approximation of its original appearance. Several works by Leighton's contemporaries hang here, including Burne-Jones, Sir Lawrence Alma-Tadema, Millais and Evelyn de Morgan.

Beyond the Hall, past red Caserta marble columns, is the **Arab Hall**. Designed by Aitchison from drawings which he had made in Spain and Sicily, particularly of the Palace of La Zisa in Palermo, the room provided a showcase for Leighton's large collection of 13th, 16th and 17th-century polychrome tiles, variously retrieved by Leighton himself, the explorer and scholar Sir Richard Burton, and the architect, archaeologist and museum director Sir Caspar Purdon Clarke from Damascus, Rhodes, Cairo and elsewhere. The room remains richly evocative of the artist's fascination with the Ottoman world. In the centre of the room, above a fountain trickling into a pool cut from a single block of black marble, hangs an ornate copper chandelier also designed by Aitchison. The dome was also purchased in Damascus, decorated with a mosaic frieze designed by Walter Crane and supported on columns with alabaster capitals designed by Caldecott. Beyond is a Moorish wooden alcove or *alhacen*.

Upper floor
Returning to the Hall, stairs lead up past a stuffed peacock placed here by Leighton above a seat adapted from a Persian inlaid chest, as well as paintings by his contempories, and Leighton's *Elisha Raising the Son of the Shunamite* (1881), *Orpheus and Eurydice* (1864) and a copy of Michelangelo's *Creation of Adam* from the Sistine Chapel, painted when Leighton was nineteen.

The landing, now the **Silk Room**, was used by Leighton as a small music studio and music room. At the far end is a *zenana* or lattice window with a seating area overlooking the Arab Hall. Several paintings hang here, including *Shelling Peas* (1889) by John Everett Millais, and Leighton's *Rustic Music* (1861), *Bianca* (c. 1881) and an oil sketch, *Picture of a Street in Damascus* (1872), probably taken from life. In one corner is a bronze bust of Mrs Emilie Russell Barrington, along with a pair of Leighton's easels, and in another an armchair given to Leighton by Queen Alexandra when Princess of Wales, and covered in silk embroideries worked by her. On the left is Leighton's bedroom,

Frederic Leighton: *Clytemnestra from the Battlements of Argos Watches for the Beacon Fires which are to Announce the Return of Agamemnon* (c. 1874)

now hung with early photographs of his work, on loan from the V&A.

To the right of the landing is the **Great Studio**, where Leighton produced most of his work. Several of his larger paintings hang on the north wall, notably his *Clytemnestra* (*pictured left*). There is also *The Uninterpreted Dream* by Edward Burne-Jones, and a bronze bust of the artist by Sir Thomas Brock, later responsible for the Queen Victoria Memorial, and who also sculpted Leighton's own memorial in St Paul's cathedral. In the apse of the west wall is a tall door through which large canvases could be lowered. An archway at the east end leads into the Winter Studio and Upper Perrin Gallery, both used for temporary exhibitions. Right of the archway is a door leading to a staircase to the servants' quarters, which was also used by the artist's models and (indicating their status in Leighton's eyes) by art dealers. On the south wall are casts of part of the Parthenon frieze and of Michelangelo's 'Taddei Tondo' (which can be seen in the Royal Academy), underlining the classical and academic influences on Leighton's work.

In the garden behind the house is Leighton's monumental sculpture *Athlete Struggling with a Python* (1877, bronze), and Brock's *Moment of Peril* (1880), a striking group representing a Red Indian on horseback spearing a large snake.

LIBRARY AND MUSEUM OF FREEMASONRY

Freemasons' Hall, 60 Great Queen Street, WC2B 5AZ
Tel: 020-7395 9257; www.freemasonry.london.museum
Open Mon–Fri 10–5
Free
Tube: Holborn/Covent Garden
Map p. 382, 2B

Freemasons' Hall (built 1927–33) is a monumental building intended as a memorial to the freemasons who died in the First World War. Steel-framed, more than 900 tons of marble were used in its construction, 500 in the Grand Temple alone. The museum proper is prefaced in the Library, with small displays illustrating the history of English freemasonry. Divided into five sections, it traces the development of freemasonry from the craft of the medieval stonemasons up to the modern day and the activities of masonic charities. On the way, it covers the initiation of Elias Ashmole in 1646, the emergence of masonic lodges in private dining rooms of the late 17th century, and the formation of the Grand Lodge in 1813.

The one-room museum, first founded in the 1830s, displays the most important collection of masonic items in the world. Of particular interest are the examples of the applied and decorative arts. English pottery and porcelain is very well represented, from Wedgwood creamware and early Worcester to Sunderland lustre and Doulton. Also impressive are the displays of Meissen porcelain, some of it commissioned by the Order of the Mopses. These were 18th-century German freemasons, who chose the pug dog as their mascot and accepted both male and female members. Notable is an early Meissen figure of Augustus the Strong, the Grand Master of the Mopses, who was also instrumental in the establishment of the Meissen factories. Another large part of the exhibition is taken up with regalia and medals, notably aprons and sashes from the 18th century onwards, including the aprons of King Edward VII as Prince of Wales, the Duke of Windsor and other members of the Royal Family. The regalia of Winston Churchill, initiated into Studholme Lodge no. 1591 in 1901, can also be seen, along with that of Tommy Gould, the only Jewish recipient of the VC during the Second World War (for service in the Mediterranean on the submarine *Thrasher*). Some of the medals are masterpieces of the goldsmith's and enameller's art.

Among the curious artefacts to be found here are the 'Wren Maul', the mallet traditionally taken to have been used by Charles II in laying the foundation stone of St Paul's Cathedral in 1675, presented by Christopher Wren; some relics claiming to be from Solomon's temple; a 1937 boxed relief map of Jerusalem from the American Colony Store; and a silver elephant cigar lighter or *hogdan* made out of molten rupees. Most recently, the museum acquired a mysterious masonic desk, discovered in Scotland, containing a secret scale model of the tabernacle of Moses.

The guided tour takes visitors beyond the library and museum, beginning with the Grand Officer's Robing Room and the Ceremonial Suite before making its way beneath painted coffered ceilings and interiors of marble, mosaic, mahogany and stained glass, towards the War Memorial itself, commemorating the 3,553 brethren who died in the First World War. The highlight of the tour is undoubtedly the opportunity to see inside the Grand Temple, beyond massive bronze doors decorated with symbols by Walter Gilbert. The ceiling of the Temple is an extraordinary mosaic of gold stars set in pale and Garter blue. Masonic symbols on an epic scale surround raked seating for some 1,700 people.

LINLEY SAMBOURNE HOUSE

18 Stafford Terrace, Kensington, W8 7BH
Tel: Mon–Fri 020-7602 3316, Ext. 305; Sat–Sun 07976 060160
www.rbkc.gov.uk/linleysambournehouse
Open for guided tours only. Weekdays only for pre-booked groups;
Sat–Sun tours at 10, 11.15, 1, 2.15, 3.30
Admission charge. No disabled access
Tube: High Street Kensington
Shop
Map p. 379, 3D

No. 18 Stafford Terrace is the very carefully preserved Victorian and Edwardian family home of the Sambourne family. Edward Linley Sambourne (1845–1910), chief political cartoonist of *Punch*, known to his wide circle of friends and acquaintances as Linley, or Lin, bought the house in 1875, four years after securing a staff job on the top satirical magazine, having spent four contributing as a freelancer. The year before he had inherited from his artistic aunt, a great encourager of his drawing talent, the modest private income that allowed him to marry Marion Herapath, a match that her family, living in Phillimore Gardens nearby, considered disappointing. A year later, their first child was born: Maud, later Maud Messel, and mistress of Nyman's in the Sussex Weald, with its fabulous gardens. Their son Roy (b. 1878) later inherited this house.

In 1901, Sambourne was promoted to 'First Cartoon', having established a reputation as an illustrator of books, including Charles Kingsley's *The Water Babies* (1886), and completed what he always considered his masterwork, which can be seen here, a large and intricately designed Diploma card for the International Exhibition of Fisheries (1883). Around the same time he developed a passion for photography, eventually converting his bathroom into a dark room and his attic into a studio. On Marion's death in 1914, Roy Sambourne took possession of the house, and dedicated his life to pleasure with such single-mindedness that on his death in 1946 he left the property to his sister largely unaltered. She encouraged her daughter Anne, later Countess of Rosse, to use it as her London home. It was here, in 1958, along with Sir John Betjeman and Sir Hugh Casson, that Lady Rosse and her husband founded the

Victorian Society, to champion the then-unfashionable arts and crafts of the period. In 1980 she sold the house and its contents to the Greater London Council. Pictures, works of art and furniture are arranged much as the family left them, the whole ensemble giving a vivid, almost uncanny insight into a successful artistic household from the turn of the last century.

Tour of the House

Viewable only on pre-booked guided tours, most conducted by costumed actors, a visit begins in the basement, with a video introduced by the photographer Lord Snowdon, Lady Rosse's son by her first marriage, telling the story of his family's occupation of the house. The **Hall** and **Staircase** set the tone of the house, with stuffed gamebirds in glass cases, engraved glass inner doors and black marbled skirting. The stair carpet is from the 1960s, designed by William Morris' trainee and successor Henry Dearle; it was spotted by Lady Rosse in a station hotel. On the first floor landing, the water tank and fountain are the most immediately striking of Sambourne's original modifications to the house, along with the stained glass window featuring the intertwined initials of him and his wife. Here also is the Diploma card that he designed for the International Exhibition of Fisheries.

The **Dining Room** contains the most expensive piece of furniture bought for the house: the sideboard—which on the whole reveals Sambourne's skill at achieving clever effects on a shoestring. The decoration of the walls, hung with Chinese export china and photographic reproductions of Old Masters, has changed hardly at all since his day. The next-door **Morning Room** was where Marion Sambourne spent much of her time, writing letters, entertaining callers and organising her staff. The wallpaper in this room gives the most accurate impression of how much of the wall-covering of the rest of the house would have looked: William Morris 'Pomegranate' on the ceiling and up to the plate rail, Morris 'Diaper' design paper above. The furniture is lighter than in other rooms, of late Victorian manufacture in 18th-century Sheraton-style.

Upper floors

The first floor is entirely taken up by the L-shaped **Drawing Room**, the centrepiece of the house, crowded with the results of Sambourne's ardent shopping sprees. He designed the large back window himself. The furnishings and general style reflect an enthusiasm for the Aesthetic movement, and especially the fin-de-siècle craze for Japanese designs. Oriental rugs cover the floor, but like the furniture, none is of museum quality. Instead, they faithfully represent middle-class taste of the period.

On the second floor are the **Principal Bedroom**, used by Maud Messel and later Lady Rosse, who redecorated early in the 1960s with Morris 'Norwich' wallpaper and new curtains and carpets. Beside the bed is a pencil portrait of Maud by her son, the theatre designer Oliver Messel. Next door is the **Spare Bedroom**, later used by Roy: an Edwardian bachelor's bedroom decorated with some of the best of his father's book illustrations, including those for *The Water Babies*, and signed photographs of his actress intimates. In the **Bathroom** the massive marble bathtub remains, used by Sambourne as a developing tank for his photography, a good sample of which is displayed here, some revealing the jolly, sociable cartoonist to have been a comic actor manqué, striking burlesque poses in a variety of different costumes. Others are the result of his candid experiments with erotic portraiture, early examples of glamour photography.

On the top floor is the **Maid's Room**—mocked up in a surprisingly squalid state— and the **Studio**. Sambourne's slide filing system, in old film cartons, line the walls at picture rail level. Some of his equipment has also been put back in place.

LONDON CANAL MUSEUM

12–13 New Wharf Road, King's Cross, N1 9RT
Tel: 020-7713 0836; www.canalmuseum.org.uk
Open Tues–Sun and bank holidays 10–4.30
Admission charge. Disabled access to most of the building
Tube: King's Cross
Shop
Map p. 379, 2D

Located in a former ice warehouse on the Battlebridge Basin of the Regent's Canal, the museum illustrates the story of the building and its unusual purpose as well as the London canal system in general. Built in 1860, the warehouse was adapted to receive and store natural ice imported from Norway by Carlo Gatti. By 1901, United Carlo Gatti Stevens Ltd was the largest ice merchant in London. On the ground floor, two ice wells dug in the 1860s can be seen, along with pairs of ice dogs (large tongs designed to assist in handling the frozen blocks), and some mid-19th-century zinc-lined ice boxes, forerunners of the fridge. Also here is a walk-in narrowboat, *Coronis*, the unpowered 'butty' of the *Corona*, enlivened by a recorded dramatisation of a bargeman's homecoming to his wife at the end of the working day.

On the first floor, the building's other use as a wagon depot is illustrated by a pair of reconstructed stables complete with model horses. Colourful information boards sketch the early history of canals in the mid-18th century, their decline after the development of road and rail, and their recent revival at the hands of enthusiasts and pleasure boaters. An illuminated push-button map of England charts the course of the country's canals, revealing Brindley's 'Grand Cross', which by the end of the 18th century had connected the four great river basins of Trent, Mersey, Severn and Thames. James Brindley (1716–77) built his first canal for the Duke of Bridgwater, to facilitate the transport of coal from the ducal mines to the factories of Manchester. The project was so successful that he was soon employed to build canals across the Midlands. He died whilst surveying a canal on Merseyside, of a diabetic attack.

Outside, in Battlebridge Basin, is the *Bantam IV*, a pusher tug built in 1949–50, designed to push a barge rigidly coupled to the tug, around 40% more effective than pulling it.

LONDON FIRE BRIGADE MUSEUM

94a Southwark Bridge Rd, SE1 0EG
Tel: 020-7578 2894; www.london-fire.gov.uk
Open Mon–Fri by guided tour 10.30 and 2
Admission charge
Tube: Borough
Shop
Map p. 383, 3D

Located in the London Fire Brigade's Training Centre at Winchester House, this old-fashioned museum presents the most comprehensive range of artefacts related to fire-fighting in the UK. The house was built in 1820 on land formerly part of the Bishop of Winchester's estate, and became the home of the Brigade's Chief Officer, Captain Eyre Massey Shaw, in 1878. Credited with introducing steam engines at all fire stations and pioneering the use of the telegraph, Massey Shaw lived here until 1891. The building remained the London Fire Brigade's HQ until 1937, when it moved to the Albert Embankment. The Brigade was formed in 1833 with James Braidwood from Edinburgh as its first Chief Officer. In charge of a full-time team of 80 firemen operating from 13 different stations, Braidwood was the first to encourage the entering of burning houses to tackle the source of conflagrations and invented one of the earliest forms of breathing apparatus. He himself was killed in 1861 by a collapsing wall while fighting a fire at the Tooley Street Warehouse. His funeral procession drew massive crowds.

Three rooms on the first floor are arranged in chronological order, and begin with the Great Fire of London in 1666 and a large selection of 17th-century firemarks: insurance companies' badges that guaranteed a house would receive the attentions of the company's brigade in the event of a fire (*see p. 55*). The second and third rooms cover the development of the Brigade up to, during and after the Second World War. The guided tour (informative rather than hands-on; not aimed at under-12s), goes into considerable detail on the history of the Brigade and also includes the Appliance Bay, with its impressive collection of early fire engines and firefighting appliances.

LONDON TRANSPORT MUSEUM

Covent Garden Piazza, WC2
Tube: Covent Garden
Map p. 382, 2B

Closed for redevelopment at time of writing, due to re-open in 2007, the London Transport Museum occupies the old flower market, a remarkable Victorian cast iron building on Covent Garden 'piazza'. The origin of the museum was a small collection of buses from the 1920s and 30s formed by the London General Omnibus Company. The collection now includes horse, motor and trolley buses, trams and underground railway rolling stock. The collection of London Transport posters includes work by some of the leading British graphic artists of the 20th century.

LORD'S TOUR AND MCC MUSEUM

Lord's Cricket Ground, St John's Wood, NW8 8QN
Tel: 020-7616 8595; www.lords.org
Tours daily April–Sept at 10, 12 and 2; Oct–March at 10 and 2. Visitors are advised to book ahead. No tours on major match days
Admission charge. Almost all of tour accessible to disabled visitors
Tube: St John's Wood
Pub and shop
Map p. 379, 2D

The guided tour of Lord's is the easiest way (without a match ticket) to see the spiritual home of English cricket. Many tours are led by passionate members of the MCC (Marylebone Cricket Club), which owns and runs the ground—and is not to be confused with MCCC (Middlesex County Cricket Club), which plays here. The MCC was founded in 1787 at a match played between Middlesex and Essex in Dorset Fields, Marylebone, now Dorset Square. The match was organised by Thomas Lord, who gives his name to today's cricket ground. The following year, the Club laid down a Code of Laws which it continues to arbitrate and which govern the rules of the game. Since 2000, following an initiative led by former England captains Ted Dexter and Lord Cowdray, the Code also enshrines The Spirit of Cricket.

The tour starts in the **Long Room**, the 'Holy of Holies' at the heart of the members' pavilion built in 1890. Three large windows look out over the hallowed turf. The **Committee Room**, surprisingly small, where the Code of Laws are displayed, is decorated with a fine portrait of Lord and other committee members ancient and modern.

Leaving the pavilion, the tour continues with a look at the **Real Tennis court** built in 1900, replacing the court that was built on the east side of the ground in 1838. Originating in the 13th century, with rules perhaps even more arcane than those of cricket, the game is mentioned by Shakespeare in five of his plays, and has only recently been called 'Real' in order to distinguish it from the modern game of Lawn Tennis. Real Tennis is played today in the UK, USA, Australia and France.

The **Museum** describes and illustrates the origins and history of cricket. Its most famous exhibit is on the first floor: the small urn containing the 'Ashes', for which Test Matches between England and Australia are fought. They remain at Lord's even when Australia wins. Numerous mementoes of the game are displayed; among the collection of cricket bats is one used by W.G. Grace. There is also the oldest known cricket ball, from 1820, used to score 278 runs in an MCC v. Norfolk match; Don Bradman's cap worn during the 1930s Australian tour; and Shane Warne's boots from

1997. Another popular curiosity is a stuffed sparrow killed by a fast ball bowled by Jehangir Khan at Lord's on 3 July 1936.

MALL GALLERIES

17 Carlton House Terrace, SW1Y 5BD
Tel: 020-7930 6844; www.mallgalleries.org.uk
Open daily 10–5 during exhibitions
Free
Tube: Charing Cross
Café
Map p. 382, 3A

The Mall Galleries are the home of the Federation of British Artists, an organisation which comprises several artists' societies, some with distinguished histories, which use the galleries for their annual exhibitions. Although the address is Carlton House Terrace, the main exhibition space is entered via The Mall side of Nash's imposing creation, in the basement with its row of sturdy Doric columns. Chief among the societies are the New English Art Club (NEAC) and the Royal Society of Portrait Painters. The NEAC was established in the late 19th century by a group of artists including Stanhope Forbes, John Singer Sargent and Wilson Steer. Later members included Walter Sickert, Augustus John, Stanley Spencer, Paul Nash, Duncan Grant and Mark Gertler, a roll-call of significant early 20th-century British artists. Today the society champions figurative art and has an exhibition every December. The Royal Society of Portrait Painters was founded in 1891. Its lively annual show (every April) includes work by members and selected work by non-members, including portraits of principally British figures, from the Queen to actors, politicians, distinguished academics, or the completely unknown. Quality varies from excellent and penetrating to hilariously dreadful (although the latter is increasingly rare). The gallery can organise commissions.

MARBLE HILL HOUSE
(English Heritage)

Richmond Road, Twickenham, TW1 2NL
Tel: 020-8892 5115; www.english-heritage.org.uk/visits
Open Apr–Oct Mon–Sat 10–2, Sun and bank holidays 10–5;
Nov–March by pre-booked appointment
Admission charge
Station: St. Margaret's (from Waterloo)
Café open March–Oct (in March open Wed–Sun only)
Map p. 378, 3B

Built in 1724–29 for Henrietta Howard, later Countess of Suffolk, and mistress of George II, Marble Hill is often cited as a perfect example of a Palladian villa. Overlooking the Thames at Twickenham, it is a simple, pure exercise of symmetry, the three central bays of the south elevation topped by a pediment, flanked by a further bay on either side, giant Ionic pilasters decorating the north front. Inside, the principal room, the Great Room on the first floor, is a perfect cube at the heart of the building. It is not quite known who designed the house, which has been attributed to both Henry Herbert, Earl of Pembroke, the 'architect earl', and the Palladian architect Colen Campbell (who remodelled Lord Burlington's town residence, now the Royal Academy; *see p. 244*). Two early designs for the house are certainly by Campbell, the first with side pavilions never executed, the second, published in the third volume of his *Vitruvius Britannicus* in 1725, with an external staircase leading up to the *piano nobile*, in the end also omitted. Mrs Howard seems to have considered, rejected and accepted elements of the design herself. The final design of Marble Hill was constructed by Roger Morris, then Colen Campbell's draughtsman, under the supervision of Lord Pembroke, Mrs Howard's architectural advisor. Balconies on the south front, breaking the Palladian purity, allowed contemplation of the fine prospect over the river, towards Ham House and Richmond Hill.

The House and its Mistress

Henrietta Howard (1688–1767), wife of Charles Howard, fifth son of the Earl of Suffolk, had become, at the accession of George I, a Woman of the Bedchamber of the Princess of Wales. By 1720 the Prince of Wales, the future George II, was said to be spending 'every evening of his life, three or four hours in Mrs Howard's lodging'. An early Hanoverian 'blue-stocking', she was said to keep a 'philosophical' expression and, in her own words, enforced 'every argument with that gesticulation of the hand for which I am so famous'. A patron and correspondent of men of letters, she gathering about her at her new summer villa at Twickenham a literary circle that included Alexander Pope, the Earl of Chesterfield, John Gay and Jonathan Swift. Pope's 'On a Certain Lady at Court' refers to Mrs Howard, and his 'Bounce to Fop' is an epistle addressed to her lap-dog Fop from Pope's own Great Dane, Bounce. In 1731 she had become the Countess of Suffolk, on her husband's accession to the title. He died in 1733, around the same time she fell from favour with the king, and in 1734 she retired from court service, marrying the following year George Berkeley. In her declining years Horace Walpole, her near neighbour at Strawberry Hill, was a regular visitor; between 1759 and 1766 he filled notebooks with her conversation and anecdotes.

On Mrs Howard's death in 1767, the estate passed to her nephew, the 2nd Earl of Buckingham, in whose family's possession it remained, let out to a succession of tenants, until sold in 1824. In 1887 the contents were auctioned but the house remained unsold. In 1902, under threat of demolition, it passed into public ownership and opened to visitors in 1903. Over the decades successful efforts have been made to return to it the original, or similar, pictures and furnishings and to present the rooms as they would have been lived in during its early Georgian heyday.

South front of the Palladian Marble Hill House.

Tour of the House

The **Hall**, with its four columns, is decorated with four marble profile reliefs of gods and goddesses, Jupiter, Juno, Ceres and Bacchus (French c. 1720), installed in the room in 1750–51, the only works of art to remain at the house in 1903. Mrs Howard also had a model of Shakespeare here. To the left is the grandest room on the ground floor, the **Breakfast Parlour**, with an elaborate alcove at the north end and a curious frieze, an adaptation of motifs derived from Inigo Jones. The **Dining Parlour** was created for Mrs Howard in 1750–51 by Matthew Brettingham. Originally decorated with Chinese wallpaper, it introduced a touch of Rococo spirit to the Palladian interior. The grand mahogany staircase leads to the stately **Great Room** on the first floor, the central reception room and the most important room in the house. The principal pictures hung here, including the *capriccio* views of classical Roman ruins by G.P. Panini, 1738, set over the doors and chimneypiece, were returned to the house in stages, as they appeared on the art market. Copies after van Dyck and Rubens by Charles Jervas hung here in Mrs Howard's day (the works after van Dyck seen here now are not original to the house). The chief splendour of the room is its carved and gilded decoration by James Richards, Grinling Gibbons' successor as Master Sculptor to the King: panels of flowers and foliage above the pictures and pier glasses, eagles above the doors and antique masks in the cornice. Owls appear on the inside of the shutters and two large putti lean on the overmantel pediment. The marble-topped console table, with heavy

Kentian gilded carving incorporating a peacock, the attribute of Juno, one of an original set of four, was returned to the house after its discovery in Australia. **Lady Suffolk's Bedchamber** retains its screen of Ionic columns at the north end marking the bed space. Hung here are pictures of the correct period—but not original to the house—including Richard Wilson's *Thames at Marble Hill* (c. 1762) and Charles Phillips's portrait of George II, standing in the anteroom to William Kent's New Library at St James's (demolished), built for Queen Caroline's vast collection of books, seen in shelves in the room beyond, behind a statue of Minerva, goddess of wisdom. Rysbrack's bust of Caroline is shown above the door.

From the mahogany staircase the Stone Staircase leads to the floor above, the chief room being the **Picture Gallery**, originally hung with full-length portraits of George II, Queen Caroline and Mrs Howard. The majority of Mrs Howard's pictures were displayed at her Savile Row town house, but at Marble Hill she had a quantity of porcelain, a large proportion of it displayed in a detached cottage in the grounds, in a chamber with carved and gilt-edged display shelves.

In the gardens, which had been laid out by Charles Bridgeman, with the involvement of Alexander Pope, was a **Grotto**, accidentally rediscovered in 1941 following the felling of a tree, and re-excavated in 1984. Now restored to an approximation of its original c. 1739 appearance, it has walls lined with shells and a floor with circles of pebbles. The original cavern-mouth entrance was decorated with coral, flints and blue glass. Since disappeared is the other garden addition, the Priory of St Hubert, a 'gothic' barn dedicated to the patron saint of hunting, a sport which Mrs Howard is said to have pursued with a violent passion.

MARIANNE NORTH GALLERY
(Royal Botanic Gardens)

Kew, Richmond, Surrey, TW9 3AB
Tel: 020-8332 5655; www.rbgkew.org uk
Open daily from 9.30; closing time varies according to season (approx. 4pm in winter, 6pm in summer)
Admission charge
Tube: Kew Gardens
Cafés and shop
Map p. 378, 3C

Situated, at the artist's request, in a quiet corner of the Royal Botanic Gardens, away from the main gate and other places of refreshment, the Marianne North Gallery survives almost unaltered since the day of its opening on 9 June 1882. Red brick with a veranda, typical of European dwellings of that period in India, the building was expressly designed to display Marianne North's oil paintings, 832 studies of nature from life in countries all over the world, executed between 1871 and 1885. Many were painted in circumstances of considerable discomfort and hardship, so Marianne North also wanted the gallery to remind visitors of the hospitality offered to the weary traveller in far-flung places, stipulating to that end that the gallery should serve 'tea or coffee and biscuits, nothing else, at a fair price'.

After the death of her beloved father, MP for Hastings, in 1869, Marianne North (1830–90) devoted her life to travelling and painting. In 1871 she visited North America, Jamaica and Brazil. Two years later she crossed America on her way to Japan, returning via the East Indies and Ceylon. 1880 found her in Australia and New Zealand, at Charles Darwin's suggestion. Immediately after the opening of her gallery, which she provided for, curated and arranged herself, she visited South Africa. Finally, despite declining health, she travelled to Chile in 1884.

The three-room building was designed by her friend, the architectural historian James Fergusson, using natural light on principles learned from the study of ancient Greek temples. Neatly numbered, labelled and arranged in geographical order, her direct, colourful, uncomplicated oil paintings, none much larger than twelve inches by six, fill the walls completely above the dado, itself made of some 250 vertical strips of different types of timber. Lit from above by clerestory windows, the pictures depict over 900 different species of plant, as well as various views, landscapes and architecture, all framed in uniform black with a gold fillet. Directly ahead of visitors upon entering are 'Plants Sacred to the Hindus': the sacred lotus or Padma; the all-curing Neem; and the foliage, fruit, and flowers of the tree sacred to Krishna, the Banyan. Clockwise from this point are pictures of plants and scenes from Singapore, Borneo, Japan, Java, New Zealand, Australia, Chile, Brazil, Jamaica, America, Ceylon, and back to India. Above the main entrance is picture no. 1, *Victoria Regia*, an extraordinary waterlily, followed by no. 2, *Common Tobacco*. Along with surprising juxtapositions, these hard-earned holiday snaps also occasionally allow for humorous titles: no. 735, for example, *Australian bears and Australian pears*. In the smaller inner sanctum of the gallery are more pictures from Australia, as well as from the Cape of Good Hope, the Seychelles, South Africa, Tenerife and India again.

MARITIME GREENWICH

Map p. 379, 3F

'Maritime Greenwich' is an invented entity. It was awarded World Heritage Site status by UNESCO in 1997, in recognition of the fact that its blend of architecture and royal and maritime history is of international significance. The buildings of the Old Royal Naval College, together with the Queen's House, constitute a unique ensemble of buildings by leading architects such as Inigo Jones, Sir Christopher Wren and Nicholas Hawksmoor; the magnificent river view of them inspired Canaletto. Greenwich has had royal associations since the 15th century. The site of an important royal palace, renamed Placentia by Henry VII, it was the birthplace of Henry VIII and

Elizabeth I, and a favourite location for jousting, tilting and hunting for Tudor and early Stuart monarchs. The palace was the official reception point for important visitors, such as foreign ambassadors, who arrived downriver at Gravesend. After the Restoration, Charles II demolished the Tudor palace and began work on a vast new one, designed by John Webb. Greenwich Park, which stretches up the hill beyond the Queen's House, was given axial tree-lined avenues, grass terraces, or Giant Steps (the remnants of which can be made out to the east of the Observatory), and an elaborate parterre with fountains designed by the French court garden designer André Le Nôtre. Greenwich is also the home of Greenwich Mean Time. The foundation of the Royal Observatory within the Park (a public space since 1830) in 1675, and the presence of the Navy on the palace site since 1694, placed Greenwich at the heart of astronomical discovery and maritime endeavour.

OLD ROYAL NAVAL COLLEGE
GREENWICH HOSPITAL

King William Walk, SE10
Tel: 020-8269 4747; www.greenwichfoundation.org.uk
Open (grounds) daily 8–6; (Chapel) daily 10–5, Sun 11am service;
(Painted Hall) daily 10–5, sometimes closed Sat 4.30 for weddings;
(Visitor Centre) daily 10–5
Free
Café and restaurant

Established by Royal Charter in 1694, the Royal Hospital for Seamen was the wish of Queen Mary II, who desired a charitable institution for injured Royal Navy seamen, their widows and children. She gave over royal land at Greenwich for the purpose, John Webb's vast new palace for Charles II having been abandoned in 1669 with the completion of only one block. Mary died in 1694 but her husband, William III, respected her wishes. Sir Christopher Wren was appointed the Hospital's Surveyor, with Nicholas Hawksmoor as Clerk of the Works. The Queen's House, however (*see p. 179*), remained in royal ownership and its vista to the river was to be preserved. Wren's plan, therefore, was to use it as a distant visual centrepiece, with in front of it four symmetrical blocks, the two furthest from the river (the King William and Queen Mary blocks) with matching domes and colonnades. On the river, the King Charles block **1** (Webb's earlier building) was mirrored by the Queen Anne block **2** . Building was a piecemeal exercise which spanned 55 years and which witnessed successive Surveyorships (Vanbrugh 1716, Colen Campbell 1726, Thomas Ripley 1729), but the resulting ensemble is one of the grandest Baroque sites in England. Greenwich Hospital's magnificence reflected the charitable munificence of the Crown and the importance of the Navy. The King Charles block, enlarged and with Webb's architecture altered internally and externally, was the first to be completed; in 1705 the pensioners moved in.

In 1869 Greenwich Hospital closed and in 1873 the site became home to the Royal Naval College, which occupied the buildings until the mid-1990s. In 1997 the buildings were transferred to the Greenwich Foundation, established to administer the site and to oversee its conversion for the University of Greenwich (which now occupies the King William, Mary and Anne blocks) and Trinity College of Music (King Charles block). Visitors can see the grounds as well as the Painted Hall and Chapel.

Visiting the Building

Entrance to the Hospital is via the west gates, which date from 1751 and were moved to their present position in 1850. Their gigantic celestial and terrestrial stone spheres, 6ft in diameter, have their latitudinal and longitudinal lines marked in copper bands. The Pepys Building, on the left, decorated with busts of naval heroes, was built in 1874–79, with additions in 1882–83, as a sports facility for the Naval College. It now houses the Greenwich Visitor Centre. The history of Greenwich, its status as a World Heritage Site, and the histories of the Hospital and the Royal Naval College are explored in a series of displays which include architectural models of Wren's design, and early 18th-century carved stone heads (Neptune; Galatea etc) by Robert Jones, originally intended for the exterior of the King William block. Beyond the Pepys Building, directly ahead, is the main Hospital complex, with a statue of George II by Rysbrack (1735) in the centre of the Grand Square.

The **Painted Hall** occupies the length of one wing of the King William block ➌. Painted by Sir James Thornhill in stages (for £3 per yard), between 1708 and 1726, it is one of the most magnificent and impressive Baroque painted interiors in the country, and Thornhill's masterpiece. Its hugely complicated iconography necessitated the publication of Thornhill's *Explanation* of it in 1726/7. The main body of the hall, the Lower Hall, where the pensioners ate, was painted first, between 1708 and 1714, the ceiling glorifying the Protestant constitutional monarchy of William and Mary (*Peace and Liberty Triumph over Tyranny*), and the Naval and maritime foundation of Britain's power and mercantile prosperity. Below the seated figures of the monarchs, a cowering Louis XIV clutches a broken sword, and Architecture points to a large elevation of the King William block. The appearance of Tycho Brahe, Copernicus and John Flamsteed on the ceiling (on the north side of the arch leading from the entrance vestibule) alludes to the importance of astronomy to maritime navigation. Flamsteed holds a document inscribed 'Apr: 22 1715', the date of his predicted eclipse of the sun (which proved accurate). The Upper Hall, where the officers ate, was completed in 1718–25. Queen Anne and her husband, Prince George of Denmark, Lord High Admiral, appear on the ceiling; the Prince of Orange, later William III, is welcomed by Britannia on the south wall (in grisaille), and on the north wall George I lands at Greenwich (also grisaille). The great west wall, mainly the work of Thornhill's assistant Dietrich Ernst André, celebrates the Protestant Hanoverian succession, with George I and his family surrounded by Peace and Justice and other Virtues, the great dome of St Paul's Cathedral, symbol of Anglicanism (and Thornhill's other great painting commission), rising in the background. Thornhill himself

MARITIME GREENWICH

1   King Charles block
2   Queen Anne block
3   King William block
4   Queen Mary block
5   National Maritime Museum
6   Queen's House
7   Royal Observatory

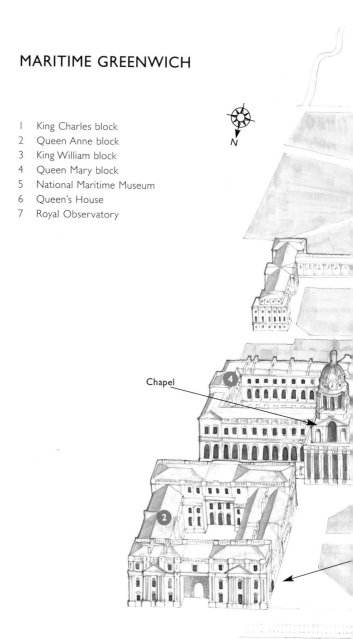

Chapel

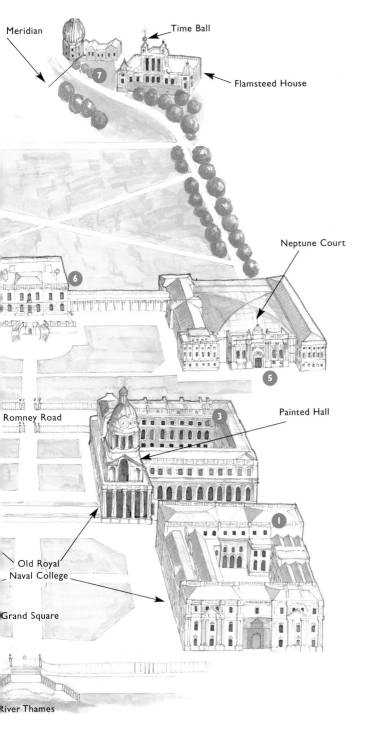

Meridian

Time Ball

Flamsteed House

Neptune Court

Romney Road

Painted Hall

Old Royal
Naval College

Grand Square

River Thames

appears to the right of the steps. The entrance **Vestibule**, painted with cartouches inscribed with benefactors' names, with seated charity boys, was completed by 1726.

The **Chapel** is directly opposite the Painted Hall, in the Queen Mary block ④, the least magnificent of the four and externally a simpler (cheaper) version of the King William. Originally completed in 1750, the chapel was gutted by fire in 1779 and remodelled by James 'Athenian' Stuart (author, with Nicholas Revett, of the influential *Antiquities of Athens*). The distinctive bracketed gallery repeats the earlier one, but the plasterwork ceiling is Stuart's design, its delicate neo-Grecian modelling in startling contrast to Thornhill's overwhelming Baroque. The 25-ft altarpiece, *St Paul Shipwrecked at Malta*, was commissioned from Benjamin West in 1781, and the statues of Faith, Hope, Charity and Humility in the vestibule were also designed by him. From 4th–7th January 1806, Nelson's body lay in state in the Painted Hall before being taken by funeral barge to St Paul's Cathedral. The 1810–12 Nelson Pediment above the colonnade of the King William block was designed by West. Forty feet wide and ten feet high and stylistically heavily influenced by the Elgin Marbles, recently arrived in London, it shows Neptune delivering Nelson's mortal remains to Britannia. It is made of Coade Stone (*see below*).

Coade Stone

An artificial, frost-resistant material first manufactured by Mrs Eleanor Coade (d. 1821) of Lambeth in 1769, Coade Stone was extolled in its day as the equal of marble, for its sharpness of definition. The mixture, to which fine-ground quartz was added, was fired at very high temperatures so that it practically vitrified. In the 18th century its trade name was Lithodipyra, from the Greek meaning stone (*litho*) twice (*di*) fire (*pyra*). The stone, in fact, was semi-ceramic, the secret of its durability. The Coade family was originally from southwest England, and it is surmised that they knew of and used china clay, which was —and still is— mined around St Austell in Cornwall. The success of Mrs Coade's enterprise came largely thanks to the enthusiasm for her product of influential architects and sculptors. Robert Adam, on his return from the Grand Tour, found it the ideal medium for producing the ornamental Grecian urns which he made fashionable. Sir John Soane was another user. On the façade of his house in Lincoln's Inn Fields are two Coade Stone figures (*see p. 267*), and there are others at Pitshanger Manor, his country villa (*see p. 236*). The sculptor John Flaxman also appreciated the material's qualities. His figures of Tragedy and Comedy on the Royal Opera House in Covent Garden are of Coade Stone.

Coade Stone ceased manufacture in 1840, but its presence still endures. Captain William Bligh's tomb at the Museum of Garden History (*see p. 188*) is made of it, and there is a Coade Stone lion standing at the southern end of Westminster Bridge, outside old County Hall, on the site of the original Coade Stone manufactory.

THE NATIONAL MARITIME MUSEUM

Romney Road, Greenwich, SE10 9NF
Tel: 020-8858 4422; www.nmm.ac.uk
Open daily 10–5 (6pm in summer)
Free
Cafés
Map p. 379, 3F

The National Maritime Museum ❺ (the name was supposedly supplied by Rudyard Kipling), founded in 1934 and opened by George VI on 27 April 1937, tells the story of the Royal Navy, Britain as a seafaring power and the history of maritime exploration, navigation, astronomy and the measurement of time. As well as the main museum, it includes the historic Queen's House, where its important collection of maritime art is displayed, and the Royal Observatory (*see separate entries below*). As well as paintings the museum's 2.5 million objects include cartography, ship models and plans, an exceptional collection of scientific and navigational instruments, important collections relating to national heroes such as Nelson and Captain Cook, and an important library housing books and manuscripts dating from the 15th century onwards.

The Museum Collection and Buildings

The Museum's foundation collection was an amalgamation of others established much earlier, mainly the Greenwich Hospital collection of over 300 naval portraits and paintings which had been established in the Painted Hall (*see p. 171 above*) in 1823, and the Naval Museum's collection of ship models and other memorabilia, which had been established at the Hospital when the Royal Naval College arrived in 1873. Added to this was the personal collection of the Scottish millionaire ship owner Sir James Caird (1864–1954), one of the Museum's first trustees, which included the A.G. Macpherson collection of 11,000 maritime prints, paintings, drawings and atlases which Caird had purchased in 1927–28 with the establishment of a national museum in mind. Caird was a generous benefactor to the Museum and his bronze bust by William Reid Dick is displayed in the Library vestibule, or Rotunda, which was remodelled by Sir Edwin Lutyens especially to display it.

The Museum's buildings were formerly those of the Royal Naval Asylum (renamed the Royal Hospital School in 1892), a charitable educational institution for orphans of war. In the early 19th century the Queen's House was transferred for the Asylum's use, and the colonnades either side of it (respecting Inigo Jones's architecture), leading to east and west wings, were built between 1807 and 1811 to the designs of Daniel Asher Alexander. In 1861–62 an L-shaped extension was added to the west wing by Philip Charles Hardwick, creating a three-sided square, and in 1872–73 a roofed gymnasium, one of the first indoor gymnasiums in Europe, was added to the middle. Its magnificent north entrance front with a giant order Doric screen, with the royal arms and a Neptune keystone above the door, is now the Museum's main entrance, the school having moved to Suffolk in 1933. In 1996–98 the National Maritime Museum underwent a major refurbishment. The gymnasium was demolished (its iron structure was moved to the Childe Beale Wildlife Park, Berkshire) and in its place is the new Neptune Court (Rick Mather, with the Building Design Partnership), a vast space spanned by a steel-framed glass roof. The lower level is divided into 'streets' surrounding a central exhibition space, above which are the 'Upper Deck' coffee bar and walkway links to the 19th-century wings.

Tour of the Museum

Approaching the Museum from Romney Road the air is filled with the sound of crashing waves, an audio innovation of the 1990s. The north entrance leads straight into **Neptune Court** where large-scale highlights from the collection are displayed, including the working paddle engines from the steam paddle-tug *Reliant* (built in 1907 for service on the Manchester ship canal) and Prince Frederick's barge, a 'floating coach' designed by William Kent in 1732 with carved and gilded work by James Richards, the King's Master Carver. Used for state occasions on the Thames, it would have been accompanied by another barge with a 'set of Musick'.

The new displays on the ground floor, to the east, north and in the centre of Neptune Court, are aimed chiefly at school parties. To the sound of creaking decks, 'Explorers' gives a brief overview of the history of exploration, from Vasco da Gama and Christopher Columbus to Sir John Franklin's ill-fated 1845 attempt to find the Northwest Passage. In cases set into ice-lined walls, with the sound of howling wind, are items such as the snow boot of one of Franklin's party who died in Starvation Cove. Displays in 'Exploring the Deep' are set in an underwater world, around the rusting hulk of a ship. Important early navigational instruments—astrolabes and quadrants from the 13th to the late 16th centuries—are on show in 'Navigation', as well as the magnificent late 16th-century **Drake Jewel and Cup**: the former sun-shaped, decorated with rubies and opals, the reverse containing a miniature of Elizabeth I; the latter a coconut shell set elaborately in silver, the cover surmounted by an exquisite model of the *Golden Hind*. Presented to Sir Francis Drake by Elizabeth I to mark his historic circumnavigation, it is rather lost in the overwhelming display design of twinkling stars, compass lines criss-crossing the floor and accompanying harp music. 'Maritime London' contains an interesting painting by William Parrot of Isambard Kingdom Brunel's great ship *Leviathan*, renamed *Great Eastern* before its launch in 1858, its massive hulk, surrounded by scaffolding, dominating Greenwich. A rather confusingly arranged collection of reproduction photographs tell the story of London's docks and wharves. 'Rank and Style' explores naval uniform. Exhibits are shown in cases sunk

Rear Admiral Sir Horatio Nelson, by Lemuel Abbott. In his hat Nelson wears the *chelengk* presented by the Ottoman Sultan. Abbott did not paint the likeness from life, and had never seen the *chelengk,* which was surmounted by diamond-studded filaments. This is his artist's impression.

into the floor, or in cupboards which visitors are encouraged to open. In one of them is Edward VIII's Admiral of the Fleet full-dress uniform of 1936. 'Passengers' explores the age of the passenger liner and the rise of shipping lines such as Cunard and P&O. A model of the famous Cunard steamship *Mauritania* is shown at a dizzy slant, a recreation of its publicity posters which demonstrated its size in relation to the Great Pyramid at Giza. Recreations of Mauritania's cabins highlight the difference between first class and steerage and, through port holes, photographs are displayed, e.g. the first class lounge of the *Aquitania*, 1914, redolent of a glamorous era.

Upper level
Around the Upper Deck café are cases containing items from the museum's unrivalled collection of navigational instruments: 16th- and 17th-century Iranian, North African and European astrolabes for measuring the height of the sun above the horizon in order to calculate latitude; sun-centred Copernican armillary spheres engraved with signs of the zodiac; and terrestrial and celestial globes, such as Isaac Habrecht's clockwork example, shouldered by Atlas with engraved figures of the heavens.

Leaving Neptune Court, 'Trade and Empire' examines the rise of trading companies such as the East India Company, the slave trade and the expansion of the British Empire. Nineteenth-century views of China are on show, with a mixture of Chinese and European shipping; the 1819 figurehead of *HMS Seringapatam*, a carved representation of Tipu Sultan (*see p. 333*) holding a parasol and riding a roc, a mythical bird; and paintings by William Hodges, the artist on Cook's second voyage to the Pacific in 1772–75, including his beautiful *Waterfall in Dusky Bay*. On show in 'Art of the Sea' is Willem van de Velde the Younger's best and largest painting, *The Gouden Leeuw at the Battle of the Texel 11 August 1673*, the Dutch fleet's final victory of the Anglo-Dutch Wars; van de Velde the Elder's graphite and wash sketch of the *Battle of the Sound*, drawn in the heat of battle; as well as several examples of his works in pen and ink on oil, incredibly detailed monochrome studies.

Third level
'Oceans of Discovery' displays early sea charts and atlases as well as items relating to Cook's voyages of discovery. Zoffany's unfinished portrait of the dying hero is on show; works by John Webber, artist on Cook's third voyage; Cook's own journals; collected botanical specimens; and a model of the *Endeavour*, including her cargo and crew, which included the naturalist Sir Joseph Banks (*see p. 127*), the botanist Dr Daniel Solander, two artists and an astronomer. Further on, the search for the ever-shifting Magnetic Poles is examined (discovered in 1831 and 1909), as well as *HMS Challenger*'s scientific circumnavigation of 1872–76, with jars of preserved marine specimens collected by her crew. 'Ship of War' displays models of the Royal Navy's historic 17th- and 18th-century warships, most of which came from the Royal Naval Museum and are of immense historic value (almost no plans survive for 17th-century ships). One of the finest models is the *Royal George*, launched in 1756. Unplanked on one side, her cabins, internal arrangement and structure can be examined in detail.

The 'Nelson Gallery' shows items from the Museum's important collection of arte-facts relating to the nation's great hero, Admiral Lord Nelson. Chronologically arranged, there is a miniature of Nelson aged eight; a chart showing his rise through the Navy's ranks; François Rigaud's excellent portrait of him, begun in 1777 but not completed until 1786, by which time he was a Captain; Lemuel Abbot's portrait commissioned in 1800 by Nelson's biographer, John McArthur; a brass garrison gun captured at Copenhagen in 1801; an examination of his battle tactics; Pococke's 1808 painting *The Battle of the Nile (1 August 1798)*, and dress swords, with crocodile hilts, owned by Nelson's Captains who formed the Egyptian Club following their victory. Emma Hamilton is represented by Romney's portrait of her, traditionally described as in the pose of Ariadne. The most compelling exhibits are the clothes Nelson wore at the Battle of Trafalgar, the fatal musket ball hole visible just below the left epaulette of his coat. An invitation card to his public funeral is displayed, with the mourning ring worn by his nephew beside it. Touchingly personal items include the lace overskirt from his wife, Frances Nisbet's, wedding dress, and a gold toothpick case given to Nelson by her, with a hidden inscription 'love and kisses, home sweet home'.

THE QUEEN'S HOUSE
Open as National Maritime Museum

The Queen's House **6**, a perfectly proportioned architectural masterpiece, is usually taken as the first—and one of the finest—truly classical Renaissance buildings in England. Designed by the great architect Inigo Jones on his return from his influen-tial last trip to Italy (*see p. 27*), it symbolises the refined aesthetic of the early Stuart court. The Queen's House was in fact built in three main stages for successive queen consorts: Anne of Denmark, wife of James I; Henrietta Maria, wife of Charles I; and Catherine of Braganza, wife of Charles II. Anne of Denmark was granted Greenwich as her private residence in 1613 and commissioned the building in 1616. It stands almost exactly on the site of the gatehouse of the old Tudor palace, which marked the demarcation between the private palace gardens and Greenwich Park, to which the queen desired easy access. The Queen's House is in fact two buildings, one on the palace side, the other on the park side, linked by first-floor bridges which span what was then a public highway. On Anne's death in 1619 only the bottom storeys of the two blocks were complete. In 1629 Greenwich was granted to Henrietta Maria, and work resumed. Between 1629 and 1638 the upper storeys were added, including the central bridge room and the elegant loggia overlooking the park, and a programme of elaborate interior decoration was undertaken.

The Interior
The double-height, single cube galleried **Hall**, the centrepiece of the Queen's House, had its black and white marble floor laid in 1636–37, its pattern mirroring the white and gold compartmented ceiling above. The latter originally contained nine canvases by the

friend and follower of Caravaggio Orazio Gentileschi, *The Allegory of Peace and Arts under the English Crown*, which were removed in 1708 when the Queen's House became the official residence of the Governor of Greenwich Hospital. They were re-erected at Marlborough House, where they still are today. Other important Gentileschis were commissioned for the house, including the large *Finding of Moses*, which was sold at the 1649 Commonwealth sale following Charles I's execution (it is now in the National Gallery; *see p. 209*). The Hall was used for the display of classical and modern sculpture. Just off it are the so-called **Tulip Stairs**, though the motif in the fine wrought iron balustrade is in fact probably intended as a fleur-de-lis, Henrietta Maria's Bourbon family emblem. The stairs lead to the principal rooms on the *piano nobile*. The **Queen's Bedchamber** has a coved ceiling painted with important Italianate grotesque work, possibly by the King's Serjeant Painter John de Critz. Guido Reni was commissioned in 1637 to paint the central canvas, but it was never installed. The most sumptuous room is the Queen's **Withdrawing Room**, the beams of the compartmented ceiling bearing festoons of fruit and flowers and the frieze and cornice cartouches the monograms of Charles I and Henrietta Maria. The room would have contained the great cycle of 22 paintings commissioned from Jacob Jordaens, which took as their theme Cupid and Psyche and courtly Neoplatonic love. Eight paintings had arrived by 1641, but the cycle was never completed and none of the canvases is known today.

Between 1661 and 1663 the Queen's House was repaired and enlarged for Catherine of Braganza. The two other bridge rooms were built, some of the rooms were redecorated and some had their functions changed. The Queen's Bedchamber became, for instance, Catherine of Braganza's Presence Chamber, while the Queen's Antechamber was used as a chapel. In the 1980s a large restoration of the Queen's House was undertaken, which presented the building in its 1660s state. Silk hangings were reproduced, as were other furnishings, and photographic reproductions of the Gentileschis were installed in the Hall ceiling. The recent reappraisal of the Queen's House has thankfully seen most of these interventions swept away, although some have been retained, such as chimneypieces made according to Inigo Jones designs.

The Collection

The Queen's House is now used to display the National Maritime Museum's excellent collection of paintings, including marine paintings, portraits of naval heroes and portraits and landscapes relevant to Greenwich's royal history. Portraits of Tudor monarchs are on show, including *Elizabeth I* by John Bettes, as well as early battle pieces such as the German School *Battle of Lepanto* of 1571. Netherlandish panoramas of Greenwich show the old Tudor palace, while slightly later views, e.g. by Danckerts (c. 1670) or Vorsterman (c. 1680), with leisurely spectators on the hill above the Queen's House, show the demolished palace replaced by the beginnings of Webb's scheme (*see p. 170 above*). William Dobson's portrait of the elderly Inigo Jones (c. 1644) is shown in a room devoted to the history of the Queen's House. Upstairs, in the open gallery surrounding the Hall, are portraits of famous 17th-century admirals, e.g. Sir Cloudesley Shovell, from the series by Kneller and Dahl. Displays on Samuel Pepys and the 17th-century Anglo-

Dutch Wars include a view of the 1667 Dutch raid on the Medway, seen from a height with ships burning in the estuary; Bakhuysen's *The Captured Flagship Royal Charles Entering Dutch Waters*; and Lely's celebrated 'Flaggmen' series, portraits of the flag-officers who served under James II, Lord High Admiral, when Duke of York, at the Battle of Lowestoft in 1666. Other works by Lely include his early portrait of Peter Pett, with the *Sovereign of the Seas* in the background, and his excellent double portrait of Sir Freshville Holles and Sir Robert Holmes. James II himself appears in a swaggering, almost comic, full-length by Henri Gascars. A display devoted to the van de Veldes, the first great marine artists to work in Britain, who settled in London in 1673/4, occupies the room they were given by Charles II to use as a painting studio. Eighteenth-century works include Hudson's portrait of the unfortunate Admiral Byng, who failed to prevent the French capture of Minorca, was court-martialled and shot in 1757. Seapieces by Dominic Serres, the only marine artist to be admitted a founder member of the Royal Academy, are also on show, as well as portraits by Reynolds. *Rear-Admiral the Hon. Augustus Keppel* (1752–53), shows Keppel, a faithful patron of Reynolds, full length before a stormy sea, and is said to be the picture which established Reynolds as a leading artist. Another portrait of Keppel is nearby, with the mezzotint after it as well as the plate from which the mezzotint was printed—a rare and interesting trio.

THE ROYAL OBSERVATORY
Open as National Maritime Museum

Standing high on Observatory Hill, with a spectacular panoramic view over the Hospital, the river and London stretching into the distance, is Flamsteed House **7**, the earliest building of the Greenwich complex which comprises the Royal Observatory. Built in 1675–76 by Sir Christoper Wren, with the assistance of Robert Hooke, it was the first purpose-built scientific research facility in the country. The Observatory at Greenwich is no longer used to make positional observations (due to atmospheric pollution, the Royal Observatory began the move to Herstmonceaux, Sussex, in 1948), but its historic buildings remain a site of extraordinary significance for the history of astronomy, timekeeping and the search for the calculation of longitude. At the International Meridian Conference in Washington in 1884, Greenwich was recognised as marking the Prime Meridian, Longitude 0°, and Greenwich Mean Time was internationally adopted. Outside the gates of the courtyard is the Shepherd 24-hour clock, erected in 1852, the year the Greenwich Time Service started sending signals. Greenwich is the official starting point of each new day. The large red **Time Ball** on the east turret of Flamsteed House is the world's first visual time signal. Since 1833 it has been hoisted half-way up the mast at 12.55, to the top at 12.58, and dropped at precisely 1pm.

As visitors enter the courtyard, with Flamsteed House directly ahead and the Meridian Building on the left, a brass line in the ground marks the **Prime Meridian**. It runs straight through the Meridian Building, linking the North and South Poles and marking the division between the Eastern and Western Hemispheres. Visitors can thus stand astride the line, in two hemispheres at once. The Meridian is seen most dramatically at dusk when the green laser beam projected from the Observatory stretches into the evening sky, across Greenwich Hospital and the river towards the distant lights of the tall modern buildings of Canary Wharf.

History of the Observatory

The Royal Observatory was the product of the 17th-century scientific revolution, a great era of investigation and discovery. One of the crucial problems demanding a solution was the calculation of longitude, vital for accurate navigation at sea which, for a maritime nation, was of obvious importance. The Royal Observatory was founded by Charles II, with John Flamsteed appointed the first 'Astronomical Observator' in 1675, with this specific task in mind. Flamsteed's aim was to facilitate the calculation of longitude through lunar observation, specifically the annual passage of the moon against the stars, by compiling accurate star catalogues and lunar tables. He moved into Flamsteed House, his official residence, in July 1676 and began his observations from the top floor observatory in September.

Tour of the House

On entering the house there is first a display of early navigational instruments: early Islamic astrolabes, 16th- and 17th-century European gilt-brass terrestrial globes of astonishing craftsmanship, and planispheric astrolabes. Flamsteed's downstairs living quarters can be seen, displayed with contemporary oak furniture, simple pewter utensils and a gently ticking brass bracket clock, but none of it Flamsteed's own. Upstairs is the spectacular **Octagon Room** (known by Flamsteed as his Octagonal Great or Star Room), Wren's fine, airy interior with tall windows suitable for observing the heavens through long telescopes. It appears today much as it did in an etching by Francis Place published in 1676, with its plasterwork ceiling with a frieze of roses, oak leaves and the royal arms, full-length portraits of Charles II and James II after Lely (the latter a copy of 1984), and Flamsteed's and other (18th-century) observational instruments set up against the windows. The three clocks, with 13-ft pendulums behind the walnut-grained wainscot, were used by Flamsteed for checking the regularity of the Earth's rotation. The original movements and dials were made by the great Thomas Tompion but in 1719, after Flamsteed's death, were sold by his widow (Flamsteed had paid for his own instruments). One was purchased by the British Museum in the 1920s and another was returned to the Observatory in 1994 and is displayed in a case with its movement and pendulum visible. Flamsteed's immense contribution to astronomical observation was published soon after his death (*Historia Coelestis Britannica*, 1725; *Atlas Coelestis*, 1729) and he is celebrated on the ceiling of Thornhill's Painted Hall (*see p. 171 above*).

From the Octagon Room stairs lead down to displays of historically important timepieces, the most important of which is the **'Search for Longitude'**. In separate cases are John Harrison's four ground-breaking marine chronometers (on loan from the

Hydrographer of the Navy), which changed maritime navigation forever. Instead of using the moon as an astronomical clock, Harrison, a Yorkshire carpenter and self-taught clockmaker, worked towards the perfection of a clock that would keep accurate time while on a temperature-variable rolling ship at sea. His first prototype, H1 (1730–35), was based on his early wooden clocks but was fitted with a temperature compensation device. It was followed by H2 in 1737–40, and H3 between 1740 and 1759. The latter can be seen in the background of Harrison's portrait by Thomas King, as well as the precision pocket watch made for him, according to his specifications, by John Jefferys. H4 was Harrison's triumphal marine timekeeper. In the form of a compact watch, inspired by the Jefferys watch, it has pivot-holes of rubies and pallets of diamonds. It was H4 that was awarded the £20,000 prize for solving the Longitude problem, which the Board of Longitude had been seeking to give away since 1714.

The Octagon Room is not truly aligned north–south and Flamsteed had made further astronomical observations from instruments fixed to the wall, 'trewly built in the meridian', in the courtyard. Early views of the Observatory show his 60-ft refracting telescope appearing above the courtyard wall. He also erected the northeast Summer House, his solar observatory, a Sextant House, for his seven-foot Equatorial Sextant, and a Quadrant House. The latter was added to by succeeding Astronomers Royal, Edmund Halley (d. 1742), of comet fame, and James Bradley. These buildings now make up the **Meridian Building**, where Mural Quadrants can be seen; Bradley's 12-ft Zenith Sector Telescope (1727); and successive Transit Instruments, culminating with Airy's Transit Circle. Observations made on the latter had the effect of moving the Greenwich Meridian 19ft east, the equivalent of .02 seconds, and its optical axis still defines the Greenwich Meridian. Inside the distinctive onion-shaped **Dome** of the Great Equatorial Building (built 1857) is Sir Howard Grubb's great 1893 28-inch refracting telescope which was used at Herstmonceaux until 1971 and then returned to Greenwich. In 1894–99 two further buildings, ornamental structures of red brick and terracotta, were added to the complex: the Altazimuth Pavilion and the South Building. They are currently closed for major redevelopment work, the Time and Space project, due for completion in Spring 2007, which will include a new, technologically more advanced **Planetarium**, galleries exploring modern astronomy, and an astronomy learning centre. In the meantime a temporary Planetarium has been erected in the Neptune Court of the National Maritime Museum, with regular shows presented by an astronomer.

MARTINWARE COLLECTION

Southall Library, Osterley Park Road, Southall, UB2 4BL
Tel: 020-8574 3412; www.artguide.org.uk
Open Mon, Fri, Sat 9–5; Tues–Thur 9–7.45; Sun 2–5
Free
Station: Southall (from Paddington)
Map p. 378, 3B

Displayed in a room on the first floor of the Library is an interesting display of the distinctive salt-glaze stoneware produced by the Martin brothers, Robert, Walter, Edwin and Charles, pioneers in the production of Victorian studio pottery. Robert, trained as a sculptor, was the founder of the firm in 1873, which moved from Fulham to Havelock Road, Southall, in 1877. Their extraordinary bird jars, with anthropomorphic expressions, are probably the most famous Martinware products but also on show are tiles, clockcases, teapots and reliefs, as well as vases and jugs. Photographs of the workshop and the brothers at work are also displayed. There is another, larger, collection of Martinware at Pitshanger Manor (*see p. 236*).

MUSEUM IN DOCKLANDS
(Museum of London)

No. 1 Warehouse, West India Quay, Hertsmere Road, E14 4AL
Tel: 0870 444 3857; www.museumindocklands.org.uk
Open daily 10–6
Admission charge
Tube: Canary Wharf; Station (DLR): West Ferry/West India Quay
Café, restaurant and shop
Map p. 379, 2E

A branch of the Museum of London, the Museum in Docklands opened in 2003. The idea originated with the Museum of London's record-gathering exercise during the demise of the main docks on the Isle of Dogs. The first purpose-built cargo-handling docks and warehouses in London were built here, at West India Quay in 1802. The museum now occupies the superb, three-storey, brick-built, wooden-floored Warehouse No. 1. Extended in 1827, for the next half-century the building was one of the city's largest tea warehouses, serving the East India trade and racing tea clipper ships. Later it was used to store sugar, dried fruit, molasses, shells, steel and canned fish. One of only two West India Quay warehouses to survive the Blitz, it was closed in 1968 and is now the only sizeable Georgian harbour warehouse preserved in the UK.

Floor Three
A visit begins here. 'Thames Highway' sketches the founding of *Londinium* in AD 43, illustrated by a first-century amphora for storing fish sauce or *garum*. Then follows the establishment of Saxon *Lundenwic* along the Strand around 600, evidence of the new settlement's troubles being a Viking battleaxe found in the river; and the development of *Lundenburgh* and medieval London up to 1600. Gaming pieces carved from walrus tusk from this period are shown, along with a meticulous scale model of the first London Bridge. 'Trade Expansion' then charts the rise of the port during the two centuries after 1600. The oil painting *Westminster Waterfront around 1771*, by William Marlowe, shows the Adam brothers' Adelphi block (the Royal Society of Arts; *see p.*

256) under construction, almost complete behind wharves busy with lighters and small sailing boats. The carved wooden figure of c. 1750 that can be seen here has been taken to represent the Native American Virginian Pocahontas—hence the tobacco-leaf skirt—and was probably used as a tobacconist's shop sign. An earlier survival from the period is the East India Company's coat of arms from 1618. This carved keystone coat of arms decorated the main gate of the Company's new yard at Blackwall after its move from Deptford in 1614, and was discovered by chance during the closure of the shipyard in 1988. 'Legal Quay' is a reconstruction of some of the different aspects of the late 18th-century docks, a counting house, beams and barrels complete with creaking woodwork and whistling stevedore sound effects. It introduces 'Execution Dock' and the display of an iron gibbet cage from around 1750, used to exhibit the decomposing corpses of condemned pirates. The *Rhinebeck Panorama* of 1806–11 (*pictured overleaf*), an eight-foot watercolour acquired by the museum in 1998, is recreated here, showing a bird's-eye view of the city towards the end of the 18th century. Painted on four panels, it was the work of three unknown artists, one of them a specialist in depicting ships, another in church towers and steeples. 'The Coming of the Docks' then illustrates the development of the first of the city's docks between 1796 and 1828. A key role was played by Trinity House, established since 1540 and responsible for navigation on the Thames. Possessing considerable influence as the sole agent with the right to sell ballast, the organization policed the river and went on to oversee the construction and maintenance of lighthouses around Britain's coast. Coloured aquatints by William Daniell show West India Docks and Poplar in 1802, Wapping in 1803. A large portrait by Sir Thomas Lawrence depicts George Hibbert in 1811, with his hand resting on plans for the docks. One of the first directors of the West India Dock Company, past agent for Jamaica, patron of the arts and editor of Ovid's *Metamorphoses*, Hibbert was a prominent Whig and friend of Prime Minister William Pitt, who laid the foundation stone of the docks in 1800.

Floors Two and One

The story of the period is expanded up to 1840 in 'City and River' on Floor Two. The construction of Warehouse No. 1 is described, followed by displays on the West Indian sugar plantations. The library table belonging to Thomas Fowell Buxton, MP for Weymouth, can be seen, upon which was drafted the abolition bill of the Anti-Slavery Society, founded in 1823. Slavery was finally abolished in 1834. Other displays cover the last Frost Fairs on the frozen river (*see p. 190*), the demolition of the medieval bridge, and construction of the new London Bridge in 1831. 'First Port of Empire 1840–1900' describes the role of London's docks at the heart of colonial trade. A large painting of *Tilbury Fort Wind against the Tide in 1849* by Clarkson Stanfield, an ex-seaman and theatre scenery artist, who also worked for the engineer Robert Stephenson, shows the hazards faced by small craft on the Thames. The worst ever maritime disaster in British coastal water involved the paddle steamer *Princess Alice*. In 1878, while returning from the Rosherville pleasure gardens in Gravesend, the steamer was practically cut in half by the steam collier *Bywell Castle*, killing 640 pas-

The 18th-century *Rhinebeck Panorama* (artists unknown), showing shipping on the Thames.

sengers. A celebrated subject of sombre fascination to the Victorians, the *Princess Alice*'s nameplate can be seen here, along with a macabre model illustrating the moment before impact. A showcase of unusual Thames shipwrights' tools introduces a 1:96 scale model of the paddle steamer *Great Eastern*. Five thousand hours in the building, capable of steaming to Australia without re-coaling, she laid the first two transatlantic telegraph cables between Ireland and Newfoundland. She was ready for sea at Millwall on 5 September 1859; her designer, Isambard Kingdom Brunel, was photographed hatless on her deck days before he collapsed from a stroke. 'Warehouse

MUSEUM OF GARDEN HISTORY **187**

of the World 1890–1939' includes a reconstruction of the Dock Warehouse office originally on the ground floor of the museum's building. The first and second floors were entirely given over to tea handling from 1834–82. A tea weighing station is shown and a small display covers Joseph Conrad and the *Torrens*, showing a model of the square-rigger that he called 'a good seaboat in heavy weather', and on which he was first mate while writing his first novel *Almayer's Folly*.

On Floor One, accessible from here, is the Thames Gallery, presenting an array of working and pleasure boats, ship models and reconstructed premises relating to the river from 1850 until 1950. Antique skiffs and peter-boats evoke the heyday of pleasure boating in the 1920s and 30s. Models of bawley-boats, barges, tugs and coasters are a reminder of some of the different types of working vessel that used the port at its busiest, in 1935, as many as 1,000 of them each week.

Back on Floor Two, the story of the port continues with 'Docklands at War', describing the devastation of the area by enemy action in 1940–45. The work of the war artists, especially William Ware (1915–97), illustrates the displays, along with artefacts such as a molten iron girder, wartime testimonials and archive film. *Rotherhithe in 1933* by Duncan Grant shows the river scene before the bombing, probably sketched from the terrace of the Mayflower public house. 'New Port New City' describes the recession that hit the docks in the 1950s; the Enterprise zone set up under the auspices of the London Docklands Development Corporation in 1981; and the coming of the Docklands Light Railway.

On the Ground Floor is the Mudlarks Gallery, a very popular interactive play area with a vaguely riparian theme for the under-12s. The Chris Ellmers Gallery stages temporary exhibitions.

MUSEUM OF GARDEN HISTORY

Lambeth Palace Road, SE1 7LB
Tel: 020-7401 8865; www.museumgardenhistory.org
Open daily 10.30–5 (closed mid-Dec–early Jan)
Free (but donations suggested)
Café and shop
Tube: Lambeth North/Westminster
Map p. 382, 4B

Located in the deconsecrated church of St Mary, beside the Tudor gatehouse of Lambeth Palace, the London residence of the Archbishop of Canterbury, the Museum of Garden History was founded in 1977 by the late John and Rosemary Nicholson, thus narrowly rescuing the church from demolition. It was the tomb of the Tradescant family in the graveyard that gave the Nicholsons the idea to create a museum dedicated exclusively to garden history—the first of its kind in the world. John Tradescant the Elder (1570–1638) was gardener to Robert Cecil, the first Lord Salisbury, at

Hatfield House, and later to Charles I and his consort Henrietta Maria at Oaklands, being sent on several plant-gathering trips to France. His son, John Tradescant the Younger (1608–62), was enrolled as a freeman of the Worshipful Company of Gardeners in 1634 and three years later made the first of three voyages to Virginia, bringing back the tulip tree, Michaelmas daisy and Virginia creeper, among other plants and shrubs. The family collection of curiosities became the basis of Oxford's Ashmolean Museum whose founder, Elias Ashmole, is also buried here. The elegant Coade Stone (see p. 174) tomb of Admiral William Bligh (d. 1817), best known as the captain of the mutinous HMS Bounty, stands next to that of the Tradescants. Bligh was engaged on a prize-winning mission to transplant the first breadfruit trees to the West Indies from Otaheite (now Tahiti), as an alternative food source for sugar plantation slaves after American independence threatened the usual supplies. After the mutiny, he and his men were obliged to navigate 3,600 miles by sextant in an open boat for 41 days, living off raw fish, turtles and seabirds.

In 1981, the small graveyard beneath the walls of Lambeth Palace was planted with a knot garden designed by Lady Salisbury to a pattern popular in the early 17th century, the square within a circle representing heaven on earth. All the plants and shrubs, many introduced to Britain by the Tradescants, were donated by nurserymen from around the country and are carefully labelled with their botanical and common names, first recorded date, area of origin and family.

Inside the church, the themed display explores the development of gardens down the ages, and includes material on Joseph Banks (1743–1820), the first professional plant hunter. Banks (see p. 127) accompanied Captain Cook aboard HMS Endeavour, and named Botany Bay. Artefacts illustrating the history of gardening include a Tudor watering thumbpot, late 19th-century walking-stick tools, a collection of early garden gnomes, including one perched on a swing dated 1910, antique pottery by Doulton of Lambeth, and the hand-painted jardinière of Ellen Willmott, the first woman member of the Linnaean Society. In the church porch can be seen the tomb of William Bacon of the Salt Office, London, 'killed by thunder and lightning in his window, July 12, 1787 aged 34 years'. The north transept is given over to a vegetarian café serving wholesome hot meals throughout the day.

MUSEUM OF LONDON

London Wall, EC2Y 5HN
Tel: 0870 444 3852; www.museumoflondon.org.uk
Open Mon–Sat 10–5.50; Sun 12–5.50
Free
Tube: Barbican/St Paul's
Café and shop
Map p. 383, 1D

The Museum of London is a 1976 amalgamation of two collections: that of the London Museum, which opened in 1912 in a part of Kensington Palace, and the much older Guildhall Museum, founded by the Corporation of London in 1826, originally housed at the Guildhall. Both institutions had similar collections, mainly archaeological, with other artefacts relating to the history of London. By the early 20th century one of the chief roles of the Guildhall Museum was the overseeing of archaeological excavation within the City: its collection was especially rich in Roman and medieval artefacts revealed as a result of London's constant redevelopment. The London Museum, too, had a wide range of material dating from London's earliest beginnings to modern times. Its inaugural displays included early tools, toys, pictures, torture implements, porcelain, costume, 'a milk tooth of a Mammoth found in Pall Mall' and a 'washing bowl from the Condemned cell, Newgate Prison'. For its brief move to Lancaster House in 1914, models of the 1666 Great Fire and a Frost Fair on the Thames were commissioned, still in the collection today. The decision to unite the two collections was taken in 1961. The awkward new building (Powell & Moya 1968–76), white-tiled above and of black bricks below, occupies a site on the edge of the Barbican complex, in a heavily bombed and bleakly re-planned part of the City. The entrance, not immediately obvious, is on the Aldersgate/London Wall roundabout, either up the spiral stairs to the overhead walkway above the roundabout, or the new entrance at street level. The latter is part of a recent scheme to improve the building, which added a new entrance foyer and exhibition space, and will eventually include extra gallery space. The museum is constructed very close to sections of the old Roman Wall, which once defined the city limits: occasional windows overlook the ancient remains.

The Displays

The museum has over 1.1 million objects pertaining to the physical and social history of London, from its prehistory origins, its Roman, Saxon and Medieval past, through to its more recent history, from Tudor times to the present day. The museum also has a vast archaeological archive, archaeological excavation being an essential part of the museum's work: the London Archaeological Archive & Research Centre (LAARC) is an independent branch of the museum. The displays, which incorporate salvaged period interiors and interior reconstructions, follow a chronological sequence over two floors, the upper level forming a gallery around the lower.

Prehistory ('London Before London') covers the period c. 400,000 BC–AD 50, with flint hand axes, Mesolithic tools and other items used by the people of the Thames Valley. There is a display of bronze weaponry dredged from the river and a 5,640–5,100 year-old skeleton, with a facial reconstruction alongside it, one of the oldest people to have been discovered in the London area. **Roman London** explores *Londinium*, the first city on the site, which bridged the Thames and was the largest city in Roman Britain. Craftsman's tools and jewellery (including a beautiful emerald necklace with gold links) are shown, as well as items from the museum's rich collection of Samian pottery, produced in France and shipped to London. A reconstructed interior incorporates a 3rd-century AD mosaic floor discovered in Bucklersbury in

1869, one of over 30 floors excavated from London sites. A mid-2nd-century AD wall painting, with Cupid in a columned architectural setting, from a Roman bath house, was discovered on the site of Winchester Palace, Southwark. The marble sculptures from the Temple of Mithras are major items discovered on the site of Bucklersbury House in 1954. The bust of Mithras himself dates to 180–220 AD; Mercury sitting on his rock to the 2nd century AD. Artefacts from **Saxon London** include jewellery, glassware and pottery and a hoard of Viking-age weapons discovered close to the site of the Saxon London Bridge. A c. 886 King Alfred the Great silver penny is on show, and a 7th-century brooch of garnets set in gold discovered in a grave in Floral Street, Covent Garden. An 11th-century grave slab, beautifully carved with a lion and serpent in battle and with a Norse runic inscription, was possibly part of a tomb of an individual connected to the court of King Canute.

Items from **Medieval London** underline the cultural flowering of the capital and its extensive overseas mercantile links. Pilgrim badges are on show, mementoes brought back from holy shrines, the most popular being that of St Thomas à Becket at Canterbury. The leather shoes with long pointed toes, the points kept stiff with stuffing, were fashionable in London in the 1380s. The **Tudor and Early Stuart** display includes early views of London: a c. 1559 copper plate map, the earliest known of the city, and a painting showing London's myriad church spires, the skyline dominated by the mass of old St Paul's. The palace buildings of Henry VIII–Charles I are explored; there is a reconstruction of a Jacobean bedchamber; and a model of the Rose Theatre. The remarkable Cheapside Hoard is a collection of over 230 pieces of jewellery recovered in 1912 from the site of Wakefield House, probably part of a goldsmith's trade stock. The Tangye collection of items relating to Oliver Cromwell includes his Bible, funeral escutcheon and death mask. Dirck Stoop's important painting shows Charles II's processional route through the City following his triumphal Restoration in 1660. Mortality bills from the time of the 1665 Great Plague can be seen, as well as paintings of the Great Fire which raged through the City in 1666. The Great Fire Experience combines models, lighting effects and sound, including a voice-over of Samuel Pepys' first-hand account of events.

The displays continue on the lower level with **Late Stuart London** and the modern city that rose from the 1666 ashes, directed by the great Sir Christopher Wren, architect of the new St Paul's Cathedral and several of the City churches. The City became home to wealthy merchants and financiers, made rich through the great trading companies and the emerging financial market: the interior from Poyle Park, with its painted allegorical ceiling and carved panelling, indicates the degree of comfort such families enjoyed. Abraham Hondius' 1677 painting shows the frozen Thames, a common occurrence in the 17th century and an opportunity for Frost Fairs, when booths and stalls were set up on the ice.

Eighteenth-Century London concentrates on the cosmopolitan nature of the city. It was a centre for luxury trades, such as silk weaving centred on Spitalfields. Period costumes are on show, elaborately embroidered waistcoats and dresses, such as that made for Ann Fanshawe c. 1752–53 when her father was Lord Mayor of London.

Panorama of Moorgate after the Blitz. From the collection of wartime material to go on display in the Museum of London's new 20th-century Gallery.

Items relating to the social side of polite society are on display (tea drinking; the theatre) as well as the harsher side of life in the capital. Carved panelling from Wellclose Square prison is on show, with inscriptions scored by its inmates. The elaborate Lord Mayor's Coach, with Rococo carving and painted allegorical scenes on its doors attributed to Cipriani (who also decorated the Gold State Coach; *see p. 254*), was commissioned in 1757 and is still used for the annual Lord Mayor's Procession.

London as a **World City** covers the period 1789–1914, a period which witnessed unprecedented growth (London's population rose from one to seven million) and the capital's expansion into the world's first metropolis. Personal items of Britain's great heroes are on show: Wellington's boots and hat, and Nelson's jewel-encrusted sword. Paintings capture scenes of London life, such as George Elgar Hicks' *The General Post Office: One Minute to Six* (1860), showing the rush of customers before closing time, and George William Joy's well known *Bayswater Omnibus* (1895). Items from the Great Exhibition are on show, as are theatre bills, music hall programmes and items relating to the Suffragette movement, such as a 1914 photograph of Sylvia Pankhurst being arrested. The Victorian Walk is a succession of salvaged shop fronts and signs, and reconstructed interiors include Barings Bank c. 1853. The seedier side of the city, and social reform, is explored, including photographs and paintings of poverty and hardship, such as Gustave Doré's *A Poor House* (c. 1869). Items from the museum's large photography collection and sound archive are shown throughout the displays.

The museum's London story currently ends in 1914, although a new 20th-century gallery is planned, which will show the extensive collection of 20th-century material: images and objects relating to London's experience of wartime; its post-war recovery, including a model of the 1951 South Bank Exhibition site, part of the Festival of Britain; London's printing trade, formerly concentrated on Fleet Street; and items relating to the rise of shopping: an Art Deco lift from Selfridges and a mid-20th-century Woolworth's counter.

MUSEUM NO. I
(Royal Botanic Gardens)

Kew, Richmond, Surrey, TW9 3AB
Tel: 020-8332 5655; www.rbgkew.org uk
Open daily from 9.30; closing time varies according to season (approx. 4pm in winter, 6pm in summer)
Admission charge
Tube: Kew Gardens
Cafés and shop
Map p. 378, 3C

Looking out across the Kew Gardens lake towards Decimus Burton's graceful Palm House is another, more austere, Neoclassical building also designed by Burton, known as Museum No. 1. Opened in 1857, it was the second home for the Museum of Economic Botany, founded in 1841 by Sir William Hooker when he became Director of the Royal Botanic Gardens. He held that post until 1865, and the display of his core teaching collection of specimen textiles, gums, dyes and timber was intended to complement the living plants in the gardens. A protégé of Sir Joseph Banks (*see p. 127*), who sent Captain Bligh on his ill-fated expedition to transport breadfruit aboard *HMS Bounty* (*see p. 188*), Hooker had a particular interest in the economic usefulness of plants. The museum was the first of its kind in the world, and the collections grew rapidly, with contributions encouraged from all corners of the Empire. Many, such as an intricate Hindu temple carved out of vegetable ivory, were also received from the Great Exhibition of 1851. The famous expeditions undertaken by explorers like Richard Spruce in South America and Dr Livingstone in Africa also donated a variety of exotic artefacts. Burton's new building was purpose-built, with as many windows as possible on each elevation to illuminate the showcases with natural light. By 1987, when the museum was closed for extensive refurbishment, the collections contained over 70 thousand different plants and plant products, making them not only the oldest but also the most comprehensive of their type in the world.

Curated by the Centre for Economic Botany, they now concentrate on wild and little cultivated plants, especially from Europe and the dry tropics. Museum No. 1 reopened in 1998 and visitors can now see two rooms on the ground floor, one small part of a visit to the Royal Botanic Gardens themselves.

The first room is given over to a contemporary exhibition entitled 'Plants and People' in themed showcases illustrating changing selections from the museum's collections. The central cabinet contains items chosen by staff at Kew Gardens, such as the cannibal fork and dish collected from the island of Fiji and made from dark *merbau*, a timber native to southeast Asia and the Pacific. This is the place to discover how the potato was originally developed for domestic consumption by the Incas of Peru, to see a superior brick of Chinese tea, or a very delicate lace-like collar spun from the hair of the milkweed fruit in Jamaica.

The second, smaller, room provides an introduction to the history of Kew's economic botany collections, briefly exploring the study of plants useful to people, explaining how the collections have grown over the past century and a half, and how they have been exhibited.

MUSEUM OF THE ORDER OF ST JOHN

St John's Gate, St John's Lane, Clerkenwell, EC1M 4DA
Tel: 020-7324 4070; www.sja.org.uk/history
Open Mon–Fri 10–5, Sat 10–4. Tours on Tues, Fri, Sat at 11 and
2.30. Only groups need pre-book
Free (except tours). Limited disabled access
Tube: Farringdon
Shop
Map p. 383, 1D

The castellated gatehouse spanning St John's Lane once formed the main entrance of the Grand Priory of the Order of the Hospital of St John of Jerusalem (the Knights Hospitaller of the Crusades), founded around 1113. Built shortly after that date, the priory was burnt down by Wat Tyler's Peasants' Revolt in the late 14th century, and rebuilt in something resembling its present form by Prior Thomas Docwra in 1504. The Order was one of the last to be suppressed by Henry VIII (in 1540). The king then used the gatehouse for storing tents and hunting equipment. Refounded as a Protestant Order in 1831, the British Order of St John purchased St John's Gate in 1874 and started to form a library and museum from 1888. The museum now features three galleries exploring the history of the building, the work of St John's Ambulance, and the Order of St John.

The Galleries

'Gateway to a Lost Palace' is arranged chronologically, occupying the saloon bar of the

17th-century Old Jerusalem Tavern, little altered structurally since that time. William Hogarth lived here as a young man, hence his caricature of John Wilkes as the 'champion of liberty' that can be seen here. Shortly afterwards, from 1731, the building was used by Edward Cave to publish and print the *Gentleman's Magazine*. Cave gave Samuel Johnson his first job, writing parliamentary reports for the new magazine, and received visitors such as David Garrick and Oliver Goldsmith. A copy of the *Gentleman's Magazine* from May 1738 and a copy of Dr Johnson's Dictionary, opened at M for Magazine, are displayed. Antique letters patent can also be seen, one dated 1557 by Queen Mary Tudor and King Philip of Spain restoring the Order's possessions after the Dissolution, and another dated 1422 by Henry V, exempting the Knights Hospitaller from tax.

'Time to Care' is a multimedia exhibition on the history of St John's Ambulance, from 1877 to the present day. The 'Order Gallery' displays precious artefacts relating to the Hospitallers, exploring their medical, religious and military roles. Here is the 'Rhodes Missal', a finely illuminated manuscript presented by a French Prior to the Conventual Church in Rhodes in 1504, on which the knights swore their vows of profession. Other remarkable artworks include the *Weston Triptych*, formerly the altarpiece in the Grand Priory Church, recovered in 1932, now comprising two wings of a Flemish triptych, one bearing the arms of John Weston (Prior 1476–89); and a small oil-on-copper of *The Annunciation* by Luigi Gentile in a fine silver frame, probably to a design by Alessandro Algardi. It was commissioned by Pope Innocent X, whose arms are engraved on the verso of the copper plaque. Several suits of armour worn by the Knights can also be seen here, most of Italian manufacture, as well as a bronze cannon given to Grand Master Delisle Adam by Henry VIII to help recover the island of Rhodes from the Turks. It was recovered from the sea off Famagusta in 1907. In 1530 the Order was given the island of Malta by the Holy Roman Emperor Charles V. Some of the banners captured by Napoleon when he conquered the island in 1798 can be seen here.

MUSEUM OF RUGBY

Twickenham Stadium, Rugby Road, Twickenham, Middlesex, TW1 1DZ
Tel: 020-8892 8877; www.rfu.com
Open Tues–Sat and bank holidays 10–5, Sun 11–5
Admission charge (covers museum and tour of the stadium; no tours on match days)
Station: Twickenham (from Waterloo)
Café and shop
Map p. 378, 3B

The Rugby Football Union was founded in 1871, as a result of an initiative by Edwin Ash, the secretary of Richmond Rugby Club, to standardise the rules of the game. A large market garden was bought at Twickenham by the RFU in 1907; initially it was known as 'Billy Williams's Cabbage Patch', after the committee member who had promoted the purchase of the land in the face of fierce opposition. The museum, which opened in 1996, is a state-of-the-art piece of museum design, introduced by a reconstructed 'line-out', with fully interactive multimedia coverage of the history of the game, the RFU, and individual clubs and players. Mementoes include early match programmes, the Calcutta Cup, and an 1871 England jersey. The tour of the stadium includes the England dressing rooms, the players' tunnel, Council Chamber, and Royal Box.

MUSICAL MUSEUM

High Street, Brentford, TW8 0BD
Tel: 020-8560 8108; www.musicalmuseum.co.uk
Station: Kew Bridge (from Waterloo)
Map p. 378, 3C

NB: At the time of writing the museum was closed for removal to new premises.
The Musical Museum is a remarkable collection of some 200 19th- and 20th-century automatic playing instruments. Many are in working order, and include pianolas, barrel organs, musical boxes, automatic violins, orchestrions and the only self-playing Wurlitzer organ in Europe. Their often exotic appearance and strange names—the Hupfeld Phonoliszt Violina, for example—recall a lost age of mechanical music-making.

NATIONAL ARMY MUSEUM

Royal Hospital Road, Chelsea, SW3 4HT
Tel: 020-7730 0717; www.national-army-museum.ac.uk
Open daily 10.30–5
Free
Tube: Sloane Square
Café and shop
Map p. 380, 4C

Founded at the Royal Military Academy, Sandhurst, in 1960, the official museum of the British Army moved to these purpose-built premises in 1971. The museum illustrates, celebrates and records the history of the army from 1415 to the present day, with particular emphasis on important engagements and soldiers' day-to-day lives, employing a wide range of artefacts, especially paintings, prints and uniforms, but also models, reconstructed scenes, antique weapons and archive film.

Lower ground floor: Redcoats: The British Soldier 1415–1792

The display introduces the story with the museum's oldest artefact, a bronze cannon or 'saker' mounted on a replica gun carriage, as it might have been at the siege of Boulogne in 1544. Early artillery pieces were often named after birds of prey, in this case a large falcon. Nearby there's the opportunity to feel the weight of the chain mail worn at the time.

Displays on the Civil War dispel some of the myths surrounding Cavaliers and Roundheads: neither in fact wore uniform, so distinguishing their allegiance was often difficult. Sometimes nothing more obvious than a hat ribbon denoted it, with predictably disastrous consequences. Two paintings by Jan Wyck hang here: *King William and his Army at the Siege of Namur* (1695) and *The Battle of the Boyne* (1690), as well as an eye-witness record of one of the earliest formal musterings of the British Army, a detailed sepia pen-and-ink wash by Willem van der Velde the Elder from 1687–89. Contemporary prints and portraits continue the story, alongside uniforms, including one worn by an officer at the Battle of Blenheim, the pivotal engagement of the War of the Spanish Succession (1704), and a collection of hand-embroidered British Grenadier caps. Others illustrate the Seven Years War of 1756–63. A scale model towards the end of the displays depicts the siege of Yorktown in October 1781. The surrender of General Charles Lord Cornwallis' 8,000-strong army to 20,000 American and French troops under George Washington and the Comte de Rochambeau marked the effective end of the American War of Independence, 1775–83.

First floor: The Road to Waterloo 1793–1815

This charts the army's role in the struggle against Revolutionary and Napoleonic France. Paintings include *A Rifleman in the 95th Regiment*, demonstrating this new type of soldier's dressed-down khaki uniform during the Peninsular War, and a portrait by Sir Thomas Lawrence of Lt Gen. Sir John Moore (1805). Commissioned into the 51st regiment in 1776, John Moore saw service in the American Revolution, spent six years as a Whig MP, served in Corsica, the West Indies, Ireland, Holland and Egypt, and established a training camp at Shorncliffe for Light Infantry. In 1808 he was given command of the army in Portugal. The next year his defensive action at Corunna (La Coruña, northwest Spain) cost him his own life along with that of many of his men, but allowed an army of more than 25,000 to be safely evacuated from the Peninsula. He lives on in the lines of the famous poem: 'Not a drum was heard, not a funeral note, as his corse to the rampart we hurried'. Also here is a tattered Regimental colour from the bloody Battle of Albuera in 1811.

The highlights of the gallery are the **skeleton of Napoleon's horse, Marengo**, and Captain Siborne's **scale model of the battle of Waterloo**. The model was completed in 1838 after eight years of research, and shows the battle at its crisis point, at around 7pm, using some 70,000 figures, one for every two men present on the day. Some controversy surrounded the model's first exhibition, with government support having been withdrawn and the Duke of Wellington staying away, although not actually condemning Siborne's efforts. He had originally approved of the scheme, with the caveat that the model was unlikely to be accurate, observing that 'After all, a battle is like a ball: they keep footing it all the day'. His comments undermine the suggestion that he was offended by the fact that the model portrays the moment that the Prussians saved the day. Mild controversy has also attached itself to the gallery's other highlight, with an article displayed here suggesting that Marengo was a generic name for several of Napoleon's horses and that there can be no certainty that the skeleton displayed here is that of his favourite. The skeleton does without doubt belong to one of the Emperor's horses; nevertheless its true provenance is likely to remain as mysterious as the snuffboxes displayed alongside it, which claim to be made from Marengo's hooves.

On the same floor, **The Victorian Soldier 1816–1914** charts the history of the army's role in expanding and defending the British Empire. A magnificent Sudanese helmet of Persian inspiration can be seen, recovered from the terrible slaughter at the Battle of Omdurman in 1898. Several paintings dramatise the wars against the Zulus.

Second floor: From World War to Cold War

This section is introduced by a diorama showing an episode during the Battle of Mons in 1914, called '15 rounds a minute'. There are displays on the Christmas Truce of 1914, Ypres, the Gallipoli campaign, and the Battle of the Somme, illustrated by a Vickers machine gun. Reconstructed walk-through scenes include a First World War trench and dug-out, and a Malayan jungle patrol, which introduces the Second World War galleries. A Russian PPSH 41 submachine gun recovered from North Korea can be seen, the standard weapon of the Red Army infantryman after 1942.

Third floor: The Modern Army

The display covers operations in Africa, Aden and Cyprus, the Falklands, Northern Ireland and Bosnia among other centres of operations, and features a variety of interactive exhibits illustrating soldiering skills such as range-finding, the daily lives of a contemporary tank crew, and photographs from the recent war in Iraq.

In one large room beyond, the **Art Gallery** displays the museum's collection of portraits and oil paintings, most illustrating celebrated soldiers or important engagements. They are arranged in broadly chronological order, beginning to the left of the entrance with portraits of Lord Protector Oliver Cromwell, and King James II. A portrait by Benjamin West depicts the *Honourable Robert Monckton at the taking of the Martinique* (1762). Monckton was Wolfe's second-in-command at Quebec in 1759. While Governor of New York from 1761 to 1763, he chose the young American artist to record this pinnacle of his career for posterity. The painting launched West's career in England, with such success that in 1792 he succeeded Joshua Reynolds as President of Royal Academy. John Wootton's *King George II at the Battle of Dettingen 1743* celebrates the last occasion when a reigning British monarch led his troops into battle. Francis Rawdon Hastings, created 2nd Earl of Moira, Governor General in chief of the Forces in India, in 1813, was painted by Sir Henry Raeburn. Hastings left the bizarre instructions in his will that his right hand should be amputated and preserved after his death to be laid in his wife's coffin. *The Reception of the Mysorean Hostage Princes by Marquis Cornwallis, 25 February 1792* is a large oil painting by Robert Home. It depicts a decisive moment in the conquest of India, when Governor General Lord Cornwallis received as hostages the sons of Tipu Sultan (*see p. 333*) as part of the peace settlement following the Third Mysore War (1790–92). The artist, who accompanied Cornwallis on his campaigns, making numerous sketches, was probably actually present at the occasion, and indeed included himself in the painting, in the crowd on the extreme left. The large portrait of George III by George Beechey, 1798, showing the king on his favourite horse, Adonis, is a smaller version of the one commissioned by George III that was lost in the Windsor Castle fire in 1992.

Several paintings also illustrate military misfortunes. The striking *Captain Colin Mackenzie of the Madras Army lately taken hostage in Caubool in his Affghan dress* (1842), by James Sant, depicts the Assistant Political Agent at Peshawar sent to Kabul in 1840, during the First Afghan War, and taken hostage by Akbar Khan. One of the most popular paintings in the gallery is the *Battle of Isandlwana* (1885) by Charles Fripp, illustrating one of the worst disasters to befall the army in the late 19th century, when the 24th regiment was massacred by some 20,000 Zulus. On a more positive note, the dramatic *Buller's Final Crossing of the Tugela* depicts a key moment in February 1900 during the relief of Ladysmith. *The Relief of Ladysmith on 27th February 1900*, by John H. Bacon, is known as the 'Bovril War Picture', because photogravures of the painting were offered free in 1901 to purchasers of 21 shillings-worth of Bovril.

NATIONAL GALLERY

Trafalgar Square, WC2N 5DN
Tel: 020-7747 2885; www.nationalgallery.org.uk
Open daily 10–6 (Wed until 9pm)
Free
Tube: Charing Cross/Leicester Square
Restaurant, café and two shops. On-line shop
Map p. 382, 3A

The National Gallery's collection of Western European art, spanning the period c. 1250–1900, is one of the finest in the world. The Italian early and high Renaissance collection is particularly rich, with countless works of international significance; there are important early Netherlandish works; major holdings of 17th-century Dutch and Flemish masters, including Rembrandt, Rubens and van Dyck; notable works by the French masters Claude and Poussin, as well as a significant collection of French Impressionist pictures. Although Tate Britain is the official home of British art (*see p. 288*), the National Gallery also has some seminal masterpieces of the British School, which hold their own alongside Continental works.

History of the Gallery

Compared with other European national galleries, London's was established relatively late, in 1824. Various earlier moves to found a gallery had come to nothing, but in the 1820s the artist and collector Sir George Beaumont (1753–1827) offered to the nation his collection of pictures, with two provisos: that the government purchase for the nation one of the finest private collections in London, the collection of the wealthy banker John Julius Angerstein; and that suitable accommodation be found for it. In April 1824 Parliament voted to pay £57,000 for Angerstein's 38 Italian, Dutch, Flemish and British works, the core of the National Gallery's collection. Sebastiano del Piombo's magnificent altarpiece, *The Raising of Lazarus*, was officially the first work to enter the collection (it has the accession number NG1), along with Raphael's *Pope Julius II*; Rembrandt's *Woman Taken in Adultery*; and some fine Claudes. Angerstein's collection had fulfilled the government's desire for 'large pictures of eminence', but instead of in a purpose-built gallery, they were displayed in three rooms of Angerstein's former London home, 100 Pall Mall. In 1826 they were joined there by Beaumont's own 16 pictures, a much smaller collection but one which contained several masterpieces: Canaletto's excellent *The Stonemason's Yard*; Rubens' *View of Het Steen* (Beaumont considered Rubens 'the Shakespeare of painting'); and, a reflection of the taste of the times, further Claude landscapes including Beaumont's personal favourite, *Landscape with Hagar and the Angel*, which travelled with him whenever he left London for his country home. In face of public criticism of the National Gallery's inadequate accommodation (100 Pall Mall was hardly the Louvre), the government agreed in 1831 to construct a building on the north side of the new Trafalgar Square, on the site of the old Royal Mews.

The Building

Built between 1833 and 1838 by William Wilkins, the building is dignified but somehow not imposing, its long façade punctuated with a central portico with Corinthian columns, a dome and further porticoes to east and west with column bases and capitals salvaged from the recently demolished Carlton House.

At first the National Gallery occupied only the west side of the new building, the Royal Academy having the east. But in 1868 the latter removed to Burlington House (*see p. 244*), allowing expansion for the gallery's growing collection. In 1845 Robert Vernon had bequeathed his large collection of British works, followed in 1851 by J.M.W. Turner's overwhelming bequest of over 1,000 of his own watercolours, drawings and oils. Both these collections had to be displayed elsewhere, at Marlborough House and then at the new South Kensington Museum (*see V&A, p. 315*). In 1871 the collection of the late Prime Minister, Sir Robert Peel, came to the gallery, a distinguished assembly of mainly Dutch and Flemish pictures, including Hobbema's supreme *Avenue at Middelharnis*, and Rubens' *Chapeau de Paille*. Since its foundation— and particularly from 1855, with the appointment of Sir Charles Eastlake as Director—the gallery had also been making acquisitions of its own. Eastlake travelled throughout Italy purchasing important works, mainly early Italian 'Primitives'.

A new east wing extension was added to the back of Wilkins' building. Designed by

E.M. Barry and completed in 1876, the suite of galleries was opulent and rich. Recently restored to their period glory, the central octagonal **Rotunda** (Room 36) has green Genoa marble columns, a coloured marble floor, walls of burgundy, green and blue, with white and gilded plasterwork and a domed ceiling of etched glass panels. Between 1885 and 1887 Sir John Taylor added further architecturally important spaces: the **Central Hall**, also recently restored to its Victorian splendour, with richly coloured Venetian wall fabric; and the grand Staircase Hall, an important Victorian space, originally with rich plasterwork, pink stone cladding and polychromatic decoration by J.D. Crace. At the time of writing the latter was closed for restoration, as was Wilkins' Entrance Hall, allowing for only partial viewing of the four Boris Anrep **Mosaic Pavements**, commissioned in 1928–33. The foremost mosaicist working in Britain, Anrep's themes were *The Labours of Life* (west vestibule, 1928), *The Pleasures of Life* (east vestibule, 1929) and *The Awakening of the Muses* (half-landing, 1933). *Modern Virtues* (north vestibule) followed later, in 1952. Portraits of famous British arts figures are incorporated, such as Augustus John (who appears as Neptune); Margot Fonteyn (Delectation); Edith Sitwell (Sixth Sense); and Bertrand Russell (Lucidity).

With the opening in 1897 of the National Gallery, Millbank, built with funds from the wealthy industrialist Sir Henry Tate for the display of British art (now Tate Britain; *see Tate, p. 287*) further space was released at Trafalgar Square, which was further added to in 1907–11 with new galleries behind Wilkins' west wing; and the building of the Northern Extension in 1970–75. More recently, in 1991, the **Sainsbury Wing** was completed to designs by Venturi, Rauch and Scott, who won the commission after the original scheme, the winner of an architectural competition, was famously denounced by the Prince of Wales as a 'monstrous carbuncle on the face of a much loved friend'. In a modern classical style which acknowledges Wilkins' building, the new wing's main feature is a giant, broad and tall staircase which rises from the entrance foyer up to the main gallery level, with views over Trafalgar Square. Below is the gallery's main temporary exhibition space. The most recent architectural intervention is the new Getty entrance and foyer (Dixon/Jones 2004), which allows entry directly from Trafalgar Square, rather than up the main portico stairs. The sharp white staircase with glossy black wall cladding (a rather undistinguished, corporate look) leads to the main level.

Entrance to the National Gallery has always been free. Even during the Second World War, when the collection was removed for safety to old mining caves in Wales, one masterpiece per month was shown at the gallery, at risk in the capital alongside Londoners. During its evacuation, much scholarly study of the collection was undertaken, resulting in published catalogues which set the international standard (*see p. 133*). The National Gallery is too large to see in full at one visit. Below, ordered by date and school, are the major highlights, many of which are long-established favourites.

Agnolo Bronzino's *Allegory of Venus and Cupid* (c. 1550).

The Collection

1250–1500 (Sainsbury Wing; Rooms 51–66)

The early Renaissance collection is shown in the Sainsbury Wing, the elaborate architectural frames, rich colours and punched gold leaf of the pictures set off against pale grey walls. In the early years, collecting had concentrated on Italian high Renaissance pictures (*see Italy 1500–1600, below*) but by the mid-19th century it was felt that the gallery should aim to be a complete historical collection rather than a collection of select masterpieces. Reflecting the 19th-century taste for the Gothic, Giotto was set as the starting date, and early Italian, German and Netherlandish works were actively sought. The gallery's first Director, Sir Charles Eastlake, travelled throughout Italy annually and was instrumental in acquiring major early Italian works, then known as 'Primitives', including a panel from Uccello's *Battle of San Romano*. In 1863 Queen Victoria presented a collection of early Renaissance works.

Italy: Among the earliest works are Margarito of Arezzo's 1260s Byzantine icon-like *Virgin and Child* (Room 52), the earliest Italian work in the collection, acquired by Eastlake to demonstrate 'the rude beginnings' from which Italian art grew; Giotto's *Pentecost* (Room 52), one of seven panels from an altarpiece now scattered around the world; and Duccio's *Annunciation* and *Jesus Opens the Eyes of a Blind Man* (Room 52), predella panels from his masterwork, the *Maestà*, the high altarpiece of Siena Cathedral, completed in 1311. Not Italian, but displayed with these pictures, is the outstanding *Wilton Diptych* (c. 1395; Room 53), the highpoint of painting to survive from medieval England. Possibly of French authorship, it shows Richard II being presented to the Virgin and Child, accompanied by St John, St Edmund and St Edward the Confessor.

Tuscan art 1400–50 (Room 54) includes Lorenzo Monaco's brilliantly coloured *Coronation of the Virgin* (c. 1414); the only documented painting by Masaccio, the 1426 *Virgin and Child*, part of the altarpiece for the chapel of Santa Maria del Carmine, Pisa; works by Sassetta, one of Siena's leading artists of the early 15th century; and Fra' Angelico's *Christ Glorified in the Court of Heaven* (before 1435), with its ranks of angels. Early Florentine works include Fra' Filippo Lippi's *Annunciation*, possibly part of bedchamber furniture from the Palazzo Medici, the dove hovering before the Virgin's womb in a glittering holy sphere; Uccello's *Battle of San Romano* (Room 55), also from the Palazzo Medici, showing the mercenary general Niccolò da Tolentino in a magnificent headdress, on a rearing white charger (the other two parts of this painting are in the Uffizi and the Louvre); *St George and the Dragon*, also by Uccello, the fierce dragon being speared at the entrance to his craggy cave; works by Botticelli (Rooms 57–58) including the *Mystic Nativity*, one of the gallery's best-known works, showing the Virgin kneeling in adoration, with a circle of dancing angels above the stable; important pieces by Piero di Cosimo, who was 'rediscovered' in the second half of the 19th century; and Alesso Baldovinetti's popular *Portrait of a Lady in Yellow* (Room 58), depicted in profile against a blue background, with black palm fronds embroidered on her sleeve.

THE NATIONAL GALLERY

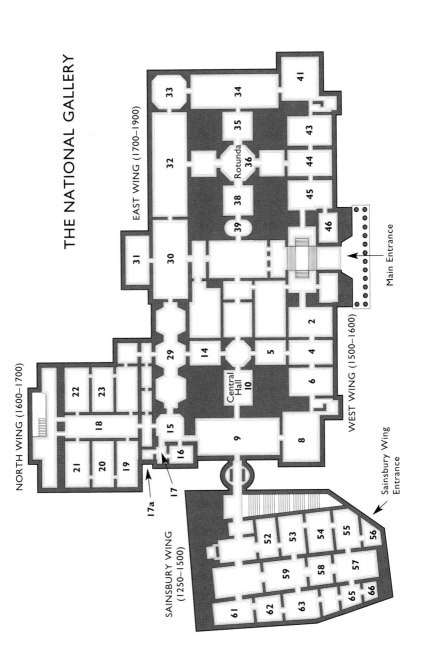

NORTH WING (1600–1700)

EAST WING (1700–1900)

WEST WING (1500–1600)

SAINSBURY WING (1250–1500)

Rotunda

Central Hall

Main Entrance

Sainsbury Wing Entrance

A separate gallery (Room 59) displays late 15th-century works by Carlo Crivelli, including *The Annunciation with St Emidius* (1486), an astonishing exhibition of his skill. Later 15th-century works from Siena and Perugia include Giovanni di Paolo's *Scenes from the Life of St John the Baptist*, the desert realised as tall, craggy mountains.

From Venice and the Veneto 1450–1500 are important works by Mantegna—who did his most important work for the Gonzaga court at Mantua—including the *Agony in the Garden* (Room 62), the slumbering apostles in the foreground with rabbits hopping on the road along which Judas conducts the Roman soldiers; Sicilian-born Antonello da Messina's *St Jerome in his Study* (c. 1475–76; Room 62), a gentle work showing the saint at his desk surrounded by the paraphernalia of learning, a pet cat sitting by potted plants and his lion hovering in the shadows to the right; and works by the great Giovanni Bellini (Rooms 61–62), including the *Madonna of the Meadows*, and his famous portrait of Doge Leonardo Loredan, in an expensive gold and silver damask robe, prominent against a blue background.

Ferrarese and Milanese painting 1450–1500 includes works by the Este court artist Cosimo Tura, such as *The Virgin and Child Enthroned* (c. 1475–76), seated on an architecturally elaborate throne; and works by Pisanello (Room 55), better known as a medallist, whose few known paintings include the *Virgin and Child* and *The Vision of St Eustace*, illustrating the saint's vision of a stag with a crucifix between its antlers, with much attention paid to the hunting dogs and other forest wildlife.

In a separate gallery (Room 66) are outstanding masterpieces by Piero della Francesca, who worked chiefly in his native Borgo Sansepolcro, Tuscany, and was recognised as a rare and extraordinary talent in the second half of the 20th century. The National Gallery has exceptional works by him, including the *Baptism of Christ*, a work of great delicacy, and *The Nativity*, an unfinished work allowing insight into his working methods.

The Netherlands and Germany: Unlike early Italian works which are painted in egg tempera, with a gradual shift towards oil as time progresses, early Netherlandish and German works are in oil on panel. The technique, in fact, is thought to have been brought from the Netherlands to Italy by Antonello da Messina. Important works in the collection include those by Robert Campin, active in Tournai in the early 15th century, including small devotional images; and penetrating portraits of a man and a woman, c. 1420–30, great observational pieces with sparkling eyes, one of the earliest surviving examples of a pair of portraits.

One of the greatest artists of his day was Jan van Eyck, who worked for Philip, Duke of Burgundy at Bruges. His outstanding work, already famous in the 16th century and today one of the most important of the National Gallery's pictures, is his remarkable *Arnolfini Portrait* (Room 56), probably a marriage portrait, the couple standing in a well furnished room, their reflections seen in the round mirror in the background.

The outstanding Netherlandish painter of his time was Rogier van der Weyden, who worked in Brussels and probably for the Burgundian court. His beautiful

Magdalen Reading (c. 1440–50; Room 56) has been cut down from a once large altarpiece. Dieric Bouts' *Entombment* is one of the most important examples of his religious painting to survive. Exceptional works by Hans Memlinc (or Memling; Room 63) include the *Donne Triptych* (c. 1475), commissioned by the English patron Sir John Donne when in Bruges, and the peaceful *Virgin and Child* (c. 1475), possibly the central panel of a private devotional painting. Works by the leading Antwerp painter Quinten Massys (or Metsys) include the *Virgin and Child Enthroned.*

Early German works, from Cologne and Westphalia, include *The Presentation in the Temple* by the 'Master of the Life of the Virgin', whose name is unknown but who was one of the leading painters of Cologne; and fragments of the high altarpiece from the Benedictine Abbey of Liesborn, including the beautiful *Annunciation*, by the 'Master of Liesborn'. Southern German painting includes *The Painter's Father* (1497), by one of the greatest European artists of his age, Albrecht Dürer (Room 65).

1500–1600 (West Wing; Rooms 2–14)

Italy: The National Gallery's Italian Renaissance collection is extensive and excellent. In the Gallery's early years it was the trustees' objective to purchase the best works by the outstanding artists, then identified as Titian, Correggio and Raphael. An astonishing number of masterpieces arrived at the Gallery throughout the 19th century. Central Hall (Room 10), at the heart of the Gallery, displays a selection of works by Titian and his contemporaries, although *The Vendramin Family* was purchased in 1929, and the late, freshly handled *Diana and Actaeon* not until 1972. Leonardo da Vinci's great *Virgin of the Rocks* (c. 1508), the central panel for the altarpiece of the oratory of the Milanese Confraternity of the Immaculate Conception, and one of the gallery's most renowned works, is displayed in Room 2, along with his large cartoon, *The Virgin and Child with St Anne and St John the Baptist* (c. 1499–1500), a large-scale preparatory drawing for a painting commissioned by Louis XII of France. Also in this room is Correggio's *Madonna of the Basket*, in excellent condition, and his well known *School of Love* (c. 1525), purchased in 1824. Early 16th-century painting of Ferrara and Bologna, and the patronage of the Este dukes, is explored in Room 6, with works by Lorenzo Costa (*A Concert*, c. 1485–95) and Garofalo.

Room 8 contains major works by Florentine and Roman artists: Michaelangelo's unfinished *Entombment*; Bronzino's outstanding *Allegory with Venus and Cupid*, the 'picture of singular beauty' mentioned by Vasari in 1568; Raphael's large *Ansidei Madonna*; his beautiful *Mond Crucifixion* and *St Catherine of Alexandria*, twisted towards the sky in a position of holy rapture; his important and influential portrait of Pope Julius II, an 1824 Angerstein foundation work; and the small and gentle *Madonna of the Pinks*, a controversial acquisition (for £22m) in 2004.

Room 9, a large barrel-vaulted room with restored plasterwork and gilding, showpieces the Gallery's magnificent works by Veronese and Venetian artists, 1530–1600: Veronese's four beautiful *Allegories of Love*, ceiling paintings commissioned either by the Holy Roman Emperor Rudolf II, or for a Venetian setting; his enormous and impressive *Family of Darius before Alexander*; and *The Rape of Europa*, which came to the gallery in 1831 and was highly esteemed in the 18th and 19th centuries. Also an 1831 purchase was Tinoretto's *St George and the Dragon*, a typically roughly finished work, the dragon being speared on a savage rocky shore. Other important works include Tintoretto's *Origin of the Milky Way* (1575–80) and Jacopo Bassano's *Purification of the Temple*.

Probably the most famous Titian in the collection is *Bacchus and Ariadne*, purchased in 1826. It hangs in Room 10, with other important works by him (his early *Noli me Tangere* (c. 1515); *Portrait of a Lady* ('La Schiavone'); and *Portrait of a Man*, the sitter's head turned to the viewer, his elaborate silver-blue quilted sleeve filling the picture space). Other early 16th-century Venetian artists include Giorgione, Palma Vecchio and Sebastiano del Piombo, whose *Raising of Lazarus*, originally part of the Orleans collection but a casualty of revolutionary Europe, was the first work to enter the collection (*see p. 199 above*).

Northern Italian works include portraits by Moroni, Moretto da Brescia and Lorenzo Lotto, excellent pieces of realism including Lotto's *Portrait of a Lady inspired by Lucretia* (c. 1530–32), and *Giovanni Agostino della Torre and his son, Niccolo* (1515), showing the 61 year-old doctor holding a work by the Greek physician Galen.

The Netherlands: The fine collection of 16th-century Netherlandish pictures can be seen in Rooms 5 and 14 including, in the latter, works by Jan Gossaert: *Adam and Eve*, with the serpent coiled in the branch of a tree at the top of the picture, nudging its head between the standing couple; his small-scale *Little Girl*, in an elaborately embroidered and jewelled dress, holding an armillary sphere; and his meticulous, tightly handled *Adoration of the Kings* (c. 1500–15), with angels hovering above the Virgin and Child, the kings bearing their costly gifts and dogs wandering across minutely observed cracked paving invaded by weeds. Room 5 has larger scale works. Important religious altarpieces by the distinguished Bruges painter Gerard David include *Canon Bernardijn Salviati and Three Saints* (c. 1501), the left hand shutter of a diptych, the goldsmith's work of the croziers meticulously painted, with a beautiful landscape background; and *The Virgin and Child with Saints and Donor*, from the altar of St Catherine in the chapel of St Anthony in St Donatian's, Bruges, a work of sophisticated splendour, painted in David's rich, bright colours. *Scenes from the Passion* by the 'Master of Delft' is painted with an incredible minute clarity. Works by Quinten Massys, the leading Antwerp painter from 1491, include *The Virgin and Child Enthroned*, an early work; *A Grotesque Old Woman*, her wrinkled skin contrasting with her fine, revealing clothes; and *The Virgin and Child with Saints*, a rare survival of a cloth painting.

Germany: The collection of 16th-century Northern painting from the Protestant states of what are now Germany and Switzerland includes works by Cranach, Hans von Aachen and others, but is of particular note for its works by Holbein. *The Ambassadors* (Room 4), one of the National Gallery's major masterpieces, dominates one wall. Painted in 1533 for Jean de Dinteville, French Ambassador at the court of Henry VIII, it shows Dinteville standing with Georges de Selve surrounded by objects symbolic of Humanist learning. The perspective of the distorted skull, bottom centre, is corrected when viewed from the right. The charming *Lady with a Squirrel and a Starling* (1526–28) has recently been identified as Anne Lovell, the animal and bird being a heraldic play on the Lovell arms and the family home at East Harling, Norfolk. *Christina of Denmark* (1538), depicting a prospective bride of Henry VIII, is a rare, early example of full-length portraiture.

1600–1700 (North Wing; Rooms 15–32)

Dutch Pictures: The large collection of 17th-century Dutch and Flemish works is largely the result of two major bequests, that of the late Prime Minister Sir Robert Peel in 1871, and the Wynn Ellis bequest of 1876. Vermeer and the painters of Delft and Leiden are hung in Rooms 16 and 17. Of the only 30 works known by Vermeer, the National Gallery has two, including the outstanding *Young Woman Standing at a Virginal* (c. 1670). Nearby is Pieter de Hooch's *Courtyard of a House in Delft* (1658), with its carefully observed brickwork. Numerous works by Gerrit Dou, the principal artist of the Leiden *fijnschilders* (literally 'fine painters'), are on show, including his *Poulterer's Shop* (c. 1670), seen through a stone window, its produce of gamebirds and a hanging hare shown in a virtuoso performance of meticulous detail. Also on show is Hoogstraten's *Peepshow* (c. 1655–60), a painted box with two viewing holes, through which the illusion of a three dimensional Dutch interior can be seen. From a black and white tiled floor a dog stares up at you, and through a doorway further rooms recede into the distance. On the other side a sleeping figure can be glimpsed in bed. Of such boxes to survive, this is the finest and most elaborate.

In Room 17a are Dutch flower and cabinet pieces: minutely observed and smoothly finished tulips by Bosschaert and van der Ast, and small landscapes by Roelandt Savery, including *Orpheus* (1628), playing his violin to an enraptured audience of flora and fauna. In Room 21 are works by Cuyp and the Dutch Italianate landscapists, most importantly Jan Both, who was in Rome in 1635–41, and the Haarlem artist Nicholas Berchem. Cuyp's brilliant *River Landscape with a Horseman and Peasants* (c. 1658–60), suffused with a beautiful golden light, was bought by the Earl of Bute in the 1760s and is supposedly the picture that stimulated the admiration of Cuyp, and his landscapes populated by cows, among British collectors. Further panoramic and low-horizoned landscapes and marine pictures hang in Room 22: works by Jacob van Ruisdael, the most famous landscapist of his day, including *A Road Winding between Trees* (c. 1645–50), an important early work; *Vessels in a Fresh Breeze* (1660–65), the muddy water slapping against the jetty; and *Landscape with a Ruined Castle and a Church* (c. 1665–70), a famous work with light playing on the fields below scudding clouds. Hobbema's *Avenue at Middelharnis* (1689), with its central avenues of trees receding into the distance, was formerly owned by Robert Peel and is one of the gallery's best-loved works.

Room 23 is entirely devoted to Rembrandt. The National Gallery has a large collection of his works, both portraits and large scale biblical pictures, many of which were bequeathed or purchased in the 19th century. The *Woman Taken in Adultery* (1644), was one of Angerstein's 1824 foundation works; the *Lamentation over the Dead Christ* was Beaumont's; and the famous *A Woman Bathing in a Stream* (1654), probably Hendrickje Stoffels, who lived in Rembrandt's household, came to the gallery in 1831. The important *Belshazzar's Feast* (c. 1635), is an early attempt by Rembrandt to establish himself as a large scale history painter. He shows the moment when, having served wine in sacred vessels looted from the Temple in Jerusalem, Belshazzar observes the appearance of Hebrew script on a wall predicting the fall of his kingdom. Other key works include *Saskia van Uylenburgh in Arcadian Costume* (1635), Rembrandt's wife shown a year after they married; *Margaretha de Geer*, wife of the wealthy merchant Jacob Trip; and *Self Portrait at the age of 63*, one of the last pictures Rembrandt painted.

The Dutch Caravaggists and the painters of Haarlem are shown in Room 25, including Hendrick ter Brugghen's *The Concert* (c. 1626). Scenes of everyday life are in Rooms 26–27: interiors by Jan Steen and Gerard ter Borch, full of symbolism and moral comment; Thomas de Keyser's excellent portrait of the ambassador and advisor to the Prince of Orange, Constantijn Huygens, surrounded by objects pointing to his intellectual and artistic interests; and townscapes redolent of the prosperity of the Dutch Golden Age.

Flemish Pictures: Early 17th-century cabinet-sized Flemish works are shown in Room 28: works by Jan Brueghel the Elder, including the meticulously detailed *Adoration of the Kings*; church interiors by Hendrick van Steenwyck and Brueghel; and tavern and brothel scenes by David Teniers (the most famous painter of such works) and Adriaen Brouwer. The large and impressive collection of works by the great Baroque artist Rubens is in Room 29. Many arrived at the gallery in the 19th century, including the *Rape of the Sabine Women* (1635–40), acquired in 1824; *A View of Het Steen in the Early Morning*, showing Rubens' country estate purchased in 1635 (part of the Beaumont bequest); and the important *Peace and War*, painted when Rubens was in England on a diplomatic mission to negotiate peace with Spain (presented by the Duke of Sutherland in 1828). Other works produced for English patrons include the portrait of the celebrated art connoisseur Thomas Howard, Earl of Arundel (*see p. 27*); an oil sketch for the allegorical ceiling painted for the Duke of Buckingham, destroyed in 1949; and, on long term loan, the *Apotheosis of James I*, a sketch for his famous Banqueting House ceiling (*see p. 20*). One of the most famous pictures in the National Gallery is *Le Chapeau de Paille*, part of the Peel collection purchased in 1871, the name of the picture dating back to the 18th century. Other important works include the early *Samson and Delilah* (c. 1609–10); and *The Watering Place*, a landscape which inspired Constable's work of the same name (*see British School, below*).

Works by Rubens' most famous pupil, van Dyck, are in Room 31. The collection is particularly rich in English period works, van Dyck being the most celebrated and influential artist working in Britain in the 17th century. The most important is the enormous *Equestrian Portrait of Charles I* (c. 1637–38), painted for the King whose official painter van Dyck was, and who knighted him for his services. *George Gage with Two Attendants* (1622–23), came with the Angerstein collection, but many of the more important works are relatively recent purchases: *Lords John and Bernard Stuart* (c. 1638), posed with a wonderful degree of confidence and flair, one of his English masterpieces, was purchased in 1988; and the excellent full-length *Abbé Scaglia* in 1999.

Italian Pictures: Room 32 contains great Italian works of the 17th century: Caravaggio's early *Supper at Emmaus* (1601), and his late *Salome Receives the Head of St John the Baptist*, with theatrical, dramatic lighting and intense passion. In contrast is Annibale Carracci's quieter, more mannerist work, such as *The Dead Christ Mourned* ('The Three Maries'; c. 1604), one of his most powerful and emotionally charged works. The large collection of Guido Reni includes his elaborate *Coronation of the Virgin* (1607), and his well known *Rape of Europa* (before 1640), painted for King Wladislaw of Poland. Guercino, the great Bolognese Baroque artist, is well represented: the still and dignified *Cumaean Sibyl with a Putto* (1651), one of his finest works, is one of an important group on loan from the collection of the distinguished Italian Baroque scholar Sir Denis Mahon. Orazio Gentileschi's large and imposing *Finding of Moses* is an important work executed in England in the 1630s when the artist was in the service of Charles I and his queen, Henrietta Maria.

French Pictures: Rooms 19 and 20 are dedicated to the two great French landscape artists Poussin and Claude. Both the foundation Angerstein and Beaumont collections contained Claude, reflecting the high esteem in which British collectors held his work. *Landscape with Hagar and the Angel* was Beaumont's favourite picture (*see p. 199 above*). The gallery's collection of his hugely influential, poetic classical landscapes, peopled by figures from classical mythology and the Bible, includes *Seaport with the Embarkation of St Ursula*, the view to the open sea bathed in a golden light; *The Enchanted Castle* (1664), which influenced Keats' 'Ode to a Nightingale'; and *Landscape with Aeneas at Delos* (1672). When J.M.W. Turner bequeathed his pictures to the nation he stipulated that two of them, *Dido Building Carthage* and *Sun Rising through Vapour*, were to be shown alongside two of Angerstein's Claudes, *Seaport with the Embarkation of the Queen of Sheba* and *Landscape with the Marriage of Isaac and Rebekah*. They hang together in Room 15, the modern genius alongside the influential predecessor.

Excellent landscapes by Poussin include *A Bacchanalian Revel before a Term*, (1632–33); *The Triumph of Pan* (1636), commissioned by Cardinal Richelieu; *Landscape with Travellers Resting* (c. 1638–39), probably executed for his major Roman patron Cassiano del Pozzo; the brilliant *Adoration of the Golden Calf* (1633–34), made for Amadeo del Pozzo, Cassiano's cousin; and the late, grand *Finding of Moses* (1651), purchased jointly with the National Museum of Wales in 1988 and shown alternately in London and Cardiff. Other French works are shown in Room 18, including

Philippe de Champaigne's full-length regal image of Cardinal Richelieu, one of several full-length variants; Mignard's extraordinary *Marquise de Seignelay and two of her Sons* (1691), where the sitter is shown as the sea goddess Thetis, surrounded by exotic shells, with coral and pearls in her hair, an allusion to her husband's post as head of the Admiralty.

Spanish Pictures: Religious works created in the service of the Counter Reformation, and other 17th-century Spanish pictures, are displayed in Room 30: the highly individual works of El Greco, including *Christ Driving the Traders from the Temple* (c. 1600); important works by Velázquez, expressing the dignity of the court of Philip IV, including the majestic 1630s full-length of the king, in a splendid costume with sparkling silver embroidery; and the exceptional *Toilet of Venus* ('The Rokeby Venus'; c. 1647–51), the only surviving female nude by the artist, famously slashed by a suffragette in 1914. Zurbarán's *St Francis in Meditation* shows the kneeling saint with uncompromising realism, in a stark interior, his face partially hidden by the dramatic shadow cast by his hood. Murillo's more gentle works, with their soft style and colouring (known as *estilo vaporoso*), include his *Self Portrait*, *Peasant Boy Leaning on a Sill*, and the sweet and gentle *The Two Trinities* (1681–82).

1700–1900 (East Wing; Rooms 33–46)

Italy: Rooms 38 and 39 show the relatively small collection of 18th-century Spanish and Italian works, including Goya's *Doña Isabel de Porcel* (before 1805) and Canaletto's excellent *Stonemason's Yard* (Room 38), the latter from Beaumont's collection. It was not until the late 19th century, however, that the foundations of a representative collection of 18th-century works were laid, with the acquisition of works by the great late Baroque artist Tiepolo and the 'Venetian Hogarth', Pietro Longhi, including the latter's *Exhibition of a Rhinoceros in Venice*. Further Canalettos include excellent views of the Grand Canal, Venice, and *The Rotunda at Ranelagh* and *Eton College*, two English works. The gallery now has a large collection of works by both Giovanni Battista Tiepolo and his son Giandomenico, as well as works by Sebastiano Ricci.

British School: Although Tate Britain is the official home of British art, the National Gallery holds some supreme masterpieces of the British School. In the Rotunda (Room 36) are important full-length works including Sir Thomas Lawrence's *Queen Charlotte* (1789–90), shown seated at Windsor Castle, in expensive pearls, with a view of Eton College chapel through the window; and Sargent's excellent *Lord Ribblesdale* (1902), a former trustee of the National Gallery. Rooms 34 and 35 display the bulk of the British pictures: Hogarth's important *Marriage à la Mode* series (Room 35), a moralising commentary on contemporary life, part of Angerstein's collection; Gainsborough's early *Mr and Mrs Andrews*, a genteel couple outdoors in their park; his full-length *Mr and Mrs William Hallett* ('The Morning Walk'), a fashionable couple out strolling; Constable's well-known *Hay-Wain* (Room 34), the quintessential image of the English countryside, as well as *The Cornfield* (1826), and *The Cenotaph to Reynolds' Memory, Coleorton*. The latter had been erected in the grounds at Coleorton, Sir George Beaumont's country home, in 1812. Stubbs' monumental *Whistlejacket*, a great rearing, riderless horse against a stark background, is a relatively recent acquisition. Other pictures include Joseph Wright of Derby's famous *An Experiment on a Bird in the Air Pump* (1768); Turner's celebrated *The Fighting 'Temeraire', tugged to her Last Berth to be broken up* (1839) in Room 34; and his *Rain, Steam and Speed—The Great Western Railway* (before 1844).

France: The French 18th-century collection (Room 33) is small but includes some good pictures, notably Drouais' portrait of Mme de Pompadour, shown seated, with her pet dog, in domestic but expensive surroundings, wearing an exquisitely embroidered dress (1763–64); and Elisabeth Vigée le Brun's charming *Self Portrait in a Straw Hat* (after 1782), where she shows herself holding a palette and brushes.

French 19th-century Academy painting (Room 41) includes Paul Delaroche's romanticised *Execution of Lady Jane Grey*; works by Géricault and Delacroix; and Ingres' *Mme Moitessier* (1844–56), the wife of a wealthy banker, shown seated in her finery. The picture, with its extraordinary porcelain finish, took Ingres 12 years to complete.

No purchases of contemporary French works were made in the 19th century; it was not until the Sir Hugh Lane Bequest of 1917 that works by the great 19th-century French Impressionists were acquired. The gallery now has an excellent collection (Rooms 43–46) which includes several outstanding masterpieces: Manet's *Music in the Tuileries Gardens*, and his *Execution of Maximilian* (1867–68), the latter the second version he painted of the execution by firing squad of Archduke Maximilian, younger brother of the Emperor Franz Joseph of Austria, who had been installed as Emperor of Mexico by Napoleon III but was captured and executed by Mexican forces after the withdrawal of French troops. The mutilated fragments of the picture were rescued and pieced together by Degas. Monet's work (Room 43) includes *Gare St-Lazare*, (1877); *The Water-Lily Pond* (1879); *The Beach at Trouville* (1870) and *The Thames below Westminster* (1871). Seurat's *Bathers at Asnières*, partly executed in his 'pointillism' technique, was acquired in 1924 through a fund established by Samuel Courtauld (*see Courtauld Institute of Art, p. 275*). Works by Pissarro include *Boulevard Montmartre at Night* (1897). Renoir's supreme *Les Parapluies* is a Hugh Lane Bequest work, and his *Boating on the Seine* was formerly owned by Courtauld. Henri Rousseau's *Tiger in a Tropical Storm* ('Surprised!'; 1891), is the first of his over 20 jungle pictures.

The final decades of the 19th century are represented with works by Cézanne (Room 45): his *Self-Portrait* (c. 1880), *Hillside in Provence* (c. 1886–90), and his well known *Bathers, 'Les Grandes Baigneuses'*, one of three large works of the same theme. Of van Gogh's work (also Room 45) the gallery has one of his *Sunflowers* (1888), as well as *Van Gogh's Chair*, painted at Arles in November 1888 when he was working in the company of Gauguin, and *A Wheatfield with Cypresses*, painted in September 1889 at the mental asylum at St-Rémy.

NATIONAL PORTRAIT GALLERY

St Martin's Place, WC2H 0HE
Tel: 020-7312 2463; www.npg.org.uk
Open Mon–Wed, Sat–Sun 10–6; Thur, Fri 10–9
Free
Tube: Leicester Square/Charing Cross
The Portrait Café (basement) is open Sat–Wed 10–5.30, Thur and Fri 10–8.30;
The Portrait Restaurant (3rd floor) is open Sat–Wed 11.45–2.45 (last orders); Thur and Fri 11.45–2.45 & 5.30–8.30 (last orders); Bar open Sat–Wed 10–5, Thur and Fri 10–8.30pm (last orders food), 10pm (last orders drink)
Map p. 382, 2A

Founded in 1856, the first establishment of its type in the world, the National Portrait Gallery's aim was to show images of those who had made Britain great. By virtuous example future generations would be instructed and inspired. As such, the gallery represents the fulfilment of a 19th-century educational ideal. Beginning with the 'Chandos' portrait of Shakespeare, the gallery's first acquisition, an exceptional collection of historical images has been collected over the decades. It includes outstanding examples of the art of portraiture by famous artists, sculptors and photographers and represents distinguished figures from nearly 550 years of British history.

History of the Gallery

In 1846, stimulated by Thomas Carlyle's *On Heroes, Hero-Worship and the Heroic in History* (1841), which argued that it was the actions of great men that shaped the world, Lord Stanhope made the first (of three) proposals to the House of Lords for the founding of a national portrait collection. In 1856 £2,000 was secured from the government for the purchase of portraits, and in 1859 the museum opened in a small house in Great George Street. Through the collecting efforts of the gallery's first Director, George Scharf (1820–95), the two rooms and staircase were soon woefully inadequate. In 1870 the museum moved to South Kensington where the collection was hung chronologically, with instructive labels (an early instance of the museum caption) and signatures and autograph letters alongside the works. Finally, in 1889, after a spell at the Bethnal Green Museum, where conditions (condensation, a leaking glass roof) proved harmful to the pictures, the government provided a permanent site next to the National Gallery.

W.H. Alexander gave £80,000 for the new building, which was designed by his chosen architect, Ewan Christian (1890–95). The north block is in Florentine Renaissance palazzo style while the principal entrance, on St Martin's Place, is inspired by the delicate terracotta façade of Santo Spirito, Bologna. The three portrait busts, by Frederick

Detail of Holbein's celebrated cartoon of Henry VIII (c. 1536–37).

Thomas, on the entrance façade are the significant figures in the museum's history: Stanhope, Macaulay (a founding trustee) and Carlyle (who became a trustee in 1857). Continuing round the building are images of artists, sculptors and historians.

The 1998–2000 Dixon/Jones alterations to the building, which swept away the curious mock-19th-century medieval-revival painted decoration in the entrance hall and stairs (part of the improvement scheme of Roderick Gradidge, 1990), have vastly improved the internal circulation. Straight ahead of the entrance lobby, with its original mosaic floor, is the bright, white hall of the new Ondaatje wing. From here, the contemporary collections are to the right; the long escalator takes visitors straight up to the second floor Tudor and Stuart galleries (and off them, the 18th-century and Regency collection); and the new stairs lead to the first floor Victorian and 20th-century pictures. On the third floor is the Portrait Restaurant (reservations essential, although there is also a bar) with its now famous bird's-eye panorama of Nelson on his column in Trafalgar Square with the Palace of Westminster and Big Ben beyond.

NB: Not all the collection can be shown at once. To minimise their exposure to light miniatures, works on paper and photographs are shown in selected rotations and a significant number of works are shown at the gallery's three main outstations: Montacute House in Somerset, Beningbrough Hall, near York (both National Trust properties) and Boddelwyddan Castle in Clwyd, Wales. The entire collection can be viewed at the terminals in the IT mezzanine gallery.

Tour of the Gallery

Tudor and Stuart Collection (Second Floor; Rooms 1–8)
The National Portrait Gallery holds one of the best collections of 16th- and 17th-century British pictures in the world, including many iconic images of famous figures from Tudor and Stuart history. The small early panel portraits of Plantagenet rulers, including Richard III, are mostly 16th-century copies of 15th-century images, but are nevertheless rare survivals. The earliest portrait in the collection is the finely painted *Henry VII* (1505), his hand resting on a stone ledge, a composition taken from early Flemish portraiture. There are few portraits of women in the early collection, unless of queens or mistresses. Henry VIII's wives Katherine of Aragon and Anne Boleyn are represented, as well as Catherine Parr, a full-length attributed to Master John, and formerly identified as Lady Jane Grey. The most important early work, probably the most important work in the gallery, is Holbein's famous 'cartoon' (*pictured on the previous page*) for the left hand side of the mural in Whitehall Palace (since destroyed) celebrating the Tudor dynasty. The King's commanding full-length pose served as the prototype for other images of him. Other Tudor figures include Thomas Cromwell; Thomas More, Henry VIII's Chancellor, beheaded in 1535, shown surrounded by his family in a copy after Holbein's lost portrait; Thomas Cranmer, burnt at the stake in 1556, by Gerlach Flicke (1545–46); and the curious anamorphic portrait of Edward VI, a distorted image which comes into line at one visual point.

NATIONAL PORTRAIT GALLERY
SECOND FLOOR

1–3: Tudor portraits
4–5: Early Stuarts
6: Enlightenment
7–8: Restoration and the
    later Stuarts
9: Kit-cat portraits
10–14: Hanoverian Britain
17–18: Regency portraits
19–20: Early 19th century and
    Great Reform Act

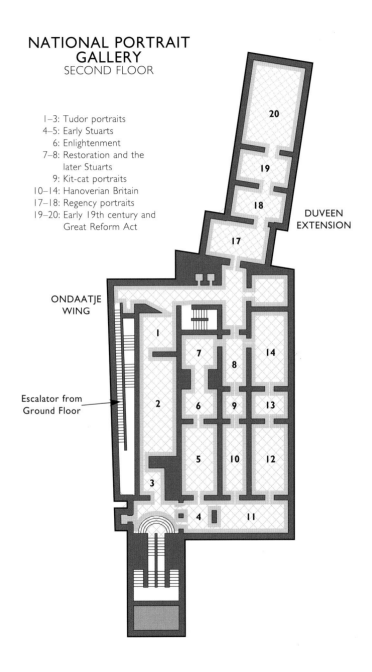

DUVEEN
EXTENSION

ONDAATJE
WING

Escalator from
Ground Floor

Mary I is represented in a portrait by Master John, and Elizabeth I in several portraits: the full-frontal 'Coronation Portrait' (actually dateable to c. 1600); the 'Darnley Portrait', showing the queen in an intricately embroidered dress with a rich rope of pearls; and the full length 'Ditchley Portrait' by Marcus Gheeraerts the Younger (*pictured opposite*), an exceptionally fine image of the deliberately ageless queen c. 1592. It was painted to commemorate her stay at Ditchley, in Oxfordshire, as the guest of Sir Henry Lee. She stands on a globe, her feet on Oxfordshire, with lightning flashes behind her (banished by her radiance) and sunshine before, all typical of the symbolic portraiture so loved by the Elizabethans. Other portraits include Elizabeth's favourite, the Earl of Leicester; the great circumnavigator Sir Francis Drake; Sir Walter Raleigh; and Shakespeare.

By James I's reign canvas had become the most common support for painting, allowing for larger pictures. As well as James himself, by Daniel Mytens, are beautiful full-lengths by Robert Peake of Frederick, Prince of Wales, and his sister Princess Elizabeth, in an intricately embroidered gown of gold and silver thread. From Charles I's reign are images of Charles himself; his queen, Henrietta Maria; and Lord George Stuart, Seigneur d'Aubigny (c. 1638), a young royalist killed at the battle of Edgehill, an excellent late work by van Dyck, who was Charles I's official painter.

One of the best works from the mid-17th century is Walker's *John Evelyn*, a wonderful study of intellectual melancholia. The later 17th-century collection is particularly rich, with several portraits by Sir Peter Lely, Charles II's official painter following the 1660 Restoration. As well as the king there are several portraits of his mistresses, including Nell Gwyn; members of the 'Cabal' government, including Lely's *Arlington*; court wits such as the Earl of Rochester and, of course, Samuel Pepys, in a portrait by John Hayls that Pepys mentions in his famous diary.

The later Stuart collection includes the ruthless Judge Jeffreys, by John Michael Wright; a particularly beautiful Lely of Mary II, as Princess of Orange; a very fine full-length of Queen Anne by Michael Dahl; Anne's close friend, and later enemy, the powerful Duchess of Marlborough, shown with her gold key of office around her waist; and Sir Godfrey Kneller's small allegorical oil sketch of the Duke of Marlborough, the famous victor of Blenheim, shown on a rearing horse.

18th-century Collection (Second Floor; Rooms 9–14)

The 18th-century collection begins with figures from the early Hanoverian art world including artists' self-portraits (Kneller, Dahl); the great architect of St Paul's, Sir Christopher Wren; Hogarth (a terracotta bust by Roubiliac); and men of letters such as the satirist and author of *Gulliver's Travels*, Jonathan Swift. Hung together are Kneller's important Kit-cat portraits, with their uniform frames, showing the politically Whig-minded members of the convivial drinking and dining club: Congreve and

The 'Ditchley Portrait' of Queen Elizabeth I (c. 1592), by Marcus Gheeraerts the Younger.

NATIONAL PORTRAIT GALLERY
FIRST FLOOR

21: Queen Victoria
22: Victorian statesmen
24: Early Victorian writers
    and artists
25: Political portraits
26: Portraits by Watts
28–29: Late Victorian portraits
30–31: 20th century (First World War
       to Queen Elizabeth II)
32: 1960–1990
33: Royal family

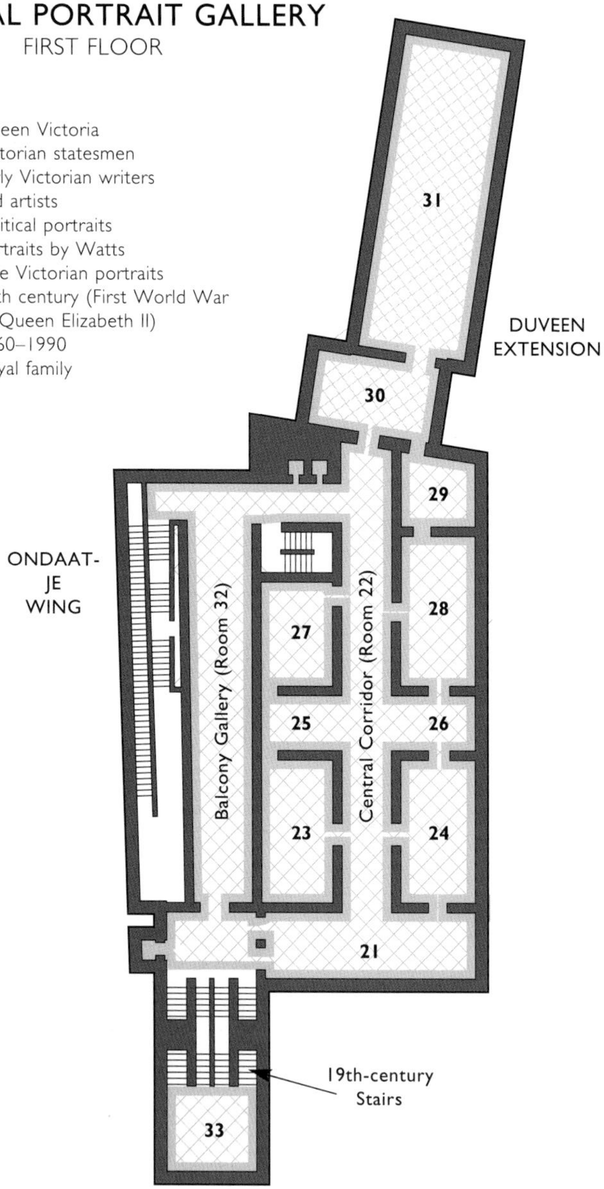

DUVEEN
EXTENSION

31

30

29

ONDAAT-
JE
WING

Balcony Gallery (Room 32)

Central Corridor (Room 22)

27

28

25

26

23

24

21

19th-century
Stairs

33

Dryden appear alongside politicians and courtiers. Philip Mercier's beautiful small-scale work (1733) shows the great art patron Frederick, Prince of Wales and his sisters playing musical instruments in the grounds of Kew Palace.

Later Georgians include the great painter Sir Joshua Reynolds, President of the Royal Academy of Arts founded in 1768. As well as his early self-portrait (c. 1749), he appears with fellow Academicians Sir William Chambers and Joseph Wilton in a triple portrait by François Rigaud. Literary figures include Dr Johnson, author of the Dictionary; and images of actors, including Sarah Siddons, painted full-length as Tragedy by Sir William Beechey, probably inspired by her famous appearance as Lady Macbeth.

There are portraits of George III and Queen Charlotte by Allan Ramsay; the expanding East India Company is the subject of Francis Hayman's important image *Robert Clive, Receiving the Homage of Mir Jaffir after the Battle of Plassey*; and dominating an entire wall is John Singleton Copley's great work *The Death of the Earl of Chatham* (on long loan from Tate), showing the dramatic collapse of William Pitt in the House of Lords.

The Regency (Second Floor; Rooms 17–20)
The recently refurbished Regency Rooms occupy the second floor of the 1931–33 Duveen extension. The peacock blue-green walls, silvered coving and black marble dados and door surrounds have more to do with the date of the architecture than the contents of the rooms. The galleries actually span the period 1789 (the French Revolution) to 1832 (the Great Reform Act) rather than the Regency itself (1811–20). The gallery possesses Sir Thomas Lawrence's autocratic profile oil sketch of the Prince Regent, as well as the great military and naval heroes of the day, the Duke of Wellington and Lord Nelson. Romantic poets and novelists include Lord Byron (in 'magnifique' Albanian costume); Benjamin Robert Haydon's portrait of the seventy-two year-old Wordsworth; Coleridge, Keats and Sir Walter Scott. Also in the collection is the delicate sketch of Jane Austen by her sister, Cassandra. The principal painting in the largest room (Room 20) is Sir George Hayter's enormous *The Reformed House of Commons* (1833), painted to commemorate the passing of the 1832 Great Reform Act, which widened the country's electorate.

Victorian Collection (First Floor; Rooms 21–29)
The Victorian displays occupy Ewan Christian's original 19th-century building, this part of which was remodelled by CZWG Architects in 1996. Immediately facing you (if you arrive via the 19th-century stairs rather than from the Ondaatje Hall) is a theatrical, pyramidal display on shelving of portrait busts of great Victorian patriarchs. Along the central corridor heading west (Room 22) is a formal procession of portraits of statesmen, interspersed with white marble busts. To either side are smaller galleries (Christian's side-lit cabinets) with thematic hangs, basically chronological, showing images of the great writers, artists, travellers, inventors and politicians of the Victorian age. The British Empire's self-confidence and evangelising spirit is summed up well in Sir George Strong Nares' *The Secret of England's Greatness*, showing Queen Victoria presenting a Bible to a kneeling African convert. Large historical portraits

include Jenny Barret's *The Mission of Mercy: Florence Nightingale Receiving the Wounded at Scutari* (c. 1856–58). As well as these ponderous pieces is James Tissot's wonderful *Frederick Gustavus Burnaby* (1870), a cavalry officer and explorer who died of a spear wound on an expedition to Khartoum. He is shown in uniform, relaxing on a sofa, with an elegantly twirled moustache.

Early Victorian writers and artists include Dickens, Thackeray and George Eliot, as well as Branwell Brontë's famous image of his three sisters Charlotte, Emily and Anne, a naïve work, discovered folded up on top of a cupboard by the second wife of Charlotte Brontë's husband. John Ballantyne's 1865 image of Landseer shows the great artist at work modelling the stone lions for the base of Nelson's column in Trafalgar Square. Several of these pictures are curiously hung on projecting wall brackets, a nod towards Christian's original intention to have screens, and to minimise the reflection from Christian's re-exposed windows.

Among the gallery's many images of inventors and men of science is Robert Howlett's early 1858 photograph of the great engineer Isambard Kingdom Brunel, standing before the massive anchor chains of his steamship *Leviathan* (later the *Great Eastern*). Shown together are G.F. Watts' 'Hall of Fame' portraits of the great men of his day, which Watts bequeathed to the gallery. His belief in the importance to history of men of intellectual power and vision, close to Carlyle's theory of the Hero, coincided with the founding mission of the gallery. Included, of course, is Carlyle (who hated his portrait); William Morris; Matthew Arnold; and the influential philosopher John Stuart Mill. The gallery also owns Watts' famous image of his wife for one year, the great actress Ellen Terry, shown at the age of 17 'choosing' (the title of the work) between the worldly camellia and the innocence of violets. Terry—who was 30 years younger than Watts—left her husband and returned to the worldly stage.

The gallery's collection includes Millais' sombre, composed portraits of the two towering political figures, Gladstone and Disraeli, and John Singer Sargent's powerful and brilliant 1908 portrait of the Earl of Balfour, a pivotal figure in British politics from the 1880s. It was thought by G.K. Chesterton to sum up not only the man but also the vague pessimism of the age. The gallery's other late Victorian and turn-of-the-century images includes the Italian Boldini's exuberant *Lady Colin Campbell*, socialite and journalist, shown in black chiffon with an impossible wasp waist; Napoleon Savory's photograph of his 'picturesque subject', Oscar Wilde, taken in New York in 1882; and portraits of the avant-garde leaders Walter Sickert, Philip Wilson Steer and Augustus John.

20th-century Collection (First Floor; Rooms 30–32)
The first floor of the Duveen wing, internally transformed in 1996 by CZWG Architects, houses the 20th-century collection up to 1960. The main gallery has large glass screens allowing the backs of pictures to be seen, at first rather disconcerting. Figures from the period of the First World War include the suffragette Emmeline Pankhurst. Sir James

Choosing (c. 1864), by G.F. Watts, a portrait of his new wife, the actress Ellen Terry.

Guthrie's large painting *Some Statesmen of the Great War* (1923–24), shows Asquith, Lloyd George and Churchill, among others, seated below the vast winged figure Nike, the Winged Victory of Samothrace (in the Louvre). Graham Sutherland's oil sketch of Sir Winston Churchill is a reminder of the original, disliked by Churchill and destroyed by his wife. Post-war images include Sir James Gunn's elegant *Conversation Piece at Royal Lodge, Windsor*, showing George VI and his family taking tea.

The period 1960–90 is shown in the Balcony Gallery in the Ondaatje wing. Works include a self-portrait by Lucien Freud; images of political leaders (Harold Wilson, James Callaghan and Harold Macmillan); actors including Sir Alec Guinness and Dame Peggy Ashcroft; and authors, including Iris Murdoch, painted by Tom Phillips in 1984–86. The first-floor landing (Room 33) is devoted to portraits of the current royal family. On the Ground Floor is the 1990s and contemporary collection, which includes works specially commissioned by the gallery.

Eminent Britons

The three men responsible for the foundation of the National Portrait Gallery, the 5th Earl Stanhope (1805–75), Thomas Macaulay (1800–59) and Thomas Carlyle (1795–1881) were all historians and biographers keenly interested in Britain's past. Stanhope was the author of a seven-volume history of Georgian Britain, Macaulay of a monumental *History of England*, and Carlyle of the famous *On Heroes* (1841), in which he argued that 'the history of the world is but the biography of great men'. All three agreed that a National Portrait Gallery should not only illustrate British history but should celebrate the individuals who had contributed to Brtain's pre-eminence, a view reflective of mid-19th-century British optimism. The gallery was to be a historical resource where images of the great and good could be venerated and could inspire emulation.

The foundations of the collection were laid by George Scharf (1820–95). An etcher and illustrator keenly interested in history, Scharf's tireless and mostly single-handed industry saw the collection grow from an original 57 pictures to over 1,000. His profound study of portraiture enabled him to authenticate as genuine or dismiss images, and his meticulous manuscript notebooks of portraits in private collections, with lively sketches and annotations, now in the gallery's archive, remain a valuable resource. Scharf did not live to see the completion of the present building. Responsibility for the new gallery passed to Sir Lionel Cust (1859–1929), who was one of the main contributors to that magnificent late 19th-century enterprise, the publication of the *Dictionary of National Biography*. Recently revised (Oxford University Press 2004), the new volumes, 12 years in preparation, provide biographies of 50,000 famous Britons through the ages and are illustrated with 10,000 images from the National Portrait Gallery's collection, reinforcing the gallery's position as the leading institution for the study of famous Britons and their iconography.

Photography (shown throughout the gallery)

Since the 1968 Cecil Beaton exhibition at the gallery, photography has been a grow-ing part of the collection. The collection actually starts much earlier, in the 1840s. It includes over 100 images by the early Victorian photographer Julia Margaret Cameron, dating from the 1860s and 70s; famous images such as Frederick Henry Evans' 1893 image of Aubrey Beardsley, and George Charles Beresford's 1902 portraits of Virginia Woolf; over 1,000 works by Cecil Beaton; and images by, among others, Norman Parkinson, Bill Brandt, Henri Cartier-Bresson and Helmut Newton. Selections from the collection are shown throughout the displays.

NATURAL HISTORY MUSEUM

NATURAL HISTORY MUSEUM

Cromwell Road, South Kensington, SW7 5BD
Tel: 020-7942 5000; www.nhm.ac.uk
Open Mon–Sat 10–5.50, Sun 11–5.50 (last admissions 5.30)
Free
Tube: South Kensington
Cafés and shops
Map p. 380, 3B

The Natural History Museum's collection was originally a department of the British Museum, where the myriad stuffed animals, fish, skeletons, botanical specimens, rocks and fossils were first displayed. A critical lack of space prompted the move to South Kensington, an idea which had been aired as early as 1853 but which only came to fruition in 1881, when Alfred Waterhouse's astonishing new building finally opened to the public. Since then the collection has grown immeasurably. Between them the five departments of Botany, Entomology, Mineralogy, Palaeontology and Zoology contain over 70 million natural history specimens and the museum—as it has always been—is one of the world's leading centres of taxonomic research (the science of classifying species). The museum gained independence from the British Museum in 1963.

The Collection

At the core of the collection is the hoard of natural history 'curiosities' of the eminent botanist and physician Sir Hans Sloane, whose entire collection constituted one of the three foundation collections of the British Museum in 1753 (*see p. 28*). Sloane's items were joined by the eye-opening specimens brought back from Captain Cook's great voyages of discovery to the South Pacific including the botanical manuscripts of David Solander and the natural history specimens and herbarium of Sir Joseph Banks, both of whom had accompanied Cook on the Endeavour in 1768–71 and were museum employees (*see p. 127*). Objects from Darwin's revolutionary voyage to the Galapagos Islands in *HMS Beagle* in 1831–36 also came to the museum as did, in 1856, the entire collection of the Zoological Society, soon followed by that of the East India Company. The burgeoning collection of specimens from parts of the globe far distant from London quickly outstripped the building's display capacity and stored items deteriorated quickly. Dr George Shaw held annual 'cremations' of Sloanian material. Of Sloane's original 1,886 mammals, 1,172 birds (or eggs or nests), 1,555 fishes and 5,439 insects only a fraction remains today, although his important 330-volume *Herbarium* has survived, as well as drawers of minerals from his pharmaceutical cabinet and his magnificently carved pearly nautilus shell.

The Building

Waterhouse's magnificent new building (1873–80), a great secular Romanesque cathedral clad in ornamental terracotta, was built on the site of the International Exhibition of 1862. Its design incorporated the ideas of Professor Richard Owen, a great comparative anatomist and palaeontologist and Superintendent of the Natural History Department from 1856. Owen was the prime agitator for a new museum and envisaged it as a great storehouse of divine creation. A broad flight of steps leads from the road up to the **giant portal**, centrally placed in the 680-ft frontage, above which, surmounting the gable, Owen desired a statue of Adam, man being creation's crowning glory (he fell off in the 1930s). Covering the façade and the interior is a veritable menagerie of birds and beasts cast in terracotta, symbolising the museum's function: to the west, where Zoology was displayed, designs of living animals; to the east, where Geology and Palaeontology were housed, extinct species. Owen's idea was brilliantly realised in Romanesque style by Waterhouse, whose beautiful designs (based on specimens and natural history drawings) are in the museum library. Extinct beasts line up on the entrance façade, monkeys scramble up arches in the entrance hall, fishes swim in rippling water around columns where further up lizards lurk, and on the stairs animals and birds—including a beautiful pair of demoiselle cranes—peep from twining plants. Waterhouse's dramatic **entrance hall** is conceived as a vast nave with a triforium above and, at the far end, the great staircase rising to the upper floors. Owen wished the Hall to be an 'Index' gallery, with displays of minerals, plants and invertebrates on one side and vertebrates on the other—a simple guide to the 'types' of the animal, plant and mineral kingdoms, carefully arranged according to the Linnaean system of classification. Owen's successor Sir William Flower introduced evolution to

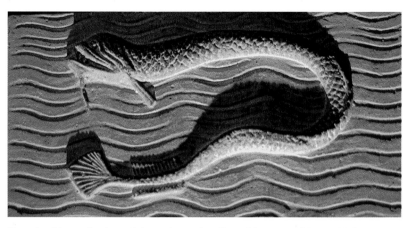

Example of the marine-themed decoration on the pillars of the present Dinosaur Hall.

the display, a theory to which Owen had not wholly subscribed. In the centre were large mammals—whales, elephants and giraffes. Today the hall is dominated by the museum's most famous inhabitant, *Diplodocus carnegii*, 150 million years old and one of the largest land mammals which ever lived, cast from the original specimen at the Carnegie Museum, Pittsburgh and given to the museum in 1905. It is a fitting tribute to Owen, who coined the name 'dinosaur' in 1841.

Tour of the Museum

The museum today offers a very different visitor experience from the museum which opened its doors in 1881. Instead of carefully arranged classified specimens in mahogany cases are interactive audio-visual life- and earth-science displays on ecology, evolution and man. This popular staging of science, which sometimes fits uneasily in a building designed for scientific knowledge of a different era, was first introduced to the museum in 1977 with the opening of the Human Biology display. It outraged scholars, who believed that the Victorian founding ideal, both to educate and to amuse, had swung too far in one direction.

Life Galleries

The mainstay of the sequence of Life Galleries are of course the ever popular **Dinosaurs**, to the left of the main entrance—a new set of animatronic ones have recently been introduced, including a vast model of *Tyrannosaurus rex*. Beyond the staircase and through the café (with Chi Chi the Giant Panda who died at London Zoo in 1972 in a case to one side, his skeleton on the other), a corridor lined with reptiles and amphibians leads to the **Mammal Hall**, almost completely filled by the vast 91-ft Blue Whale suspended from the ceiling, with the White Whale, Sperm Whale and dolphins alongside it. The Zoology department, with over 27 million specimens, is one of the most comprehensive in the world, but only a tiny fraction of the taxidermy, skeletons, jarred specimens and skins are on show. Large polar bears, tiny pigmy shrews, and skeletons of the extinct sabre-toothed tiger can be seen. To the right of the Hall is the **Bird Gallery** with a remarkable collection of stuffed specimens, some in their original Victorian display cases (only a few remain), delicately arranged against painted backdrops. Of particular note is the dodo. On the first floor is a permanent photographic exhibition 'Plant Power'; the primates section; African animals; and a separate **Evolution Gallery**, with Darwin in his study, focusing on his *Origin of the Species* (1859) and theory of natural selection. On the second floor is a cross-section of a giant sequoia tree from the Sierra Nevada, California, 1,335 years old when felled in 1892. At the time of writing the Ecology Gallery was closed for refurbishment.

Earth Galleries
The entrance to the Earth Galleries is from Exhibition Road. In the atrium, lined with extraordinary figurative sculptures, an escalator takes visitors on a journey to the top of the building through the middle of a 36-ft revolving model of Earth, of beaten copper, iron and zinc, with sound and light effects. 'The Power Within' explores volcanoes and has an immensely popular earthquake simulator. 'From the Beginning' takes you from the Big Bang, the formation of Earth 4,560 million years ago, to the creation and sustaining of life. 'Earth's Treasury' has a display of minerals and gemstones, including the Latrobe gold crystal, a fraction of the museum's collection of 180,000 specimens. The 'Earth Lab' explores the diversity of rocks and fossils, drawing on the museum's great mineralogy and palaeontology collections, which include 160,000 rocks and ocean bottom deposits, 3,000 meteorites and 30,000 ores, many collected on great expeditions such as that of *HMS Challenger* in 1872–76 and Scott's second polar expedition (specimens brought back by the naturalist Edward Wilson proved that Antarctica had once been warm).

The Darwin Centre
The new Darwin Centre is the storehouse for the museum's zoological 'Spirit Collection': 22 million jarred specimens preserved in alcohol. Standing in the atrium you can look up seven storeys and see the extent of the storage. A small section on the ground floor is available for viewing, although you can take behind-the-scenes tours of other storerooms and the laboratories where over 100 scientists carry out taxonomic research. The Darwin Centre is the public face of the museum's core research work of identification and classification, but only Phase I has been completed. Phase II, the proposed new home of the Botany and Entomology departments, where, for instance, the 'dry' collections of insects and butterflies will be housed, is scheduled to open in 2007 (C.F. Møller Architects).

OLD OPERATING THEATRE, MUSEUM AND HERB GARRET

9a St Thomas' Street, SE1 9RY
Tel: 020-7188 2679; www.thegarret.org.uk
Open daily 10.30–4.45
Admission charge. No disabled access
Tube/Station: London Bridge
Shop
Map p. 383, 3E

The operating theatre for the women's ward of the original St Thomas's Hospital was constructed in 1822 in the roof space of the church of St Thomas the Apostle adjoining the hospital ward. It was designed to satisfy the new legal requirement that surgeons and their apprentices-in-training observe live operations. Partly dismantled and forgotten when the hospital moved west 40 years later (*see p. 84*), the operating theatre was only rediscovered in 1956. Following careful restoration, it opened as a museum in 1962, and is now the only surviving example of its type in the country. With its plaster ceiling, bare wooden floor, matchboard walls, and plain operating table of deal, with sawdust box below to catch the blood, the small theatre with its five tiers of standings serves as a salutary and atmospheric reminder of 19th-century surgical practice.

Access is via a steep winding stair to the church belfry, where the discovery was made through a hole in the wall 15ft above floor level. The church and bell tower, on the site of a 13th-century foundation, were rebuilt in 1703 by Thomas Cartwright, master mason to hospital governor Sir Christopher Wren. By the early 19th century, the timbered roof space of the church was already in use as a herb garret for the storage and preparation of medicinal compounds. The museum now exhibits examples of the type of herb that might have been found here: liquorice, comfrey, rosemary, hops, elderflowers, couchgrass, dill (used for gripe water), and marigold (a little less effective against smallpox and measles than saffron). Displays also illustrate the history of surgery, complete with instruments used for bloodletting, scarification and cupping, alongside the revolutionary discovery of antisepsis by Joseph Lister at the Glasgow Royal Infirmary in 1847.

ORLEANS HOUSE GALLERY

Riverside, Twickenham, TW1 3DJ
Tel: 020-8892 0221
Open Tues–Sat 1–5.30, Sun 2–5.30
Free. Partial disabled access
Station: St. Margaret's (from Waterloo)
Map p. 378, 3B

The handsome octagon room, designed by James Gibbs c. 1718, is all that remains of the 1710 villa on the Thames built by John James for James Johnstone, Secretary of State under William III. A garden pavilion, it was supposedly built for the reception of Caroline of Anspach, wife of the future George II. The most famous resident of the house, after whom the place is now named, was Louis-Philippe, Duc d'Orléans, King of France from 1830–48, who leased it from 1815–17. The main house was demolished in 1926–27 but the Octagon survived, saved by the Hon. Mrs Ionides, who bequeathed it to the borough on condition that it was used as a public art gallery. The interior comprises a magnificent domed room adorned with elaborate, not quite Rococo, stucco, executed by the Swiss-Italian specialists Giuseppe Artari and Giovanni Bagutti, whom Gibbs described as 'the best fret-workers that ever came to England'. The pediments of the chimneypiece and doors support boldly modelled figures, while in the round niches inside the dome are busts possibly representing George I. On either side of the chimneypiece are portrait medallions of George II and Queen Caroline, when Prince and Princess of Wales; a third, above the east door, is possibly later, and may represent Louis-Philippe. The full-length portrait of Queen Caroline c. 1728 is attributed to Herman van der Mijn.

The Gallery, built on the site of the old house, displays selections from its important collection of paintings, drawings and prints, mostly early 18th-century to present day topographical views relating to the area, including works by Leonard Knyff, Samuel Scott, Peter de Wint, and Corot. Peter Tillemans' early 18th-century *The Thames at Twickenham* is the earliest known view of the area. At the heart of the collection is the Ionides bequest of over 400 works.

OSTERLEY PARK
(National Trust)

Jersey Road, Isleworth, Middlesex, TW7 4RB
Tel: 020-8232 5050; www.osterleypark.org.uk
Open April–end Oct Wed–Sun and bank holidays 1–4.30; March Sat–Sun 1–4.30
Admission charge. Partial disabled access
Tube: Osterley
Shop and tea room
Map p. 378, 3B

Set in a landscaped park with several lakes—an unexpected large country estate in the suburbs of west London—this former Elizabethan house was extensively remodelled by Robert Adam with a magnificent series of state rooms. Much of Adam's original decoration and furniture has been preserved, providing a rare opportunity to appreciate the development of his style over almost two decades. The house and its contents also make useful comparison with Adam's work at nearby Syon House (*see p. 285*).

History of the Manor

A manor house, square-built in brick on three storeys, was first built at Osterley in the 1560s by Sir Thomas Gresham (?1519–79), the wealthiest English merchant of the time. He endowed Gresham College and, after the early death of his son, also contributed towards the founding of the Royal Exchange. The manor house served as a retreat from the City and also as a profitable enterprise: one of the earliest paper mills in England was established here. On Gresham's death in 1579, the estate passed through several hands without significant alteration, being owned by the parliamentary general Sir William Waller, and towards the end of the 17th century, by the speculator, entrepreneur and founder of fire insurance, Nicholas Barbon. In 1711 the property was purchased by the goldsmith Francis Child, the founder of Child's Bank at No. 1 Fleet Street. His son, Sir Robert Child, a director of the East India Company from 1719–20, was the first member of the family to live at Osterley but died unmarried in 1721. His younger brother Francis inherited the house and made several alterations to the stables and offices, modelling them on those at Hampton Court. His younger brother Samuel inherited in 1740, but it was his sons Francis and Samuel, the first of the Childs to have been brought up at Osterley, who were largely responsible for the shape of the house today. In 1761 Francis the Younger employed the most fashionable architect of the day, Robert Adam, to transform his hotch-potch Elizabethan home into a sensational Neoclassical building, eventually described by Horace Walpole as 'the palace of palaces'. On Francis' sudden death two years later, his 24-year-old brother Robert continued the great work with Robert Adam until 1772. A decade later his only daughter eloped with the Earl of Westmorland. Robert Child died—apparently from a broken heart—in the same year, leaving Osterley and his numerous other estates to his future grandchild, Lady Sarah Sophia Fane. She married the 5th Earl of Jersey in 1804. The house was never fully occupied again as a family home. In 1949 the 9th Earl of Jersey gave the property and some of its original contents to the National Trust.

The Hall and Great Stair

The house is approached through Adam's Grand Portico and across the screened courtyard, the visitor first entering the severely formal **Hall**. Completed by Adam in 1767, rectangular with alcoves at either end intended to improve the original room's proportions, the design of the grey and white marble floor echoes the plasterwork ceiling. The walls are decorated with stuccowork panels representing armorial trophies. The elongated pilasters and shallow Greek-key frieze were inspired, like the ceiling of Adam's masterful Library at Kenwood, by Diocletian's palace at Split. The niches in the apses display copies of Roman statues of Apollo, Minerva, Ceres and Hercules, and the Portland stone Adam chimneypieces are surmounted by painted grisaille bas-reliefs by Cipriani. They depict *The Triumph of Bacchus* and *The Triumph of Ceres*.

The North Vestibule, containing cases displaying part of the Childs' large collection of Chelsea and Sèvres porcelain, leads into the North Passage connecting the Great Stair with the Library, Breakfast Room and Eating Room, all except the Library designed by Adam in two stages. The austerity of the **Great Stair**, with its Corinthian and Ionic screens and wrought-iron balusters identical to those at Kenwood (*see p. 146*), is relieved by the ceiling also designed by Adam for Rubens' *The Apotheosis of the Duke of Buckingham*. A copy now replaces the original which was removed in 1949 and later lost in a fire. Rubens' sketch for the painting can be seen in the National Gallery (*see p. 208*). Three lamps, probably made by Matthew Boulton to Adam's designs, hang between the Corinthian columns of the *piano nobile*.

Adam Style

The designs of Robert Adam (1728–92), one of the pre-eminent architects of the 18th century, generated a revolution in British architectural taste and interior decoration. The particular brand of light, elegant and highly ornamental Neoclassicism which now bears his name was much imitated during his lifetime. Born in Kirkaldy, Fife, the second of four sons of the architect William Adam, his work was heavily influenced by what he had seen on his 1754–58 Grand Tour, when he travelled to Italy and beyond, met important architects such as Piranesi, and studied the remains of the Palace of Diocletian at Split, on the Dalmatian coast, which he later published in a lavish book, *Ruins of the Emperor Diocletian at Spalato*. His personal interpretation of Greek and Roman antique remains was blended with Rococo and Italian Renaissance motifs to create the highly elaborate ceilings, friezes and pilasters which are such a feature of the 'Adam style'. The 1768 publication of Sir William Hamilton's Greek vase collection (purchased by the British Museum in 1772), with their red and black decoration, inspired Adam's distinctive 'Etruscan manner', seen to startling effect at Osterley Park. These free borrowings were dismissed as mere 'filigrane toy work' by the other architectural heavyweight of the period, the academically more rigorous Sir William Chambers.

Many of Adam's architectural projects were undertaken in partnership with his brothers, James, John and William, while a group of specialist independent craftsmen was used to realise the meticulously planned interiors. Every interior element was designed by the Adam office, whose designs were advertised through the engravings after them by Francesco Bartolozzi and their publication in Robert and James Adam's *Works in Architecture* (1778). Joseph Rose and his nephew, also Joseph Rose, provided plasterwork; Thomas Chippendale, Gillows, Ince and Mahew and other cabinet makers produced furniture; and the chief supplier of elaborate metal-cast ornament was Matthew Boulton. Patterned inlaid floors or carpets mirrored the design of the ceilings, richly painted in combinations of greens, blues, lilac and pink. Inset classical scenes were painted by Antonio Zucchi (who had travelled with Adam to Split), Giovanni Battista Cipriani and the Swiss-born Angelica Kauffmann. The latter, admired throughout Europe for her skill, worked with Zucchi on a number of Adam projects before their marriage and departure for Rome in 1781.

The Principal Floor

The striking white-painted **Library**, monochromatic like the Hall at Syon, was designed in 1766 to accommodate the Fairfax library (sold in 1885 to save the house from demolition) and is more of a piece than many of the other rooms on this floor. The ceiling in very low relief is characteristic of Adam's middle years, with paintings by Antonio Zucchi set into the walls illustrating scenes from the lives of classical writers. Above the door is *Britannia Encouraging and Rewarding the Arts and Sciences*. The exceptionally high-quality marquetry furniture, inlaid with motifs emblematic of the liberal arts, was probably designed and manufactured by John Linnel (c. 1768). Next door, at the end of the North Passage, the Breakfast Room, decorated with reserved pictures from the V&A, provides fine views over the park.

The **Eating Room** was one of the first rooms designed by Adam for the house, in 1766, and decorated up to the cornice in cheerful pinks and greens. As he later wrote of such rooms in his *Works in Architecture* (1772), 'Instead of being hung with damask, tapestry etc. they are always finished with stucco, and adorned with statues and paintings, that they may not retain the smell of the victuals'. The ceiling came first, decorated with appropriate Bacchic motifs (vines, wine ewers, and decorated staves) very similar to early work by Joseph Rose. Paintings and roundels by Zucchi with mainly classical themes are set into the walls. Above the remarkably large chimneypiece is Giovanni Battista Cipriani's *An Offering to Ceres*: women and children paying homage to the goddess of the harvest.

Next door is the **Long Gallery**, running the full width of the garden front and now hung with some important late 17th- and 18th-century Venetian paintings, representative of the kind that might originally have been seen here. Some are drawn from the National Trust's own collection; others are on loan from private collections, including two from the Royal Collection. On the North End Wall, nearest the Eating Room, hangs Sebastiano Ricci's *Christ and the Woman taken in Adultery*. At the opposite end of the room is his *Miracle at the Pool of Bethesda*, also on loan from the Royal Collection, and both part of a series of seven paintings with New Testament subjects commissioned around 1725 for the palazzo of Consul Smith, patron of Canaletto. On the East (Chimneypiece) Wall hang the limpid *Shipping on the Maas at Dordrecht* by Albert Cuyp (1650s) and a still-life by Rubens' pupil and sometime collaborator Frans Snyders. Over the North Chimneypiece is Marieschi's *View of the Rialto Bridge and the Palazzo dei Camerlenghi, with the festive entry of the Patriarch Antonio Correr in 1737*. The painting is one of the young contemporary of Canaletto's masterpieces, and is unusual in being a *capriccio* or architectural fancy that also celebrates an actual historical event. Further along the same wall hangs Gaspard Dughet's *Wooded Rocky Landscape with Classical Figures*. Apprenticed to his more famous brother-in-law, Nicolas Poussin, Dughet adopted the same surname, and his work became especially popular with English Grand Tourists. This painting's stormy sky is typical of his innovative approach to landscape. On the opposite wall, *Aeneas and Achates wafted in a cloud before Dido, Queen of Carthage, with Cupid at her feet* by Jacopo Amigoni, is from the Wombwell Collection at Newburgh Priory, the largest of the artist's works not painted directly onto a wall but probably commissioned specially for Newburgh. It depicts an early episode in the tragic story of Dido and Aeneas from Book I of the *Aeneid*. The Long Gallery itself has been returned as far as possible to Adam's original pea-green colour scheme with pier glasses for easier viewing of the paintings. The seating furniture is attributed to John Linnel.

Next door is the **Drawing Room**, counterbalancing the Eating Room and designed around the same time, much richer in concept, with a ceiling modelled on the Temple of the Sun at Palmyra, inspired by the nave of West Wycombe church. Most probably it was Francis Dashwood, the owner of West Wycombe Park, who recommended Robert Adam to Francis Child. The carpet was designed by Adam in response to the ceiling and was manufactured by Thomas Moore of Moorfields. Horace Walpole, not always an admirer of Adam's work, considered the room 'worthy of Eve before the Fall'. The tall pier glasses are also by Adam, along with the inlaid, purely ornamental commodes. The grate in the chimneypiece, itself not entirely of a piece with the room, is made of *paktong*, an alloy of copper, zinc and nickel, and the only one of such pieces by Adam to remain *in situ*.

The State Apartment

The Drawing Room gives onto the highlight of the tour of the house: the sumptuous State Apartment, already practically out of fashion when commissioned by Robert Child in 1772, though now providing three superb examples of Robert Adam's style at its most confident and mature. The **Tapestry Room** has a delicate ceiling, which as usual came first, the central medallion depicting *The Dedication of a Child to Minerva*. The carpet, again manufactured by Thomas Moore, was designed by Adam to mirror the ceiling and also the Gobelins tapestries on the walls. These were designed by the painter François Boucher (1703–70) and represent the Four Elements in the shape of the loves of the gods: Venus and Vulcan (Fire), Aurora and Cephalus (Air), and Vertumnus and Pomona (Earth). The mirror on the window wall stands in for Water. Over the chimneypiece are Cupid and Psyche. The eight armchairs are backed with oval frames holding Boucher's *Jeux d'Enfants*, designed specially for Madame de Pompadour in the early 1750s: the cartoons were not released for use by other clients until 1770. Moving next door, from France to England, from Fire to Earth, the **State Bedchamber** is dominated by the domed State Bed of 1776, one of Adam's most ambitious pieces of furniture. Green forms the basis of the colour scheme, as can be seen from the sketch now in Sir John Soane's Museum. The dome and canopy echo those designed by Adam for George III's box at the Italian Theatre in Haymarket. The last room is Italian in style, with a colour scheme based on pale sky blue to represent the Air. The other most striking feature of the **Etruscan Dressing Room** is the wall decoration, inspired by ancient Greek vases and the engravings of Piranesi, and the only surviving example of this type of design by Adam. The room has survived remarkably unaltered, apart from some restorative cleaning. It now looks much as it might have done when first seen, though one corner remains to demonstrate the effect of decades of grime.

PERCIVAL DAVID FOUNDATION OF CHINESE ART

53 Gordon Square, WC1H 0PD
Tel: 020-7387 3909; www.pdfmuseum.org.uk
Open Mon–Fri 10.30–5
Free
Tube: Russell Square
Map p. 382, 1A

Sir Percival David (b. 1892), a scholar and collector of great distinction, presented his library and collection of Chinese ceramics to the University of London in 1951. The Foundation, based in a 19th-century Bloomsbury townhouse, opened in 1952 and is administered by the School of African and Oriental Studies (SOAS), where the Chair of Chinese Art and Archaeology established by Sir Percival at the Courtauld Institute in 1931 was transferred. The claim that the collection is second only to the former Imperial Collection, now in the National Palace Museum, Taipei, is no idle boast. Sir Percival had a profound knowledge of Chinese ceramics and, from 1912, accumulated a collection of intellectual precision, quality and beauty. He travelled to Beijing to study the then rather neglected Imperial Collection in the Forbidden City, where he mounted an exhibition of the more important pieces. In 1927 he was able to purchase 40 items from the Yuin Yeh Bank sale of Imperial pieces left as collateral by the Dowager Empress in 1901. In 1930–31 he travelled to China again to inventory the rich contents of the various halls in the Forbidden City and took the opportunity to make further purchases from dealers.

The collection today, supplemented with 171 mainly monochrome pieces from the collection of Mountstuart Elphinstone, has over 1,400 pieces, mainly reflecting the court taste of the Song, Yuan, Ming and Qing dynasties (10th–18th centuries). The collection is especially strong in wares from the important kilns of the Song dynasty, the great age of Chinese ceramics renowned for its elegance and simplicity of design and decoration. There are fine examples of Ding; pieces with the famous 'shadow blue' and 'blue white' glazes and shades resembling prized jade; stoneware pieces from the Jun kilns of an exquisite lavender blue, some with purple copper splashes; examples of the very rare Ru ware; and a beautiful, refined 12th–13th-century Guan ware vase of a delicate blue, its lip banded in copper and the crazing in the glaze spiralling round its elegant, long neck. This piece, from the Imperial collection, was Sir Percival's favourite and was exhibited at the 1935 Chinese art exhibition at the Royal Academy, the first such exhibition in Europe, which he organised with the collectors George Eumorfopoulos and Oscar Raphael (whose collections are now at the British Museum). Other pieces of Song ware were owned by the Emperor Qianglong (1736–95), who had poems and other inscriptions added to them expressing his admiration of them. Later pieces, including blue and white Ming, are displayed upstairs. The collection is rich in pieces inscribed with dates and names at the time of manufacture, making them invaluable historical documents. The 'David' temple vases, dated 1351, are two such examples.

PETRIE MUSEUM OF
EGYPTIAN ARCHAEOLOGY

University College London, Malet Place, WC1E 6BT
Tel: 020-7679 2884; www.petrie.ucl.ac.uk
Open Tues–Fri 1–5; Sat 10–1 (NB: School parties visit the museum on
Tues and Wed mornings)
Free. Limited disabled access
Tube: Goodge Street
Shop
Map p. 382, 1A

Located on the first floor of the DMS Watson Library in Malet Place (signs guide you
to the lift), the Petrie Museum is attached to the Institute of Archaeology, University
College London (UCL) and is used as a teaching resource. It was founded in 1892 by
the novelist, journalist and travel writer Amelia Edwards (1831–92) who left to the
college, as well as her collection of Egyptian artefacts and library, a sum of money for
the establishment of a chair of Egyptology, the first in the country. The professorship
was filled by the great Egyptologist and excavator Sir Flinders Petrie (1853–1942),
through whose digs in Egypt and Palestine the collection was further enhanced. In
1913 Petrie sold his personal collection to the museum; that collection is now recognised as one of international importance. Amelia Edwards' passion for Egypt was
stimulated by a trip she took in 1873, which resulted in her bestselling book *A
Thousand Miles up the Nile* (1877). Horrified by the neglect of ancient monuments
there, in 1882 she founded the Egypt Exploration Fund, which sponsored excavations. Finds from these digs not wanted by the Egyptian authorities were sanctioned
for export and through this method Flinders Petrie, the Fund's chief excavator, was
able to direct many valuable artefacts to the British Museum. Amelia Edwards was
admiring of Petrie's careful, scientific and controlled archaeology, but in 1903 he fell
out with the Fund (now Society) and set up his own British School of Archaeology in
Egypt based at UCL. The Petrie Museum, rather than the British Museum, became the
main recipient of his finds.

The museum contains many items, including mummy portraits, from Petrie's excavations at the Roman-period cemetery at Hawara in the Fayum; from Amarna, the city
of Akhenaten; and from Abydos. It also has a great quantity of pottery, displayed on
shelving in tall wooden cases. Petrie was one of the first to recognise the importance
of pottery finds, from which he derived his system of sequence dating for the Pre-
dynastic period. Also displayed are textiles; costume, including a unique 1st–2nd-
century AD beaded dress of a dancer; papyri and sculpture.

Only partial display of the 80,000 objects is possible but a new museum is planned,
on three floors of the new university 'Panopticon' building, due to open in 2008. Until
then torches are available for the keen to combat low light levels.

PHOTOGRAPHERS' GALLERY

5 & 8 Great Newport St, WC2H 7HY
Tel: 020-7831 1772; www.photonet.org.uk
Open Mon–Wed, Fri, Sat 11–6; Thur 11–8; Sun 12–6
Free
Tube: Leicester Square
Café and bookshop
Map p. 382, 2B

Founded in 1971 at 8 Great Newport Street, a former Lyons Tea Shop, the Photographers' Gallery was one of the first independent spaces in the UK devoted specifically to photography. It expanded in 1980 into 5 Great Newport Street, and in 2008 moves to 16–18 Ramillies Street. Exhibitions of the work of well-established and up-and-coming photographers are staged here, and the Gallery also awards the annual Citibank Photography Prize. The Print Sales Gallery holds work by some 100 photographers, with an emphasis on contemporary British work.

PITSHANGER MANOR

Walpole Park, Mattock Lane, Ealing, W5 5EQ
Tel: 020-8567 1227; ealing.gov.uk/services/pm+gallery+and+house
Open Tues–Fri 1–5, Sat 11–5
Free
Tube/Station: Ealing Broadway
Map p. 378, 3C

Built in 1800–03, Pitshanger Manor was the showpiece country villa of the architect Sir John Soane (Ealing at that time was a rural village retreat from the city). Soane retained the new wing of the previous house (owned by the Quaker banker and City merchant Thomas Gurnell), which had been erected in 1768 by George Dance, for whom Soane then worked. Soane rebuilt the rest of the property to his own very individual design. He was keen for the house to reflect his rising status, his originality as an architect and, through the display of his collection, his learned connoisseurship. It was a burdensome cost, however, and in 1810 Pitshanger was sold for £10,000. Until relatively recently the house was a public library, but painstaking conservation has brought it back as near as possible to how it was in Soane's day. Soane's crowded possessions, however, are at his London town house, 13 Lincoln's Inn Fields (*see p. 267*).

Tour of the House

In the summer of 1804 Soane and his wife Eliza played host and hostess to a stream of visitors to Pitshanger. In Soane's words, a succession of 'intellectual banquets' took place. Visitors included clients, fellow Academicians and friends such as the painter J.M.W. Turner. Soane liked to convey his guests on a tour of the property. The entrance front, of yellow London stock brick and Portland stone, was fashioned as a triumphal arch with great Ionic columns and sculptural figures, of Coade Stone (*see p. 174*), based on those at the Temple of Pandrosus at Athens. Through this, visitors entered the Hall and Vestibule where they were bathed in a golden light from stained glass in the fanlight (still existing) and amber glazing in windows above. They would then be taken to the Drawing Room (now the Small Drawing Room) where Hogarth's *The Rake's Progress* series was proudly hung. From this room a door led to the Conservatory (sadly demolished c. 1901). Filled with antique fragments and statuary among the plants, Soane liked to imagine it dramatically lit by moonlight. The Library and Breakfast Room, next on the tour, are the boldest of Soane's interiors, with shallow canopied ceilings, reflective mirrors and emphatic lines. The Library has a painted trellis-work ceiling and walls of painted imitation golden satinwood. The Breakfast Room is of a more overpowering stylised classicism, with bronzed caryatids in the corners, sombre marbled walls and a diagrammatic Greek Key design on the ceiling. In Soane's day, visitors were finally taken downstairs to the extraordinary Monk's Dining Room, a Gothick fantasy room with real Gothic fragments eerily lit through stained glass, and inhabited—so Soane informed his guests—by a hermit. The room today is only an approximation of its original appearance.

George Dance's 1768 rooms are also part of the tour, and the house is set within what is now Walpole Park, which retains elements of Soane's original garden. The 'ruined forum', with half buried columns to puzzle the antiquarian, has unfortunately gone. The PM Gallery, with exhibitions of contemporary art, occupies its site.

Pitshanger Manor is also home to the Hull Grundy collection of Martinware pottery. The largest collection of Martinware in the country (there is another collection in Southall Library; *see p. 183*), it includes a unique fireplace made for the Billiard Room of Buscot Park, Oxfordshire.

POLLOCK'S TOY MUSEUM

1 Scala Street, W1T 2HL
Tel: 020-7636 3452; www.pollockstoymuseum.com
Open Mon–Sat 10–5
Admission charge
Tube: Goodge Street
Shop
Map p. 382, 1A

This small-scale, rambling, six-room museum above a shop selling traditional toys and cardboard theatres, takes its name from Benjamin Pollock (d. 1937), one of the last of the Victorian printers and publishers of toy theatres. The museum occupies two interconnecting Georgian houses where the upstairs rooms and staircases are crowded with displays of antique toys, dolls, dolls' houses, puppets, prints and games. Guaranteed to intrigue, it is ideally suited for children aged 7–12 as many of the exhibits are at child's eye-level.

PRINCE HENRY'S ROOM

17 Fleet Street, EC4Y 1AA
Tel: 020-7936 2710
Open Mon–Sat 11–2
Free
Tube: Blackfriars/Temple/Chancery Lane
Map p. 382, 2C

A fine timbered house built in 1610 just inside the Temple Bar which marks the boundary of the City of London, 17 Fleet Street is one of the very few Jacobean houses in the City to have survived the Great Fire of 1666, which died out near St Dunstan's, Fetter Lane, nearby. When the house was newly built, a room on the first floor was used by Henry, Prince of Wales, the son of King James I, until his early death from typhoid at the age of eighteen in 1612. For the last two years of his life, Henry is believed to have held meetings here to administer the Duchy of Cornwall. The Jacobean plasterwork ceiling is very well preserved, as is one oak-panelled wall, divided into three parts by carved strips with a patterned frieze above. Oak chairs and an elaborately carved refectory table are also of the period, but with no known connection to the room, which now also houses a small display on the indefatigable diarist Samuel Pepys, one of the great chroniclers of the Fire. A letter signed by him can be seen, alongside pictures and information panels on Pepys' life and times and his work as a naval administrator.

THE QUEEN'S GALLERY

Buckingham Palace Road, SW1A 1AA
Tel: 020-7766 7301; www.royal.gov.uk
Open daily 10–5.30 (last admissions 4.30)
Admission charge
Tube/Station: Victoria/Green Park
Shop (free entry)
Map p. 381, 2E

The Queen's Gallery at Buckingham Palace, with its separate entrance on Buckingham Palace Road, is a permanent display space for changing displays and exhibitions of objects from the enormous and outstanding Royal Collection. The original gallery was built in 1962 on the site of the bomb-damaged private chapel. Discreet, small and inadequate, it has recently undergone a major redevelopment (John Simpson & Partners, 1998–2002) which has tripled the display space. The new classical revival gallery, with echoes of Nash (*see p. 50*) and Soane (*see p. 267*), has a welcoming Doric portico, but interiors of an elaborate fussiness. From the light, double-height entrance hall, with friezes of Britain's patron saints, visitors should keep straight ahead for the staircase hall, lined with green columns, and the tall and imposing staircase, with its balustrade of bronze and alabaster lamps, which leads up to the seven display galleries.

The Royal Collection

The Royal Collection is one of the finest picture collections in the world, formed by Britain's monarchs over the centuries from Henry VIII onwards. Many works were part of the exceptional collection of Charles I, a great connoisseur and lover of art, who bought part of the renowned Gonzaga collection of pictures, employed the great van Dyck as his Principal Painter, and owned works by Giulio Romano, Tintoretto, Titian, Raphael and Rubens, among many others. It was Charles I who purchased Raphael's important 'Acts of the Apostles' cartoons (now in the V&A; *see p. 324*) as well as Mantegna's *Triumphs of Caesar* (at Hampton Court; *see p. 117*). Following Charles I's execution his collection was dispersed by the Commonwealth government. While some works were eagerly purchased by international bidders, and have now found their way into the great national museums of Europe, many items were either bought back or returned to the restored Charles II by loyal supporters and constitute an important part of the royal picture collection today. The collection also includes major work by British artists; fine Canalettos which entered the collection during the reign of George III; and one of the world's best collections of 17th-century Dutch pictures, including Vermeer's *A Lady at the Virginals with a Gentleman* and Rembrandt's *Agatha Bas*. Other highlights include Lorenzo Lotto's *Andrea Odoni*; works by Dürer and Holbein, and drawings by Leonardo da Vinci. The Royal Collection is rich in other areas. Also displayed are important items of furniture, sculpture, porcelain, silver and gold, miniatures, jewellery and Fabergé and other decorative arts objects.

Displays constantly change, and works from the Royal Collection are also shown at other royal residences in and out of London, as well as at properties administered by Historic Royal Palaces (chiefly Hampton Court Palace and Kensington Palace).

Johan Zoffany's *Queen Charlotte* (1771). Charlotte of Mecklenburg-Strelitz was the consort of King George III.

RAGGED SCHOOL MUSEUM

46–50 Copperfield Road, E3 4RR
Tel: 020-8980 6405; www.brlcf.org.uk
Open Wed, Thur 10–5; first Sun of the month 2–5
Free
Tube: Mile End; Station: Limehouse (DLR)
Café and shop
Map p. 379, 2E

Opened in 1990, the Ragged School Museum is the inspiring result of a local East End initiative to save three historic canalside warehouses from a proposed extension to Mile End Park. The warehouses were built in 1872 and used to store lime juice (hence the name of the local station) and general provisions. Five years later, Dr Thomas Barnardo rented two of the buildings (now No. 46) and added an imposing pediment to them for his Copperfield Road Ragged School for the children of the poor. Here boys and girls aged five to ten, regardless of race or creed, were given a free education, breakfast and dinner. By 1896 they numbered more than a thousand, with almost two and a half thousand attending the Sunday school, the largest in London. Even after expanding into No. 48, the day schools on this site were considered unsuitable for education and closed down by the London County Council in 1906, the children being dispersed to council schools, although evening classes and the Sunday school continued to be run here for another nine years. From 1915 until 1983, and the founding of the Ragged School Museum Trust, the buildings were used as garment factories and warehouses.

The ground-floor display presents the history of the local borough (Tower Hamlets) and the people that have lived and worked here. Snapshots and personal recollections complement artefacts, such as a model of the Bryant and May matchworks in Bromley by Bow, and a tiny model of the *Great Eastern* made by Bob Hamill, caretaker of Westwoods Engineering on West Ferry Road, where the ship was originally built. Pad hooks used by dockers to grip sacks of sugar, coffee and cocoa are typical of the items used to illustrate life in the East End over the last two centuries.

On the first floor is a re-created Ragged School classroom for 60 to 100 children from c. 1896. Painted in the chocolate brown and primrose yellow stipulated by Dr Barnardo, the room would originally have been lit by gas and heated by one small fire. Pupils studied reading, writing, arithmetic, recitation, grammar and geography and were examined at six standards in each of those six subjects. Teaching made heavy use of the blackboard and repetitive chants, with the pupils seated in ranks of wooden desks equipped with slates and slate pencils, the cost of paper and lead pencils being prohibitive.

RANGER'S HOUSE
(English Heritage)

Chesterfield Walk, Blackheath, SE10 8QX
Tel: 020-8853 0035; www.english-heritage.org.uk
Open end March–end Sept Wed–Sun 10–5; Oct–Dec and March by
appointment
Admission charge
Station: Greenwich/Blackheath (from Charing Cross/London Bridge)
Shop
Map p. 379, 3F

Standing between Blackheath and Greenwich Park, over which it has fine views to the
Royal Observatory, Ranger's House is a handsome mansion built in 1700–20 for
Captain, later Admiral, Francis Hosier (1673–1727). Due to its proximity to the royal
palace, and later to the Naval College and surrounding shipyards, it was a spot
favoured by courtiers and seafaring men. The core of the house is Hosier's, who made
a fortune through the sale of ship's cargoes. The principal entrance is on the
Blackheath side of the house. The delicate but imposing wrought iron gates date from
the 1770s. The fine red brick exterior has a Portland stone centrepiece, a modest
Baroque flourish, with a carved mask of Neptune above the entrance door. In 1748
the house was owned by Philip, 4th Earl of Chesterfield (1694–1733), politician and
wit, and author of the celebrated letters to his son, who built the south wing of yellow brick, containing a large Gallery probably designed by Isaac Ware (completed
1750). Chesterfield spent every summer here for the last 23 years of his life. The north
wing was added by the lawyer and art collector Richard Hulse in the 1780s. In 1807
the house was leased by Augusta, Dowager Countess of Brunswick, sister of George
III, and in 1815 it became the official residence of the Ranger of Greenwich Park, by
now purely an honorary office. The first Ranger to take up residence was Princess
Sophia Matilda of Gloucester (1777–1848). Other occupants of the house include the
young Prince Arthur of Connaught, Queen Victoria's third son, and Field Marshal
Viscount Wolseley, who relieved General Gordon at Khartoum.

The House
The Entrance Hall, with its chequered black and white stone floor, dates from Hosier's
day. He furnished it with plain mahogany hall furniture but during Chesterfield's
occupation it had plaster busts displayed on wall brackets. To the right of the Hall is
Hosier's Crimson Camblet Parlour, used by Chesterfield for cards, which leads to the
New Gallery, a spacious room with triple bow windows in the centre and at each end.
Here Chesterfield displayed his Old Master paintings, with sculpture busts and porcelain in the niches. Hosier's principal parlour was the Green Silk Damask Parlour,
which leads to the Dining Room, where Hosier had crimson damask curtains and a
suite of silvered furniture. The room was substantially altered in 1749–50 by Ware.

The 1710 Oak Staircase leads up to the Long Gallery or Passage, which retains its original early 18th-century panelling. Off it Hosier had a 'Cockloft', a gazebo from which he could train his telescope on ships on the Thames.

The Wernher Collection

The house was purchased by the then London County Council in 1902 and restored in 1959–60. Until recently it displayed the important Suffolk Collection of paintings but these have now been moved to Kenwood (*see p. 150*) to make way for the important Wernher Collection of pictures, jewellery and *objets d'art*, on permanent loan from the Wernher Foundation since 2002. Sir Julius Wernher (1850–1912) was a German diamond merchant who made his fortune (£11 million at his death) in South Africa in the 1870s when his operation merged with De Beers. He settled in England and in 1903 purchased the great Bedfordshire mansion Luton Hoo, which was redecorated in lavish style. Luton Hoo was sold in the 1990s and several key items from the collection were also auctioned, including Titian's portrait of Giacomo di Agostino Doria, now at the Ashmolean, Oxford. What remains is nonetheless impressive. There are pictures by Joos van Cleve, Hans Memling and Gabriel Metsu; English works by Reynolds, Romney and Hoppner; 18th-century French tapestries; Renaissance bronzes, ivories and enamels; pieces by Fabergé; silver; and porcelain. The important collection of enamelled and gem-studded Renaissance jewellery is shown in the jewel vault.

RED HOUSE
(The National Trust)

Red House Lane, Bexleyheath DA6 8JF
Tel: 01494 755588 (Mon–Fri 9.30–4)
Open March–Sept Wed–Sun and bank holidays 11–5; Oct–Dec and mid–end Feb Wed–Sun 11–4.15 (last admissions 45mins before closing) by guided tour only. Telephone to book. Closed Jan–mid Feb, Mon–Tue (except bank holidays)
Station: Bexleyheath (from Charing Cross/Waterloo East/London Bridge)
Map p. 379, beyond 3F

Recently acquired by the National Trust (2003), Red House is a seminal building of the Arts and Crafts Movement and holds an important place in the history of domestic architecture in Britain. Designed by Philip Webb for his friend the artist and designer William Morris, and built on the site of an old orchard, it was completed in 1859 and became the Morris family home for the following five years. Webb's first independent commission, the house is generally regarded as the first Arts and Crafts building, although it predates by a quarter of a century the coining of the term. Together with the garden, which 'clothes' the house, and its interior, designed by Morris, with Rossetti and Burne-Jones, the house encapsulates the aesthetic of Morris, which rejected heavy Victorian opulence and mass production in favour of simplicity and good craftsmanship and design. The experience of Red House inspired Morris's foundation, in 1861, of the interior design firm Morris, Marshall, Faulkner & Company, which produced the wallpapers, fabrics and stained glass furniture so well known today (*see p. 349*). From 1952–2002 Red House was owned by the Hollamby family, who were sympathetic to its history and who reclaimed much of its original feel, with whitewashed or wallpapered walls, medieval details, such as the staircase with its tall newels, fixed items of furniture such as the hall settle, with unfinished paintings by Morris on the cupboard doors, and stained glass. Continuin̬ restoration will fully restore the house to how it looked in Morris's day.

ROYAL ACADEMY OF ARTS

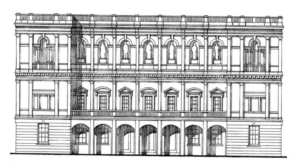

BURLINGTON HOUSE, PICCADILLY

Burlington House, Piccadilly, W1J 0BD
Tel: 020-7300 8000; www.royalacademy.org.uk
Open daily 10–6 (until 10pm on Fri); Fine Rooms Tues–Fri 1–4.30; Sat–Sun 10–6. Free guided tours Tues–Fri 1pm
Admission charge
Tube: Green Park/Piccadilly Circus
Restaurant and shop
Map p. 381, 2E

Founded in 1768 under the patronage of George III, with the distinguished portraitist Sir Joshua Reynolds as its first President, the Royal Academy's aim was and still is the promotion of art and design through its teaching Schools; its Summer Exhibition of contemporary British work, an annual event since 1769; and the staging of international loan exhibitions. It is for the latter that the Royal Academy (RA) is perhaps best known today, being one of the main venues in London for major national and international shows. The RA has always been a self-governing institution, its President elected from its body of Academicians (RAs) composed, since the 18th century, of leading painters, sculptors and architects and, from the 19th century, engravers. As well as Reynolds, past Presidents include great figures such as Benjamin West, Sir Thomas Lawrence, Lord Leighton (*see p. 156*), Sir Edwin Lutyens and, more recently, Sir Hugh Casson.

Burlington House

In 1837 the RA moved from its elegant purpose-built premises in Somerset House (*see p. 272*) to the new National Gallery building in Trafalgar Square and from there, in 1868, to Burlington House where it has been ever since. The present building, largely the work of Sydney Smirke (1866–76), encases a much older one. Smirke's alterations for the RA included the construction of large exhibition galleries to the rear, and heightening and altering the existing building. The house, begun c. 1664 by Sir John Denham, then bought and completed in 1668 by the 1st Earl of Burlington, was one of London's foremost private mansions. In the early 18th century it underwent radical alterations, first by James Gibbs for Juliana, Duchess of Burlington; and in 1717–20 by Colen Campbell for the Duchess' son, the famous architect and promoter of Palladianism, the 3rd Earl of Burlington (*see Chiswick House, p. 57*). The current façade, the block directly facing you as you pass through the central archway from Piccadilly, has Campbell's Palladian ground and first storeys and Smirke's third, a heavy addition with niches containing statues of British and Italian Renaissance painters and sculptors. The wings creating the courtyard, by Banks & Barry 1868–73 in Italian Renaissance style, house learned societies: to the left, the Linnaean Society, Royal Astronomical Society and Society of Antiquaries; to the right, the Royal Society of Chemistry and the Geological Society. The pleasant fountain jets in the centre of the courtyard are placed, apparently, according to Reynolds' horoscope.

Internally Burlington House has been extensively altered by a succession of architects. The low-ceilinged entrance hall, remodelled in 1899, contains ceiling paintings by West (*The Graces Unveiling Nature*, with the *Four Elements*) and Angelica Kauffmann (*Composition, Design, Painting* and *Invention*) removed from the RA's old meeting room in Somerset House. The central grand staircase by Samuel Ware (1815–18) leads to the Exhibition Galleries. Further up, past Sebastiano Ricci's grand Baroque paintings *The Triumph of Galatea* and *Diana and her Nymphs*, part of a decorative scheme from Gibbs' old staircase (c. 1712–15), and Kent's ceiling painting of *Architecture* with the portrait of Inigo Jones (c. 1720), are the RA's Fine Rooms (*see below*).

The Exhibitions

Smirke's **Exhibition Galleries**, a succession of large, grand spaces with a central octagonal hall, are where the Summer Exhibitions took place from 1769 and the Winter Old Master Exhibitions from 1870, from which the RA's current but more elaborate exhibition programme has evolved. The galleries witnessed spectacular crowds, especially in the 1880s and 90s during Leighton's successful Presidency when 350–400,000 visitors flocked to see popular masterpieces such as Sargent's *Carnation, Lily, Lily, Rose*, Logsdail's *St Martin-in-the-Fields* and Anna Lea Merritt's *Love Locked Out* (all now owned by the Tate). In was also here, in the octagonal hall in 1896, that Leighton's body lay in state. The Summer Exhibition (working hard to shake off its reputation as a bastion of conservatism) still takes place here as do the RA's excellent major loan exhibitions.

Norman Foster's **Sackler Galleries** (1985–91) on the third floor have created additional exhibition space, dramatically approached via a glass lift (or staircase) in the narrow space, now glazed, between the back of Burlington House and Smirke's Exhibition Galleries, affording an extraordinary close-up view of the architecture. Displayed outside the galleries is the Academy's greatest treasure, Michelangelo's carved marble *Madonna and Child with the Infant St John*, the so-called 'Taddei Tondo', a work of great beauty and spirituality, bequeathed to the RA in 1830. A further space behind the RA, approached from Burlington Gardens, has occasional loan exhibitions and art fairs while its future development is considered. A rich, Italianate building designed by Sir James Pennethorne for the University of London in 1867–70, until 1997 it was the Museum of Mankind and housed the British Museum's Ethnographic collection.

Fine Rooms and Permanent Collection

Overlooking the courtyard on the first floor are the recently restored John Madesjki Fine Rooms, splendid historic interiors which now display the RA's permanent collection. The rooms were the principal apartments of old Burlington House, which over the years have been altered by several architects on behalf of various owners and which from 1868 were the RA's administration and meeting rooms. Originally decorated, and perhaps designed, by William Kent for the 3rd Earl of Burlington, some were altered by John Carr for the 3rd Duke of Portland in 1771–75 and then remodelled again by Samuel Ware in 1815–18 for Lord George Cavendish. The **Saloon**, with its pedimented doorcases with large putti, rich gilding and ceiling by Kent, *The Marriage Feast of Cupid and Psyche*, is the most intact of the Burlington interiors. The **Secretary's Room** has another Kent ceiling but others are by Ricci, taken from the old staircase decorated for Juliana, Duchess of Burlington. The **Council Room** has Ricci's old staircase ceiling; The **General Assembly Room** his *Triumph of Bacchus*, originally on the staircase wall; and the Riccis either side of the current staircase are also from the dismantled scheme.

Throughout the rooms are paintings, sculpture and architectural drawings from the RA's significant permanent collection which includes Diploma Works presented by RAs on their election as members (a requirement since 1768); plaster casts after the antique (used for teaching in the RA Schools); portraits of RAs; and other works either collected or bequeathed. Among the paintings by Fuseli, Turner, Gainsborough and Millais; sculpture by Flaxman and Chantrey; and architectural drawings by Soane and Waterhouse, is Reynolds' *Self-portrait with a bust of Michelangelo*; Constable's famous *Leaping Horse* (exhibited at the RA in 1825); Sargent's *An Interior in Venice* (his Diploma work); Stubbs' anatomical drawings for his *Anatomy of the Horse*; and many more works by other and more modern members. Not all works can be shown: the selection changes approximately every 18 months (five months for works on paper).

Further works are displayed on the **Norman Shaw staircase**, which leads to the restaurant in the basement, a handsome space also designed by Shaw with murals by Harold Speed (*Autumn*, 1898), Fred Appleyard (*Spring Driving away Winter*, 1902) and most recently a large scene by Leonard Rosoman (1984–85).

The Baroque in England

The dramatic art and architecture of the Baroque, with all its theatricality and direct appeal to the senses and emotions, took hold in Britain following the triumphant restoration to the throne of Charles II in 1660, when 'all arts seemed to return from their exile'. An international court language which bolstered the absolutist regimes of much of Europe, it flourished in Britain until the early 18th century. The period witnessed the architecture of Sir Christopher Wren, Nicholas Hawksmoor and Sir John Vanbrugh, the vast illusionistic mural paintings of Antonio Verrio, Louis Laguerre and Sir James Thornhill, and the virtuoso limewood carving of Grinling Gibbons. In 1660 Charles II and his courtiers set about equipping the Stuart monarchy with a magnificent setting suitable for the restored regime, inspired by the visual splendour witnessed at the courts of Europe. Baroque culture, with its emphasis on vastness of size, immense cost and grandeur, as well as the theatrical etiquette and ceremony which accompanied it, was used by the Stuart court to underline the power of the monarch and reinforce it in the minds of the people. Outside London, Verrio decorated the ceilings of the remodelled Windsor Castle with vast allegorical scenes celebrating the might of the crown. In London, following the Great Fire of 1666, Sir Christopher Wren's new St Paul's Cathedral rose glorious from the ashes, a magnificent symbol of the Anglican nation, its great dome decorated by Thornhill. William and Mary created their great Baroque palace, Hampton Court, in conscious competition with Louis XIV's Versailles, its painted ceilings and sculpture symbolic of William as the Protestant victor of Europe. Greenwich Hospital, with Thornhill's supreme masterpiece, the Painted Hall, reflected the magnificence, munificence and charity of the crown.

In an age which, following the 1688 Glorious Revolution, saw the curbing of the absolute authority of the crown and the championing of civil liberty, Whig adherents increasingly associated the reigns of the old Stuart monarchs as periods of aggressive Roman Catholicism, tyrannical government and extravagant ostentation. The Baroque, inextricably bound up with the Stuarts, fell from favour. In its stead came Palladianism, rooted in the ideals of ancient Rome, and hailed as a purer and more restrained form of art. Symptomatic of this change was the renewed interest in the unsullied Classicism of the architecture of Inigo Jones, particularly championed by Lord Burlington and his circle, who saw in its 'still unravished' lines a style and culture which better reflected the decorum and gravitas of the new Augustan age.

ROYAL ACADEMY OF MUSIC MUSEUM

1 York Gate, Marylebone Road, NW1 5HT
Tel: 020-7873 7373; www.ram.ac.uk/museum
Open Mon–Fri 12.30–6.30, Sat, Sun 2–5
Free
Tube: Baker Street/Regents Park
Shop
Map p. 379, 2D

The Royal Academy of Music was founded in 1822 at the instigation of the keen ama-
teur composer Lord Burghersh, later Earl of Westmorland, and granted its Royal
Charter by George IV in 1830. It was the original venue for the Proms, the
'Promenade Concerts' devised by the impresario Robert Newman in 1895 to 'train the
public' to appreciate classical music. All that survives of the original building,
destroyed by bombing, are five carved busts representing Beethoven, Mozart, Bach,
Haydn and possibly Purcell, now displayed in the basement lobby. The Royal
Academy of Music (since 1999 a college of London University) moved here in 1911.

The museum is now housed in York Gate, designed in 1822 by John Nash (*see p.
50*) as a main entrance to his new Regent's Park. The collections include a number of
treasures: a Renaissance-style lute by Venere of Padua, dating from 1584 and still with
its original back; a horn used by Alfred Brain, principal horn of 20th Century Fox.
'The Violin Family' features selections from a collection of more than 200 stringed
instruments, kept in playing order by the resident luthier, whose workshop can also
be seen. The collection includes the Archinto violin (1696), the Rutson
violin (1694), and the Maurin violin (1718), all by Stradivari, as well as instruments
made by the Amati brothers. They form a representative selection of most of the
famous names. Violins seem to have originated in eastern Lombardy, in the craftwork
traditions of Cremona, native town of Stradivari and the Amati and Guarneri families.
A Turkish violin here from 1737 was made by Giuseppe Guarneri del Gesù, who
incorporated the Jesus monogram into his label and was popularised by Paganini. The
instrument has been played by the great Russian interpreter of Brahms Jaschka
Heifitz; Isaac Stern,; and Polish violinist Henryk Szeryng, best known for his recordings of Bach and Mozart. The Savage-Stevens bequest of 1865 includes an important
collection of 17th- and 18th-century Italian manuscripts, purchased in 1817. The
Goetz Library of full scores was donated in 1902 and the David Munrow collection in
1993. Conductors' libraries include those of Otto Klemperer, Henry Wood and John
Barbirolli. On the second floor, the Piano Collection demonstrates the technical development of the grand piano in the first half of the 19th century and contrasts it with
the daintier Viennese style, illustrated by nine examples. The sequence of English
square pianos traces half a century of changes responding to composers and players.

ROYAL COLLEGE OF MUSIC
MUSEUM OF INSTRUMENTS

Prince Consort Road, SW7 2BS
Tel: 020-7591 4346; www.rcm.ac.uk
Open Wed, Thur in term-time, 2–4.30 or by appointment
Admission charge
Tube: South Kensington
Map p. 380, 3B

Close to the Royal Albert Hall, in a building by Sir A.W. Blomfield in 'French baronial' style, the College owns a remarkable collection of musical instruments, comprising some 800 items dating from the end of the 15th century to the present day. Founded in 1883, with Sir George Grove as its first Director, the college received important collections from, among others, Rajah Sourindro Mohun Tagore (1884); the Prince of Wales, later King Edward VII (1886); founder of the College Sir George Donaldson (1894), curator of the historic music rooms for the International Inventions Exhibition in the Royal Albert Hall in 1885; and A.J. Hipkins (1911), first honorary curator at the College.

The museum is housed in a purpose-built 1970s split-level room. In the far left-hand corner at ground level is a clavicytherium of c. 1480, the oldest known stringed keyboard instrument in the world. Probably made in Germany, it features an elaborately carved miniature Gothic rose window and was preserved in the Contarini and Correr collections near Venice until it was exhibited in London in 1885 and then acquired by Donaldson. A working copy, which can be seen—and occasionally heard—here, was commissioned by the College from Adlam-Burnett in 1973. One of the earliest harpsichords to survive can be seen nearby, dated 1531, by Alessandro Trasuntino of Venice, the inside of the outer case decorated with a voluptuous Venus and Cupid painted by the school of Paris Bordone, c. 1580. The remarkably well preserved polygonal virginals by Giovanni Celestini (1593), also the oldest surviving of its type, was decorated in Venice towards the end of the 16th century with miniature paintings of the contest between Apollo and Pan, Apollo pursuing Daphne, and Orpheus playing to the animals. Items with historical associations include a clavichord that was once owned by Haydn; a spinet supposed to have been given to Handel by his friend A.G. Leamon, from whose descendants it was acquired by Hipkins; and trombones that belonged to Elgar and Holst. Among the organs, rare examples are the German table regal of the late 17th century, the portable Bible regal from the early 18th century, designed to fold up like a book, and the chamber organ attributed to the important Restoration builder Bernard Smith, from around 1702. Displayed with several percussion instruments is an early 19th-century glass harmonica of the type invented by Benjamin Franklin. Both Mozart and Beethoven composed for glass harmonica, an instrument which is notoriously difficult to play. Among the wind instruments is an early 19th-century Northumbrian smallpipe and a rare Scottish stock-and-horn, of which only one other original survives. These last two both once belonged to the artist and caricaturist Charles Keene.

On the gallery level are the bowed and plucked stringed instruments, and the College's ethnographic collection of Asian and African instruments. The bowed strings include the oldest-known baryton, from 1647, a very rare example of an instrument that was played like a viol and made some time before being brought into vogue by Haydn and Prince Nikolaus Esterházy. Among the plucked instruments is a very well-preserved lute-like instrument, a chitarrone from 1608, made by Magno Tieffenbrucker of Venice, and a late 16th-century cittern that once belonged to Rossini, and was used, according to a label discovered inside, as a model by Titian. Also particularly fine is the museum's ten-strong collection of guitars. They include the earliest known guitar in the world, from 1581, complete with its original back, made by Belchior Diaz of Lisbon. The Asian and African instruments, composed largely from the collections donated by Tagore and King Edward VII, include a rare 17th-century Afro-Portuguese ivory horn; a Tibetan dragon horn; Indian stringed instruments, including a *vina* decorated with carved depictions of scenes from the life of Krishna; and an arched harp, shaped like a boat, from Burma, a type of instrument that appears in the very earliest Egyptian and Sumerian sources. Several of the museum's most precious instruments can be heard in action on a computerised 'virtual tour'.

The collection of portraits, selections from which are displayed in the museum, contains depictions of the greatest composers, instrumentalists, singers and conductors of all nations, although the emphasis is on British musicians or those who worked in Britain. Outstanding items include Houdon's terracotta bust of Gluck; Burne-Jones's portrait of Paderewski (1890) and Epstein's bust of Vaughan Williams.

ROYAL HOSPITAL MUSEUM
CHELSEA HOSPITAL

Royal Hospital Road, Chelsea, SW3 4SR
Tel: 020-7881 5203; www.chelsea-pensioners.org.uk
Free
Open daily 10–12 and 2–4. Closed on Sun Oct–Mar, and bank holidays
Tube: Sloane Square
Shop

Founded by Charles II in 1682 for invalided and elderly soldiers, the Royal Hospital, Chelsea appears much as it did in the 17th century. Sir Christopher Wren's magnificent building dominates Royal Hospital Road, with its elegant central Doric portico, surmounted by a small tower and cupola, with ranges of red brick to east and west. Here around 420 Chelsea Pensioners still have lodgings, and the governing routines of the Hospital are little changed since its foundation. The 1961 Infirmary to the east is due to be replaced with a building by Quinlan Terry.

Sir Christopher Wren's restrained and elegant Royal Hospital, Chelsea (1692).

As you stand in the central Octagon Porch, to the east is the **Chapel**, with fine oak carving, its apse filled by the *Resurrection*, an unexpected splash of Baroque verve, painted by Sebastiano Ricci in 1716 (the oil sketch for the work is at Dulwich Picture Gallery). To the west is the magnificent **Hall**, where the Pensioners eat. The west wall is filled with a mural by Antonio Verrio, an equestrian portrait of Charles II in the centre, the king surrounded by marine deities, the Royal Hospital in the background. Recently restored, it was started in 1687, Verrio being assisted by the artist Henry Cooke. Straight ahead from the Octagon Porch is **Figure Court**, a wide, magnificent courtyard enclosed by ranges to either side, the north range with a handsome open colonnade. In the centre is Grinling Gibbons's statue of Charles II, a classical image of Imperial authority, recently regilded and dazzling in the sun. Presented to Charles II by Tobias Rustat and placed here in 1685, every Founder's Day (Oak Apple Day, 29 May, Charles II's birthday and the day which celebrated his Restoration to the throne) it is wreathed with oak leaves. The south end is open, with a vista over the beautiful Hospital grounds to the river. Originally laid out as water gardens, the gateways retain their original Jean Tijou wrought ironwork.

In the range to the west of the main Hospital buildings is the small **Museum**, refurbished in 2001. A model of the Hospital shows it c. 1745, with, adjoining the Hospital gardens to the west, the famous Ranelagh Pleasure Gardens with its celebrated Rotunda (Canaletto's view of the inside of the Rotunda is at the National Gallery). Pictures include George Jones's *Battle of Waterloo*, and a full-length of the Duke of Wellington by John

Simpson. There is a mock-up of a pensioner's 'berth', the 9ft-square panelled living accommodation (a 1990s improvement on Wren's original 6ft-square spaces) ranged in succession down the Long Wards; examples of the Chelsea Pensioners' distinctive uniforms, bright scarlet coats for summer, dark blue for winter; and a display of military service medals bequeathed by Pensioners over the years.

ROYAL INSTITUTE OF BRITISH ARCHITECTS

66 Portland Place, W1B 1AD
Tel: 020-7307 3770; www.architecture.com
Open Tues–Fri 10–9, Sat 10–5
Free
Tube: Regent's Park/Great Portland Street
Café and bookshop
Map p. 379, 2D

Designed by G. Grey Wornum (1888–1957) and purpose-built for the RIBA, the building opened in 1934. One of the first 'modern' buildings to be listed Grade II, the stern Art Deco exterior of Portland stone is decorated with sculpted figures and reliefs showing a painter, a sculptor, an architect (Sir Christopher Wren), an engineer and a labourer. The huge cast bronze doors depict in relief the river Thames and its London buildings, including St Paul's and the Houses of Parliament. Most striking on passing through them is the stairwell ascending from the entrance hall. The treads are in figured Dema marble and black birdseye marble, framed by four large columns clad in pink Ashburton marble. On the landing ceiling are six moulded plaster illustrations of the main periods of English architecture. The stairs lead up to the Henry Florence Memorial Hall, an impressive space taken up with a café and temporary exhibitions. The plaster ceiling reliefs illustrate different building trades, while the window piers of carved Perrycot stone show 'man and his buildings through the ages'.

ROYAL INSTITUTION FARADAY MUSEUM

21 Albemarle Street, W1S 4BS
Tel: 020-7409 2992; www.rigb.org
Open Mon–Fri 10–5
Admission charge
Tube: Green Park
Map p. 381, 1E

NB: At the time of writing, the Faraday Museum was due to close for 12 months.
Behind an impressive rank of Corinthian columns, modelled on the Temple of

Antoninus in Rome, is the Royal Institution of Great Britain, founded in 1799 to promote 'the application of Science to the common Purposes of Life'. In the basement, in the area occupied until 1872 by his laboratory, is a small museum devoted to the scientific discoveries of Michael Faraday (1791–1867). Born the son of a blacksmith, and initially apprenticed as bookbinder, Faraday discovered electro-magnetic rotation (the principle behind the electric motor) and—even more importantly for 19th-century industry—electro-magnetic induction (the principle behind transformers and generators), as well as benzene, the magneto-optical effect, diamagnetism and field theory. He himself was discovered by Humphry Davy, the second professor of chemistry at the Royal Institution. In 1812, at the age of 21, inspired by Davy's final four lectures, Faraday had presented his notes to the great man in application for an interview. It was granted, but no position was available. The following year, a fight between the Instrument Maker and Chemical Assistant resulted in the latter's dismissal, giving Davy the opportunity to appoint Faraday as his assistant. From October that year until April 1815, he accompanied Davy and his new wife Jane on a scientific tour of the continent. They travelled on a passport from Napoleon allowing the couple a maid and also a valet, a job description that caused Faraday some distress but gave him the opportunity to witness scientific research in Paris, Italy, Switzerland and Germany. Back in London, he helped Davy develop his celebrated miner's safety lamp. In 1821, he published his first piece of original research, on electro-magnetic rotation, followed ten years later by his discovery of induction. The site of his original laboratory was restored in 1973, guided by eight watercolours painted by Harriet Jane Moore during the 1850s: the result is an ordered chaos of cabinets, bottles, bell jars, table stands, and a hand-operated vacuum pump. In the adjoining exhibition area are shown further pieces of his equipment, including the Great Cylinder Machine built in 1803, which he used to observe the nature of electrical discharge, a stool insulated with glass legs, the voltaic pile (prototype of the battery) given to him by Alessandro Volta, the original discoverer of electro-magnetism in 1800, and an electric egg that Faraday used to demonstrate electrical discharge in gases. Variations under different pressures allowed Faraday to identify the 'dark discharge' near the cathode now known as the Faraday Dark Space.

ROYAL LONDON HOSPITAL MUSEUM

St Philip's Church, Newark Street, Whitechapel, E1 2AA
Address for correspondence: c/o Royal London Hospital, Whitechapel Road, E1 1BB
Tel: 020-7377 7608; www.brlcf.org.uk
Open Mon–Fri 10–4.30
Free
Tube: Whitechapel
Café (in hospital) and shop
Map p. 379, 2E

Located in the crypt of the hospital's former church of St Philip and St Augustine, now a medical library, the museum tells the story of The London Hospital (founded 1740), once Britain's largest voluntary hospital. Refurbished in 2002 and arranged in chronological order in three sections covering the 18th, 19th and 20th centuries, some of the items were originally collected by Henry Wellcome (*see p. 265*). Displays cover the history of healthcare in the East End generally, as well as of the hospital itself, featuring sections on children and health, early surgery, Victorian doctors, Dr Barnardo, early X-rays and the hospital in the two world wars. A display on forensic medicine sponsored by crime writer Patricia Cornwell covers the Whitechapel 'Jack the Ripper' murders, and Christie's murders at Rillington Place. Other highlights include a video about Joseph Merrick (the elephant man), the last letter of Edith Cavell—the nurse executed by the Germans in 1915 for helping Allied soldiers to escape occupied Belgium—and a fragment of George Washington's false teeth.

ROYAL MEWS

Buckingham Palace Road, SW1
Tel: 020-7766 7302; www.royalresidences.com
Open March–July and Oct daily except Fri 11–4, Aug–Sept daily 10–5
Admission charge.
Tube: Victoria/Green Park
Shop (free entry)
Map p. 381, 3E

The Royal Mews is a working department of the Royal Household, responsible for the care and maintenance of the sovereign's horse-drawn carriages of state, official cars and internal mail. Likened by members of the Royal family to a small village, it now occupies the south corner of the gardens of Buckingham Palace, beyond the conspicuous pediment of the **Riding House**. Designed by Sir William Chambers in 1765–66, this was one of George III's early improvements to his new purchase, Buckingham House. The pediment was adorned in 1859 with a sculpted relief of Hercules and the Thracian Horses, the man-eating mares whom Hercules tamed by feeding them their master's flesh. Queen Victoria watched her nine children learn to ride here, where royal horses are still trained to become accustomed to the sounds of marching bands, crowds and flag waving. Beyond the Riding House are the main quadrangle, stables, coach houses and clock tower, all designed in 1825 by John Nash, as part of his renovation of Buckingham House for George IV (*see p. 47*).

The Royal Transport

Queen Alexandra's State Coach is considered to be the finest built in the collection, converted by Hoopers into a 'glass state coach' in 1893. Decorated with 67 different crowns, it has now been adapted to carry the Imperial State Crown to the State

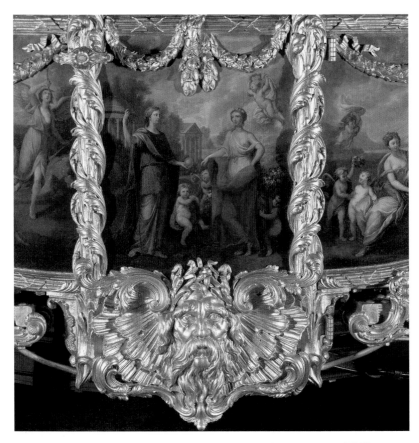

Gilded Neptune by Wilton and side panels by Cipriani on the Gold State Coach (1762).

Openings of Parliament. On these occasions, the Queen normally travels in the **Irish State Coach**, originally built by Hutton's of Dublin 1803–04. First favoured by Queen Victoria after the death of Prince Albert, and later severely damaged by a fire, it was meticulously restored, and carried Princess Margaret and the Queen Mother to the Queen's coronation in Westminster Abbey in 1953. The 1902 **State Landau**, built by Hoopers for King Edward VII, is used by the monarch to meet visiting heads of state. Prince Charles travelled to St Paul's in this open coach for his wedding to Lady Diana Spencer in 1981. She herself was conveyed to the cathedral in the **Glass Coach**, first used for King George V's coronation in 1911. The **Scottish State Coach** was built in 1830 and used at the coronation of King William IV. In the late 60s, on the wish of the Queen, it was adorned with the Order of the Thistle and Royal Arms of Scotland

and refurbished by the St Cuthbert's Co-Operative Society in Edinburgh. Also on display are some of the five royal **Rolls-Royce Phantoms IV to VI**. In place of the marque's 'Spirit of Ecstasy', a silver statuette depicts St George and the Dragon, designed by Edward Seago.

Some of the **Queen's horses**, the famous Windsor greys and Cleveland bays, can also be seen in loose boxes on the south side of the quadrangle. Apart from the thoroughbred bays, their names are each chosen by Her Majesty.

The extraordinary **Gold State Coach** was built for George III in 1762 to a design approved by William Chambers, costing eight thousand pounds. It has been used at every coronation since that of George IV in 1821, weighs nearly four tonnes and is pulled by eight horses proceeding at a walk. William IV likened the ride to 'a ship tossing in a rough sea'. After the death of Prince Albert, Queen Victoria refused to use it, complaining of the 'distressing oscillations'. A fantastic showpiece designed to trumpet British sea power, the gilded body framework carved by Joseph Wilton comprises eight palm trees, each of the four corner trees rising from a lion's head, and supporting trophies symbolising British victories against France in the Seven Years War (1756–63). The body is slung on braces of morocco leather held by four gilded tritons or bearded sea gods, half-man half-fish, the front pair blowing conch shells, the winged pair behind holding trident fasces, symbols of the King's maritime authority. Putti symbolising England, Scotland and Ireland stand at the centre of the roof, supporting the royal crown. The design of the wheels is based on those of an ancient triumphal chariot. Eight side panels painted by Wilton's assistant, the Florentine artist Giovanni Battista Cipriani (1727–85), depict classical scenes celebrating the wealth and success of Britannia. The carriage is displayed here complete with four model horses in full harness and livery, ridden postillion by two mannequins also in livery. Encircling the room is a frieze painted by Richard Barrett Davis, animal painter to King William IV, showing the carriage and that monarch's coronation procession in 1831. King William had wanted a relatively quiet affair compared to that of his predecessor George IV ten years earlier, which had cost 240 thousand pounds. At the Duke of Wellington's insistence, parliament voted 50 thousand pounds for the event; it in fact ended up costing slightly less.

ROYAL SOCIETY OF ARTS

8 John Adam St, WC2N 6EZ
Tel: 020-7930 5115; www.rsa.org.uk
Open to the public on first Sun of every month (except Jan), 10–1;
otherwise open by appointment
Free
Tube: Charing Cross
Map p. 382, 2B

Founded in 1754 as the Society for the Encouragement of Arts, Manufactures and Commerce, the RSA (as it now known), sprang out of the speculative coffee-house culture of the Strand, a patriotic pressure-group designed to recognise, accredit and reward hard-working entrepreneurs. Founder William Shipley, a drawing master from Northampton, wrote that his aim was 'to render Great Britain the school of instruction as it is already the centre of traffic to the greatest part of the known world'. The Society mounted the first public art exhibition in 1761, the preface to its catalogue penned by Dr Johnson, and went on to help in the organisation of the Great Exhibition of 1851 and of the establishment of the National Training School of Music, predecessor of the Royal College of Music, in 1876. It also had a hand in the Festival of Britain in 1951.

In 1863 the Society instituted the annual Albert Medal for 'distinguished merit in promoting Arts, Manufactures and Commerce', the first recipient being Sir Rowland Hill for his part in setting up the Penny Post. Subsequent awards have gone to the discoverer of electro-magnetism Michael Faraday (1866; *see p. 252*), the pioneer of antisepsis Joseph Lister (1894), Bauhaus architect Walter Gropius (1961), ornithologist Sir Peter Scott (1970), architectural historian Sir Nikolaus Pevsner (1976), musician Yehudi Menuhin (1981), conductor Sir Simon Rattle (1997), and lager beer entrepreneur Karan Bilimoria (2004). In 1935, in conjunction with the Royal Academy, the RSA mounted the first important exhibition of industrial design, which led to the establishment of the Design Council and also the RSA's own faculty of Royal Designers for Industry: among those appointed members are architect Sir Norman Foster, fashion designer Issey Miyake and the designer of the iMac, Jonathan Ive.

The Building

In 1770 the architect brothers John, Robert, James and William Adam began work on a sumptuous riverside development called the Adelphi, meaning 'brotherhood'. Almost the only part of their original edifice now surviving is the home that Robert and James completed for the Society four years later at No. 8 John Street (now John Adam Street). Robert Adam's elegant Palladian façade frames a large, arched Venetian window, surmounted by a stucco crescent of plaster, the epistyle of the entablature inscribed 'Arts and Commerce Promoted'. In the entrance hall and grand stairwell, both re-modelled in the 1920s, the columns imitate the Adams' front porch, and wall panels list those honoured as RDIs (Royal Designer for Industry), as well as the Presidents of the RSA, and recipients of the Albert Medal. The staircase, decorated with one portrait of Prince Albert and another of Queen Victoria looking over the plans for the Great Exhibition, leads up to the landing and the Great Room. Near the door sits the President's Chair, a massive piece designed by Sir William Chambers in 1759, and still used by the current president when attending lectures or award ceremonies.

The Great Room

The Great Room, designed by Robert Adam as an assembly room for discussions, debates and presentations, is dominated by James Barry's epic series of mural paintings, *The Progress of Human Knowledge and Culture*. Left and right within his scheme are portraits of two early presidents: *Robert, Lord Romney* by Joshua Reynolds and *Jacob, Lord Folkestone* by Thomas Gainsborough. In 1774 ten artists including Barry had been invited to undertake the decoration of the room, but all declined. Three years later Barry offered to do the job free of charge, in exchange for his board, canvas, paints and models. In his own 'Account' of the six pictures in the series, he writes that they were intended to 'illustrate one great maxim or moral truth, that the obtaining of happiness, as well individual as public, depends on cultivating the human faculties'. Impressive to behold, their symbolism certainly seems to be at least as important as their art, a stirring allegory of the aims and objectives of the Society.

On the west wall, left upon entering the room, the first painting, *Orpheus*, shows 'the founder of Grecian theology' with his lyre, surrounded by 'people as savage as their soil', their cave-dwelling children prey to wild beasts. Barry defended his depiction of a woman shouldering a dead deer by reminding his more delicate readers that 'the value and estimation of women increases according to the growth and cultivation of society'. All the paintings emphasise struggle and competition as fundamental characteristics of progress. The second painting, *Thanksgiving to the Rural Deities*, is perhaps the least portentous. It depicts a 'Grecian harvest-home', with Ceres and Bacchus looking down upon an Arcadian group happily dancing around Sylvanus and Pan. But as Barry points out: 'It is but a stage at which we cannot stop, as I have endeavoured to exemplify by the group of contending figures in the middle distance, where there are men wrestling.' The third painting, *Crowning the Victors at Olympia*, runs the full length of the north wall facing the door and was originally the backdrop for the Society's own award ceremonies. Representing the climax of Ancient Civilization, the composition features many famous faces from the Golden Age of Greece, and some too from Barry's own time: Pericles appears as William Pitt the Elder, and the artist Timanthus as a younger version of Barry himself. The next painting blends myth and reality more boldly: *Commerce, or the Triumph of the Thames* shows Father Thames being borne along by tritons in the shape of the great navigators Drake, Raleigh, Cabot and Cook. The white cliffs of Dover can be seen in the background, behind a strange landmark monument added by Barry in 1801: 'a combined mausoleum, observatory and lighthouse which the Tritons have erected in tribute to the first Naval Power'. The penultimate painting, *The Distribution of the Premiums in the Society of the Arts*, features many of the people involved in the early years of the Society standing in front of Chambers' Somerset House with the dome of St Paul's in the background. Founder William Shipley sits in the bottom left-hand corner, the instrument of the institution in his hand; Dr Johnson 'points out Mrs Montagu to the Duchesses of Rutland and Devonshire as worthy their attention and imitation'; William Locke and Dr Hunter look over a youth's promising drawings; the agriculturalist Lord Arthur Young, who had quarrelled with Barry, is shown in unflattering profile.

The final painting, *Elysium or the State of Final Retribution*, running the length of the south wall, shows a gathering of 'those great and good men of all ages and nations, who were cultivators and benefactors of mankind'. A pelican in her piety (feeding its young with its own blood), a symbol of Christ's love and sacrifice—perhaps also a reminder of Barry's ardent but necessarily covert Catholicism—here apparently 'typifies the generous labours of those personages in the picture, who had worn themselves out in the service of mankind'. Among the 150 or so personages included are Archimedes, Descartes, Copernicus, Galileo, Columbus, Hogarth and, in Barry's words, the 'glorious sextumvirate of Epaminondas, Socrates, Cato, Lucius Junius Brutus, Marcus Brutus and Sir Thomas More, which Swift so happily brought together in his account of the island of Glubbdubdribb'. Swift himself appears in the company of Erasmus and Cervantes. Among the legislators, Alfred the Great stands proudly centre stage with William Penn and Trajan looking over his shoulder. In the bottom left-hand corner are the dark shades of Tartarus, with a volcano vomiting flames and men, an uncomfortable home for a 'malicious whisperer', a vain man wearing the Order of the Garter, a worldly Pope and 'a wretch holding the Solemn League and Covenant', the Scottish protestants' oath against King Charles I.

The Tour
In the 20th century the RSA's house expanded into Nos. 6, 4 and 2 John Adam Street, and the tour includes other Adam rooms, their correct proportions preserved and several featuring doors and fireplaces rescued from Bowood House in Wiltshire. The Romney room in particular has been carefully restored to its original colour scheme, with ceiling panels showing 'Pan celebrating the feast of Bacchus' by the school of Antonio Zucchi and his wife Angelica Kauffmann. The Shipley Room also has a fine decorative ceiling. The back yard of No. 8 was converted in the late 1980s into a glazed atrium and staircase (Green Lloyd) leading down to the 18th-century brick vaults. In the Durham Street Auditorium, the mid-19th-century street running down to the river from the Strand has been exposed and preserved.

The RSA also holds one of the largest single collections of paintings on loan from the Arts Council Collection. These include works by Lucien Freud, Norman Adams, Elizabeth Frink, Frank Auerbach and Gillian Ayres. Specially commissioned by the RSA in 1991 to commemorate 50 years of royal patronage, Justin Mortimer's portrait of the Queen displays an unusually fresh but not irreverent approach to its subject. A portrait by Stuart Pearson Wright of HRH Duke of Edinburgh, commissioned in 2002 to celebrate the half-century of his presidency, did not find favour: 'As long as I don't have to have it on my wall,' the Prince is reported to have declared.

SAATCHI GALLERY

County Hall, South Bank, SE1
Tel: 020-7823 2363; www.saatchi-gallery.co.uk
Open Sun–Thur 10–8; Fri, Sat 10–10
Admission charge
Tube: Westminster/Waterloo
Map p. 382, 3B

Selections from the attention-grabbing Saatchi collection of over 2,500 recent British and American artworks can be seen in the surprisingly formal setting of County Hall. These grand offices of the London County Council and its successor, the Greater London Council, were designed by Ralph Knott from 1902–22, when they were occupied by the LCC, and finally completed in 1974. Following the abolition of the Greater London Council in 1986, County Hall has hosted an eclectic variety of tenants, all attracted by the central riverside location beside Westminster Bridge. These tenants were joined in 2003 by the Saatchi Gallery, relocating from its white-walled, top-lit home in a former paint factory on Boundary Road, St John's Wood, where it had first opened in 1985. Seven years later, picking up on the success of 'Freeze', a show curated in 1988 by Goldsmiths College Fine Arts graduate Damien Hirst, Charles Saatchi mounted a show at Boundary Road entitled 'Young British Artists I'. The YBAs, such as Hirst, Tracey Emin, Jake and Dinos Chapman, Sarah Lucas and Gavin Turk, predominantly conceptual artists and sculptors, have since monopolised the public's perception of the Saatchi Collection, especially since the success of the 'Sensation' exhibition at the Royal Academy in 1997, itself perhaps an inspiration for the move into the establishment confines of County Hall. Recent shows here, entitled 'The Triumph of Painting', have begun to address other forms of art represented in the Saatchi Collection, while continuing to promote both established and up-and-coming artists working in all media.

A tour of any exhibition here entails a circuit of the parquet-floored corridors of former bureaucracy, with detours into the empty offices of erstwhile Council functionaries. These small individual rooms, windowless and wood-panelled, with stopped clocks above the municipal mantelpieces and cold grates below them, are intensely evocative—and also sometimes highly appropriate—spaces for the display of individual artworks or groups of work. Most exhibitions also make a feature of the Rotunda Room, formerly the Council's conference room, with its domed, coffered ceiling and convenient bays between marble Corinthian columns. Another permanent fixture is the installation '20:50' (1987) by Richard Wilson, a formal room filled up to the door handles with engine oil, a steel walkway let into the middle, creating a mirror image of the room. The effect is disorientating and pungent.

ST BARTHOLOMEW'S HOSPITAL MUSEUM

North Wing, St Bartholomew's Hospital, West Smithfield, EC1A 7BE
Tel: 020-7601 8152; www.brlcf.org.uk
Open Tues–Fri 10–4. For guided tours of St Bartholomew the Less, the Hospital Square, North Wing (staircase and Great Hall), St Bartholomew the Great and the Cloth Fair, meet at 2pm on Fridays at the Henry VIII gate
Free
Tube: St Paul's/Barbican
Café (in hospital) and small bookshop
Map p. 383, 1D

St Bartholomew's Hospital, one of London's major hospitals, was founded in 1123, with the Priory of St Bartholomew, by Rahere, a former courtier of Henry I. St Bartholomew appeared to him in a vision, demanding the establishment of a hospital for the poor and sick. The hospital's small museum tells the history of this ancient charitable and medical institution, from the 12th century to the present day. Entry is through the Henry VIII gate, which leads to the hospital's main square, built in the 18th century by James Gibbs, whose designs replaced most of the medieval architecture. The museum is under the north wing archway. On show is Rahere's 1137 grant, an ancient document which has been at the Hospital without interruption, except perhaps at the time of the 1666 Great Fire. There are also a magnificent 1546 charter which refounded the Hospital following the dissolution of the Priory, with Henry VIII's Great Seal; displays relating to William Harvey, the famous discoverer of the circulation of the blood, who was physician to Barts (as the hospital is popularly known) from 1609–43; and historic surgical, medical and apothecary's equipment.

The museum's other magnificent attraction is Gibbs's 1730–32 North Wing, with its grand staircase leading to the vast Great Hall, the highly decorated, official and ceremonial rooms of the hospital. The staircase is decorated with large biblical New Testament **scenes by William Hogarth**, *The Pool of Bethesda* and *The Good Samaritan*. Hogarth carried out the work for free, and was elected a governor of the hospital in return. He wrested the commission from the Venetian artist Jacopo Amigoni (who was instrumental in persuading Canaletto to visit London) in 1734. Beyond charitable philanthropy and the desire to be a hospital governor, Hogarth had several reasons for wanting the project: Barts was personal to him, since he was born in the area; he could avenge his late father-in-law Sir James Thornhill's humiliation at having had his great Baroque works at Moor Park replaced with those of Amigoni; he could champion the work of the British School; and he could establish himself as a serious, large-scale history painter. Hogarth himself recognised the ambitious challenge he had set himself of painting figures 'seven foot tall'. In April 1736 the *Pool of Bethesda* was complete, and the *Good Samaritan* the following year, by July when the scaffolding was taken down. The governors thanked Hogarth for his pictures 'which illustrate the Charity extended to the Poor, Sick and Lame of this Hospital', which quickly became one of the sights of London. Several elements of Hogarth's dignified scenes draw on Raphael's 'Acts of the Apostles' cartoons, then at Hampton Court, now at the V&A (*see pp. 116 and 324*), regarded at the time as the high point of artistic excellence. The figure of Christ, for example, is based on Raphael's *Feed My Sheep*. Hogarth had also carefully observed the patients at Barts for the sick being cured by Christ (an infant with rickets, a man with gout, and an emaciated old woman). The landscape background is attributed to Hogarth's fellow artist and friend George Lambert; the scenes are set within feigned Rococo plasterwork, executed by a Mr Richards; and below are grisaille scenes showing Rahere's vision and establishment of the hospital, and a sick man being carried into the hospital on a stretcher.

ST BRIDE'S CRYPT MUSEUM

St Bride's Church, Fleet Street, EC4Y 8AM
Tel: 020-7427 0133; www.stbrides.com
Open Mon–Fri 9–6, Sat 11–3
Free
Tube: Blackfriars
Map p. 382, 2C

A small display in the crypt of the famous Wren church (1675) illustrates the history of the church and also of the printing industry, for which Fleet Street was once famous. An apprentice of William Caxton's, Wynkyn de Worde, set up a press near here in the early 16th century. A Roman pavement discovered on the site during repair of the devastating Second World War bomb damage can be seen.

SCIENCE MUSEUM

Exhibition Road, South Kensington, SW7 2DD
Tel: 0870 870 4868; www.sciencemuseum.org.uk
Open daily 10–6. Often crowded at weekends and during school holidays
Free
Tube: South Kensington
Cafés and shop
Map p. 380, 3B

Like the Victoria & Albert Museum, the origins of the Science Museum lie in the Great Exhibition of 1851. In the following year the Museum of Manufactures was opened on the first floor of Marlborough House, maintaining a permanent collection of selected Exhibition items, later transferred to the South Kensington Museum. In 1870, following the museum's acquisition of a collection of mechanical instruments, the Scientific and Educational Department of the South Kensington Museum merged with this new collection and the Patent Office Museum collection, a hybrid which came to be known as the 'Science Museum'. In 1924 the Museum acquired the contents of James Watt's workshop and four years later moved into its present site on Exhibition Road, where it has continued to grow, presenting the development of science, technology and medicine from the early 18th century to the present day. The focus of acquisitions has been on artefacts that demonstrate developments in concepts and theory as well as practice, in the processes of discovery and invention, and in their relationship to economics and society. Artefacts associated with important historical events in science, individuals, groups of people and institutions have also found a home here. To mark the millennium the Wellcome Wing was opened, purpose-built to display the latest developments in digital, biomedical and electronic science.

The Collections

Ground Floor

The recently renovated 'Energy Hall' introduces the collections with a riveting display of early engines, including Boulton and Watt's rotative steam engine (1788) and the much later Harle Syke red mill engine (1903), awesome when in steam. The 'Space' gallery re-creates the race for the moon and beyond with a replica of the *Apollo 11* lunar lander, describing developments in missile technology and investigating the future of space exploration. The main part of this floor is devoted to the museum's core collection in 'Making the Modern World', an exhibition depicting the development of technological society using some of its landmark products, beginning with *Puffing Billy* (1815), the oldest steam locomotive in the world. It worked for nearly 50 years on a five-mile stretch between Wylam colliery near Newcastle, and Lemington on the Tyne. George Stephenson's *Rocket* can also be seen here, which reached a record-breaking speed of 29mph at the Rainhill trials of 1829. The pace of change is demonstrated by the *Columbine* (1845), recognisably a modern steam locomotive, as well as by the oldest surviving traction engine in the world, an Aveling and Porter steamroller from 1871, the type of machine that paved the way for the internal combustion engine. Nearby the Portsmouth Block-Making Machines (1803), designed by Marc Isambard Brunel, father of Isambard Kingdom, and manufactured by Henry Maudslay, are the first purpose-designed and integrated system for quantity production in the world, in use for more than a century, supplying 100 thousand pulley blocks each year to the Royal Navy during the Napoleonic era. The idea was adopted for the navy by Samuel Bentham, brother of the Utilitarian philosopher Jeremy Bentham. Nearby, the Holmes Lighthouse generator (1867), in operation until 1900, was installed at Souter Point near South Shields, showing the most powerful light in the world at the time, visible from some 20 miles off the coast.

The transport theme continues with vintage cars and aircraft. More recent innovations on display are *Mad Dog 2*, the UK's most successful solar-powered racing car, coming first in the stock class of the 1998 World Solar Rally in Japan; and a Magnetic Resonance Imaging scanner from 1983, of the type used at the Royal Aberdeen Infirmary, where the first clinically useful image was achieved three years earlier.

'Technology in every day life 1750–2000' displays artefacts in common use from five periods, each laid out according to a contemporary system of classification. The period 1750–1820 is arranged according to an order suggested by the *Encyclopédie* (1751–80) edited by Denis Diderot and Jean d'Alembert. The period 1820–80, covering the Great Exhibition, is laid out according to Lyon Playfair's scheme specially devised for the event, with British exhibits divided into four sections: Raw Materials, Machinery, Manufactures and Fine Arts. Thirty different classes were identified under these headings. Under Manufactures, for example, fell 'Class XV. Mixed Fabrics, including Shawls, but exclusive of Worsted Goods (Class XII)' or 'Class XVIII. Woven, Spun, Felted and laid fabrics, when shown as specimens of Printing or Dyeing'. Fine Arts was allotted just one category: 'Class XXX. Sculptures, Models and Plastic Arts'.

Enigma encryption machine from the Second World War.

The layout of artefacts dating from 1880–1939 employs a system devised by the pioneer Scottish sociologist and town planner Patrick Geddes (1854–1932); the period 1939–62 uses the catalogue of the Festival of Britain in 1951, organised into five areas: Art, Architecture, Science, Technology and Industrial Design; finally, the period 1968–2000 is arranged according to an order suggested by *The Next Whole Earth Catalog* of 1980, first published in the US in 1968. Among the objects exhibited from this period are an Apple II desktop computer (1977), a lap-top (1982), a radar speed-trap (1992) and a wheelclamp (1999).

First Floor

'The Steel Experience', designed by Simple Productions, is a wrap-around audio-visual insight into steel production from raw material to finished product. Other displays deal with telecommunications, featuring an Enigma 'cypher' machine and operational telephone exchange from 1950, followed by the History of Agriculture, an unusual series of 51 dioramas showing agricultural developments since 1500 BC, as well as artefacts such as 'Bell's Reaper' (1826), the first mechanical corn cutter, alongside a bright red Massey-Ferguson combine harvester (c. 1953–62). The 'Surveying' gallery displays instruments for mapping the earth's surface from chains and theodolites to Global Positioning Satellite receivers. 'Time Measurement' features a particularly fine collection of antique clocks and their mechanisms, such as the 14th-century example from the cathedral at Wells, one of the earliest mechanical timepieces in the country. Watson's Astronomical Clock (1695) was the first instrument in England to show the sun fixed on the Copernican principle.

Second Floor
The History of Mathematics and the History of Computing face each other across the building, their stories inextricably entwined. The Pegasus Computer (1959), the last valve-based computer still operational and one of the first to be built for general-purpose use by large businesses, can be compared with a recently completed working copy of Charles Babbage's 'Difference Engine No. 2', designed in 1847–49. The 'Ship Gallery' beyond displays the museum's unusually comprehensive collection of model ships, an important historical record of many long-lost actual vessels as well as an impressive overview of different types of craft from around the world.

Third Floor
'Science in the 18th Century' is a traditional display based on King George III's collection of scientific apparatus, illustrating the type of equipment used at the birth of the Industrial Revolution. Artefacts include an air pump made by leading scientific instrument maker George Adams in 1761; a mechanical model of the solar system—the original orrery made for the Earl of Orrery in 1712—and another example, much more ornate, enlarged in 1733 to include Saturn. The 'Optics' gallery explains the nature of light, illustrates Victorian and modern developments in the field, including microscopy, and demonstrates with examples the invention of holography by Hungarian scientist Dénes Gábor in 1948. The small prism and mirror from around 1800 with which William Herschel explored the spectrum beyond the visible region, discovering infrared, can be seen here, along with the massive lighthouse optic (1881) from Anvil Point, Swanage. Nearby is the Great Rosse Telescope Mirror from Birr Castle, Ireland. Made in 1845 for Lord Rosse, it remains the largest metal mirror ever manufactured for a telescope. The 'Photography and Cinematography' gallery features a reconstruction of Beard's Studio, the first photographic portrait studio in Europe, used to produce daguerrotypes, and a series of display cases illustrating the development of cameras and processing equipment. The 'Flight Gallery' offers rides on a motion simulator. Classic aircraft crowd the floorspace and ceiling, and a raised walkway provides access for closer viewing. The de Havilland 60 Gypsy Moth *Jason* from 1928 is the biplane in which Amy Johnson made her solo flight from England to Australia in 1930. The Fokker E. III from 1916 was the type of aircraft fitted with synchronised machine guns that wreaked havoc on the Royal Flying Corps in the middle years of the First World War. Early jet aircraft include a Gloster E. 28/39, from 1941, the first in Britain, and a Messerschmitt Komet of 1944, designed to defend Germany from Allied daylight bombing raids.

Fourth and Fifth Floors

These are devoted to the Wellcome Museum of the History of Medicine. The collections of Sir Henry Wellcome FRS (1853–1936) were given to the museum in 1977. Born the son of a poor pastor in northern Wisconsin, Henry Wellcome founded a very successful pharmaceutical company which patented the word 'tabloid' for its pills. An obsessive collector, he became a naturalised British citizen and was knighted in 1932. On the stairs a display case contains striking oddments from the collections, such as shrunken heads from South America, Florence Nightingale's moccasins, a lock of the Duke of Wellington's Hair, Captain Scott's medicine chest, Nelson's razor and Napoleon's field toilet case (almost complete with 19 different implements, sadly short of his comb and mirror). On the Fourth Floor, 'Glimpses of Medical History' is a series of diorama models depicting scenes in the development of medicine: trepanning in Neolithic times; the treatment of Roman battle casualties; eye-couching in 11th-century Persia; an anatomical theatre in Padua around 1594; and the effects of plague in 17th-century Rome. On the fifth floor, 'The Science and Art of Medicine' is an impressive exhibition presenting the history of medicine, mainly in western but also in other cultures around the world. Included is a 1.66 model of the temple of Asclepius at Epidaurus, a site where faith met science: a sort of cross between Lourdes and a sanatorium. There is also the Giustiniani Medicine Chest of 1565. Made for Vincenzo Giustiniani, Genoese governor of the Aegean island of Chios from 1562 until the Turkish invasion of 1566, it was bought by Henry Wellcome in 1924 and contains 126 bottles and pots for drugs, several retaining their 16th-century contents. While the governors of Genoa supported Holy Roman Emperor Charles V against the French, the city state's wealth also provided the economic power behind the Spanish exploitation of the New World. This explains the American origins of several of the drugs in the chest. There are also two small pieces claiming to be unicorn horn, although they are probably narwhal tusk.

The Wellcome Wing

Bathed in an eerie blue light, the Wellcome Wing extension extends over four floors in a cunning open-plan design by Richard MacCormac (2000). On the ground floor, 'Antenna' is the largest of the galleries, updated weekly and dedicated to the very latest developments in science, the displays exploring anything from MRSA superbugs to nanotechnology and the footfall-sensitive flooring of the future. The first floor of the gallery asks the question 'Who am I?' with a bleeping array of 'Bloids', computerised interactive puzzles and games arranged under four categories, 'Human Animal', 'Family Tree', 'Identity Parade' and 'Live Science', each designed to explore themes ranging from 'Where did you get your looks from?' to allowing visitors to participate in current research projects. On the second floor, 'Digitopolis' looks at the future of digital technology, including audio-visual developments and the everyday digitial networks connecting people, with an array of interactive computer terminals. The third floor asks the question, 'In the Future, how will life be different?'. Interactive computerised board games encourage visitors to debate subjects such as 'Choosing the sex of your baby', comparing responses with previous participants.

SERPENTINE GALLERY

Kensington Gardens, Kensington, W2 3XA
Tel: 020-7402 6075; www.serpentine.org
Open daily 10–6 (late nights Fri to 10pm in summer)
Free
Tube: South Kensington or Lancaster Gate
Shop
Map p. 380, 2B

Founded by the Arts Council in 1971, the Serpentine is one of the leading venues for modern and contemporary art exhibitions, staging bold, creative shows and retrospectives of established names. The Serpentine's setting is unique, in a 1934 tea-pavilion (by Henry Tanner) on the edge of Kensington Gardens. On one side is the road that divides Kensington Gardens from Hyde Park, and the bridge (by Sir John and George Rennie, 1828) over the Serpentine. On the other is the parkland, extensive lawns and beautiful trees of Kensington Gardens, dotted with occasional statuary. The most atmospheric approach is on foot from the direction of Kensington Palace, when the gallery suddenly emerges in the grounds. Its recent redevelopment (John Miller + Partners, 1998) has retained the character of the Grade II listed building whilst the programme of Serpentine Pavilions provides each year an interesting architect-designed temporary structure which houses the Pavilion café (past architects have included Zaha Hadid, 2000, and Daniel Libeskind, 2001).

SHAKESPEARE'S GLOBE

21 New Globe Walk, Bankside, SE1 9DT
Tel: 020-7902 1500; www.shakespeares-globe.org
Open daily 10–5
Admission charge
Tube: Southwark/London Bridge/St Paul's/Mansion House
Shop
Map p. 383, 3D

The museum and exhibition attached to the reconstructed Globe Theatre provide an informative introduction to the regular tours of the theatre and a space in which various themes related to the Elizabethan stage can be explored. From 1599–1613, when the Globe Theatre was destroyed in a fire started by a prop cannon during a performance of *Henry VIII*, it was one of the most popular in London. American actor, producer and director Sam Wanamaker first conceived the idea of recreating the theatre in 1949. In 1970 he founded the Shakespeare Globe Trust and, along with the architect Theo Crosby, drew up plans for the reconstruction, to be undertaken as close as possible to the site of the original building. The first part of the exhibition details the meticulous techniques—many authentic to the period—that were employed in the construction project, finally completed in 1997. 'All the World's a Stage' illustrates life on Bankside in the early 17th century. A large model of a Frost Fair held on the Thames in 1621 (on loan from Museum of London) can be seen, along with contemporary bowling balls and hazelnut shells, a late 16th-century dagger, whistles, and spoons. Another model shows Middle Temple Hall, the venue for the first performance of *Twelfth Night*. Separate displays cover special effects in the Elizabethan theatre, and the question of Shakespeare's identity (who wrote the plays?), examining the claims of Christopher Marlowe, Edward de Vere and Francis Bacon. Downstairs there is a temporary exhibition area and performance space, along with listening booths where early recordings of speeches from Shakespeare by famous actors can be heard, courtesy of the British Library's National Sound Archive.

SIR JOHN SOANE'S MUSEUM

13 Lincoln Inn's Fields, WC2A 3BP
Tel: 020-7405 2107; www.soane.org
Open Tues–Sat 10–5 (first Tues in the month 6pm–9pm by candlelight)
Free
Tube: Holborn
Shop
Map p. 382, 1B

This extraordinary house on the north side of Lincoln's Inn Fields, the largest square in central London, was the home of Sir John Soane (1753–1837), one of England's most important and original architects. The façade, of Portland stone and red brick, with its projecting loggia and incised lines representing pilasters, daringly modern in its day and considered by many a 'palpable eyesore', and with two large standing Coade Stone caryatids, based on those from the Erechtheion on the Acropolis, hides the most unexpected interior in London. Designed by Soane to house his ever-growing collection of antiquities, marbles, plaster casts, porcelain, paintings, watercolours, books and an enormous array of architectural drawings, the unusually-shaped rooms are crowded with works of art. Cunning use is made of surprise vistas and changes of level. Carefully positioned mirrors reflect light and judiciously placed possessions; ceilings are punched through to admit shafts of light at desired angles, dramatically falling on walls encrusted with sculpture and architectural fragments. Windows of rooms overlook courtyards packed with sculpture, and in the basement are solemn Gothic cloisters and cells, originally lit by light faintly penetrating through stained glass. The whole creates an overwhelming labyrinthine effect. In March 1825 Soane threw a three-day party to celebrate his most magnificent purchase, the sarcophagus of Sethi I. Eight hundred and ninety guests, among them J.M.W. Turner, Coleridge,

Robert Peel, Lord and Lady Liverpool and Sir Thomas Lawrence, viewed his home-cum-museum by lamp and candlelight, the flickering light shimmering in the mirrors and illuminating the spaces with dramatic chiaroscuro. The drama of the presentation was deliberate, and the museum today is open for evening candlelight viewings.

The House

Soane's house is in fact spread over three. In 1793 he purchased No. 12 Lincoln's Inn Fields, which he demolished and rebuilt to his own design, converting the back to house his architectural office. Here he and his wife Eliza and their two children lived until 1813, when they moved next door, to No. 13, which Soane had purchased in 1807 and architecturally transformed in 1812. No. 13's long-suffering sitting tenant, George Booth Tyndale, moved to the front portion of No. 12 in a swap, the back being joined to No. 13 which extended Soane's office and created the dramatic Dome area, used to display his architectural and sculptural fragments. This area was further extended in 1824 with the purchase of No. 14. Again, Soane rebuilt the old terrace house, the front being let to tenants while the back was appropriated for his own use, linked to No. 13: the Picture Room was created (where he displayed his important Hogarths), with the Monk's Parlour below. At Lincoln's Inn Fields Soane was able to continue and perfect architectural ideas he had used elsewhere: at his magnificent Bank of England (*see p. 17*), his country villa at Ealing, Pitshanger Manor (*see p. 235*) and at Dulwich Picture Gallery (*see p. 69*), as well as countless other public and private commissions. Throughout his life Soane was remodelling rooms and rearranging his extending collection. In 1816 he had purchased the collection of antique marbles collected in Rome in the 1790s by Charles Heathcote Tatham for Henry Holland, and in 1818 he bought from Robert Adam's sale a large number of marbles, terracottas and casts. He considered a ring with a strand of Napoleon's hair one of his most treasured possessions. Today the collection of Greek, Roman and Egyptian antiquities, casts, bronzes, gems and medals, ceramics, oil paintings and watercolours, 8,000 books, 30,000 architectural drawings (including those by Adam) and 150 architectural models, displayed in their astonishing surroundings, is one of Soane's most extraordinary legacies. By the end of his life Soane was already referring to the ground floor of Lincoln's Inn Fields as 'the Museum'. He bequeathed it to the nation by Act of Parliament in 1833.

Tour of the Museum

NB: At the time of writing the museum was undergoing restoration in certain areas. While completed restoration will better achieve Soane's intended effects and placement of his collection, the following description may have altered in parts.

The **Hall** is painted in imitation of porphyry, its staircase, with its occasional niches and alcoves, winding up to the top of the house. To the right of the stairs is the **Library and Dining Room**, conceived as one space, the Library at the front of the property, the Dining Room at the rear. Painted a rich, glossy Pompeian red, an arcaded screen-like division, suspended from the ceiling, divides the two spaces, its two mirrored piers on either side of the room arranged with objects, including the model of the Soane Monument. Made in 1816 after the death of Soane's wife Eliza, the actual monument stands in the burial ground of St Giles-in-the-Fields (now St Pancras Gardens, near St Pancras Station). Elizabeth Soane, his son John and Soane himself are buried there. Mirrors in the recesses above the bookcases, made for the room by John Robins, give an impression of a room beyond. The mythological ceiling paintings, with scenes from the story of Pandora, were commissioned from Henry Holland and positioned in 1834. Over the Dining Room chimneypiece is Sir Thomas Lawrence's portrait of Soane (1828–29), one of his last works, and below it a model of the Board of Trade offices which Soane

Architectural plaster casts illuminated by a yellow glow populate the Dome Area of Sir John Soane's Museum.

designed at the entrance to Downing Street. Convex mirrors, canted forward, reflect the entrance from the Hall, and mirror-backed niches contain sculpture. It was in this room that Soane exhibited his large collection of antique vases, or 'Grecian urns', the most celebrated being the large 'Cawdor Vase', an Apulian krater of the late 4th century BC. The Dining Room window overlooks the astonishing **Monument Court**. Soane designed for its centre a tall 'pasticcio' composed of capitals representing various styles of architecture, topped by a cast-iron finial, which was dismantled in 1896.

Approached from the Library is Soane's **Study**, a small room also painted Pompeian red, crammed with marble fragments from the Tatham collection, displayed on shelves and brackets of 'bronzed' green. Above the door to the Dining Room is a large cast of the *Apotheosis of Homer*, taken from the marble relief purchased by the British Museum in 1819, originally in the Palazzo Colonna, Rome. The oak-grained **Dressing Room**, with an elaborate ceiling in Soane's late manner, contains Giovanni

Bandini's terracotta model for the figure of Architecture, one of two which flank the tomb of Michelangelo in Santa Croce, Florence, designed by Giorgio Vasari in 1564, as well as G.B. Guelfi's terracotta model for his monument to James Craggs in Westminster Abbey. The **Corridor** is a forest of architectural plaster casts, lit by a long skylight, in Soane's day filled with tinted yellow glass admitting a mellow light. On the east wall is a convex mirror with a view westwards down the Colonnade, below it an 18th-century terracotta plaque showing *Britannia*, possibly by John Bacon (1740–99). To the right an aperture offers a glimpse into the Picture Room Recess.

The buildings at the back of the house were designed for Soane's 'Museum' but also for drawing rooms and offices for his successful architectural practice. At the north end of the Corridor, up the stairs, is the **Upper Drawing Office**, its walls lined with architectural fragments and casts. The long drawing desks, their drawers originally filled with drawings and plans to aid his pupils, are sited away from the walls; the gaps admit light to the ground floor below. The **Picture Room** occupies the rear of No. 14 Lincoln's Inn Fields, its suspended ceiling a curious mix of classical and Gothic forms. Here Soane displayed his best paintings, hung on an ingenious method of hinged panels, or 'moveable planes' which swing out, revealing different layers. Prized by Soane were his original ink-and-wash views of Paestum by Giovanni Battista Piranesi (1720–78) but the chief pictures are those by Hogarth: the celebrated eight-canvas *Rake's Progress* series (1732–33) and the magnificent four-canvas *Election* series (c. 1745). The former was purchased at Christie's auction house by Mrs Soane (Soane being unwell) in 1802 from Alderman Beckford's collection. The latter was purchased at Christie's in 1823, at Mrs Garrick's sale, for £1,732. In addition Soane possessed watercolours by Turner; an oil sketch for Sir James Thornhill's Baroque ceiling for the Queen's State Bedchamber at Hampton Court; and a fragment of a tapestry cartoon, from the studio of Raphael, for the 'Life of Christ' tapestries for the Scuola Nuova in the Vatican. In the inner recess of the south wall, formerly glimpsed from the Corridor, is the plaster nymph by Sir Richard Westmacott, a friend of Soane's, who was invited to dinner to admire the placement of his sculpture.

In the basement is the **Monk's Parlour**, or the 'Parloir of Padre Giovanni' as Soane was amused to called it, the first of a series of theatrical spaces for his medieval and Gothic treasures, inspired by, and satirising, the taste for gothic novels and medieval antiquarianism, an elaboration of the sombre reclusive hermit theme begun at Pitshanger (*see p. 236*). Ancient stained glass and coloured glazing was set into windows and doors, rearranged in the 1890s for its greater protection, with yellow light filtering down from the Picture Room recess. The walls are covered with casts and genuine Gothic fragments, many from the old Palace of Westminster. In this odd environment Soane would entertain close friends to tea. From the window is a view onto the **Monk's Yard**, with its cloister with further fragments from the old Palace of Westminster, demolished in 1823, including pieces from the House of Lords, the celebrated Painted Chamber, and carved Gothic canopies from St Stephen's chapel; the Monk's Tomb; and the grave of his wife's dog, Fanny. The **Monk's Cell**, with a niche for holy water, displayed Soane's medieval illuminated manuscripts.

Leaving the Monk's Parlour, to the left are plaster models by the celebrated Neoclassical sculptor John Flaxman, a personal friend of Soane's. There are over 60 of his works in the museum, many given to or purchased by Soane from Maria Denman, Flaxman's sister-in-law, after the sculptor's death (many more were presented to University College; see UCL Art Collections, p. 312) including the fine plaster relief for the monument to Mrs Helen Knight, at Wolverley, Worcestershire. The plaster figure of the reclining Penelope Boothby is the model for Thomas Bank's monument to her at Ashbourne, Derbyshire. In the **Anteroom** is a large cast of *Venus at her Bath*, from the collection of the painter George Romney. Soane probably intended this entire area to mimic the atmosphere of a sepulchral vault. The **Catacombs** house Roman and other antiquities; in the **New Court** is one of the original capitals from Inigo Jones's Banqueting House, removed when the building was refaced in 1829; and in the **West Chamber** a colossal bronze head of Jupiter (Italian 18th century) and cork models of the Temple of Fortuna Virilis in Rome, of Stonehenge and of three Etruscan tombs. Looking east is the staggering vista down the **Crypt**, the basement area below Soane's Dome. Immediately ahead is the Sepulchral Chamber, light flooding down from the dome above, bouncing off the walls encrusted with marbles, sculpture and architectural fragments. The space is dominated by the colossal bulk of the sarcophagus of Sethi I, Soane's most expensive and triumphant purchase, made in 1825. Excavated by the colourful strongman and hydraulic engineer Giovanni Belzoni, it had been offered to the British Museum by the British Consul-General in Egypt, Henry Salt, but had been turned down on grounds of cost. Huge and translucent, covered in hieroglyphics, it was the centrepiece of Soane's flamboyant party held over three evenings soon after its arrival.

Returning to the main floor is the **Colonnade**, supported by ten Corinthian columns. Crowding into the area are antique fragments and sculptures by Soane's friends and contemporaries. A female torso is from the frieze of the Erechtheion on the Acropolis, although its identity was not realised in Soane's day. The **Dome** continues the overwhelming assemblage of architecture and sculpture. Large and dominating is the *Apollo Belvedere*, a cast formerly in the collection of Lord Burlington at Chiswick House, of which Soane was exceedingly proud, not least because of its provenance. Lined up on the balustrade surrounding the opening to the Crypt below, with a view down onto the Egyptian sarcophagus, are antique vases and urns, and Sir Francis Chantrey's bust of Soane. Beyond the Dome an arch opens into the **New Picture Room**, with a pair of fine console tables in the style of William Kent, from Walpole House, Chelsea, demolished by Soane in 1809 to make way for the new Infirmary he had designed for the Royal Hospital. The greatest treasure is Soane's prized Canaletto, a view of Venice, one of his very finest, which Soane purchased from the sale of Fonthill Splendens in 1807. The **Breakfast Parlour** remains almost unaltered from Soane's day. The ceiling is a beautiful flattened dome, almost floating in the air, to either side openings rising to skylights with coloured glass. In the four corners of the ceiling are convex mirrors, and nearly 100 more punctuate the surfaces of the room, some merely small glittering orbs. On the north wall is a large watercolour of

Mrs Soane's tomb, Flaxman's figure of Victory having been positioned in front of it by Soane just ten days before he died in 1837. The dog portrait by James Ward is Mrs Soane's pet, Fanny, who is buried in the Monk's Yard.

Returning to the inner Hall, the stairs lead up to the Drawing Rooms, passing on the way the **Skakespeare Recess** and other niches with sculpture busts.

SOMERSET HOUSE
COURTAULD GALLERIES, GILBERT COLLECTION
AND HERMITAGE ROOMS

Somerset House, Strand, WC2R 0RN
Tube: Temple
Map p. 382, 2B

Somerset House, built largely between 1776 and 1801, is the masterpiece of the architect Sir William Chambers (1723–96), former architectural tutor to George III and from 1769 Comptroller, and effective head, of the King's Office of Works. The complex was designed to house various government offices, in particular the Navy Office (which occupied the river block), as well as three learned societies under royal patronage: the Royal Society, the Society of Antiquaries and the Royal Academy of Arts. The latter were housed in the Strand block, with their Fine Rooms on the first floor. The learned societies vacated the building in the 19th century and until very recently the site was almost wholly occupied by government departments, and the magnificent courtyard by civil servants' cars. However, since the Courtauld Institute Gallery, and Institute, moved into the Strand block (1989–90) and the Gilbert Collection and Hermitage Rooms into the river block, Somerset House has enjoyed a cultural regeneration. Now free of vehicles, the courtyard is one of the most elegant public spaces in London, with café tables from which one can enjoy Chambers' dignified architecture as well as the rectangular 55-jet fountain (Dixon/Jones 1999–2000). Over Christmas and New Year the latter is covered with a temporary ice rink which, on a dusky winter afternoon with its lighted flambeaux and Palladian surroundings, is extremely atmospheric.

The Building

Chambers intended Somerset House as a public showcase for English architectural and sculptural design. Its façades are enriched with the work of leading Royal Academician sculptors, maritime glory and royal patronage, symbolic of the building's function, the themes. The Strand façade, for instance, is surmounted by the arms of the British Empire, supported by *Fame* and the *Genius of Britain*, by John Bacon Sr (renewed in 1896); below this stand *Prudence*, *Justice*, *Moderation* and *Valour*, by Agostino Carlini and Giuseppe Ceracchi, the qualities, according to a 1781 description, upon which dominion is built; and the bearded heads on the keystones of the

The dignified courtyard of Somerset House, with the famous 55-jet fountain.

arcade, mainly by Joseph Wilton, represent Ocean and the great rivers of England. From the Strand one enters the elegant Vestibule, with its coupled Doric columns and vaulted plaster ceiling. To left and right, above the entrances to the learned societies, are carved busts by Wilton: Newton, on the left, for the Royal Society; Michelangelo, on the right, for the Royal Academy (now the entrance for the Courtauld Institute Gallery. *For the rich interiors of the societies' Fine Rooms, see p. 276 below*). From the Vestibule there is a view out to the great courtyard beyond. Centrally placed is Bacon's large bronze statue of George III with a reclining Father Thames below, completed in 1789. Sculpture, by Bacon, Wilton, Thomas Banks and Richard Rathbone continues on the courtyard façades.

Chambers' building was built on a site originally occupied by Lord Protector Somerset's 1547–52 town house (hence the name Somerset House) which, after the latter's execution, was ceded to the Crown. In the 17th century Somerset House served as the official residence of successive Stuart Queen Consorts. Following the Restoration of the monarchy in 1660, the palace was refurbished for Henrietta Maria, queen of Charles I and now the Queen Dowager, which included the lavish refitting of her Roman Catholic chapel and the building of a new gallery along the river. Samuel Pepys was a frequent visitor to Somerset House and found the new works 'might fine and costly'. Although probably by John Webb, Chambers believed the gallery, which along with the rest of the palace was demolished to make way for the new building, to be the work of the revered Inigo Jones, and its pure Classicism inspired his Strand façade. Under Catherine of Braganza, Portuguese queen of Charles II, Somerset House and its chapel remained a gravitational centre for Roman Catholics. Steep steps in front of the west wing lead down to a subterranean passage under the courtyard, the Dead Room, where funerary tablets, the only remnants of the palace's religious past, can be seen (*guided tours only, twice daily first Saturday of every month, tickets from the Seamen's Hall*).

Access to the Collections

The Embankment entrance, through the low central arch of the great rusticated façade, originally intended as access for boats (before the river was embanked the building was right on the water's edge), is best for the Gilbert Collection (*see p. 278 below*) which is immediately to the right. Stairs in the foyer also lead down to the small permanent Old Palace Exhibition, useful for an historical overview of Somerset House pre-Chambers. Among the exhibits are excavated architectural fragments.

Edouard Manet: *A Bar at the Folies-Bergère* (1881–82), part of the Courtauld Collection, and one of the world's most famous images.

Running along the length of the space is the mid-18th-century Royal Navy Commissioners' barge, with gilded carving along a maritime theme. It would have been used by officials travelling downriver to the Royal Dockyards and Greenwich Hospital.

Having entered from the river, the rest of Somerset House is up another level. Visitors should take either the lift or the more sedate eighteenth century Stamp Stair (which originally served the Stamp Office). The Hermitage Rooms (*see p. 279 below*) are off the Seamen's Hall, in the centre of the river block, from which there is also access to the grand River Terrace. Down the long corridor heading west from the Seamen's Hall is the magnificent Navy Stair (renamed the Nelson Stair), its elegant curved flights leading to the Navy Board Room (*open by appointment only*).

THE COURTAULD INSTITUTE OF ART GALLERY

Tel: 020-7848 2526; www.courtauld.ac.uk
Open daily 10–6
Admission charge; Courtauld free 1st Mon of every month 10–2
Courtauld/Gilbert/Hermitage joint ticketing system: concessions if two collections visited, further concession if all three
Café, restaurant and shop

Part of the Courtauld Institute of Art, one of the colleges of the University of London, the Courtauld Institute Gallery is made up of a series of private collections, the first and arguably most important being the superlative Impressionist and Post-Impressionist collection of its founder, Samuel Courtauld (1876–1947). Now removed from Woburn Square, the Gallery's intimate but hard-to-find home since 1958, and installed in the elegantly decorated 18th-century interiors of the Strand block of Somerset House, these masterpieces can be appreciated in an atmosphere of calm and restrained luxury.

Courtauld and the Collections

Descended from a Huguenot family active as London silversmiths in the 18th century, later as silk weavers and textile manufacturers, Samuel Courtauld became chairman in 1921 of the multinational company (still in existence today) which in the early 20th century had become a leading producer of the artificial textile rayon. As well as giving £50,000 to the nation for the purchase of works of art for the National Gallery and the Tate Gallery (among them van Gogh's *Sunflowers* and Seurat's *Bathing Party*) Courtauld also built up a private collection, concentrating mainly on the 'modern' French school. Manet's *A Bar at the Folies-Bergère* (1881–82); Monet's *Antibes* (1888); Renoir's *The Theatre Box* ('La Loge'; 1874); and Cézanne's *The Montagne Sainte-Victoire* (c. 1887), are just a handful of the now internationally famous works which once hung at Courtauld's private London house, the historic Home House in Portman Square, built by Robert Adam in 1774.

After the death of his wife in 1931 Courtauld gave over Home House and the majority of his collection (the rest was bequeathed on his death) to a new art history teaching institute (there was no other in the country), which opened its doors as the Courtauld Institute of Art in 1932. Viscount Lee of Fareham (1868–1947) was another of the founding fathers. As well as donating Chequers to the nation, for the use of Prime Ministers, he also gave his personal collection to the Courtauld. Wide-ranging, it included the richly carved and painted 1472 Morelli-Nerli *cassoni* (marriage chests for household linen); masterpieces such as Rubens' sketch for *The Descent from the Cross*, the great altarpiece for Antwerp Cathedral; and Cranach's *Adam and Eve*. Although Gainsborough's *Portrait of Mrs Gainsborough* (1778–79) came through Courtauld, most of the Gallery's important British pictures are part of the Lee collection, including Hans Eworth's extraordinary allegorical portrait of Sir John Luttrell, rising half naked out of the sea with a shipwreck behind him, and Sir Peter Lely's *The Concert*, one of the rare landscapes he painted when he first came to England in the 1640s.

The collections were further enhanced by the painter and art-critic Roger Fry (1866–1934), who had been a key adviser to Courtauld on his Impressionist purchases. As well as a number of his own works, he bequeathed an important group of Bloomsbury Group paintings and Omega Workshops ceramics, as well as works by other artists including Walter Sickert. Sir Robert Witt (1872–1952), the third player in the institute's foundation, gave over 4,000 Old Master drawings as well as his important photographic archive. Further gifts followed: the Mark Gambier-Parry bequest of 1966, consisting mainly of early Italian works; Dr Alistair Hunter's collection of British artists including Ben Nicholson's *Painting 1937*; and in the late 1970s came the major benefaction of Count Antoine Seilern (1901–78), known as the Prince's Gate Collection (Seilern's London address). Astutely advised by curators, scholars and dealers, Seilern built up an exceptional collection of Old Master Dutch, Flemish and Italian paintings, extremely rich in works by Rubens and Tiepolo, but also including Oskar Kokoschka's 1950 *Prometheus* triptych, the artist's largest work, commissioned by Seilern for the ceiling of his Prince's Gate house.

The Fine Rooms

This rich collection is displayed in decorative interiors of the highest historical importance. Designed by Chambers, with beautifully ornamented plasterwork ceilings, the Fine Rooms on the first floor were designed to reflect the dignity of the learned societies which occupied them. Originally three separate suites—although the Royal Society and Society of Antiquaries shared some rooms—they are now seen as one set of intersecting galleries. At ground floor level, Gallery 1 was originally the Royal Academy's Academy of the Living Model, but is now much altered. Through the Doric screen, flanked on either side by casts of the Furietti Centaurs, which occupy their original positions, the stairs rise to the public rooms. Several of the ceiling paintings, by Academician artists, were removed to Burlington House (*see p. 244*) when the Royal Academy vacated Somerset House in 1836. Chambers' original colour scheme, with ceilings of pale green, pink and lilac, has been restored. The rooms are as fol-

Paul Cézanne: *The Montagne Sainte-Victoire* (c. 1887).

lows: The **Royal Academy Anteroom and Library** (Gallery 2): The ceiling has a copy of Reynolds' *The Theory of Art*; Cipriani's *Nature, History, Allegory* and *Fable* decorate the cove; The **Royal Society Meeting Room** (Gallery 3): A ceiling of enriched coffering with plaster medallions of Charles II, the Society's founder, and George III, its patron at the time; The **Royal Society and Society of Antiquaries Joint Anteroom** (Gallery 4): Decorated by Cipriani with *Apollo*, surrounded by the signs of the zodiac, the *Four Elements* in the cove; The **Society of Antiquaries Meeting Room** (Gallery 5); The **Royal Academy Council and Assembly Room** (Gallery 6): The most important room, with tinted photographs replacing paintings by Benjamin West and Angelica Kauffmann (*The Graces Unveiling Nature*, surrounded by the *Four Elements*, now in the RA; *see p. 244*) the **Royal Academy's Antique Academy** (Gallery 7): An elegant plaster ceiling featuring the initials of the Royal Academy and pairs of brushes at the four corners. The niche at the west end originally held a stove in the form of an obelisk. At present it displays 18th–19th-century Courtauld silver, on loan from Courtaulds Ltd.

Upper floor

The steep, narrow ascent to the second floor, up to the realm of the Muses, is the route to the Royal Academy Great Room, where the famous annual Summer Exhibition took place from 1780–1836. The precipitous climb was wittily satirized by Thomas Rowlandson in his c. 1800 image *The Exhibition Stare-case*, showing eager exhibition visitors tumbling down it, with the billowing hindquarters of Albacini's completed *Venus Callipygos* in a niche, an amusing symbol of both exhibitionism and voyeurism. The empty plaster frame once housed Cipriani's *Minerva with the Muses on Mount Parnassus*. Gallery 8 is the Anteroom to the Great Room, with above the door to the latter the Greek inscription 'Let no one uninspired by the Muses enter here'. To maximize display space, an understandable requirement, the Great Room is currently subdivided into smaller galleries, which is nevertheless a disappointment for viewing this great historic room. Up above one can see the lantern, but not the famous 'line', the wooden moulding running round the gallery. Large paintings were hung on the line, canted forward, smaller ones below, and others above, dismissed to an invisible oblivion. With paintings covering the walls from floor to ceiling, it was one of the sights of London.

GILBERT COLLECTION

Tel: 020-7420 9400; www.gilbert-collection.org.uk
Open daily 10–6
Admission charge. Courtauld/Gilbert/Hermitage joint ticketing system: concessions if two collections visited, further concession if all three
Café and shop

The property millionaire Sir Arthur Gilbert, who was born in London in 1913 but emigrated to California in 1949, bequeathed his extraordinary collection of *objets d'art* to the nation in 1996. The museum in Somerset House was developed especially to house it. The collection is particularly rich in 19th-century Roman micromosaics (images made up of thousands of opaque glass tesserae), a technique which especially fascinated Gilbert, as well as Florentine hardstone mosaics, or *pietre dure*. Plaques of the latter, dating from the 16th–19th centuries, are found set into elaborate cabinets, table tops and pieces of jewellery. The large collection of silver includes ornamental works by leading European silversmiths, most also dating from the 16th–19th centuries, including pieces by the important early 18th-century London-based Huguenot silversmith Paul de Lamerie. There are also exquisitely crafted solid gold objects; enamel portrait miniatures; and an immense collection of gold snuff boxes, displayed in darkened rooms in spotlit display cases. The most important are the six from the collection of Frederick the Great of Prussia, made for him in Berlin in the mid- to later 18th century. Made of gold, with bodies and lids of mother of pearl, chrysoprase or agate, and encrusted with flashing diamonds and other gemstones, they repay close scrutiny (magnifying glasses can be borrowed from the ticket desk).

Downstairs, to the left of the ticket desk, is an introductory gallery with information about Gilbert, who died in 2001. Beyond this, most unexpectedly, is a mock-up of his study in Beverly Hills. A waxwork of the man himself, dressed in tennis shorts, sits behind a Louis XVI-style desk and reaches for the telephone to bid for antiques. On the walls are family portraits and 19th-century micromosaic views of the sights of Rome.

HERMITAGE ROOMS

Tel: 020-7845 4630; www.hermitagerooms.org.uk
Open daily 10–6
Admission charge. Courtauld/Gilbert/Hermitage joint ticketing system: concessions if two collections visited, further concession if all three
Shop

An outpost of the State Hermitage Museum in St Petersburg, the Hermitage Rooms have two exhibitions a year featuring items from the Hermitage's outstanding collections. Formerly the private collection of the Russian Imperial family, it is now one of the richest national collections of European paintings and decorative arts in the world. Past exhibitions in London have featured items from the collection of Catherine the Great, and oil sketches by Rubens. Although the space is actually quite small, its exuberant decoration is supposed to evoke the splendours of the Winter Palace. Exhibitions usually run for about five months, with a month between each for installation.

SOUTH LONDON ART GALLERY

65 Peckham Road, SE5 8UH
Tel: 020-7703 6120; www.southlondongallery.org
Open Tues–Sun 12–6
Free
Bus: 12 from Trafalgar Square; 36 or 436 from Victoria; 171 from Waterloo Road (Tate Modern)
Map p. 379, 3E

The South London Art Gallery, the first London gallery to be open on Sundays (for the 'convenience of the artisan and poorer classes of South London'), evolved from the 1868 exhibition space opened by a local tradesman, William Rossiter. After several moves and with the private backing of artists and wealthy benefactors, including Lord Leighton (*see p. 156*), Burne-Jones and G.F. Watts, a new gallery opened in Peckham Road in 1891 (with a fine marquetry floor designed by Walter Crane), independent of the South London Working Men's Club with which it had been connected. The library, lecture room and exhibition space followed in 1893, funded by J. Passmore

Edwards. The gallery's foundation was part of the lofty Victorian ideal of bringing improving culture to the working class. In 1898 Camberwell College of Art opened next door and a new façade, by Maurice Adams (1902), was built physically to unite the two. The permanent collection has Victorian paintings (over 40 donated by Leighton, and others by Ford Madox Brown, Ruskin and Millais) as well as earlier works dating from the 17th century onwards. Its 20th-century collection of paintings was begun in 1953; that of prints in 1960, with examples by John Piper, Duncan Grant, Patrick Heron and Graham Sutherland. All these are rarely on show, but can be seen by appointment. The gallery's exhibition space concentrates mainly on contemporary art, both international and British.

SOUTHSIDE HOUSE

3–4 Woodhayes Road, Wimbledon Common, SW19 4RJ
Tel: 020-8946 7643; www.southsidehouse.com
Open Easter–end Sept Wed, Sat, Sun and bank holidays for 60-min guided tours. Tours at 2pm, 3pm, 4pm. No need to pre-book, but phone to check house open, as it is often hired for private events
Admission charge. Disabled visitors should phone ahead
Station: Wimbledon, then bus 93
Map p. 378, 4C

In a semi-rural corner of Wimbledon, on Woodhayes Road, off the south side of the common, is Southside House with its late 17th-century Anglo-Dutch façade, usually dated to 1687 (the date carved on one of the chimneypieces inside). Robert Pennington, a Chancery official, bought the property in 1665: the substantial new entrance front brought a fashionable regularity to the old farmhouse behind. Descendants of the Pennington family have been in ownership ever since. In 1910 Hilda Pennington Mellor married the Swedish doctor and philanthropist Dr Axel Munthe, author of the bestselling *The Story of San Michele*, and the house is now run by the Pennington Mellor Munthe Trust.

The house is seen by guided tour only, an eccentric but entertaining experience. En route are fine Stuart portraits mainly from the collection of Philip, Lord Wharton (connected to Southside through his daughter's marriage into the Kemeys family of Cefn Mably). Most of Wharton's van Dycks, an exceptional collection of at least 32 works, were sold in 1725 to Sir Robert Walpole and thence to Catherine the Great and are now in the Hermitage, but the full-lengths at Southside, in the Dining Room, bypassed the sale and came to the house in the 20th century (not with the other Wharton heirlooms). In the same room is Burne-Jones's *St George*. A number of trophy relics with colourful and elaborate provenances can be seen, among them Anne Boleyn's vanity case, which she had with her in the Tower before her execution; Marie Antoinette's pearl necklace which she wore at the guillotine and which was presented to John Pennington by Josephine Bonaparte; and the emerald and gold ring of the last King of Serbia, whose proposal of marriage Hilda Pennington Mellor declined. The Hall, with its Baroque embellishments, was badly bomb-damaged: its painted ceiling was restored and repainted by Hilda and Axel Munthe's artist son, Viking. Other pictures by him are hung throughout the house. The platform, upon which Emma Hamilton performed her classical 'attitudes', and ceiling hooks for curtains, is in the Music Room, as is her portrait by Romney. She, Lord Nelson and Sir William Hamilton were guests at Southside when they were living at nearby Merton Place (demolished) in the years before Trafalgar.

SPENCER HOUSE

27 St James's Place, SW1A 1NR
Tel: 020-7499 8620; www.spencerhouse.co.uk
Open Sun (except Jan and August) for guided tours only, every 20mins, starting at 10.45. Last tour 4.45
Admission charge
Tube: Green Park
Sales counter
Map p. 381, 2E

Spencer House was designed by John Vardy, a pupil of William Kent, as a palatial Neoclassical mansion for John, 1st Earl Spencer, great-grandson of Sarah, Duchess of Marlborough. The work began in 1756, the year after Earl Spencer had secretly married Georgiana Poyntz. The house was intended to establish their reputation in London society. After two years, once he had completed the shell and ground floor rooms in austere Roman style, Vardy was replaced by James 'Athenian' Stuart, irrepressible compiler of the The Antiquities of Athens (1762), partly funded by the Society of Dilettanti, of which Spencer was a member. This group of Whig grandees believed in emulating at home the classical styles they had admired on their Grand Tours. For the next eight years Stuart was given free rein; the result is the earliest purely Greek Neoclassical interior in Europe. He himself undertook some of the work in the Painted Room, which remains his masterpiece and the most complete surviving example of his designs. Relatively untouched by a succession of tenants, the room was damaged by a bomb blast in 1944, destroying the ceiling. In 1985 the house was bought by Lord Rothschild's bank, RIT Capital Partners, which has completed a thorough and detailed reconstruction of the interiors of most of the 18th-century rooms on the ground and first floors. Viewable on guided tours on Sundays only, the house now provides an insight into mid-to-late-18th-century aristocratic taste, and is an outstanding example of the craft of period replication, largely designed by David Mlinaric and carried out by Dick Reid and his workshop.

Tour of the House

The tour begins in the **Anteroom**, originally the family's private dining room but altered to suit its current role by Henry Holland, architect of Brooks's Club, for the Second Earl Spencer. The ceiling, dating from the 1750s, is original. Paintings from the period hanging here include a small *Virgin and Child* by Jan Gossaert or Mabuse and an *Allegory of Art* by Carlo Maratta and Giuseppe Chiari from around 1706, showing the Genoese banker and patron of the arts Niccolo Pallavicini having his portrait painted as he is guided into the Temple of Fame by Apollo. Next door, the **Library** was also altered by Holland, now restored with replica Vardy bookcases, and a meticulous reproduction of the original marble fireplace. Six hand-coloured Italian engravings by Antonio Giuseppe Barbazza (1752) depict the spread of Christianity through stone, marble and metal. Figures on the mantelpiece originally came from Castle Howard. The **Dining Room** features scagliola columns designed by Holland in imitation of Siena marble, and Vardy's original ceiling has been restored, the design based on Inigo Jones's at Banqueting House (*see p. 19*). Paintings include three by Benjamin West, on loan from the Royal Collection, originally commissioned by George III as inspiring models of stoical fortitude. They are *The Death of Wolfe* (1771), *The Death of Chevalier Bayard* (1772), and *The Death of Epaminondas* (1773). The **Palm Room** is the most extraordinary room on the ground floor, designed by Vardy as the gentlemen's retiring room. Lavishly decorated in white, gold and green, Corinthian half- and quarter-columns double as palm trees, symbolizing marital fertility. The original furniture has been reconstructed.

On the first floor, the **Music Room** gives little indication of Stuart's exuberant designs beyond. A set of 24 hand-coloured Italian engravings published in 1781 record the paintings found in Nero's Golden House in Rome, an inspiration to Raphael when first discovered in the 16th century. **Lady Spencer's Room** is a faithful reconstruction of her private drawing room, where Stuart's ceiling was based on the Baths of Augustus in Rome, with the frieze adapted from the Erechtheion in Athens. The paintings in this room include some by Benjamin West and also Sir James Thornhill. The **Great Room** follows, the largest state room in the house, with a coffered ceiling and frieze based on the Temple of Concord and Victory in Rome. The monumental paintings *Oedipus at Colonus* (1781) and *Philoctetes on Lemnos* (1781), by Giovanni Battista Cipriani, have been reframed here in copies of Stuart's original design to match the door and window architraves derived from the Erechtheion. Other paintings here include *Mrs Trecothick* and *Lady Frances Wyndham* by Sir Joshua Reynolds, and *L'Allegro* (1770) and *Il Penseroso* (1780) by George Romney. The **Painted Room** provides the climax of the tour, a room decorated in celebration of the Triumph of Love. Restoration in the 1950s painted the walls' background green darker than the original, but otherwise the work of three artists depicting exuberant classical scenes remains well preserved on every flat surface, including the designer James Stuart himself on the pilasters.

SUTTON HOUSE
(National Trust)

2 & 4 Homerton High Street, Hackney, E9 6QJ
Tel: 020-8986 2264; www.nationaltrust.org.uk
Open Feb–Dec Fri, Sat 1–5; Sun and bank holidays 11.30–5
Admission charge
Station: Hackney Central (Silverlink from Highbury & Islington)
Café, shop and art gallery (open Feb–Dec Wed–Sun 11.30–5)
Map p. 379, 2E

Sutton House is the oldest domestic house surviving in the East End of London. Built in 1534–35 by Ralph Sadleir, a wealthy soldier and diplomat, secretary to Thomas Cromwell and later knighted as King Henry VIII's Principal Secretary of State, the house was first known as 'the bryk place', being one of the very few brick-built residences near the villages of Hackney and Homerton. The ragstone tower of St Augustine's church nearby is the only other building to remain from the period. Constructed on the familiar Tudor 'H' plan, the building has been altered several times since—notably around 1620, in 1741–43 and in the early 19th century—but the original form remains remarkably intact. As such it represents an important London example of the development of the medieval hall house, with cross-wings and servants' quarters. In 1550 the house was purchased by John Machell, made Sheriff of London five years later. The property passed to his son John on his wife Jane's death in 1565, and later in part to Thomas Sutton, who according to the diarist John Aubrey was the type for Ben Jonson's Volpone. Made wealthy by investments in Durham coal mines, Sutton founded the Charterhouse Hospital and School in 1611. Under different names the house passed through several hands, becoming a girls' school until the mid-18th century, a boys' school in the early 19th century, and from 1890–1930 the St John's Institute, a recreational church club for 'men of all classes', known as the 'Tute'. In 1938, thanks to a bequest from the Robertson family in memory of two brothers killed in the First World War, the National Trust was able to purchase the property and it was let out to a variety of tenants, including the Association of Scientific, Technical and Managerial Staffs trade union. When the union moved out, the house was squatted for a period in the early 80s, when it was known as the 'Blue House'. After the eviction of the squatters, period fixtures began to be stolen, although some were later recovered. A local pressure group, the Sutton House Society, formed in 1987, helped devise a scheme that would forestall the National Trust's plans to divide the house into flats. In 1993, after a three-year restoration project, the property was opened to the public and local community as a focal point for the exploration of the heritage of Hackney.

Tour of the House
The exterior of the west (right-hand) wing retains its Tudor diaper brickwork. The first room of great historical interest is the **Linenfold Parlour**, at the front of this

wing. The small room is lined with very fine mid-16th-century carved-oak linenfold panelling. Originally the wood was painted pale yellow with green in the folds, a colour scheme that can still be seen behind hinged panels in one wall. Other panels reveal what may have been tradesmen's sketches for the room's interior decoration. Quite possibly it was in this room that Sir Ralph Sadleir held negotiations during the Dissolution of the Monasteries, which carved up the wealth of the Church. The fireplace is original, with a modern reproduction fireback. In the cellar beneath is a small exhibition on the different types of brick used in the house. To the south of the west wing is the Dining Room and a modern entrance to the Courtyard, where the two wings and general plan of the house can best be appreciated. On the opposite side of the courtyard are the **Old Kitchen**, with a display on Tudor cuisine and several original surviving features; and the **Georgian Parlour**, panelled in 1740 and restored to represent a simple mid-18th century parlour. At the back of the house, the Wenlock Barn is a performance and conference venue also housing a display of ephemera on the St John's Institute.

Crossing the courtyard again, and ascending to the first floor in the west wing, the **Painted Staircase** has elaborate patterned and *trompe l'oeil* wall paintings dating from around 1620. Turning right at the top leads into the **Gallery**, a space for temporary exhibitions that also contains a particularly well-preserved fireplace from around 1630 and fragments of late 18th-century wallpaper. Turning left at the top is the **Little Chamber**, above the linenfold parlour in the west wing, with more oak panelling, but dating from slightly later in the 16th century. Above the shop and former Great Hall is the **Great Chamber**, the most important room in the house when built, where the 16th- and 17th-century panelling has been hung with portraits from the period, including one of Sir Ralph's grandson. The replica fleur-de-lis panels replace those stolen in the 1980s. On the opposite side of the Great Chamber, in the east wing, is the **Victorian Study**, restored to its mid-19th-century appearance and also containing a Tudor garderobe. Further up the stairs on this side of the house is an exhibition room displaying preserved examples of the squatters' artwork around the fireplace and providing information on the various architectural changes to the house over the centuries. Throughout the restoration of the building, the aim has been to reveal these changes wherever possible, rather than opting for a mock-up of a single historical period.

SYON PARK

Brentford, Middlesex, TW8 8JF
Tel: 020-8560 0882; www.syonpark.co.uk
Open end March–end Oct Wed, Thur, Sun and bank holidays 11–5
Gardens open daily 10.30–5 or dusk
Admission charge
Nearest station: Kew Bridge (from Waterloo), then bus 237, 267
Cafés and shops
Map p. 378, 3B

The London seat of the Dukes of Northumberland, set in 200 acres of parkland, Syon is chiefly famous for its magnificent Adam interiors and furnishings, its collection of British historical portraits, and grounds laid out by Lancelot 'Capability' Brown.

History of the House

The house occupies the site of a medieval Bridgettine abbey (named after Mount Zion in the Holy Land), founded by Henry V in 1415. After the dissolution of the monasteries the estate became crown property, and it was at Syon that the unfortunate Catherine Howard, fifth wife of Henry VIII, was held between her trial and execution. In 1547 the estate was granted to Protector Somerset (after whom Somerset House is named; *see p. 273*), who built a house on the site of the abbey, and after his execution in 1552 it was presented to John Dudley, Duke of Northumberland (no relation to the present family). His daughter-in-law, Lady Jane Grey, was offered the crown at Syon. The estate was acquired by the powerful Percys, Earls of Northumberland, in 1594 and in 1750 passed through the earl's wife to Sir Hugh Smithson, later 1st Duke of Northumberland, who assumed the Percy name. Finding Syon 'ruinous and inconvenient', and unfit for his new status, he commissioned Robert Adam to refashion the interiors in 1761. The somewhat gaunt external form of the present house, comprising a castellated block c. 100ft square with square corner turrets (refaced c. 1825), dates from the mid-16th century and does nothing to prepare the visitors for the splendours of Adam's state rooms, with their rich ornamentation and carved and gilt furniture. The Northumberland lion of lead which tops the east front of the house is from Northumberland House on the Strand, the family's grand London town house demolished in 1874.

The Adam Rooms

Within the shell of the Jacobean house, Adam planned a progression of state rooms continuing round all four sides. The result is a thoroughly Neoclassical interior. The **Great Hall**, in the form of a Roman basilica, is austerely decorated in tones of white and black, with Roman statuary and fine plasterwork by Joseph Rose. A striking contrast to this cool restraint is the lavish **Anteroom**. Twelve columns of *verde antico* marble (some ancient, dredged from the Tiber and brought to Syon in 1765), cleverly arranged to transform the rectangular space into a square, support jutting entablatures and heavily gilded free-standing classical figures. Gilded trophies, by Rose, decorate the walls and the vibrantly coloured floor is a magnificent example of scagliola (selenite) work. The **Dining Room**, Adam's first interior at Syon, is decorated in white and gold with copies of antique statues, ordered by Adam, in niches. The **Red Drawing Room**, next in the sequence, has a coved ceiling with intricately painted medallions by Cipriani, a fireplace with ormolu decoration by the famous Matthew Boulton, doorcases with large panels of ivory with applied gilded lead ornament, in Italian Renaissance style, and an exceptional Adam-designed carpet made by Thomas Moore of Moorfields, signed and dated 1769. This room also contains pictures worthy of note, in particular Sir Peter Lely's double portrait, *Charles I and James Duke of York*, painted probably in 1646 when the King was under house arrest at Hampton Court. Occasionally he was allowed to ride to Syon to see his children in the care of Algernon Percy, 10th Earl of Northumberland, a distinguished collector of pictures. The **Long Gallery**, with its intricate enrichment of almost every surface (in the words of Adam, decorated 'in a style to afford great variety and amusement'), is one of the highlights of the house. The original Jacobean long gallery, Adam punctuated the wall with carefully positioned doors and chimneypieces, and pilasters in between, to detract from its vast length. Much of the furniture, as in the other rooms, was designed by Adam for this space.

Other Rooms and Grounds

Other (non-Adam) rooms on the public route include the **Print Room**, with Lely's portrait, as a child, of the great 17th-century heiress, Lady Elizabeth Percy, who was married three times between the ages of twelve and fifteen. Her second husband, Thomas Thynne of Longleat, was murdered in Pall Mall in 1681 by assassins hired by the Swedish Count Königsmark, a rival suitor. A suite of rooms previously closed to the public includes the **Green Drawing Room**. Among the portraits is van Dyck's *Mrs Endymion Porter*, most likely bought by the 10th Duke, an important patron of the artist.

In the **Grounds**, which contain rare trees and plants, 'Capability' Brown swept away the formal walled gardens, established spacious lawns and vistas to distant trees and created the ornamental lake. The Great Conservatory was built of gunmetal and Bath stone for the 3rd Duke in 1830 by Charles Fowler, designer of Covent Garden Market. Joseph Paxton is said to have studied it closely when designing Crystal Palace.

Finally the visitor should note, on the London Road, Adam's delicate **Screen** or 'Lion Gates' (1773), supporting a Northumberland lion, boldly silhouetted against the sky.

TATE

Tate is a family of galleries whose large collection is displayed over four sites: the two major London galleries, Tate Britain and Tate Modern, as well as Tate Liverpool and Tate St Ives, in Cornwall. For many, the name Tate is synonymous with modern art and the controversies that surround it: the infamous 'Bricks' and the annual Turner Prize. Tate in fact has two roles: it houses the national collection of British art, from 1500 to the present day (displayed at Tate Britain); and the national collection of post-1900 international art (displayed at Tate Modern and outside London). This dual purpose dates back to the early years of the gallery's foundation, in 1897, by the sugar magnate Sir Henry Tate. An annexe of the National Gallery, the Tate displayed Sir Henry Tate's personal collection of British art, which he had presented to the nation, as well as other British works transferred from Trafalgar Square. The gallery's role soon expanded to incorporate modern foreign art for which, at the time, the National Gallery's administration had little enthusiasm. It was not until 1955 that the Tate gained full independence. The gallery's site on Millbank became increasingly inadequate to display these two collections and in the late 20th century decisive action was taken, resulting in the opening in 2000 of Tate Modern, in the dramatically transformed Bankside power station. The old Millbank site, rebranded Tate Britain, has reverted to its founding concept, as a gallery dedicated to British art.

Both galleries command imposing positions on the river: on Millbank, just beyond the Palace of Westminster; and at Bankside, opposite St Paul's Cathedral. The two are linked by the Tate riverboat service (*every 40mins during gallery opening hours*). Tate Britain's angular steel pier is designed by David Marks and Julia Barfield (designers of the London Eye), and its evening light effects by the artist Angela Bulloch. The exterior of the sleek catamaran (coloured spots) was designed by Damien Hirst.

Below is an outline of each gallery (*for Tate's early history see Tate Britain, below*), their buildings and the major collection highlights. It should be noted that displays at both change annually, and by no means the entire collection is on show at one time. Modern and contemporary British art is shown at both sites.

TATE BRITAIN

Millbank, SW1P 4RG
Tel: 020-7887 8008; www.tate.org.uk
Open daily 10–5.50
Free (except for special exhibitions)
Tube: Pimlico
Restaurant (reservations: 020-7887 8825), café and shop
Map p. 381, 4F

Foundation and Building

Sir Henry Tate (1819–98), originally in the Liverpool grocery trade, began refining sugar in 1862 and was the pioneer producer, at his second refinery in London, of the new, patented commodity, cubed sugar. With the wealth this brought he began collecting modern British art, which he displayed in his picture gallery at his mansion, Park Hill, Streatham Common. In 1889, the offer of his collection to the National Gallery having been refused for lack of space, he donated £80,000 for the erection of a new gallery. Work began in 1894 on the site of the old Millbank Penitentiary, formerly the largest prison in Europe, from where felons were dispatched to Australia. Sidney Smith's design, the first having attracted criticism for its excessive ornamentation and 'pretentious' air, still retains much decorative elaboration. Domed and temple-like, it overlooks the river, its central pedimented Corinthian portico—surmounted by Britannia flanked by the lion and the unicorn—jutting forward, the entrance up an imposing flight of steps. Sphinxes and griffins perch on top of pilasters above a heavy rusticated basement and to either side of the entrance are two bronze sculptural compositions: to the right *The Rescue of Andromeda* by H.C. Fehr (1893) and to the left *The Death of Dirce* by Sir Charles Lawes-Wittewronge (1908).

The river front block is Smith's original gallery, which over the decades has been added to six times to provide extra space for the ever-expanding collection. To the right is the 1980s Clore Gallery, housing the Turner collection (*see p. 297 below*), and on Atterbury Street, to the left, is the new basement entrance, created as part of the gallery's Centenary Development (John Miller + Partners 1997–2001), reached by long ramps behind a wall of glass. At the corner of Atterbury Street and John Islip Street, greeting visitors as they approach from Pimlico tube, is the statue of the great Pre-Raphaelite painter Sir John Everett Millais, holding his palette and brushes. Intensely interested in Tate's new temple to British art, he died in 1896, a year before its completion.

History of Tate Britain

The gallery opened in 1897 with displays of Tate's collection, rich in Victorian sentimental narrative pictures (Luke Fildes's *The Doctor*; Stanhope Forbes's *The Health of the Bride*) as well as Pre-Raphaelite works (Millais' *The Vale of Rest*, and *Ophelia*; *see pp. 293 and 294 below*). A gallery was dedicated to the pictures of one of the leading artists of the day, G.F. Watts (*see p. 220*), which he had presented, as well as a selection of modern British works transferred from the National Gallery. From its foundation the Tate was an annexe of the National Gallery. Works purchased through the Chantrey Bequest, the fund established by the sculptor Sir Francis Chantrey (d. 1840) for the purchase of works of art produced in Britain, which he hoped would constitute the core of a future National Gallery of British Art and which came into effect on the death of his widow in 1875, were also displayed here, as were an increasing number of modern Continental works. In 1917 the Tate became the official home of modern foreign art as well as British, the latter role now extending to historic works as well as modern. It was at the Tate that the great French Impressionist and Post-Impressionist pictures presented through the Hugh Lane Bequest and the Courtauld Fund were first shown, necessitating the building of new galleries to accommodate them. Funded by Lord Duveen and designed by Romaine-Walker, the tall, grand galleries with marble doorcases and dados along Atterbury Street, which today display historic British works, opened in 1926. The gallery's conservative approach to modern art was, however, a defining feature of the Tate's early years. It was slow to acquire works by Cézanne; in the 1930s there was no German Expressionism, no Surrealism, and in the post-war years no Cubist works were purchased. This reluctance to engage with the avant-garde hampered the formation of a modern art collection of weight and distinction.

Following a disastrous flood in 1928 which engulfed the lower galleries, damaged 18 works beyond repair and submerged J.M.W. Turner's portfolios and watercolours, which had to be spread out to dry on the upper floors, Duveen funded the building of new galleries for the display of sculpture. Built in 1935–37 by the New York architect J. Russell Pope with Romaine-Walker and Jenkins, the imperious, monumental Duveens stretch like a great cathedral nave, vast and echoing, down the spine of the building. The Tate was badly damaged by bombing in 1940–41, sustaining almost nightly damage, including two bombs through the main dome (shrapnel wounds are clearly visible on the Atterbury Street façade) and renovations took until 1949. Post-war additions to the gallery include the large 1979 extension; the 1987 Clore Gallery (*see p. 297 below*); and the 2001 redevelopment by John Miller + Partners which created, as well as the new Atterbury Street entrance, new temporary exhibition galleries and remodelled display galleries on the main floor, accessed via the new grand staircase.

The old river front entrance is still the most impressive. From here the view down the Duveens is immediately visible, with galleries to either side. To the left are stairs, with a large stained glass window (1947) designed by the Hungarian emigré artist Ervin Bossányi, which, although branded 'abhorrent' when it arrived, was nevertheless installed, as it had been paid for through public subscription. (Other windows by Bossányi adorn Canterbury Cathedral.) The stairs lead to the inviting Restaurant (crisp white tablecloths and an excellent wine list), the original Refreshment Room, with lighthearted murals by Rex Whistler, *The Expedition to Pursue Rare Meats* (1925).

The Tate gained official independence from the National Gallery in 1955. It seems always to have attracted controversy. In the first half of the 20th century the mediocre, sentimental Chantrey pictures were criticised, as was the gallery's failure fully to embrace developments in modern art. In 1952 Zsa Zsa Gabor caused a minor stir, photographed at the gallery with a leg indecorously draped over a sculpture plinth. In the 1960s and 70s the Tate became closely identified with contemporary art, staging live performance art and a succession of enthusiastically received contemporary exhibitions. On 25 October 1971, 90 white pigeons were released on the gallery's steps to celebrate Picasso's 90th birthday. Acquisitions such as Carl Andre's *Equivalent VIII*, the famous 'Bricks' (held by Tate Modern) have caused public protest and bafflement, as does the Turner Prize exhibition, held at Tate Britain every autumn (*see p. 297 below*).

The Collection

NB: Because of Tate Britain's many thematic hangs, it is not always possible to give room numbers for chronological collections. Room numbers when given indicate where a large proportion of the works mentioned may be found.

Tudor & Stuart Collection (Rooms 1–2 & 3)

Tate Britain's displays are shown in a broadly chronological sequence, beginning with the Tudor and Stuart collection, shown in two new galleries, part of the 2001 redevelopment, at the top of and to the left of the Manton staircase. The earliest picture is the collection is *Man in a Black Cap* (1545) by John Bettes, who possibly trained in Holbein's studio. Other portraits include wealthy ladies in elaborate costumes, denoting rank and status, by Hans Eworth, who worked for Mary Tudor. The love of surface ornament and decoration is particularly apparent in Hilliard's *Elizabeth I*, the 'Phoenix Portrait' (c. 1575–56), the only large-scale (as opposed to miniature) work known by the artist. Rich in symbolism, the picture shows the queen holding a Tudor rose, while the Phoenix

Jewel at her breast alludes to her youthfulness, celibacy and the continuation of her dynasty. The Queen's Painter, Marcus Gheeraerts the Younger, is represented through a number of works, the most extraordinary being the full-length *Captain Thomas Lee*, 1594, shown as an Irish footsoldier with open shirt and bare legs. Lee was a kinsman of Sir Henry Lee of Ditchley (*see p. 216*), and this portrait of him is similar to Gheeraerts's 'Ditchley Portrait' of Queen Elizabeth in its use of elaborate symbolism. One of the most popular works is *The Cholmondeley Ladies*, a regional portrait of two women born, married and brought to bed on the same day: they sit in bed, stiffly painted in large starched ruffs, holding their tightly swaddled babies. The full-length *James Hamilton, 1st Duke of Hamilton*, standing in a deeply shadowed interior in fine red stockings, was painted by Daniel Mytens, who brought to England a new realism.

Anthony van Dyck, who settled in England in 1632 and became Charles I's Principal Painter, revolutionised portrait painting in Britain with his sophisticated handling of paint and the courtly swagger of his poses. The gallery has a good collection of works by Sir Peter Lely, Charles II's Principal Painter, including his beautiful *Ladies of the Lake Family*; and an excellent collection of works by Sir Godfrey Kneller, the official painter of William and Mary, Anne and George I. His style influenced generations of British painters. His portrait of John Banckes, a London merchant (1676), was the first work he painted in England, and the imposing *Philip, Lord Wharton* (1684), shown seated in Parliament robes, is among his finest. The second half of the 17th century witnessed a proliferation of new genres. The Tate has paintings, drawings and etchings by Francis Barlow, the first native-born landscape and animal artist; landscapes by Jan Siberechts, including his beautiful *Landscape with Rainbow, Henley on Thames*; and still life pieces by Edward Collier, collecting together objects symbolic of the transience of life.

Early 18th Century (Room 4)

This collection is rich in works by one of Britain's great painters, William Hogarth, as well as his contemporaries. By Hogarth is his famous self-portrait, *Portrait of the Painter and his Pug*, the palette in the foreground bearing the 'Line of Beauty', central to Hogarth's ideas on harmony and beauty in art. Further works include *Heads of Six of the Artist's Servants*; *The Beggar's Opera VI*; *O The Roast Beef of Old England*, full of anti-Gallic patriotic feeling; his genteel conversation piece *The Strode Family*, the small-scale figures elegantly taking tea; and one of his finest portraits, *Benjamin Hoadly*, seated in his Bishop's robes. By Highmore are scenes illustrating Samuel Richardson's best-selling moral novel, *Pamela*; and by Francis Hayman the large *See-Saw*, one of numerous pictures produced to decorate the supper boxes at the fashionable Vauxhall Pleasure Gardens. Urban and landscape views include Balthasar Nebot's *Covent Garden Market*; Samuel Scott's views of the Thames, including his large *An Arch of Westminster Bridge*; and George Lambert's *A View of Box Hill, Surrey*, a favourite picnic spot.

Later 18th Century (Rooms 5–7)

Grand Manner works include portraits by Sir Joshua Reynolds, the Royal Academy's

TATE BRITAIN
LEVEL 2

Rooms 1–17: Historic British Art
Rooms 18–31: Modern British Art
Rooms 35–45: Turner Collections

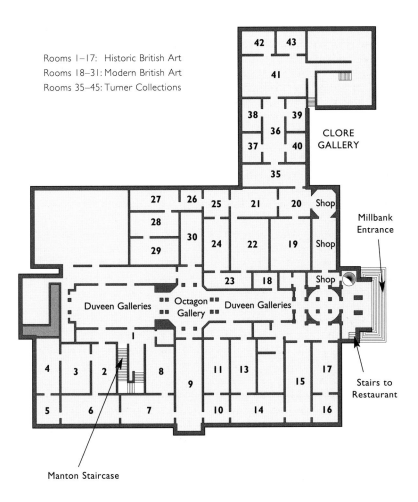

first President. His ennobling portraits, elevated to the status of history painting, include *Three Ladies Adorning a Term of Hymen* ('The Montgomery Sisters'; 1773), showing the sisters paying homage to the Greek god of marriage, and *Admiral Viscount Keppel*.

Tate has a large collection of works by Thomas Gainsborough, the other great portrait painter of the age, including an image of the vivacious Italian dancer Giovanna Baccelli, and the dignified full-length *Benjamin Truman*. Gainsborough's preferred inclination was landscape painting of which the gallery has several important examples, ranging from early views of his native Suffolk to grander, more idealised scenes such as *Sunset: Carthorses Drinking at a Stream*. Further portraits include key pieces by Cotes; Zoffany (including *Col. Mordaunt's Cock Match*, an early view of the British in India); Romney (*The Beaumont Family*; *Lady Hamilton as Circe*) and Wright of Derby, the latter's *Sir Brooke Boothby* (1781) shown relaxing and contemplative in a shady wood.

The lofty ideals of Neoclassical history painting are demonstrated in well-known images such as Benjamin West's *Cleombrotus Ordered into Banishment by Leonidas II, King of Sparta* (1768) and works by Gavin Hamilton; dramatic pieces such as James Barry's *King Lear Weeping over the Dead Body of Cordelia* (1786–88); and John Singleton Copley's large and famous *The Death of Major Peirson, 6 January 1781*, in which the majesty of antiquity is applied to contemporary history.

Of the later 18th-century landscape painters Tate has a good selection of works by the leading master Richard Wilson: landscapes of Italy, such as *Rome: St Peter's and the Vatican from the Janiculum*, inspired by the classical landscapes of Claude, as well as native views such as *Llyn-y-Cau, Cader Idris*; and major works by the famous painter of horses, George Stubbs: *Mares and Foals in a River Landscape*; the idealised vision of country toil, *Haymakers and Reapers*; and *A Horse Frightened by a Lion*, and *A Horse Devoured by a Lion*, more elevated pieces, the horse's pose based on an antique sculpture. Eighteenth-century romantic landscape is nobly represented by Wright of Derby's *An Iron Forge* and *Vesuvius in Eruption*, and the terror of the sublime in de Loutherbourg's *Avalanche in the Alps*.

The Blake Collection (Room 8)
The Tate is well known for its collection of works by the visionary genius, artist and poet William Blake (1757–1827). Blake's works have been an important component of the collection from its earliest years. In 1913 the gallery staged a Blake exhibition, by which time it already owned some important tempera works, and Blake's work provided the subjects for Boris Anrep's mosaic pavement (1923) commissioned for the octagonal gallery which terminates the west wing of Sidney Smith's 1897 gallery. The collection is of international importance and includes Blake's illustrations to Dante's *Divine Comedy*, and other works which demonstrate Blake's very personal philosophy and iconography. Highlights include the large colour-print *Newton*; *Elohim Creating Adam* (1795); the Frontispiece to the 'Visions of the Daughters of Albion'; and *The Ghost of a Flea*.

The Constable Collection (Rooms 10–11)

Also of outstanding importance is the collection of works by John Constable (1776–1837), one of Britain's most famous and internationally admired landscape artists. The collection ranges from early works painted in and around his native Suffolk, at East Bergholt, Flatford and Dedham, to grander works, painted in London but based on previous sketches. Constable placed enormous emphasis on observation from nature, and on show are numerous rapidly executed and evocative sketches, of entire scenes or details such as scudding clouds. Highlights include *Flatford Mill*; *Fenn Lane, East Bergholt*; *Hampstead Heath with the House called 'The Salt Box'*; *Chain Pier, Brighton*; *The Valley Farm*; and the *Sketch for 'Hadleigh Castle'*, a full-size sketch for a work exhibited at the Royal Academy in 1829, a working method Constable used when creating his famous 'six-footers'.

Early to Mid-19th Century

Landscape painting includes the Norwich School artists (John Crome's *The Poringland Oak* and John Sell Cotman's *The Drop Gate*); John Linnell (*Kensington Gravel Pits*) as well as more monumental works, such as John Ward's mighty *Gordale Scar*, a work of breathtaking proportions. Nightmarish apocalyptic scenes include Francis Danby's *The Deluge*, and John Martin's trio, *The Plains of Heaven*, *The Last Judgement* and *The Great Day of His Wrath* (all in Room 14). At the same time small-scale domestic genre pictures were popular, animal pictures 'inspiring delicate sympathies', and historical scenes from national history and literature. It was precisely this type of picture that was enjoyed by Robert Vernon, a London horse dealer who had bequeathed his collection of modern British pictures to the National Gallery. Displayed at the V&A, and later transferred to the Tate, they include William Mulready's *The Last In*; Sir Edwin Landseer's *The Hunted Stag* and *Dignity and Impudence* (two dogs); J.F. Herring's *The Frugal Meal* (horses); C.R. Leslie's *Sancho Panza in the Apartments of the Duchess*; and E.M. Ward's *The South Sea Bubble*. David Wilkie's *Blind Fiddler* was part of Sir George Beaumont's founding gift to the National Gallery.

The Victorian Collection (Rooms 9 & 15)

Tate's collection of Pre-Raphaelite and later Victorian works is outstanding. Among the many well known major masterpieces are Ford Madox Brown's *The Hayfield* and *The Last of England*; William Holman Hunt's *The Awakening Conscience* and *Our English Coasts, 1852* ('Strayed Sheep'); Dante Gabriel Rossetti's *Ecce Ancilla Domini!*, *Beata Beatrix*, *The Beloved* ('The Bride') and *Monna Vanna*; and Sir John Everett Millais' *Christ in the House of His Parents*, *The Vale of Rest*, *The Order of Release* and *Ophelia*, one of the stars of Sir Henry Tate's collection and one of the gallery's most popular pictures. There is also a relatively recent Millais purchase, *Mariana*, an illustration to Tennyson's poem of the same name. Other familiar works are Arthur Hughes's *April Love* and Henry Wallis's *Chatterton*, a highly romanticised view of the poet shortly after his suicide. Later works include Sir Edward Coley Burne-Jones's *King Cophetua and the Beggarmaid* and *Love and the Pilgrim*, and Waterhouse's *Lady of Shalott*.

As well as the works presented to the Tate by G.F. Watts on its foundation in 1897, the Tate's collection of late Victorian works includes Frederic, Lord Leighton's heroic sculpture *An Athlete Wrestling with a Python* and his monumental *And the Sea Gave up the Dead Which Were in It*. William Powell Frith's *Derby Day*, described by Ruskin as 'of the entirely popular manner of painting', created a sensation when exhibited at the Royal Academy in 1858, and was taken on a world tour. Sentimental narratives, ever popular pictures at Royal Academy Summer Exhibitions, include Sir William Quiller Orchardson's *The First Cloud* (a married couple's first argument), as well as more substantial pieces such as Sir Luke Fildes's *The Doctor*, his most famous painting, the light of the sombre interior falling on the dying child. Stanhope Forbes's *The Health of the Bride* and Sir Frank Bramley's *A Hopeless Dawn*, key works of the Newlyn School, show the drama of ordinary lives.

James Abbott McNeill Whistler abandoned the Academy-led insistence on the importance of narrative and focused instead on the effects of light and atmosphere. His 'art for art's sake' aesthetic was fiercely attacked by Ruskin: *Nocturne in Blue and Gold: Old Battersea Bridge* was painted during the famous trial for libel after Ruskin had accused him of throwing a pot of paint in the face of the public—which Whistler won, but received damages of just one farthing. The Tate has an important collection of portraits by John Singer Sargent. As well as the slick society Wertheimer portraits, the most famous picture is *Carnation, Lily, Lily, Rose* (1885–86), showing the pink glow of Chinese lanterns in the evening dusk.

Early 20th Century (Rooms 19 & 21)
The response to Continental Post-Impressionism saw the emergence in England of a vigorous, innovative avant-garde. The Camden Town Group, established in 1911 by Walter Sickert and others, was influenced by Post-Impressionism's emphasis on realism and the effects of light. The sombre, realist, mainly urban, scenes include Sickert's *La Hollandaise* (c. 1906) and *Ennui* (c. 1914); Spencer Gore's *The Cinder Path* (1912); Harold Gilman's *Café Royal*; Charles Ginner's *Piccadilly Circus* (1912); and works by Robert Bevan. Bloomsbury Group works, influenced by Cézanne, include works by Duncan Grant, Vanessa Bell, and Henry Lamb's *Lytton Strachey* (1914). Mark Gertler's highly original *Merry-go-Round* (1916) is a strident anti-war statement while Matthew Smith's *Nude, Fitzroy Street* (1916), in its vivid use of colour, displays the influence of Matisse. Wyndham Lewis's *Workshop* (c .1914–15), David Bomberg's *The Mud Bath* (1914) and *In the Hold*, and works by Christopher Nevinson and other Vorticists, with their diagonals, fragmented geometry and emphasis on urban industrialism, display the influence of Cubism and Futurism.

The great pioneers of modern sculpture in Britain were Jacob Epstein and Henri Gaudier-Brzeska (*Red Stone Dancer*, c. 1913). One of the most important and popular works is Epstein's massive *Jacob and the Angel* (1940–41), the angel's wings a great slab of alabaster. *Torso in Metal* from 'The Rock Drill' (1913–14) is Epstein's major work of the pre-First World War period, a former 10-ft looming robotic figure which he dismantled in 1916, casting the head and torso only in bronze.

The years following the First World War saw a return to more traditional, figurative painting. The dominant figure was Stanley Spencer, whose greatest work, *The Resurrection, Cookham* (1924–27), is a personal, religious vision of modern life. Completed in 1927, it was exhibited and immediately purchased for the national collection, hailed by *The Times* as 'the most important picture painted by any English artist in the present century'. Also in the collection is his popular *Swan Upping* (1914–19); John Nash's sleepy views of rural England, including *The Cornfield*; and works by Sir Alfred Munnings, Augustus John, Meredith Frampton; and Cedric Morris's portrait of his sister's bull terrier, *Belle of Bloomsbury* (1948).

Mid-20th Century

Tate has an excellent collection of works by the outstanding figures of English abstraction, Barbara Hepworth, Henry Moore, Ben Nicholson and Paul Nash. In touch with abstract artists in Paris, through the Seven and Five Society and Unit One, they promoted 'the expression of a truly contemporary spirit'. Works include Nicholson's *Guitar* (1933) and *White Relief* (1935); Paul Nash's *Equivalents for the Megaliths* (1935); Edward Wadsworth's *The Beached Margin* (1937), with its hint of Surrealism; and Victor Pasmore's *Spiral Motif in Green, Violet, Blue and Gold: The Coast of the Inland Sea* (1950). Hepworth's *Three Forms* (1935), three white polished marble shapes of the utmost purity and simplicity, and *Pelagos* (1946) reflect her preoccupation with form. Henry Moore was the leading British sculptor of the mid-20th century and one of the leaders in the revival of direct carving. Tate has a large collection of important works including *Recumbent Figure* (1938), of Hornton stone; *Reclining Figure* (1951); and *King and Queen* (1952–53). By 1939 Nicholson and Hepworth had moved to Cornwall, near St Ives, where the 'naïve primitive' amateur artist Alfred Wallis was discovered and to where a younger generation of artists was attracted. The St Ives School included Terry Frost (*Green, Black and White Movement*, 1957, showing boats bobbing on the water in St Ives harbour), Patrick Heron (*Horizontal Stripe Painting: November 1957–January 1958*), Roger Hilton and Peter Lanyon.

The leading British Pop artists of the late 1950s and 60s were Richard Hamilton (*She*, 1958) and Peter Blake (*Self Portrait with Badges*, 1961). A second phase of Pop was taken up by a group of artists trained at the Royal College of Art, including David Hockney (his Typhoo tea painting, *Tea Painting in an Illusionistic Style*) and works by Patrick Caulfield. The 'New Generation' of British sculptors, who moved from carved work to abstract constructions in industrial metals, brightly painted steel or modern materials such as fibreglass and plastics, is represented by Anthony Caro's *Early One Morning* (1962) and *Night Movements* (1987–90), four large, dark crouching shapes of steel; Phillip King's *Tra-La-La* (1963) and works by Eduardo Paolozzi and William Turnbull.

Later 20th Century

Twentieth-century works continuing the Realist or Figurative tradition include Graham Sutherland's landscapes and his portrait of Somerset Maugham; Lucien

Gilbert and George: *Happy* (1980).

Freud's *Girl with a White Dog* (1950–51) and *Standing by the Rags* (1988–89); Michael Andrews' *The Deer Park* (1962), as well as works by Frank Auerbach, R.B. Kitaj and Leon Kossoff. The Tate has important works by David Hockney, such as his endur-ingly popular *Mr and Mrs Clark and Percy* (showing the fashion designer Ossie Clark, a white cat on his lap, his toes buried in a hairy shagpile carpet, with his wife, the textile designer Celia Birtwell), and his witty Californian work *The Bigger Splash*. The large collection of works by one of the most important 20th-century British artists, Francis Bacon, includes *Three Studies for Figures at the Base of a Crucifixion* (c. 1944), and another grand triptych, *Triptych: August 1972*, its blurred and fused images of contemporary man based on the work of the pioneer stop-action photographer Eadweard Muybridge (*see pp. 154–55*).

Since the 1970s conceptual art and installations have been an important component of British modern art, such as Gilbert and George's 'action' works, Richard Long's sculptural interventions in the natural environment and indoor installations (*Slate Circle*, 1979), and Tony Cragg's *On the Savannah* (1988). Anish Kapoor's *As if to Celebrate, I Discovered a Mountain Blooming with Red Flowers* (1981), peaked shapes covered in a vibrant red, loose, pure pigment, refers to the birth of the goddess Devi out of a fiery mountain composed of the bodies of male gods, while Cornelia Parker's *Cold Dark Matter: An Exploded View* (1991) fills a gallery with suspended charcoal fragments, the remains of an exploded solid form, lighting casting dramatic shadows.

The Turner Prize
The annual Turner Prize takes place at Tate Britain every autumn, with an exhibition of the work of the four shortlisted artists. The televised announcement of the winner usually takes place in October. Past winners include Howard Hodgkin and Gilbert and George, and exhibitions have showcased the work of the Young British Artists, or YBAs, such as Damien Hirst and Tracey Emin, now household names. 'YBA' works in the collection include Hirst's *Pharmacy* (1992), a room-sized installation of a pharmacy interior, its shelves and cabinets stacked with drugs, those for the head at the top, those for the stomach in the middle, and so on; Gillian Wearing's *Signs That Say What You Want Them To Say …* (1992–93); Rachel Whiteread's *Untitled* ('Stairs'; 2001), the cast of the stairs and the space between the landings of a house in Bethnal Green; as well as works by Emin and the photography, film and video artist Sam Taylor-Wood.

The Clore Gallery and Turner Collection (Rooms 35–43 & Rooms 44–45 on Level 3)
Arguably the most famous of all British artists is J.M.W. Turner (1775–1851). His subjects were classical mythology and history, contemporary events and natural disaster, painted with a concern for the changing atmospheric effects of light: golden sunsets, raging storms, tossing waves and enveloping mists. Even in his own lifetime Turner was recognised as one of the greatest of all landscape painters. His early inspirations were Claude and Willem van de Velde the Younger. As his style developed, it became increasingly romantic and original, culminating in the great proto-Impressionist works for which he is so celebrated today. His brilliant image of the shadowy dome of the Salute looming out of the mist of the Venetian lagoon seems 'reminiscent' of Monet, even though it pre-dates Monet by almost half a century. Some of his work,

J.M.W. Turner: *The Shipwreck* (1805).

where concrete forms are dissolved and diffused by the effects of light and colour, are almost abstract in feel. Turner had bequeathed his unsold pictures, watercolours, sketchbooks and other paraphernalia to the nation, but for lack of space at the National Gallery they were shown first at Marlborough House, then at the V&A. In 1910 new Turner galleries opened at the Tate, but following the 1928 flood (*see p. 288 above*) the works on paper and archive material were removed to the British Museum. In 1987 the Clore Gallery, designed by James Stirling, Michael Wilford and Associates and funded by the Clore Foundation, reunited the Turner Bequest. It is a brash Post-Modern building linked to the 1897 river block, in red brick, cream and bright green, with its own entrance through a large glass void in the shape of a classical pediment. Inside, the walls are dark peach with purple and pink details. A tall staircase leads up to the main gallery level. The vast collection incorporates all periods and aspects of Turner's art, as well as personal items such as his paint boxes. Highlights include his early *The Shipwreck*, exhibited in 1805; *Crossing the Brook*; *Snow Storm: Hannibal and his Army Crossing the Alps*; *Childe Harold's Pilgrimage*; *Snow Storm: Steam-Boat off a Harbour's Mouth*; *Peace: Burial at Sea*; *Norham Castle, Sunrise*, as well as a wealth of watercolours and sketches demonstrating his evolution as an artist, his working methods and his sketching tours around Britain and the Continent.

TATE MODERN

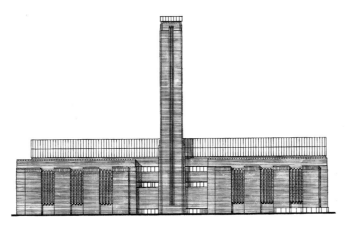

TATE MODERN (BANKSIDE POWER STATION): RIVERFRONT ELEVATION

Bankside, SE1 9TG
Tel: 020-7887 8000; www.tate.org.uk
Open Sun–Thur 10–6; Fri, Sat 10–10
Free (admission charge for special exhibitions)
Tube: Southwark. Tube/Station: Blackfriars and London Bridge
Restaurants, cafés and shops
Map p. 383, 3D

Tate Modern is one of the most popular museums of modern art in the world. Opened in 2000, in its first five years over 22 million visitors passed through its doors. Converted from Sir Giles Gilbert Scott's Bankside Power Station, built after the Second World War to provide the City with electricity, it looms heavy and massive on the south bank of the Thames. An international architectural competition for the conversion of the site was won by the Swiss firm Herzog and de Meuron, who retained the stark industrial character of the building. Externally it has been little altered. A powerful horizontal mass of red brick, alleviated by immense vertical windows, is bisected by a tall central chimney. A two-storey light box has been added to the roofline, a gleaming white beam at night, housing a restaurant with spectacular views over the river to the City and St Paul's Cathedral. The new pedestrian Millennium Bridge links Tate Modern to the north side of the river. Designed by Sir Norman Foster with Anthony Caro, an architect-sculptor partnership, it was quickly nicknamed 'the wobbly bridge' when it was found to sway alarmingly underfoot, a problem since rectified at considerable expense.

The entrance is either from the riverfront or through the great west entrance, down a vast concrete ramp straight into the **Turbine Hall**. Five hundred feet long and 150ft high, this is the heart of the building, the mighty nave of an industrial cathedral. Stripped of its turbine engines, the cavernous space is now a dramatic arena for the display of sculpture and installations of enormous scale. Specially commissioned pieces have included Louise Bourgois's giant, crouching spider; Anish Kapoor's *Marsyas*, a massive Triffid-like organic form suspended in the air and coloured the dark maroon of flayed flesh; and, most spectacularly, Olafur Eliasson's *The Weather Project*, with the vast space of the Hall bathed in the golden light of a huge setting sun positioned at the east end. Crowds were drawn to it, sitting silent and transfixed beneath the mirrored ceiling.

In the riverfront block new floor divisions have been created, with galleries for the display of the permanent collection and temporary exhibitions. Of varying heights, many have dramatic side-lighting from the original vertical strip windows, stretching from floor to ceiling with unexpected views of St Paul's. Although the power station was decommissioned in 1981, an operational switch station remained in part of the south building, but a multi-million-pound redevelopment of this area of the gallery is planned, providing further display space for installations, film and video.

The Collection

Tate Modern is devoted to the Tate's collection of post-1900 international art. In the early decades of the 20th century the gallery's administration viewed modern art with conservative caution, resulting in the collection's weaknesses in this area, weaknesses which are still apparent today. In the post-war era, however, modern art was acquired with enthusiasm, particularly from the 60s and 70s, and Tate has many major works, spanning painting, drawing, sculpture, installation and conceptual art, photography, film, video and artists' books. The collection of Surrealist works, for example, is particularly strong, as is the modern and contemporary collection of British art, which Tate represents comprehensively and in depth. Although Tate Britain is officially the home of British art, 20th-century British works are shown at both sites: the rich collection of works by Henry Moore, Francis Bacon and David Hockney, for example, allows for major works by these artists to be shown at both buildings. The collection covers mainly Western art, Latin America and Asia are also included.

The permanent collection displays have discarded the traditional chronological progression through the modern art movements, or 'isms', in favour of a thematic approach, by some regarded as a brave, fresh move, by others as a recipe for confusion. At time of writing the themes are divided into four broad sections based on the main painting genres: history painting; portraiture and figurative art; landscape; and still life. Change is due in 2006, when, for the next six years, themes will focus on the collection's strengths, on artistic movements, and also on international cultural exchange.

Post-Impressionism

The Tate's history is inextricably linked to to that of the National Gallery, and many of the latter's fine Impressionist and Post-Impressionist works were originally displayed at the Tate on Millbank (*see p. 287 above*). The dividing line between Tate Modern and the National Gallery is now accepted as 1900, although there are some exceptions. Tate's collection of Post-Impressionists, and stylistically associated younger generation artists, contains fine works, the most exceptional and well known probably being Monet's large *Water-Lilies* (after 1916), the focus of the large canvas the evanescent play of light on the pond and its flowers. Also in the collection is Manet's *Nude on a Couch* (1915); Camille Pissarro's *Self-Portrait* (1903); Cézanne's *The Grounds of the Château Noir* (1900–06), and *The Gardener Vallier* (c. 1906); Seurat's *Le Bec du Hoc, Grandchamp* (1885); van Gogh's *Farms near Auvers* (1890); and Gauguin's *Faa Iheihe* (1898), painted in Tahiti. Degas' famous *Little Dancer Aged Fourteen* (1880–81, cast c. 1922), of bronze, with a muslin skirt and satin hair ribbon, the largest and most important of his sculptures, was purchased in 1952 for £8,000, a sum which caused controversy at the time. Rodin's *The Kiss* (1901–04) shows the lovers Paolo and Francesca from Dante's 'Inferno', naked and locked in their first embrace, their polished bodies contrasting with the hewn rock they sit on. Bonnard's *The Table* (1925) was bought a year after it was painted, and *The Bath* (1925) is one of the many paintings Bonnard made of his wife, Berthe, bathing. Ever popular are Raoul Dufy's brightly coloured *Open Window at Saint-Jeannet* (c. 1926–27) and *The Wheatfield* (1929).

Early to mid-20th century

Matisse's *The Snail* (1953), the greatest of his late 'cut gouaches', composed of vividly coloured rectangles of cut paper arranged roughly in the spiral of a snail, was one of the gallery's major acquisitions, though it also caused controversy when bought, in 1962. Cubist works include still lifes by Braque, including *Clarinet and Bottle of Rum* (1911), and a large collection of works by Picasso. An early work is the melancholic *Jeune Femme en Chemise* (c. 1905). Even earlier is his *Flowers* (1901), the first Picasso to enter the collection. Purchased in 1933, its conservatism is evidence of the gallery's resistance at the time to the more radical elements of modernism. *The Three Dancers* (1925) is a major work and *Weeping Woman* (1937), an allegory of republican Spain, is one of several painted following the bombardment of Guernica. Other works include Juan Gris's *The Sunblind* (1914); Fernand Léger's *The Acrobat and his Partner* (1948); and several sculptures by Jacques Lipchitz.

Early 20th-century sculpture includes works by the influential Romanian artist Brancusi, including his bronze, metal and wood *Fish* (1926), and *Maiastra* (1911), a bronze bird standing on a stone base; Jean Arp's bronze *Pagoda Fruit* (1949); Modigliani's elongated *Head* (c. 1911–12); and the Futurist Umberto Boccioni's bronze *Unique Forms of Continuity in Space* (1913, cast 1972). Of great importance is Marcel Duchamp's *Fountain*, a urinal offered for exhibition in 1917. The most famous of his 'ready-mades', ordinary objects designated works of art by the artist, it is an important precursor to Surrealist works, as well as to conceptual art.

Surrealism

Tate has a large and important collection of Surrealist works, the movement launched in Paris in 1924 by French poet André Breton. Salvador Dalí's dream-like works, windows onto the mind, include his important *Metamorphosis of Narcissus* (1937), while *Lobster Telephone* (1936) confronts the rational with its impossible combination of objects. Other works include Joan Miró's *Head of a Catalan Peasant* (1925); Magritte's *The Reckless Sleeper* (1928) and *Man with a Newspaper* (1928); and Max Ernst's *Celebes* (1921), *Men Shall Know Nothing of This* (1923), and *Forest and Dove* (1927). Georgio de Chirico's *The Uncertainty of the Poet* (1913) shows a classical antique torso in a piazza with a bunch of bananas. *Eine Kleine Nachtmusik* (1943) is one of Dorothea Tanning's best known works, showing a girl on a wide landing coming upon a giant sunflower. The sculptor Alberto Giacometti, better known for his skeletal figures—*Man Pointing* (1947)—was a former Surrealist, and Tate has his *Hour of the Traces* (1930).

Abstraction

Works by one of the pioneers of abstraction, Kandinsky, include *Cossacks* (1910–11) and the highly geometric *Swinging* (1925). Other important early abstract pieces are Malevich's *Dynamic Suprematism* (1915/16) and works by the Dutch De Stijl artist Piet Mondrian: *Sun, Church in Zeeland* (1910) and *Composition with Grey, Red, Yellow and Blue* (1920–c. 1926). Tate has an important collection of works by the Russian constructivist Naum Gabo, a pioneer of abstract sculpture, including *Head No. 2* (enlarged version 1964), *Model for 'Column'* (1920–21) and *Construction in Space with Crystalline Centre* (1938–40), all of them sculptural explorations of form and space. American Abstract Expressionist pieces include de Kooning's *The Visit* (1966–67) and several works by Jackson Pollock. His major early drip painting is *Summertime: Number 9A* (1948), the paint splashed in a rhythmic pattern. Vast-scale colour-field Abstract Expressionist pieces include Mark Rothko's famous 'Seagram Murals', commissioned in 1958 for a restaurant in Mies van der Rohe's Seagram building on Park Avenue, New York. Rothko changed his mind about their destination and they came to Tate instead, which had begun negotiations with the artist about a possible donation of a work in the mid-1960s. It is said that as the works arrived at the gallery, news came of Rothko's suicide. The large, magnificent, luminous works, combinations of maroon and black, are among the gallery's major holdings.

Later 20th century

American Pop Art, inspired by consumer culture, Hollywood and celebrity, advertising and commercial mass production, includes Jasper Johns' *Dancers on a Plane*; Roy Lichtenstein's well-known *Whaam!* (1963); Andy Warhol's *Marilyn Diptych* (1962); and the sculptor Claes Oldenburg's *Soft Drainpipe: Blue (Cool) Version* (1967). The Continental European equivalent to Pop was Nouveau Réalisme. Tate has works by, among others, Tinguely, Yves Klein and Arman, one of its leading exponents, including *Condition of Woman I* (1960).

The large collection of conceptual art includes works by the American Bruce Nauman and the hugely influential pioneer of performance art, the German Joseph Beuys, whose installations use organic materials such as fat, wax and rock. Works include *Fat Transformation Piece* (1972), and *The End of the Twentieth Century* (1983–85), 40 basalt columns lying on the ground, each with an 'eye'—a polished cone of stone fixed with clay and felt. Works incorporating real objects as the stuff of art include Marcel Broodthaers's *Casserole and Closed Mussels* (1964), and Rebecca Horn's *Concert for Anarchy* (1990), a grand piano suspended upside down with its keys spilling out. American minimalist pieces include Carl Andre's infamous 'Bricks' (*Equivalent VIII*; 1966), plain bricks arranged in a neat rectangle, which caused a storm of indignation and hilarity when acquired in 1972, and have ever since been taken as evidence of the meaninglessness of modern art. Other works include Frank Stella's *Six Mile Bottom* (1960); Sol LeWitt's *Two Open Modular Cubes/Half-Off* (1975); Donald Judd's *Untitled* (1980), units of steel, aluminium and perspex marching up the wall in a vertical stack; and Robert Morris's *Untitled* (1965/71), four large reflective cubes of mirror-plate glass on board. In 1971 Morris famously constructed a minimal gymnasium at the Tate which invited the active involvement of exhibition visitors. Eventually it had to close due to injury of members of the public as well as to the exhibit. Other sculpture includes works by Richard Serra, and David Smith's *Cubi XIX* (1964), brushed stainless steel geometric forms, balanced on top of each other.

THEATRE MUSEUM
(Victoria & Albert Museum)

1E Tavistock Street, Covent garden, WC2E 7PA
Tel: 020-7943 4700; www.theatremuseum.vam.ac.uk
Open Tues–Sun 10–6, also alternate Fridays 10–9pm. Free guided tours daily at 12
Free
Tube: Covent Garden
Map p. 382, 2B

Housed in the old Covent Garden flower market since 1987, the Theatre Museum grew out of the Victoria and Albert Museum's receipt in 1924 of Gabrielle Enthoven's vast collection of some 100,000 playbills, programmes, play-texts and prints. Now part of the museum's archives, the collection was joined in 1971 by the Harry R. Beard collection of some 20,000 operatic and theatrical prints, and three years later by the collections of the British Theatre Museum Association and Richard Buckle's 'Friends of the Museum of the Performing Arts', which included important material on the Ballets Russes. Since then the museum has acquired numerous other collections, the Diaghilev costumes and scenic cloths, the archives of the Royal Court Theatre and of the D'Oyly Carte company, as well as the largest play library in the UK. In 1992 the museum launched the National Video Archive of Performance. In 1994 the Royal National Theatre loaned it the important Somerset Maugham Collection of theatrical paintings. A branch of the V&A, the museum is also the National Museum of the Performing Arts.

Introduced by the gilded elephants and voluptuous caryatids of the original boxes of the Palace Theatre of Varieties (1904) in Glasgow, demolished in 1977, the permanent galleries cover 400 years of theatre in Britain and Europe, illustrating the theme chronologically with displays arranged in glass-fronted viewing boxes. Dominating one wall are two of Denis van Asloot's large paintings of *The Ommegang: The Triumph of Archduchess Isabella, Grand Place, Brussels, 31st May 1615*. These expansive and detailed canvases are a pair of six commissioned by the Archduchess to record her patronage of the City and Guilds of Brussels, depicting the colourful annual procession dedicated to the Blessed Virgin that was initiated in the mid-14th century. Displays cover the Shakespearean theatre, featuring a small model of the second Globe; and the Stuart Masque 1605–49, illustrated by drawings of costume designs by Inigo Jones, a portrait of him, and also of Ben Jonson, the pre-eminent writer of court masques for James I. The story of the Garrick family and likewise later of the Kemble family is also told. Under the heading 'Costumes, Scenery and Machinery' are costumes for Diaghilev's Ballets Russes, and an embroidered silk apron worn by Lavinia Fenton as Polly Peachum in the first production of John Gay's *The Beggar's Opera* in 1788. Henry Irving, the first actor to be knighted, and manager of the Lyceum from 1878, who promoted his leading lady Ellen Terry with stratospheric success, is covered in some depth, as is Edward Gordon Craig (1872–1966), the actor generally credited with exploding imitative and interpretative theatre. Another exhibition looks at the Redgrave theatrical dynasty. The choreographer Kenneth Macmillan is celebrated with a series of sliding panels illustrating his portrayal of sex and death on the stage.

In a separate room is the Somerset Maugham collection and other paintings in a display entitled 'Picturing the Players 1759–1846'. Many of the paintings are by Samuel de Wilde. The actor John Bannister features regularly, to particular effect in *The Children in the Wood* by Thomas Morton, painted by de Wilde in 1794. Johan Zoffany's portrait of Edward Shuter, John Beard and John Dunstall in *Love in a Village* by Isaac Bickerstaffe depicts a scene from the ballad opera that was almost as popular as the *Beggar's Opera*. Other paintings include a portrait of David Garrick between the Muses of Tragedy and Comedy by Joshua Reynolds, and Edmund Kean as Richard III by an unknown artist.

TOWER OF LONDON
(Historic Royal Palaces)

HM Tower of London, EC3N 4AB
Tel: 0870 7515177; recorded information 0870-756 6060; www.hrp.org.uk
Open Mar–Oct Tues–Sat 9–5, Sun–Mon 10–5; Nov–Feb Tues–Sat 9–4,
Sun–Mon 10–4
Admission charge
Tube: Tower Hill
Cafés and shops
Map p. 383, 2F

The Tower of London, the most important and complete secular medieval edifice to survive in the city, is a place intimately and continuously involved in British history since the Norman Conquest. As the foremost royal fortress, palace, prison and place of execution, it played a central role in the defence of crown and state until the mid-19th century. In the Victorian period the Tower became the tourist attraction that it remains to this day, grimly associated with the use, abuse, or pursuit of royal power, as well as with the notable people who have suffered death or imprisonment within its walls. Remarkably well-preserved, it contains not only the Crown Jewels, but also part of the Royal Armouries, a series of reconstructed medieval rooms and restored medieval towers, a Norman keep and chapel, a Tudor church, the Regimental Museum of the Royal Fusiliers, several ancient ravens and an army garrison. Quite distinct from the latter are the famous Yeoman Warders, a body of about 40 men chosen from retired warrant and non-commissioned officers of the army. They live in the Tower of London, wear uniforms said to date from the time of Henry VII or Edward VI, and are better known as 'Beefeaters', probably because of the rations that they once received. Guided tours led by Yeoman Warders leave the Lanthorn Tower at regular intervals and remain the best possible introduction to the castle.

History of the Tower

The White Tower is the oldest part of the fortress that takes its name. It was constructed on the orders of William the Conqueror in the late 11th century as the most important of a series of keeps designed to secure London for the crown and protect the new capital from Danish invasion. A Roman wall, part of which can still be seen outside Tower Hill underground station, protected the eastern boundary of the tower's precincts. Not until the reign of Henry III (1216–72) was the White Tower fully fortified, with the addition of the Wakefield and Lanthorn towers on the waterfront, a new wall protecting the western approach, and finally, at enormous expense and more than doubling the acreage of the castle, a curtain wall complete with nine new towers and a moat. Around this time the Tower began to be used as a prison: the Welsh Prince Gruffydd died in an escape attempt here in 1244. Many of Henry III's new towers, Constable, Martin, Brick, Bowyer, Flint and Devereux, still survive much as built. Edward I (1272–1307) continued his father's work, building the Beauchamp Tower and then enclosing the whole castle on all sides with another great curtain wall and moat, providing a landward entry from the west through the Middle and Byward towers and a river entry through St Thomas's Tower, later known as Traitors' Gate, the shape substantially assumed by the Tower today. The Scottish rebel Sir William Wallace was executed here in 1305, while David II of Scotland (1346–57) and John of France (1356–60) were both held prisoner in the Tower, as was James I of Scotland for part of his long imprisonment in England from 1406–26. Until the reign of Henry VIII (1509–1547) the Tower was also used by monarchs as a safe haven in times of civil unrest, notably by the 14-year-old Richard II (1377–99) who took refuge here for two days during the Peasants' Revolt of 1381. Over the course of the next century, and especially during the Wars of the Roses, other royal residents were less safe: Henry VI (1422–61, 1470–71) was secretly murdered here, as

THE TOWER OF LONDON

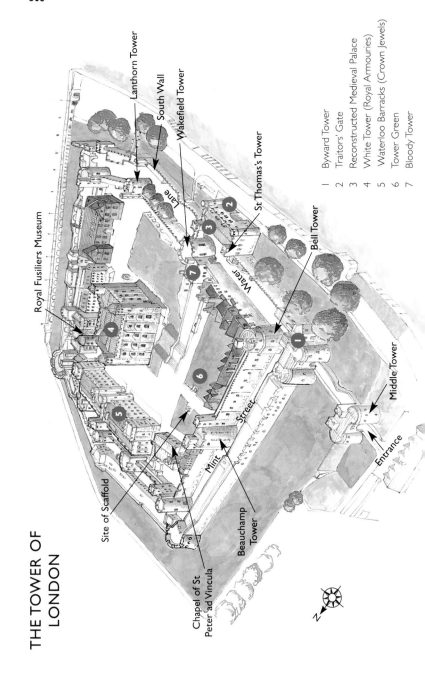

Lanthorn Tower

South Wall

Wakefield Tower

St Thomas's Tower

Bell Tower

Lane

Water

Middle Tower

Entrance

Street

Mint

Beauchamp Tower

Chapel of St Peter ad Vincula

Site of Scaffold

Royal Fusiliers Museum

1 Byward Tower
2 Traitors' Gate
3 Reconstructed Medieval Palace
4 White Tower (Royal Armouries)
5 Waterloo Barracks (Crown Jewels)
6 Tower Green
7 Bloody Tower

later were Edward IV's brother, George Duke of Clarence, 'drowned in a butt of a malmsey' in 1478, and the young Edward V and his brother, 'the Princes in the Tower', dispatched here five years later.

Official executions characterise the continuation under the Tudors of the Tower's gloomy history, beginning with the beheading of Sir Thomas More and Bishop Fisher in 1535, canonized as Catholic martyrs for refusing to accept King Henry VIII as head of the Church of England. Henry had married Katherine of Aragon here, and also Anne Boleyn, who was beheaded on Tower Green in 1536. Henry's fifth wife, Catherine Howard, suffered the same fate in 1542. Among the many prisoners of Henry's daughter 'Bloody' Mary (1553–58) were Lady Jane Grey, proclaimed Queen on the death of Edward VI (1553), and beheaded nine days later, along with her husband, Lord Guildford Dudley. Mary's half-sister, daughter of Anne Boleyn, the future Queen Elizabeth I (1558–1603) was held in close confinement here for two months. Thomas Cranmer and Sir Thomas Wyatt, by whose followers the Tower had been attacked, for the last time in its history, were imprisoned here and beheaded in 1554.

During Elizabeth's reign, the Duke of Norfolk was executed here for intriguing in favour of Mary Queen of Scots. The Earl of Essex, Elizabeth's favourite, was beheaded on Tower Green in 1601. Sir Walter Raleigh was confined here three times (*see p. 310 below*). The monarch that signed the order for his execution, James I (1603–25), was the last to use the Tower as a residence. In 1605–06 Guy Fawkes was tortured here. During the Civil War (1642–49), the castle was seized by the Parliamentarians and garrisoned with regular troops by Oliver Cromwell, later Lord Protector. Charles II (1660–85), the last King to sleep at the Tower, passed the night here before his Coronation in 1661. Simon Fraser, Lord Lovat, was one of the many noble prisoners brought here after the Jacobite uprisings of 1715 and 1745, and was the last person beheaded in England, on Tower Hill in 1747. Later prisoners in the Tower included John Wilkes (1763) and the Cato Street conspirators (1820). During the Second World War, Rudolph Hess and several U-boat crews were held here, and spies were executed by firing squad within its walls.

Traitors' Gate and the Royal Palace

The main entrance to the Tower is near the southwest corner of the castle, through Edward I's Middle Tower, rebuilt in the 18th century, over the dry moat and through the **Byward Tower** (1280) ❶. This main gatehouse to the Outer Ward and entrance through the outer circuit of walls is usually closed to the public, but it is well worth asking a Warder to see inside. Along with the Tower's original portcullis, now the symbol of Her Majesty's Government, one room reveals a remarkable painted chimney breast dating from around 1400. On the left, the figures of the Virgin Mary and John the Baptist can be clearly seen, while on the right stand St John the Evangelist and the Angel of Judgement. The wall painting once had a background pattern of fleur-de-lis, lions, and birds on a green and gold ground, which can still be seen decorating the main beam of the room. The central figure of Christ was destroyed during rebuilding of the chimney piece in the early 1600s and the other figures, which formed part of a continuous composition around the walls, were covered in limewash. The Byward Tower was once the home of the First Gentleman Porter, known as John of London, and much later the prison of the Jacobite rebel Lord Lovat.

Opposite the Byward Tower is the **Bell Tower** (1190; *closed to the public*), the prison of Fisher, More, Princess Elizabeth and Monmouth, where curfew continues to be rung at twilight. Running north between the two towers is Mint Street, named after the Royal Mint established here in the late 13th century, lined with casemates constructed against the walls in the early 18th century. Isaac Newton lived in the first of them while Master of the Mint, and they currently house the 34 Yeoman Warders. Water Lane runs east from here, parallel to the river, beneath the windows of the Queen's House (home to the Governor of the Tower and closed to the public), where Guy Fawkes was interrogated in the Council Chamber. Beneath St Thomas's Tower is **Traitors' Gate** ❷, its great stone arch constructed between 1275 and 1279. Many illustrious prisoners hardly deserving the name of traitor have passed beneath it, among them Sir Thomas More, Anne Boleyn, Thomas Cromwell, Catherine Howard, Essex and Monmouth.

St Thomas's Tower is now the entrance to the **reconstructed Medieval Palace** ❸ A small turret off the first room contains an oratory, originally overlooking the river and dedicated to St Thomas à Becket. The Wakefield Tower, traditionally the site of Henry VI's murder, was built in the 1220s as Henry III's bedchamber and later became Edward's audience chamber. It was restored in 1993 to something like its appearance at that time, featuring a reproduction of an 11th-century candelabra or corona. Lastly on the tour of the Medieval Palace is the Lanthorn Tower, built for the queen around the same time as the Wakefield Tower, but demolished in 1776 and only rebuilt in 1883. It contains a small exhibition on daily life in the palace of Edward I.

The White Tower and Royal Armouries

Leaving the Lanthorn Tower, visitors are standing close to the line of the Roman city wall, with a good view of the **White Tower** ❹. Probably built by Bishop Gundulf, also the builder of Rochester Cathedral, with walls up to 15ft thick and rising to a height of 90ft, it was whitewashed in the reign of Henry III. The exterior has been much restored since then, notably by Wren, who altered all the windows but four on the south side. The tower is entered via an external staircase to the first floor, where in many ways the most evocative room comes first: the Chapel of St John the Evangelist (1087). It rises through the height of two floors, the massive round columns and arches of the nave supporting an unusual continuous tribune gallery above, daylight filtering through heavy round-arched windows. It is the earliest piece of Norman ecclesiastical architecture in London and also one of the most important in England. The squared stonework, austere and bare, was quarried at Caen in Normandy, but was probably once brightly decorated with colourful paintings. In 1399 Henry IV created 46 knights in the chapel, which remains closely connected with the Order of the Bath; Henry VI lay in state here after being murdered; Lady Jane Grey used it during her nine days reign in 1553, and a year later it saw Mary I betrothed by proxy to Philip of Spain. In the rooms beyond, new exhibitions recount the building of the White Tower, and take visitors past a Norman garderobe or lavatory.

Exhibitions from the **Royal Armouries** occupy the rest of the rooms, recently redesigned to explore the idea of the Tower as the first museum in England. One highlight is the armour of the Tudor and Stuart kings and princes: King Henry VIII's armour comes first, a suit from 1515 with a skirt highly ornamented with the gilt brass initials H and K (for his first wife Katherine of Aragon), entwined with true lovers' knots. It was probably made for the Greenwich tournament in 1516. Some of the king's fearsome horse armour (Flanders, c. 1514) can also be seen here. Another suit of armour, engraved with designs by Hans Holbein, was made for Henry when he was forty-nine and had become seriously overweight. By contrast, the Presentation Armour of King James I shows him to have been a slight man, as does the short armour (1612) of Charles I, probably first made for his elder brother Henry, Prince of Wales, and superbly decorated in gold leaf. The 'Line of Kings' claims to be one of the earliest museum displays in Britain, dating from around 1690. Following the restoration of Charles II, the general public was allowed to visit the armouries here for the first time. The 'Line of Kings', a rank of mounted armoured figures representing English monarchs since William the Conqueror, was one of the most popular attractions. The wooden horses and heads of the kings were carved by, among others, Grinling Gibbons (third from the left), and John Nost (fifth from left). Nearby, also side by side, are the suits of armour of John of Gaunt (6ft 9in) and Richard, Duke of York (3ft 1.5in), one of the princes supposedly murdered in the Bloody Tower. Equally popular in the 17th century was the Spanish Armoury, also recreated here, which once claimed to display booty captured from the Spanish Armada: among the harnesses, thumbscrews, bilbos and shackles, a pollaxe can be seen, along with the execution block of Simon Fraser, Lord Lovat.

The Crown Jewels

Facing the White Tower from the north are the Waterloo Barracks (1845) **5**, built on the orders of the Duke of Wellington, then Constable of the Tower. Once home to almost 1,000 soldiers, they now contain the strong-room where the Crown Jewels have been kept since 1994. Crowds are channelled slowly through a procession of rooms where videos of royal ceremonies are shown, notably the live televisation of Queen Elizabeth II's coronation in 1953, the last time the regalia were used. The ancient regalia were dispersed or destroyed during the Commonwealth. Only three swords and the silver gilt Coronation Spoon, probably made for Henry II or Richard I some time in the 12th century, survive from before that time. Some of the items, most prominently the Orb and Sceptre, have been used at every coronation since that of Charles II, by whom they were commissioned. St Edward's Crown (1661), used for the actual crowning of the sovereign, may have been made from the gold of the Saxon diadem. The Ampulla and Spoon, the oldest items on display, are used at the most solemn moment of the ceremony, when oil is poured from the Ampulla eagle's beak into the Spoon, for the Archbishop to anoint the sovereign's head, breast and palms. The Ampulla was redecorated in the 17th century but may in essence be the golden eagle used at the coronation of Henry IV (1399). As well as their historical and symbolic interest, the regalia incorporate some spectacular gemstones. The Sceptre contains the largest top-quality cut diamond in the world, Cullinan I or the 'Star of Africa'. The Koh-i-Noor diamond, or 'Mountain of Light', which sits in the platinum crown made for the Queen Mother at the coronation of George VI (1937), was given to Queen Victoria by the Maharajah of Lahore as part of the treaty annexing the Punjab in 1849. Queen Victoria's Small Diamond Crown is the lightest and smallest in the collection, only 3.7 inches in height, designed to be worn on her widow's cap. The Imperial State Crown (1937), carried by the monarch after the coronation and subsequently for the state openings of Parliament, contains sapphires associated with Edward the Confessor and Alexander II of Scotland, pearls once in the possession of Catherine de' Medici and Mary Queen of Scots, a ruby possibly worn by Henry V at Agincourt, and the second largest top-quality cut diamond in the world, Cullinan II or the 'Second Star of Africa'.

Close to the Jewel House shop is the **Regimental Museum of the Royal Fusiliers**, the City of London regiment once stationed at the Tower. It contains relics relating to the history of the regiment from 1685 to the present day. Among a variety of special displays is one on the terrible Battle of Albuera in 1811. Though nominally a victory, only some 1,500 men survived out of a total of 4,000.

Tower Green and the Bloody Tower

Described by Macaulay as the 'most melancholy spot on earth', **Tower Green** ⑥ is the site of the scaffold reserved for politically sensitive executions where the following were beheaded: Queen Anne Boleyn, accused of adultery (1536); Margaret Plantagenet Pole, Countess of Salisbury, with some difficulty, having been implicated in 'The Pilgrimage of Grace' (1541); Queen Catherine Howard, fifth wife of Henry VIII, accused of adultery, along with her lady-in-waiting Jane, Viscountess Rochford (1542); the 16-year-old Lady Jane Grey, the 'nine days queen' (1554); and the Earl of Essex (1601). All are buried nearby within the altar rails of the Chapel Royal of St Peter ad Vincula, consecrated in the early 12th century, rebuilt at the end of the 13th, burnt and then rebuilt in 1512. Finally fully restored in 1971, the church also contains the tombs of Fisher, More and the Jacobite lords executed in 1746–47, along with more recent memorials to distinguished soldiers. In the north aisle is the impressive monument to the Duke of Exeter (1447), formerly in St Katherine's, Regent's Park.

Across Tower Green is the semicircular **Beauchamp Tower** (1280). The walls of the upper chamber are covered with inscriptions and carvings made for or by former prisoners down the ages, including Lady Jane Grey and the Dudley family. On the way back onto Water Lane is the **Bloody Tower** (1225) ⑦, traditionally the site of the murder of the Princes in the Tower. It was the prison of Cranmer, Raleigh, Laud and Judge Jeffreys, who died here in 1689. One room has been furnished as it might have been during Raleigh's imprisonment. Sir Walter Raleigh was first imprisoned in 1591 for secretly marrying Elizabeth Throckmorton, Elizabeth I's Maid of Honour, but released after five weeks. In 1603, King James I placed him in the Tower for conspiring to crown Lady Arabella Stuart. Condemned to life imprisonment, he resided here, conducting experiments in the hen house, growing tobacco and writing his *History of the World*. 'Only my father,' remarked Henry, Prince of Wales, 'would keep such a bird in such a cage.' In 1616 Raleigh was released to search for El Dorado. His expedition failed and involved the sacking of the Spanish settlement of Santo Tomé. To placate the outraged Spanish, Raleigh was beheaded in Old Palace Yard, Westminster in 1618.

TOWER BRIDGE EXHIBITION

Tower Bridge, SE1 2UP
Tel: 020-7940 3985; www.towerbridge.org.uk
Open April–Sept daily 10–5.30; Oct–March daily 9.30–5
Admission charge. Limited disabled access
Tube: Tower Hill
Shop
Map p. 383, 3F

Designed by Sir John Wolfe Barry, son of the architect of the Houses of Parliament, and Sir Horace Jones, Tower Bridge opened amid much fanfare in 1894, and remained the only bridge downriver of London Bridge for the next century. The towers of the bridge

Tower Bridge, looking towards Docklands, with *HMS Belfast* on the right.

support suspension cables and contain lifts to reach the high-level footbridge, originally intended for use when the bascules—or mechanical arms—of the lower bridge are raised. Each weighs around 1,000 tons. This is an impressive sight when it happens, usually a few times each day. The exhibition takes visitors up the four storeys of the north tower, to the enclosed east walkway between the towers, which has magnificent views over Docklands. Returning along the west walkway, with more superb views of the Tower of London, St Paul's, the London Eye and Big Ben, visitors descend again and cross the bridge to the basement of the south tower. Here can be seen the cast-iron boilers, flywheels and accumulator tanks of the lifting mechanism, a triumphant feat of Victorian engineering made sadly redundant by electrification in 1976.

UNIVERSITY COLLEGE LONDON: COLLEGE ART COLLECTIONS AND STRANG PRINT ROOM

Gower Street, WC1E 6BT
Tel: 020-7679 2000; www.ucl.ac.uk
Strang Print Room open Wed–Fri 1–5 during term time; other collections on application
Free
Tube: Warren Street/Euston Square
Map p. 382, 1A

The art collection of University College London, founded in 1826, comprises the Strang Print Room, the Slade collection and the **Flaxman Gallery**. Housed in the College's fine building by William Wilkins, with its dignified flights of steps leading up to a ten-columned pedimented Corinthian portico and central dome, the Flaxman collection dates back to 1847, when the group of sculpture models and drawings by the celebrated Neoclassical sculptor John Flaxman (1755–1826) was presented to the college. The gift was made by Maria Denman, Flaxman's sister-in-law and executor of his estate, through the good offices of Flaxman's friend Henry Crabb Robinson, one of the College's founders. It is an unrivalled collection of drawings and sculptures, which are displayed both in the Strang Print Room but also under Wilkins's fine 19th-century dome, a lofty architectural setting. Most of the sculptures are sketch models for church monuments, and take the form of antique stelai against which figures are silhouetted in high or low relief. All show Flaxman's characteristic blending of classical influence with Christian sentiment. They include the 11-ft full-size plaster model for his most famous sculpture, *St Michael overcoming Satan* (1822; Petworth House) and the striking high relief for the monument to the orientalist Sir William Jones (University College, Oxford; 1796–98), which shows the scholar at work on his *Digest of Hindu and Mohammedan Law* in consultation with three Orientals, palm trees in low relief behind him. Works on paper include his *Self-Portrait aged Twenty-Four*, and illustrations to Homer's *Iliad* and *Odyssey* and Dante's *Divine Comedy*.

The collection of the **Strang Print Room** includes important 16th-century German works, Baroque prints and drawings, Rembrandt etchings, an early edition of Dürer's 'Apocalypse' woodcuts and early states and proofs from van Dyck's *Iconologia*. It also includes drawings by Turner, and the early proofs and states of his *Liber Studiorum* and of Constable's *English Landscape Scenery*. Selections from the collection are shown through temporary exhibitions, usually three a year during term time.

In addition, UCL also houses the collection of **Slade School of Art** prize-winning works, dating from the 1890s to the present day. Important 20th-century British artists include Stanley Spencer, Augustus John, Edward Wadsworth and Paula Rego. Slade staff and students, including Henry Tonks and David Bomberg, have also presented works. The works are displayed in the Strang Print Room but also throughout the College. The College is also custodian to a one-off curiosity, the 'Auto-Icon' of the political economist Jeremy Bentham (1748–1832): his embalmed body, as he instructed in his will, 'in the attitude in which I am sitting when engaged in thought'.

VICTORIA & ALBERT MUSEUM

Cromwell Road, South Kensington, SW7 2RL
Tel: 020-7942 2000; www.vam.ac.uk
Open daily 10–5.45. Also Weds and last Fri of the month 10–10
Free
Tube: South Kensington
Cafés and shops
Map p. 380, 3B

The Victoria and Albert Museum (V&A) is one of the world's outstanding museums of applied arts. Its collection spans several centuries and encompasses sculpture, furniture, ceramics, glass, silver and metalwork, dress, textiles and jewellery. In addition, the V&A houses the National Art Library; an architectural collection which has recently been joined by that of the Royal Institute of British Architects; a collection of paintings which has, as its core, what in the 19th-century was intended as the embryonic National Gallery of British Art; and a vast prints, drawings and photography collection. The museum also has a distinguished collection of British portrait miniatures, and is home to the national collection of British watercolours.

The museum and its collections are enormous. Stretched over a 12-acre site, the building itself is often said to be a work of art, competing with the exhibits. Neither can possibly be seen in one visit; below is a brief outline of the V&A's history, its remarkable interiors and its collection highlights.

History of the Museum

The museum's origins lie in the School of Design, which opened in 1837 at Somerset House, established for the instruction of the application of art to industry. Works of

ornamental art were collected by the School as instructional aids: plaster casts, elec-
trotypes, modern pieces from Minton's; and medieval and Renaissance porcelain,
majolica, glass and metalwork from the important Bernal collection, which came up for
sale in 1855. In 1852 the School and its collection (now the Museum of Manufactures)
had moved to Marlborough House and was under the control of the government
Department of Science and Art, headed by the mighty figure of Henry Cole (1808–82).
Cole, with the Prince Consort, had masterminded the Great Exhibition of 1851, a phe-
nomenally popular success: almost 100 thousand visitors mobbed it on one of the days,
flocking to view the raw and manufactured products of the nations of the world, many
of the chief exhibits being purchased for the Museum. With the Exhibition's profits a
plot of land was purchased in South Kensington (then known as Brompton) for the
establishment of a cultural complex, crossed and bordered by four new roads (Cromwell
Road, Exhibition Road, Kensington Gore and Queen's Gate). The Royal Albert Hall
(begun 1868) and the Natural History Museum (*see p. 223*) were to become part of this
development but first, on the site of what is now the V&A, the South Kensington
Museum was established, an accumulation of collections, schools and departments
housed in an assortment of buildings. The School of Design and the Museum of
Manufactures (which in 1853 had been renamed the Museum of Ornamental Art)
moved to the site in 1857, accommodated in hastily built wooden huts and the supposedly temporary Iron Building. The latter, constructed by Charles Young and
Company, specialists in 'iron structures for Home and Abroad', was quickly nicknamed
the 'Brompton Boilers'. Clad in corrugated iron, striped green and white and given a
portico with iron pillars to improve its appearance, the three-span iron frame structure
leaked, caused condensation and wild temperature fluctuations. It was not until 1866
that it was partially dismantled (parts were re-erected for the Bethnal Green Museum;
see p. 24), and in 1899 the remainder was demolished. Thus were displayed the V&A's
first objects, a miscellaneous collection of sculpture, architecture, 'animal products' (fur,
feathers, bristles, human hair etc), 'patented inventions' and construction and building
materials, jostling for space alongside items of Ornamental Art, brought together to
encourage excellence in contemporary British design and its application to industry,
through a knowledge of the best examples.

The Building

The museum's earliest permanent buildings were those that surround the central garden
quadrangle, at the heart of the V&A. Built between 1857 and the early 1880s, they
demonstrate what was to become known as the 'South Kensington style', its trademark
being the use of ornamental terracotta. The South Kensington Museum's Construction
and Building Materials section contained samples of building stones and bricks, ceramic tiles and terracotta, and the museum itself was a demonstration of how these materials could be put to effective and skilled use. The museum's architect, Captain Fowke,
and Godfrey Sykes, who was responsible for much of the early interior embellishment,
were assisted by a band of pupils from the museum's Art Schools (now the Royal College
of Art). The first building was the 1857 Sheepshanks gallery, half of the east range of the

Ornamental bench-back along the V&A's Exhibition Road elevation.

central quadrangle, built to house the Sheepshanks collection of pictures, intended as the core of a National Gallery of British Art (*see Paintings, p. 324 below*). Abutting the north end of the Boilers, externally it had terracotta ornamentation with sgraffito medallion portraits of famous British artists. Internally it had gas illumination (South Kensington was the first museum in the world to be lit) which made evening opening possible. The latter, more convenient for working men and women, was a cherished wish of Cole's who saw museums as 'antidotes to brutality and vice'. The Sheepshanks gallery was soon joined by the Turner and Vernon gallery, which completed the east range, built to house National Gallery pictures for which there was no space at Trafalgar Square. In 1861–63 the North and South Courts were built behind the east range. The North Court (1861–62) was spanned by a great iron and glass roof designed by Fowke (which can be seen from Galleries 103–106, level 4). In 1863 it staged an exhibition of the wedding presents given to the Prince of Wales and Princess Alexandra, the first of the South Kensington loan exhibitions.

The South Court

The South Court (opened 1862) was a great deal more lavish, again of iron and glass but with highly decorated walls and elaborate cast and wrought ironwork designed by Sykes. Around the side walls, in niches, was the '**Kensington Valhalla**': full-length mosaic portraits of famous artists such as Apelles, Giorgione, Raphael, Inigo Jones and

Sir Joshua Reynolds, each holding items from the museum's collection. Designed by well known artists—G.F. Watts, Sir Edward Poynter, Frederic, Lord Leighton—they were executed in ceramic or glass mosaic by students of the Art Schools. An arcaded corridor, with the Prince Consort's Gallery above it, divided the South Court into two. On either side, below the roof, were balconies with large lunettes filled by **frescoes by Leighton**: *Industrial Arts as Applied to War* (1878–80; northeast) and *Industrial Arts as Applied to Peace*, completed in 1886 (southeast). Today, the former magnificence of the South Court is hidden from view behind false walls but the Leighton frescoes, and the highly decorated soffits above them, can be viewed on level 3, between Galleries 102 and 99 and Gallery 107 (*marked on the plan on p. 323*). Openings cut in the false walls give views onto the roof's iron structure and the decaying magnificence of the decorations. The original designs for the Valhalla figures are distributed throughout the museum, on the upper levels of the staircase leading to the British Galleries, the staircase leading to the National Art Library, and in the Lecture Theatre. Leighton's *Cimabue* and *Pisano* are displayed next to the southeast fresco. The complete restoration of the South Court is planned.

The Lecture Theatre Range

The museum's ornamentation reached a peak of elaboration in Fowke's Lecture Theatre range, the north side of the central quadrangle, completed after Fowke's death (1865) in 1868. Internally and externally it is a showpiece of complex decoration. Its façade includes terracotta columns with figurative ornament, designed by Sykes and completed after his death by his former pupils and successors, James Gamble and Reuben Townroe. A mosaic representation of the Great Exhibition (different countries presenting exhibits to a central Victoria) fills the pediment. Inside, the **Ceramic Staircase** (*see plan on p. 320*) is an ornamental masterpiece. Entirely encased in majolica and ceramic mosaic, it led up to what was then the Ceramics gallery. Designed and modelled by Frank Moody, with students from the Art Schools, in Italian Renaissance style, and executed by Minton in the new process of vitrified ceramic painting, its theme was the Arts, with stained glass windows representing Art and Science. The mosaic portrait of Cole, in a majolica frame, marks Cole's retirement from South Kensington in 1873. The **Ceramics Gallery** (now the Silver Galleries, Galleries 65–69), a long vista flanked by majolica-clad columns with elaborate ceilings designed by Moody, was equally lavish but between 1914 and the 1950s was stripped of its columns and stained glass windows and was whitewashed. The space was restored to its former magnificence as far as possible in 1995–96. The staircase off the gallery leads up to the Lecture Theatre.

On the ground floor of the wing are the old Refreshment Rooms (the museum was the first to have such a facility). The **Morris Room** (originally the Green Dining Room) was entirely decorated by Morris, Marshall and Faulkner, the firm established by William Morris in 1861, with painted panels by Burne-Jones, and stained glass designed by Burne-Jones and Philip Webb. The **Gamble Room** (the Centre Refreshment Room) has walls of ceramic tiles and mirrors, stained glass windows designed by Gamble, and paired ceramic-clad columns divide the room from its apse. The upper ceramic frieze reads: 'There is nothing better for a man that he should eat and drink, and make his soul enjoy good in his labour' (*Ecclesiasticus 2:24*). The chimneypiece, from Dorchester House, Park Lane, is by Alfred Stevens. The **Poynter Room** (Grill Room, or Dutch Kitchen), with its blue and white tiles, retains its original grill, designed by Poynter, who also designed the stained glass window (made by Crace & Co.) and the panels of the Months and Seasons.

The Cast Courts and Art Library Range

Also dating from this period of the museum's development are the **Cast Courts** (Galleries 46a and b), or Architectural Courts, built in 1870–73 on part of the site of the Boilers. Intended for the collection of large-scale casts of the most famous examples of sculpture in the world, these vast spaces were then and still are one of the museum's most extraordinary sites. Gallery 46a, decorated in the original scheme of olive green and red, is a jungle of sculpture, dominated by Trajan's Column towering towards the ceiling. Along the north wall is the Portico de la Gloria of the Cathedral of Santiago de Compostela. The dramatic spectacle is continued in Gallery 46b. On the north wall is the vast central doorway of San Petronio, Bologna, with an electrotype after one of the gilt bronze Baptistery doors of San Giovanni, Florence, Ghiberti's 'Porta del Paradiso'. The cast of Michaelangelo's *David*, a gift from the Grand Duke of Tuscany, was presented by Queen Victoria in 1857. A plaster fig leaf was made to hide his shocking nudity from visiting royal ladies; it can be seen in a case on the back of the plinth.

The Art Library range (early 1880s), which still houses the handsome **National Art Library** on the third floor (ticket holders only, though it can be viewed through the glass doors), closed the south side of the central quadrangle. Its ground floor (Galleries 22–24) has recently been restored and its black and white mosaic floor revealed. Tall windows overlook the quadrangle **Garden**. At the time of writing the latter was being relandscaped (Kim Wilkie Associates), but eventually it will have a pool of water, bordered by bands of light in the evenings, with fountain jets.

Foundation of the Victoria & Albert Museum

In 1890 Aston Webb won an architectural competition to bring sense and order to the museum's odd complex. Regular, grand façades along Cromwell Road and Exhibition Road would be the new public face of the museum, with additional gallery space behind, joined to the existing buildings. After years of delays, on 17th May 1899, Queen Victoria laid the foundation stone, at the same time announcing that henceforth the museum would be known as the Victoria & Albert Museum. Her last official public ceremony, the occasion was captured on a moving picture device, the Mutocscope (in the photography collection). By 1906 the works were largely complete. The Cromwell Road central tower, in the shape of an Imperial crown, is topped by a statue of Fame. Queen Victoria stands above the great arched entrance, flanked by St George and St Michael. Prince Albert stands directly above the doors with representations of Inspiration and Imagination to either side. In a procession of niches along the façade, between the windows, are sculpture figures of great British artists. The grand, airy, domed Entrance Hall (with a modern chandelier by the Seattle artist Dale Chihuly, a 5m drop of massed blue and green glass balls and spiralling tendrils) has to either side of its vestibule two noble staircases, with walls of pavonazzo marble, columns of violet breccia, and piastraccia steps. The new museum was officially opened by Edward VII in 1909.

The Collection

Before the 1909 opening, in order to fill, in an orderly fashion, the vast new acres of space, a Committee of Rearrangement was formed, a situation which half echoes the situation at the museum today, which is undergoing a 10-year programme of reorganisation and refurbishment. Already completed, up the stairs to the left of the Hall, are the flagship British Galleries. The stairs on the right will lead to the Medieval and Renaissance Galleries, due for completion in 2009 (for the time being the collection occupies the ground floor galleries surrounding the west, north and east sides of the central quadrangle). Other projects are underway throughout the museum; for the duration of works visitors should expect gallery closures and disruption to or displacement of displays.

The collection is displayed through two gallery types: the Period Galleries (e.g. Asia; British Galleries), which bring prime objects from different departments together to explore the development of art and design in different geographical and cultural contexts; and the Materials and Techniques Galleries (e.g. Sculpture; Ceramics), which show the V&A's extraordinary depth and breadth of holdings in specific departments.

Materials & Techniques Galleries

NB: Works executed in the materials and techniques covered below are also exhibited throughout the Period Galleries. Gallery numbers given refer to specific collections of a particular material or technique.

Sculpture (Gallery 50a; Gallery 111)

The excellent and comprehensive post-classical sculpture collection includes outstanding masterpieces, from highly important medieval ivory carvings to large-scale monuments. The Italian Renaissance collection is especially rich, being the best outside Italy, from which star exhibits are shown in the Medieval and Renaissance Galleries (*see p. 325 below*). Many of the items came to the museum under the important curatorship of Sir J.C. Robinson (1824–1913), the first Curator of the Museum of Ornamental Art.

The Gherardini collection of terracotta models (purchased 1854) included a wax model by Michelangelo, and the Gigli-Campana collection (purchased 1861) included key works by Donatello and Luca della Robbia. Major examples of German and Netherlandish wood carving include the 14th-century carved oak figures from the altarpiece in the Johanneskirche, Lüneberg.

There are pre-eminent examples of **British sculpture**, from medieval alabaster altarpiece panels, mainly scenes of the *Passion* and the *Life of the Virgin*, to excellent works of the 18th and 19th centuries by Rysbrack, Roubiliac, Flaxman, Wilton and Banks. As well as portrait busts there are terracotta sketch models, such as Rysbrack's for Newton's monument in Westminster Abbey, and Flaxman's youthful *Self-Portrait* roundel (1778). Many of the principal items are shown in the British Galleries (*see p. 327 below*).

As well as in the Cast Courts (*see p. 317 above*), where reproductions of monumental European masterpieces are shown, large-scale items from the collection are shown in Gallery 50a, Webb's top-lit East Court. In the centre, spanning its width, is the massive **roodloft from the Cathedral of St John, 's-Hertogenbosch**, acquired in 1871, the removal of which sparked outcry in the Netherlands and the establishment of a national policy for the protection of ancient monuments. The recumbent effigies of Sir Moyle and Lady Finch (c. 1630) are by Nicholas Stone, removed from St Mary, Eastwell, Kent. The massive **Cappella Maggiore** from Santa Chiara, Florence (c. 1493–1500), 1,110cm high, was acquired following the church's deconsecration in 1842.

Gallery 111, level 3, an open corridor with magnificent vistas over both the Cast Courts, has smaller pieces, the displays emphasising the various materials and techniques of craftsmanship.

Silver & Metalwork (Galleries 65–69; Galleries 114 a–e)

The museum's fine collection of silver and gold objects is spread throughout the museum, but also in the sumptuous Silver Galleries (Galleries 65–69, level 3), one of the most lavish interiors of the 19th-century museum (*see p. 316 above*). As well as contemporary *tour-de-force* works, exhibited at the 19th-century International Exhibitions, 19th-century interest concentrated on heavily decorated 15th-, 16th- and 17th-century European pieces. It was not until the 20th century that the museum started collecting English silver with any seriousness, but its collection is now unrivalled.

The displays include important items (although some key works are shown in the British Galleries) but emphasise the history of silversmithing and the ceremonial and domestic use of objects. Ceremonial salts are on show; examples of lavish post-Restoration goldsmith's work; the c. 1680 'Sizergh Toilet Service'; and a vast wine cistern by Thomas Jenkins (1677–78). Eighteenth-century works include elaborate candelabra; presentation cups and works by celebrated masters such as Paul de Lamerie, Charles Kandler and Matthew Boulton. The **Ashburnham Centrepiece**, or epergne, by Nicolas Sprimont (1747) is a major example of English Rococo silver. In the centre of the gallery is an electrotype copy of the celebrated and enormous 1737 **Jerningham Wine Cooler**, made by Kandler over four years, with Bacchanalian scenes modelled by Rysbrack (the original is in the Hermitage).

European silver 1400–1800 is also on show, with items from France, Spain, Italy and Scandinavia, and an outstanding **collection from Southern Germany**, one of the greatest centres of European silversmithing. At the end of the gallery are three electrotype lions by Elkington & Co, copies of the 17th-century silver lions which protect the Throne Room at Rosenborg Castle, Denmark. The gallery includes displays of contemporary silver commissioned by the museum.

As well as silver, the museum has a large collection of flatware, brass, pewter and cast and wrought iron (the museum's first recorded purchase was a pair of 17th-century

VICTORIA & ALBERT MUSEUM
BASEMENT AND LEVEL 1

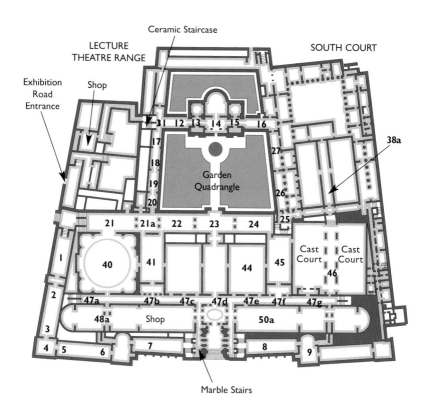

Ceramic Staircase

LECTURE
THEATRE RANGE

SOUTH COURT

Exhibition
Road
Entrance

Shop

Garden
Quadrangle

Cast
Court

Cast
Court

Shop

Marble Stairs

1–7: Europe 1500–1800
8–9: Europe and America 1800–1900
11–20: Renaissance 1400–1600
21–24: Renaissance 1200–1650
25–27: Northern Europe
38a: Photography
40: Dress (Fashion Gallery)

41: Asia
44–45: Asia
47a–g: Asia
46: Medieval 300–1500
48a: Raphael Cartoons
50a: Sculpture

German hinges). The long **Metalwork Gallery** is on level 3, Galleries 114a–e, famously described by H.G. Wells in his 1900 novel *Love and Mrs Lewisham*: 'As one goes into the South Kensington Art Museum from the Brompton Road, the Gallery of Old Iron is overhead to the right. But the way thither is exceedingly devious and not to be revealed to anybody … the gallery is long and narrow … and set with iron gates, iron-bound chests, locks, bolts and bars, fantastic great keys, lamps and the like'. One of the major works is the 'Hereford Screen'. Designed by Sir George Gilbert Scott, it was hailed as 'the grandest, most triumphant achievement of modern architectural art' at the International Exhibition of 1862. It has recently undergone an £800,000 restoration.

Ceramics (Level 6, Galleries 132–145)

NB: At the time of writing, the Ceramics Galleries were closed until further notice.
Ceramics have been an important component of the museum since its foundation. The Ceramics Galleries occupy the entire top floor, making immediately apparent the astonishing range, depth and sheer magnitude of the collection. Key examples are shown in the various period galleries, but it is here that the history of pottery and porcelain manufacture can be studied uninterrupted. The collection is truly international, ranging from the Far East and Imperial China to the Ottoman Empire and Europe. Among the outstanding examples are nine pieces of **Medici porcelain**, the first European attempts at copying Chinese blue and white porcelain, which reached Europe in the 16th century. Made in the Grand Duke of Tuscany's workshops in the Boboli Gardens, Florence, only 60 of these rare and precious pieces are known.

As well as grand Exhibition pieces, the **19th-century collections** concentrated on Italian majolica, French Renaissance pieces and Limoges, important examples of which came from the collection of Ralph Bernal (sold through Christie's over 32 days); the Soulages collection; and that of George Salting, whose astonishing collection, covering several areas, came to the museum in 1910.

Much 18th-century European porcelain came with the Jones collection in the 19th century (*see Europe 1500–1800 below*), and excellent British pieces from the collection of Lady Charlotte Schreiber. The **British collection** includes medieval pottery, English delft and comprehensive collections of the great potteries and porcelain manufacturers, well known names such as Lowestoft, Coalport, Wedgwood, Chelsea, Worcester and Bow.

Twentieth-century pieces include British studio pottery, works by Bernard Leach and Lucie Rie, and European works such as Picasso's c. 1954 vase, *An Artist at his Easel*.

Glass (Level 4, Galleries 129 & 131)

The excellent glass collection ranges from ancient Egyptian items to contemporary pieces, including commercial glass as well as works of art. Fifteenth- and 16th-century Venetian goblets, decorated with coloured enamels; 17th-century engraved glass, German goblets, early English glass, including pieces by Jacopo Verzelini, who taught the art of glassmaking in Elizabethan England; 18th-century drinking glasses, high Victorian pieces and 20th-century and contemporary items are shown in the split-level

Glass Gallery (level 4), with a staircase and balcony balustrade in rippling green glass by the glass artist Danny Lane. Of particular significance is the **Luck of Edenhall**, an exceptionally fine and pristinely preserved 13th-century Syrian beaker.

Jewellery (Galleries 91–93 & 109)

NB: The Jewellery Gallery is closed for refurbishment until 2008.

The V&A's splendid and large collection of jewellery is especially rich in Renaissance pieces. It includes precious masterpieces such as the **Canning Jewel**, an exceptional item of gold, enamelled and set with large Indian rubies, in the form of a triton, his body a great baroque pearl; and the **Heneage Jewel**, an enamelled gold locket set with diamonds and rubies with a gold medallion portrait of the Elizabeth I, with inside a portrait miniature of the Queen by Nicholas Hilliard (*see p. pp. 324–25 below*). Important 15th–18th-century pieces came from the collection of Dame Joan Evans (d. 1977), who gave her exceptional collection to the museum, while 19th-century items include the head-band, brooch and necklace designed by Pugin, in medieval style, for Helen Lumsden, but given to his eventual wife Jane Mill.

Textiles & Dress (Gallery 94; Galleries 95–101; Gallery 40)

NB: At the time of writing the textile galleries were closed until further notice.

The South Kensington Museum's collection of textiles was administered by the Department of Animal Products. Samples of silk and wool woven textiles, 18th-century Spitalfields silks, Genoese velvets and embroideries, upholstery fabrics etc, were purely a learning resource. William Morris appears to have studied the collection, elements of his designs being traceable to the specimens exhibited in the museum's early days. The serious collection of textiles began in the 1860s, but the department also encompasses costume, tapestry and carpets.

Silks and brocades from the Middle Ages include ecclesiastical vestments, for example an early 14th-century cope which belonged to the Bridgettine Convent of Syon. There are excellent examples of Indian and Persian carpets and textiles; an excellent lace collection, the largest in the world; and tapestries, including the **Devonshire Hunting Tapestries** (Gallery 94, level 3), a group of four magnificent and enormous mid-15th-century Flemish pieces formerly in the collection of the Dukes of Devonshire.

Items from the **Dress Collection** are displayed throughout the period galleries, as well as in the Fashion Gallery (Gallery 40, level 1). Historic costumes span all periods and include examples of royal and noble dress, as well as that of ordinary people, as well as shoes, boots, hats and gloves. The European collection from Stuart times to the present day is particularly strong and includes Elizabethan gloves; an unusual 17th-century Venetian jacket, of knitted silk with silver-gilt thread; 18th-century English court dress; 19th-century wedding dresses and ball gowns with elaborate silver-gilt lace; elegant designs by famous 20th-century names such as Givenchy evening wear and 'New Look' Dior; and more modern pieces such as Mary Quant yellow plastic ankle boots, and Vivienne Westwood's blue 'mock-croc' platform shoes (1993–94).

VICTORIA & ALBERT MUSEUM
LEVELS 2 AND 3

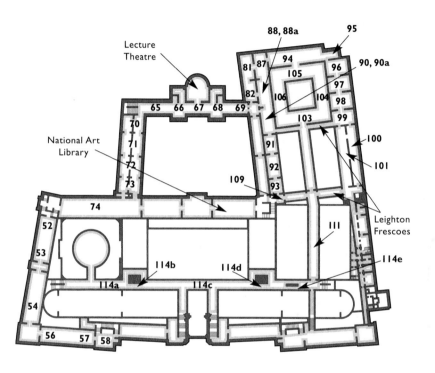

52–58: British Galleries
65–69: Silver Galleries
70–74: 20th Century
81–82: Paintings
87–88a: Paintings
90: Prints and Drawings
90a: Portrait Miniatures
91–93: Jewellery
94: Textiles (Tapestry)
95–101: Textiles
103–106: 20th Century
109: Jewellery
111: Sculpture
114a–e: Metalwork

Paintings, Prints & Drawings (Gallery 48a; Galleries 81–82 & 87–88a; Galleries 90 & 90a)

Among the V&A's most celebrated possessions are the **Raphael Cartoons** (Gallery 48a), seven of the ten executed by Raphael in 1515–16 for Pope Leo X as designs for tapestries, woven in Brussels, for the decoration of the Sistine Chapel (*see p. 116*). Among the most important surviving examples of High Renaissance art, they mark a highpoint in the traditional canon of artistic excellence. Distemper on paper, they were originally cut into strips to enable the weavers to use them as guides. Purchased by Charles I in 1623, tapestries woven after them were produced by the Mortlake Tapestry Works. In 1699 the cartoons were put back together, restored and displayed in the Cartoon Gallery at Hampton Court. Still in royal ownership, they have been on loan to the museum since 1865. The subjects, taken from the Acts of the Apostles, are: *Christ's Charge to Peter: 'Feed my Sheep'*; *The Miraculous Draught of Fishes*; *Elymas the Sorcerer Struck with Blindness*; *Paul and Barnabas at Lystra*; *Paul Preaching at Athens*; *The Death of Ananias*; and *Peter and John healing the Blind Man*. The twisted Solomonic columns in the latter were much imitated by later artists.

The V&A's Paintings Collection has at its core the **Sheepshanks pictures**, presented to the South Kensington Museum in 1857. Intended as the nucleus of a National Gallery of British Art, the gift stimulated the erection of the museum's first permanent building, the Sheepshanks gallery (*see pp. 314–15 above*). It was joined by the Turner and Vernon gallery, immediately adjacent, where the pictures are displayed today, in recently refurbished rooms (Galleries 81–82, 87–88a, level 3). John Sheepshanks (1787–1863), a Leeds clothing manufacturer long settled in London, was acquainted with a wide circle of contemporary artists. His collection included fine works by Turner and Constable, including the latter's famous *Salisbury Cathedral from the Bishop's Grounds* (1823), but his particular fondness was for early 19th-century genre pictures by Wilkie, Mulready, Landseer, C.R. Leslie, William Collins and others, of which the collection has rich holdings. Chief among them is Landseer's *The Old Shepherd's Chief Mourner*, a dog grieving at its master's coffin, exhibited at the Royal Academy in 1837 and considered by Ruskin 'one of the most perfect poems or pictures which modern times have seen'. The V&A possesses a remarkable collection of **oil sketches and works on paper by Constable**, the contents of the artist's studio given to the museum in 1888 by his daughter, Isobel Constable. The 95 oil sketches and 297 drawings and watercolours include *plein-air* oil sketches, cloud studies and sketches made in and around Flatford and his native Suffolk. In addition, the museum has sketches for two of Constable's iconic works, *The Haywain* (National Gallery) and the *Leaping Horse*.

In 1908 the Tate Gallery was officially recognised as the National Gallery of British Art, but the V&A still retains the national collection of **portrait miniatures** (shown in the British Galleries and, with Continental examples, in Gallery 90a, level 3). 'Limning' was a refined, high-status genre which flourished in England from the reign of Henry VIII. Among the many outstanding highlights by leading artists are Holbein's *Anne of Cleves*, with its carved ivory lid in the form of a rose; pre-eminent works by Hilliard, including portraits of Elizabeth I, in enamelled and jewelled lockets, or works with layered symbolism such as *Young Man Clasping a Hand from a Cloud*, and the terribly famous *Young Man Among Roses*; and key works by Isaac Oliver, such as *Unknown Woman*, known as Frances Howard. Post-Restoration miniatures include examples by the excellent Samuel Cooper, for example his exceptional *Henrietta, Duchess of Orleans*, the sister of Charles II, an intimate view with sparkling eyes and bouncing ringlets.

Gallery 90, level 3, shows changing displays from the V&A's **Prints, Drawings and Watercolours Collection**, an enormous and important resource. The principal collections are of Italian Old Master drawings; Dutch and Flemish works; and the national collection of British watercolours. The latter extends to the present day, but the bulk of the collection is of 18th- and 19th-century works, the 'golden age' of British watercolour. All major watercolourists are represented, including Sandby, J.R. Cozens (famous views of the Roman campagna), Towne (his supremely well known *Source of the Arveiron*), Girtin and Cotman. In addition there is a vast archive of prints, drawings and illustrations, including decorative arts designs, which can be viewed by appointment in the Study Room in the Henry Cole wing.

Photography (Gallery 38a)

The large and important photography collection has its origins in the 19th century. There are over 250 images by Julia Margaret Cameron, over 80 of them having been acquired for the museum in 1865 by Henry Cole, a friend and important patron who made rooms available at South Kensington for her to use as a studio. Portraits of important Victorians include images by Frederick Hollyer of H.G. Wells and William Morris. Annual displays from the collection are shown in Gallery 38a, including works by Man Ray, Bill Brandt, David Bailey and contemporary photographers.

Architecture (Level 4, Gallery 128a)

The Architecture Gallery opened in 2004 as the new display space for the museum's own architecture collection, but also for that of the Royal Institute of British Architects (RIBA; *see p. 251*), a collection of great importance which includes drawings by great names such as Andrea Palladio, Inigo Jones, Sir Christopher Wren and Mies van der Rohe. As well as preliminary designs there are original models for buildings, for example Sydney Smirke's Domed Reading Room at the British Museum; Gatwick Airport's 'beehive' terminal of 1936; Ernő Goldfinger's 1963 cinema; and roof shapes for the Sydney Opera House.

Period Galleries

Medieval & Renaissance Galleries (Galleries 11–20; 21–27; 43, 46, Cast Courts)

With new galleries due to open in 2009, for the moment the museum's key items from the period c. 300–1600 are on display on level 1, in the galleries on the west, north and east sides of the central quadrangle, to the south of it, and in Gallery 46. The latter contains a selection of pre-eminent objects, including a collection of highly important **ivory**

carvings: the small 'Symmachi' carved relief panel (Rome, AD 400), with a priestess sprinkling holy water before an altar; the 'Basilewsky Situla', or Holy Water Bucket (c. 980), probably presented to the Emperor Otto II on his visit to Milan in that year, an object of great rarity; and the Byzantine 'Veroli Casket' (c. 1000), carved with scenes of classical mythology. The **Gloucester Candlestick** is an amazing survival of early 12th-century English medieval metalwork, a great masterpiece with men and monkeys clambering through foliage, symbolic of the struggle between good and evil. Alongside Byzantine jasper and bloodstone cameos is an Egyptian rock crystal ewer (late 10th–early 11th-century) carved with foliage and birds of prey. A major treasure is the **Becket Casket** (c. 1180), made to contain relics of St Thomas à Becket, the earliest, largest and best example in Limoges enamel showing Becket's martyrdom. The 12th-century Rhenish 'Eltenburg Reliquary' is of gilt copper enriched with enamel and set with walrus ivory carvings, in the form of a church.

The Northern Renaissance 1500–1700 fills Galleries 25–27. Of great importance is the silver gilt **Burghley Nef**, a *tour de force* of Parisian goldsmiths' art of 1527. In the form of a ship, its body a nautilus shell balanced on the back of a mermaid, the tiny figures of Tristram and Iseult play chess at the foot of the main mast. Cases contain intricate goldsmiths' work; shells and hardstones mounted in precious metals; and finely carved German and Southern German religious reliefs. The charming German (Swabian) limewood sculpture *Christ Riding on an Ass* (c. 1510–20) would have been drawn through the streets on Palm Sunday.

The galleries on the north side of the central quadrangle contain highly important **Italian Renaissance** items, 1400–1600. Chief among them are works by Donatello, the most important and influential Italian sculptor of the 15th century. His *Ascension with Christ Giving the Keys to St Peter* (c. 1428–30), from the Palazzo Medici, Florence, is one of the finest surviving examples of *rilievo schiacciato* (very low relief carving). His mid-15th-century *Chellini Madonna* is another prized possession. The bronze roundel, the reverse of which can be used for a mould for glass castings, was given to his doctor, Giovanni Chellini, in 1456 but until the museum purchased it in 1976 it had gone unrecognised and had been used as an ashtray. A bust of Chellini, by Rossellino, is nearby as is Rossellino's *The Virgin with the Laughing Child* (c. 1465). Of terracotta, probably a sketch model for a larger marble, it is one of the V&A's most celebrated pieces. Among carved and painted *cassone* are important medals by Pisanello; Il Riccio's 'Shouting Horseman' (c. 1510–15); the late 15th-century Mantuan small-scale bronze and parcel gilt *Meleager*, based on an antique original; and enamelled terracottas of the della Robbia workshop: Luca della Robbia's *Labours of the Months* (c. 1450–56), a series of 12 roundels, each with the sun in the appropriate House of the Zodiac, commissioned for the ceiling of Piero de' Medici's study in the Palazzo Medici, Florence; and Andrea della Robbia's large *Adoration of the Magi* (early 16th century) in bold polychrome enamel.

Among the Renaissance 1200–1650 displays are beautiful **plaquettes with scenes from the life of Hercules**, by Moderno, a plaquette designer and gem engraver active at the courts of Ferrara and Mantua; objects in the manner of Giovanni Bologna (Giambologna), such as small bronzes by the Netherlandish sculptor Hendrick de

Keyser, and the impressive gilt bronze *Resurrection* relief, and statuettes (1581–84) from the memorial altar of Christoph Fugger by Hubert Gerhard, formerly in the Dominican church of St Magdalen, Augsburg. Giambologna's well-known **Samson Slaying the Philistine**, another V&A treasure, entered Charles I's collection in 1623.

British Galleries (Galleries 52–58 & Level 4, Galleries 118–125)

The relatively recently refurbished British Galleries house some of the museum's most prized objects produced in Britain between 1500 and 1900. Their vast chronological scope covers over 400 years of Britain's visual culture, bringing together the finest, most fashionable and most technically accomplished examples of sculpture, furniture, ceramics, silver, textiles and dress from the court of Henry VIII to the death of Queen Victoria. The incorporation of period interiors salvaged from important historic buildings lends the galleries particular authority and atmosphere. The entrance is via the marble stairs to the left of the entrance hall.

1500–1760 (Level 2): One of the earliest objects is on show is Pietro Torrigiano's famous **painted terracotta bust of Henry VII**, probably based on a death mask (*see Westminster Abbey Museum; p. 346*). A writing box of c. 1525, with painted and gilded decoration on leather, bears the arms and devices of Henry VIII and Katherine of Aragon. The important 1525–26 **Howard Grace Cup** has an ivory bowl in silver-gilt mounts, with bands of Renaissance ornament, but also with Gothic cresting on the foot, set with gemstones and pearls. Objects from the court of Elizabeth I include images of the Queen herself, powerful, carefully contrived images of monarchy, including the **Heneage ('Armada') Jewel** (c. 1600), a profile medallic image of gold and enamel, set with diamonds and rubies. Hilliard's famous image, *A Young Man among Roses*, the quintessential image of the Elizabethan court, with its emphasis on complex emblems and symbolism, shows him hand on heart, in devotion to the monarch, surrounded by eglantine roses (sweetbriar), the queen's symbol. The elaborate ceremonial **Mostyn Salt**, (1586–87) is of unusual size and weight.

Examples of tapestry—an expensive, luxury item—include one commissioned by Robert Dudley, Earl of Leicester from the Sheldon workshops, his arms in the centre. Chivalry and heraldry can be further explored in an interactive gallery: visitors can try on a gauntlet, or design coats of arms. The celebrated **Great Bed of Ware**, from an inn in Ware, Hertfordshire, mentioned in Shakespeare's *Twelfth Night*, is twice the size of any bed of the period known and was famous for the numbers it could hold. A complete panelled interior of 1606 is from a house in Bromley-by-Bow, with elaborately carved Royal Arms above the chimneypiece and a strapwork plasterwork ceiling. A rare duo is the Jacobean **portrait of Margaret Laton** (c. 1620) and, displayed alongside it, the very jacket she wears in the painting, with elaborate floral embroidery.

Among items from the time of Charles I is a large Mortlake tapestry (1619) designed by Francis Cleyn, one of a set of nine illustrating the story of Mars and Venus, the first tapestries to be woven at Mortlake, based on hangings which had belonged to Henry VIII. Also by Cleyn, probably, is the nearby chair, its back in the form of a scallop shell.

A highly important item is the **fish dish** by the celebrated and innovative Dutch silver-smith Christian van Vianen, produced in 1635 when he was in England in the service of Charles I. Another outstanding item is the **bust of Thomas Baker** by the great Baroque sculptor Bernini. Baker was commissioned to deliver to Bernini in Rome van Dyck's portrait of Charles I in three positions, from which Bernini would sculpt a bust, but took the opportunity to commission a sculpture of himself. The famous diarist John Evelyn's cabinet (1644–45), for his rare curiosities, with bronze plaques by Fanelli, stands near Honore Pelle's flamboyantly Baroque marble bust of Charles II.

An extraordinary survival is the **wedding suit of James II**, worn at his 1673 marriage to Mary of Modena, heavily embroidered with silver and silver-gilt thread, now slightly tarnished. Excellent examples of marquetry furniture are on display, as well as furniture, upholstery, wall hangings, fabrics and painted mirrors produced in the new French taste imported to Britain by immigrant French Huguenot craftsmen. Most important was the French interior designer, who had settled in Holland, Daniel Marot. A settle, probably commissioned by Lord Coningsby for Hampton Court, Herefordshire, retains its 1690s upholstery; a magnificent japanned cabinet (c. 1690–1700) has a highly elaborate carved and silvered stand in the style of Marot; a blue and white Delft tile (c. 1694), after a Marot design, is from Queen Mary's Water Gallery at Hampton Court; and behind glass, in its own room, is the exceptional c. 1700 **Melville State Bed**, from the State Apartments of Melville House, Fife. Its magnificent, theatrical hangings, of crimson Genoa velvet and ivory Chinese damask, are inspired by the work of Marot and attrib-uted to the upholsterer Francis Lapiere. The parlour from 11 Henrietta Street (1727–32), built for the architect James Gibbs, has a plasterwork ceiling by the stuc-coists Artari and Bagutti, and paintings by Damini. Nearby is Rysbrack's excellent bust of Gibbs; and the superb model of Gibbs' church, St Mary-le-Strand.

Palladianism, the new 'national' style from 1715–60, is represented by a table designed by William Kent for Chiswick House (*see p. 57*), the showpiece of Palladianism built by the style's champion, Lord Burlington. Examples of Rococo, the light, asym-metric and ornamental style fashionable from the 1740s, include porcelain and silver, Spitalfields silks, and Roubiliac's extraordinarily famous **sculpture of Handel** (1738), commissioned by Jonathan Tyers for his pleasure gardens at Vauxhall, with Handel in the guise of Orpheus with Apollo's lyre. Roubiliac's important sketch model for the Duke of Argyll's monument in Westminster Abbey (1745) shows the Duke reclining against an allegorical figure of Fame. Porcelain and silver relating to the polite pastime of tea drinking is on show, as well as the entire white and gold Music Room from Norfolk House, designed by Matthew Brettingham in 1748–56. Furnished and lit, Horace Walpole found it a scene 'of magnificence and taste'. The c. 1745 **Badminton Bed** is a supreme example of English Chinoiserie, with its delicate pagoda-shaped canopy and gilded dragons.

1760–1900 (level 4): If visitors approach the galleries by lift from 1500–1760 below, directly ahead are **items relating to Horace Walpole**, the 18th-century art historian and connoisseur, including the Walpole Cabinet (1745) designed by him, possibly with the assistance of Kent, for his collection of medals and miniatures. Three ivory figures, designed by Rysbrack, surmount it: Duquesnoy, flanked by the architects Palladio and Inigo Jones, the two giants of the Palladian style. Nearby is the limewood cravat (c. 1690) carved by the great 17th-century Grinling Gibbons, which Walpole owned and famously wore on one occasion when entertaining guests.

A section devoted to the great furniture designer Thomas Chippendale, and his influence, follows. The 18th-century passion for **Neoclassicism** was stimulated by Grand Tourists, young aristocrats, artists and connoisseurs who made pilgrimages to Italy to see classical remains. Joseph Wilton's marble bust of Lord Hastings (1761) shows him in classical garb. A glass case is filled with vases, including Wedgwood, inspired by the antique. A section from the extraordinary Glass Drawing Room, Northumberland House, designed by the great Neoclassical architect and designer Robert Adam, has panels entirely of glass, based on richly ornamented Roman interiors. Sections are backed by coloured pigments and metal shavings to give an illusion of shimmering porphyry, and some have applied decoration in gilt metal. A model of the glittering spectacle in its entirety is nearby, the furniture, ceiling and carpet also designed by Adam. Also by Adam is the complicated plaster ceiling and chimneypiece from 5 Royal Terrace, part of the Adams' Adelphi development, the home of the great 18th-century actor David Garrick. The sumptuous Kimbolton cabinet, commissioned by the Duchess of Manchester, was designed by Adam, with ormolu mounts by the famous goldsmith Matthew Boulton, and made by Ince & Mayhew.

When not in Edinburgh, Canova's magnificent **Three Graces** is on show, the famous marble sculpture commissioned by the Duke of Bedford for Woburn Abbey. It was purchased jointly with the National Museums and Galleries of Scotland after a national appeal in 1994. Examples of the new Regency taste for rich luxuriance, and for Greek, rather than Roman, sources, as well as Egyptian, include an 1804 armchair, after a design by George Smith, a blend of Greek, Roman and Egyptian forms; furniture by the famous firm Gillows; expensive, massy items of silver-gilt sold through the Royal Goldsmiths Rundell, Bridge & Rundell, whose most important customer was the Prince Regent, e.g. an 1809–10 wine cooler by Paul Storr, based on the 'Medici Krater'; and an 1806 bookcase from the Prince Regent's luxurious Carlton House, in the Greek style, possibly designed by C.H. Tatham. The famous **Rhinoceros Vase** (c. 1826) was made to advertise the skill of the Rockingham factory. A classical form, it is painted and encrusted with elaborate naturalistic ornament.

Prominent in the displays is *Bashaw* (1832–34), a large sculpture by Matthew Cotes Wyatt of the Earl of Dudley's pet Newfoundland dog. Hugely popular in its day, the 'Faithful Friend of Man', shown trampling a poisonous snake, was criticised by Ruskin. Post-1830 **Gothic Revival** pieces include works by the medievalist Wiliam Burges: the splendid painted, stencilled and gilded 'Yatman Cabinet' (1858), based on French medieval armoires, commissioned by one of Burges' early and important patrons; his 1865–66 decanter, richly ornamented and stylistically eclectic, its glass body encased in silver set with genuine antique coins, intaglios, glass and gemstones. Important items by A.W.N. Pugin, the seminal figure in the history of the Gothic Revival, include a candelabrum made for the House of Lords; and a chalice, silver and parcel-gilt set with enamels and garnets. It was made for the 1851 Great Exhibition, the world's first large-scale temporary international exhibition. A large (modern) model of Joseph Paxton's Crystal Palace in Hyde Park, where the exhibition was held, is on show. The exhibition attracted over 6 million visitors and the profits went towards the establishment of the V&A (*see p. 314 above*). Many exhibits, by firms which used the exhibition to display their most innovative techniques, were purchased for the museum. An 1851 table has a stand surrounded by herons in bulrushes, the former of cast plaster, the latter of moulded, gilded leather. Pugin's excellent cabinet was one of the most important pieces in the Medieval Court.

Purchases from the International Exhibitions which followed the 1851 exhibition include the magnificent cabinet by Alexandre Eugène Prignot, made for the Paris Exposition of 1855. Over 40 craftsmen worked on it, including Minton's and Elkington's. The enormous Minton vase was purchased from the 1862 International Exhibition in London. A great technical challenge, its floral body, with handles of gilded coiling snakes, is shouldered by three crouching bone-china cherubs. A Graeco-Roman armchair (1884–86) was designed by Sir Lawrence Alma-Tadema for an American collector's Madison Avenue residence. Sir Giles Gilbert Scott's large design for the Albert Memorial (1863) is on show, as well as Alfred Stevens' plaster and wax model for the Duke of Wellington's memorial in St Paul's Cathedral (1857), one of his most celebrated works. E.W. Godwin's sideboard is an important example of Victorian 'Japonisme'.

Items by the hugely influential interior designer and manufacturer **William Morris** include wallpaper designs, furniture, tiles and textiles produced by Morris, Marshall and Faulkner, and later Morris & Co: 'Trellis', Willow Bough' and 'Acanthus' wallpapers; stained glass panels including *Chaucer Asleep*, after designs by Burne-Jones; and an 1861–62 cabinet, designed by Paul Webb and painted by Morris. Arts and Crafts objects include a Charles Rennie Mackintosh high-backed armchair; his fireplace from the Willow Tea Room, Glasgow; wallpaper designs by Walter Crane; furniture by the innovative designer C.F.A. Voysey, for example a simple 1896 desk, with applied copper hinges; and silver by Christopher Dresser and Liberty & Co.

Europe 1500–1800 (Basement)

Below the British Galleries, at basement level, are excellent examples of European furniture, silver, porcelain and sculpture from 1500–1800, including Germany, Italy, Spain and Portugal. Adriaen de Vries' bronze portrait bust of the Emperor Rudolf II, 1609, was once in Rudolf's Cabinet of Curiosities in Prague, before entering the collection of Queen Christina of Sweden as war booty, captured during the Thirty Years War. Small, expensive, finely crafted treasures appropriate for a collector's cabinet of this date include boxwood carvings, objects of rock crystal, Venetian glass, inlaid silver boxes, enamels and ivories. Also displayed is Dieussart's bust of Queen Elizabeth of Bohemia (1641).

The early 16th-century **Portuguese silver parcel gilt dish** is a masterpiece of early

Renaissance silver, with embossed scenes of the Siege of Troy. Other items include a lavish 1577 spinet by Annibale Rossi, decorated with nearly 2,000 precious stones; the magnificent **Lomellini Ewer and Basin** (1621–22), decorated with episodes in the life of Giovanni Grimaldi of Genoa and the Lomellini arms; and the **Medici Casket** (1609–21), a jewel casket of steel, with chiselled steel figures of Mars and Minerva, made for Cosimo II, Grand Duke of Tuscany, an excellent example of High Renaissance Florentine architectural decoration.

Fine portrait busts include the terracotta of Cardinal Paolo Emilio Zacchia (c. 1650) by Algardi. Among the terracotta busts, bronze sculptures, embossed and engraved armour, rapiers and pistols and Spanish silver perfume burners are exceptional **German ivory carvings**, including a tankard by Bernhard Straus, made in Augsburg (1651), an outstanding example of Baroque ivory carving, with Hercules slaying a centaur on the lid, and mythological scenes on its body.

Part of the **Meissen service** ordered by Frederick II of Prussia for his general, von Möllendorf, as a reward for his services in the Seven Years War, is on show. Designed c. 1762 by the Meissen factory, with some of the figures modelled by Kändler, there were once over 960 pieces, now distributed over various private and public collections. The elaborate writing cabinet (c. 1750–55) was made for Frederick Augustus III, Elector of Saxony and King of Poland, by one of the leading Dresden workshops. It is a celebrated example of German Rococo cabinet making, with wood, mother of pearl, ivory and brass marquetry, and elaborate gilt mounts. It was purchased from the Rothschild collection, Mentmore Towers, in 1977.

In the 19th century there was a taste for objects with an historical or romantic connection. The glittering boudoir of the Marquise de Sérilly was in 1874 displayed with a harp in it, said to have belonged to Marie Antoinette, Sérilly having been her Lady of Honour. A display of **items from the Jones Collection** includes several other pieces with romantic provenances. John Jones (d. 1882), who established a military tailoring firm in London, was an amateur collector of great distinction who bequeathed his entire collection to South Kensington. His great passion was for French 18th-century furniture and porcelain. He owned 89 pieces of Sèvres, including important pieces such as the 'Tippoo Vase', painted with scenes after Boucher, supposedly part of the collection sent by Louis XIV to Tipu Sultan in 1788; the *bleu de roi* vase, made for Gustav III of Sweden; and a pair of vases in brilliant 'bleu nouveau' with elaborate ormolu mounts, in the form of snakes, based on a vase in the collection of the Duc de Choiseul. Other Jones items included *The Five Orders of Architecture*, possibly by Robert Arnould Drais (c. 1780), a precious, elegant object with columns of lapis lazuli set in gold; and distinguished pieces of French furniture by the best names, including Riesener and Boulle. Later 18th-century furniture includes a reading stand by M. Carlin (c. 1785) with a Sèvres porcelain plaque and ormolu mounts, given by Marie Antoinette to Mrs Eden.

Europe & America 1800–1900 (Basement, Galleries 8–9)

Of all the galleries in the museum these give the best sense of how the 19th-century museum would have been displayed. Highly decorated and gilded furniture, porcelain and silver from France, Germany, the Netherlands, Italy, Spain, Austria, Hungary, Bohemia, Russia and Scandinavia is crowded together in a scene of suffocating opulence. The showcases lined down the centre, with their massed displays, are copies of 1877 originals; the lights imitate those used in this part of the museum in 1909; and the security barriers at the sides are derived from those used at the museum in the 1860s.

The rich and dense displays include **objects acquired from the great 19th-century International Exhibitions** (1851 and beyond), but also earlier pieces. Exhibits include a c. 1800 elaborate cabinet by the great Parisian maker Jacob Frères, who supplied furniture to Napoleon and Josephine; an 1813 Sèvres vase, a copy of the 'Medici Krater' in the Uffizi; a great, Gothic oak bookcase, 'a cathedral in wood', presented by the Emperor Franz Joseph to Queen Victoria, exhibited at the 1851 Great Exhibition; a sofa (c. 1856) by John Henry Belter, originally of Hanover but who emigrated to New York, of laminated rosewood with dense, floral carving, one of the most elaborate examples of his work; an amber vase and pedestal by J. & L. Lobmeyr, Vienna (c. 1878), shown at the Paris Exposition of that year; a cabinet by Henri-Auguste Fourdinois, of ebony with inlay of various woods including box, lime, holly and pear, with mahogany and marble plaques, purchased from the Paris Exposition of 1867, where it was awarded the Exhibition Grand Prix; and Henri Fantin-Latour's gentle paintings of nasturtiums, a rare work of a single plant, as opposed to his usual vases of flowers.

Art Nouveau objects include a Carlo Bugatti armchair (Milan c. 1900); a Richard Riemerschmid dressing table (German, 1899); a firescreen by Emile Gallé, decorated with vine leaves with tendrils wrapping around its legs; and a cabinet by Louis Majorelle, with wrought iron mounts of stylised lotus blossoms. The latter two, along with other Art Nouveau objects, were purchased for the museum from the 1900 Paris Exposition by George Donaldson, a great supporter of the 'New Movement', who correctly forecast their hostile reception in London.

Twentieth Century (Galleries 70–74; Galleries 103–106)

Twentieth-century art and design is shown in Galleries 70–74, level 3 (the period galleries) and galleries 103–106, the latter rather forlorn and in need of refurbishment. Among early 20th-century items is a Gerrit Rietveld armchair (1918), a design classic by a leading figure of the Dutch De Stijl group; examples from the Omega Workshops, founded in 1913 by Roger Fry with Vanessa Bell; a 1924 table lamp by Wilhelm Wagenfeld, *MT8*, from the Bauhaus School set up in Weimar in 1919, displaying the influence of Moholy-Nagy and his ethos of beautiful but functional industrial design; and examples of artist books, such as *Klänge* by Kandinsky (1913).

Product design, and technology as an aesthetic, is further explored in later works: a c. 1934 sleek-lined electric bar heater by Christian Barman produced by HMV; Italian kettles; a 1964 Roberts radio with leopard-skin cover; an Ambrose Heal dressing table (c. 1943); a c. 1949 storage unit by the American team Eames and Eames, designers of modern furniture for mass production; and Ron Arad chairs. British studio pottery includes works by Bernard Leach and Lucie Rie, the latter dating from early works of the 1920s and 30s, produced in her native Vienna, to later works executed in England.

Asia (Galleries 41–47g)

On level 1 are the Asia Period Galleries, containing the museum's best examples of Southeast Asian, Indian, Japanese, Chinese and Korean art. **Southeast Asia** includes 11th–13th-century Cambodian bronzes; an early 15th-century double-sided Indonesian altar relief; 7th–13th-century sculptures from Thailand, including the remarkable late 15th–early 16th-century *Standing Buddha* from the workshops of Ayutthaya, then the Thai capital. A figure of great refinement, with much of its original gilding intact, it represents a high point of Thai art, reflecting the prosperity of the kingdom of Siam.

The **Indian Collection** has its origins in the 18th-century Asiatic Society of Bengal (established 1784) and the museum of the East India Company, housed at the Company's headquarters in the City. By 1808 the latter included elephant heads, Persian manuscripts, brass Hindu sculptures and one of the V&A's most famous works, 'Tippoo's Musical Tiger' (c. 1790). A wooden organ made for Tipu Sultan, ruler of Mysore, in the form of a tiger mauling a British officer (shrieking sounds emanate from it when played), it has been popular since the early 19th century. On the demise of the East India Company in 1858, its museum was transferred first to the new government India Office in Whitehall and then, in the 1870s, to South Kensington.

Tipu Sultan (1750–99)

The 'Tiger of Mysore', scourge of the British in southern central India during the late 18th century, died fighting at the Battle of Seringapatam (modern Srirangapatna) that concluded the last of the four Mysore Wars. The son of Haider Ali, who had successfully contested the first Mysore War against the forces of the East India Company and its allies, Tipu Sultan helped his father and French forces inflict another heavy defeat on the British at the Battle of Pollilur (1780).

Often quoted as saying that he would 'rather live two days as a tiger than two hundred years as a sheep', Tipu Sultan ruled Mysore from 1782, with an administrative skill admired, almost 150 years later, by Mahatma Ghandi in *Young India*, as a model of religious tolerance. Tipu also continued his father's early experiments in rocket science, equipping specially trained troops with iron-cased rocket launchers deployed to devastating effect. Even so, at the end of the Third Mysore War (1790–92), when Seringapatam had been surrounded by forces under the command of Lord Cornwallis, Tipu Sultan was forced to hand over his second and third eldest sons, Abdul Khaliq and Maiz-Uddin, aged ten and eight, as hostages against full payment of the indemnity. Received with great courtesy and ceremony by Cornwallis, the young princes were often entertained with music and dance during their captivity, and were returned to their father two years later.

Tipu Sultan's subsequent attempts to ally himself with Napoleon resulted in a final British assault on Seringapatam, where he was shot as he lay wounded after falling from the ramparts.

Important examples of **Buddhist and Hindu sculpture** include the monumental 11th–12th-century black basalt *Buddha Sakyamuri*, from Bihar; the c. 900 AD sandstone *Bodhisattva Avalokitesvara*, called the 'Sanchi Torso', beautifully carved and exceptionally elegant, from the ruined temple of Sanchi, central India; and the c. 11th-century Chola-period, small gilt copper figure of Buddha offering reassurance, excellently modelled, cast and finished, possibly the finest Buddhist metal sculpture to survive from southern India. The temple sculpture of Nandi, Shiva's sacred bull, late 16th–17th century, is carved in attractive serpentine.

Sixteenth–18th-century **Mughal art** contains early Indian painting; gold ornamental jewellery (armlets, necklaces, hair ornaments); and Mughal textile designs, including elaborate tent hangings. Intricately illuminated books illustrate the histories of the dynasty.

The **European presence in India**, and the export trade, is explored. Furniture includes the ivory table (c. 1785) given to Warren Hastings by Mani Begum. Expensive and finely crafted objects in the centre of the gallery include Shah Jahan's white jade thumb ring; his exquisite white jade wine cup (1657) in the form of a ram's head flaring to a wide bowl, perhaps the finest known example of Mughal hardstone carving; and turban ornaments and daggers ornamented with rubies, emeralds and diamonds. The agate cameo portrait of Shah Jahan (c. 1630–40) was carved by a European lapidary at the Mughal court. The golden throne of Maharajah Ranjit Singh, which was shown with other Indian Empire treasures at the 1851 Great Exhibition, was part of the state property taken by the British in 1849 on the annexation of the Punjab.

The **Islamic Near East**, covering the art of Egypt, Turkey, Iran, Iraq and Syria, was closed at the time of writing (due to open August 2006), but will contain famous items such as the Ardabil carpet (1539–40), one of the largest and most magnificent Persian carpets in the world, from the shrine of the same name in northwest Iran. Purchased in 1893, to William Morris it was 'of singular perfection'.

The earliest objects in the **China Gallery** date from the Han and Tang dynasties. Costly burial goods include the 206 BC–AD 220 large head and partial torso of a horse, the largest animal carving in jade known; a large and rare tomb model of a standing Arabian horse, 1st–2nd centuries; and a 1st–2nd-century Tang camel and rider, of lead glazed earthenware, elaborately groomed and saddled. A bronze incense burner in the shape of an angry goose, its neck outstretched, dates from the Song-Yuan dynasty (1200–1300). Domestic items include highly decorated and embroidered silk robes, table utensils such as jade cups and ewers, and Ming dynasty furniture such as the important early lacquer table (1426–35), one of the only surviving pieces from the 'Orchard Workshop', the Imperial lacquer workshop set up to the northwest of the Forbidden City. The collection is rich in pieces with an Imperial provenance, an association which early collectors particularly sought. The ornate carved polychrome lacquer throne of the Emperor Qianlong was probably commissioned in the 1780s for the Tuanhe Travelling Palace in the Nan Haizi hunting park south of Beijing.

The gallery of **Chinese export art** (more items are shown in their European setting in the British Galleries) includes a magnificent 9-ft, 17-tier porcelain pagoda (1800–15) of the type that was ordered for the decoration of the Royal Pavilion, Brighton. It is one of only ten known to exist.

The **Korean Collection** includes beautiful examples of pale green celadon ware of the Koryo dynasty (935–1392), and fine examples of porcelain, furniture and decorative objects from the Choson dynasty (1392–1910), when Seoul became the capital.

The acquisition of items from **Japan** was sporadic until the second half of the 19th century. The emphasis was on contemporary items purchased from the International Exhibitions, demonstrating extreme technical skill. The dramatic hammered iron incense burner in the form of an eagle, for example, was bought in 1875, and the ornamental bronze vase, executed by the noted bronze caster Suzuki Chokichi, was acquired at the Universal Exhibition in Amsterdam in 1883, directly from Kiritsu Koshu Kaisha of Tokyo, a company founded to promote Japanese craft industries. As well as ornamental swords and knife mounts; an excellent collection of Japanese lacquerware; and a collection of over 20,000 woodblock prints, the overwhelming bulk of the collection comprises ceramics. Historic and contemporary examples were purchased for the museum in Japan by Sano Tsunetami in the 1870s, including important late 16th-century tea ceramics.

A Woman Poking her Tongue Out, by Utagawa Kuniyoshi (c. 1855).

WALLACE COLLECTION

Hertford House, Manchester Square, W1U 3BN
Tel: 020-7563 9500; www.wallacecollection.org
Open Mon–Sat 10–5, Sun 12–5
Free
Tube: Bond Street
Restaurant and shop
Map p. 381, 1D

Built in 1776 for the 4th Duke of Manchester, Hertford House lies on the north side of handsome Manchester Square and is home to a remarkable collection of works of art. The collection was formed by successive members of the Seymour-Conway family, Marquesses of Hertford, and Sir Richard Wallace, natural son of the fourth marquess. Sir Richard Wallace's widow bequeathed the collection to the nation in 1897, on condition that nothing was added or removed from it, and so the Wallace Collection remains today, its mix of paintings, furniture and decorative arts retaining much of the atmosphere of a grand aristocratic town mansion, as Hertford House was in its heyday.

The collection comprises important 18th- and 19th-century British portraits, mainly collected by the first and second marquesses, and a large collection of 17th-century Dutch and Flemish pictures, collected by the third marquess. Its chief importance and glory, however, is the exceptional collection of 18th-century French painting, sculpture, furniture, porcelain and *objets d'art*, amassed by the fourth marquess and unparalleled in this country. In this area the Wallace collection outdoes both the National Gallery and the V&A. It was the fourth marquess who purchased two of the museum's greatest treasures: Fragonard's *The Swing*, and Frans Hals's *Laughing Cavalier*. Sir Richard Wallace added an extensive collection of medieval and Renaissance works as well as the important collection of arms and armour, the latter second only to the Royal Armouries.

Richard Seymour-Conway, 4th Marquess of Hertford (1800–70) spent much of his life in France, in Paris in an apartment on rue Lafitte, and at the Château de Bagatelle in the Bois de Boulogne. Collecting was an obsession, made possible through the extraordinary works of art on the market following the French Revolution. He purchased works by the leading 18th-century painters Boucher, Watteau, Fragonard, Lancret and Greuze, as well as items by the finest French cabinet makers such as Boulle and Riesener. On his death in 1870 Hertford House was bought by his natural son, Sir Richard Wallace, from his cousin, the fifth marquess. To contain the collection, Sir Richard and his French wife altered and extended the house, most importantly adding to the rear the Great Gallery, designed by Thomas Ambler. The collection was open to a select public, via a separate entrance on Spanish Place. Following Lady Hertford's bequest to the nation, much was done to retain the house's palatial character, which opened to the public in 1900.

Recent redevelopment (Rick Mather) has provided the museum with its first dedicated exhibition space, a watercolour gallery and a lecture theatre. The new rooms are in the basement, accessed by steps from the central courtyard, which has been glazed and is now the museum's restaurant, Bagatelle, named after the family's French house. With its fountain and potted palms, it has the air of a late Victorian or Edwardian conservatory, and is a pleasant and sedate place to eat.

The Wallace Fountain

On the front lawn of Hertford House stands a Wallace Fountain, one of the type of 50 donated by Sir Richard Wallace in 1872 to the city of Paris, where they have become known simply as 'wallaces'. Designed by Charles-August Labourg, the fountains provided a free supply of clean water, and were enthusiastically received by pedestrian Parisians. The ornamental dome of the fountain is supported by four caryatids representing the gowned goddesses of Simplicity, Temperance, Charity and Kindness, distinguishable by their knees, whether left or right, covered or bare. Eighty-two Wallace Fountains can now be found in different  parts of Paris, with at least six in other French cities and towns, and others in more than 20 cities worldwide, with one most recently installed in Macao (the second in Asia after Tokyo).

Sir Richard Wallace (1818–90) was born Richard Jackson, son of the twenty-eight-year-old Agnes Jackson, *née* Wallace, with whom the eighteen-year-old fourth marquess of Hertford had an affair. Richard was brought up in Paris by his grandmother Maria Fagnani, Lady Hertford, known as Mie-Mie. In 1935 his increasingly reclusive father purchased the Château de Bagatelle in the Bois de Boulogne, where from 1842 he employed Richard, unacknowledged as his son but having adopted his mother's maiden name, as his secretary, managing the growing collection of Hertford paintings and rare *objets d'art*.

In the year of his father's death in 1870, Richard Wallace inherited the estate and was caught up in the Siege of Paris and the painful birth of the Second Republic. Staying on in the city, he paid for an ambulance and a hospital bearing the Hertford name. Beleaguered by the Prussians and forced to accept a humiliating peace, the city's violent suppression of the Paris Commune in the following year persuaded Wallace to remove his art collection to London for safe-keeping, offering the 50 fountains as a farewell gift.

Tour of the House

Through the glass-fronted porte-cochère and to the right of the handsome Entrance Hall, is the **Front State Room** with displays of royal and family portraits, including *George II* by Allan Ramsay, presented by the king to the first marquess, and Hoppner's *George IV as Prince of Wales*, presented to the third marquess when Lord Yarmouth. The **Back State Room** displays objects relating to Louis XV and his mistress Madame de Pompadour: a French marble-topped commode (1739) by Antoine-Robert Gaudreaus and Jean-Jacques Caffieri, with applied gilt bronze mounts, extending over the front in exuberant Rococo scrolls, made for Louis XV's bedchamber at Versailles; a gilt bronze chandelier by Caffieri, the leading French metal founder and chaser, given by Louis XV to his daughter Louise-Elisabeth; several important pieces of Sèvres porcelain, including bright green, gilded and floral decorated elephant vases and a porcelain inkstand with terrestrial and celestial globes, designed by Jean-Claude Duplessis and given by Louis XV to his daughter Marie-Adelaide; and an elaborate musical clock (c. 1762), also by Duplessis, its dial surrounded by lavish flowers and surmounted by a spaniel with a game bird.

The **Dining Room** has aristocratic French portraiture, including an image by Nattier of the Marquise de Belestrat, lady-in-waiting to Louis XV's daughters; and marble busts by Houdon of Madame Victoire, one of the daughters, and Madame de Sérilly, maid of honour to Marie Antoinette. The **Billiard Room** takes a step back to the reign of Louis XIV. He appears, posthumously, in a portrait of his children with their governess. Other items include a terracotta bust (1676) of Charles Le Brun, the king's painter, by Antoine Coyzevox, the king's sculptor; a bronze bust (c. 1699) of the king, also by Coyzevox; and an exceptional example of Boulle, the great French cabinet maker, a wardrobe (c. 1715), veneered with *contre-partie* Boulle marquetry (sheets of turtleshell and brass glued together and a design cut out) with elaborate gilt bronze mounts.

Through the glass doors in the bow of the Dining Room, steps on the left lead down to the new galleries in the basement, an exhibition gallery and a **Watercolour Gallery**. On show is the exceptional group of works by Richard Parkes Bonington including his *Venice: the Piazzetta*, (1826); *Sunset in the Pays de Caux* (1828); and *A Lady dressing her Hair* (1827), in van Dyck costume of a vibrant emerald green.

The **Housekeeper's Room** contains 19th-century French pictures, principally Delacroix's *The Execution of the Doge Marino Faliero* (1825–26), which was inspired, like Donizetti's opera, by Byron's poem about the 14th-century execution.

Renaissance and Medieval Galleries and Armouries

The **16th-century Gallery** contains the remarkable collection of medieval and Renaissance treasures collected by Sir Richard Wallace, which includes Pieter Pourbus's *An Allegory of Love*; an Elizabethan standing salt and cover (1578) with elaborate Renaissance form chasing; Limoges painted enamels; Venetian 16th-century glass; and a marble bust of Christ by Pietro Torrigiano, from Westminster Abbey.

Wallace decorated his **Smoking Room** with Turkish-design Minton tiles and a mosaic floor. Further treasures can be found here: a late 16th-century German hare pendant, its body a great baroque pearl; bronze firedogs after sculptural designs by Algardi, *Jupiter Victorious over the Titans* and *Juno Controlling the Winds*, owned by Louis XV; and an important collection of Italian majolica. Of particular note is the large wine cooler (1574), from the collection of Cosimo de' Medici; and an important dish signed by Giorgio Andreoli of Gubbio, 6th April 1525, whose workshop was famous for its lustrewares, decorated with a scene of bathing maidens taken from an engraving after Raphael. The *Horn of St Hubert*, said to have been given by the Bishop of Liège to Charles the Bold, Duke of Burgundy in 1468, is encrusted with gesso, painted, gilded and decorated with champlevé enamel, while the 7th-century 'Bell of St Mura', a bell-cover of bronze adorned with Celtic tracery, crystal and semi-precious stones, is from the Abbey of Donegal.

The remaining rooms on the ground floor contain the astonishing collection of arms and armour built up by Sir Richard Wallace, mainly through the wholesale purchase of the collection of the Comte de Nieuwerkerke, Napoleon III's Minister of Fine Arts and Director of the Louvre, and the opportunity of the pick of Sir Samuel Rush Meyrick's collection, the great scholar of arms and armour in England. The **Oriental Armoury** contains objects from India, Persia and the territories of the Ottoman Empire, many of them in fact collected by the fourth marquess and of outstanding quality: the exceptionally fine 17th-century Indian dagger (arguably one of the finest in the world), made at the Mughal court for either Jahangir or Shah Jahan, with a solid gold hilt set with diamonds and a floral design of rubies, with leaves of emeralds; a late 15th-century Persian dagger, the hilt carved jade, the blade decorated with jackals and hares amid floral arabesques; silver-gilt tiger-headed 18th-century Indian ceremonial maces; Tipu Sultan's *tulwar*, a type of scimitar; and the gold and ivory sword of Ranjit Singh.

The **European Armoury I** displays 10th- to early 16th-century items, including a 10th-century sword; swords used by Crusader knights; an early 15th-century German mail shirt; a visored basinet helmet, light and close-fitting, made in Milan c. 1390; an ornate short-sword made for Cosimo de' Medici; an early 15th-century English or Flemish jousting helmet; and a late 15th-century German tournament shield, decorated with painted and gilded foliage.

The **European Armoury II** contains the most important pieces in the collection: the equestrian armour, for horse and rider, made c. 1475–85 at Landshut in southern Germany with characteristic shell-like flutings, one of the few examples known to retain its original horse-armour; and the 1555 German close helmet, made by Conrad Richter of Augsburg as part of the Golden Garniture ordered by the future Holy Roman Emperor, Ferdinand I. Alongside these items is Lord Buckhurst's suit of armour, made c. 1587 at the royal workshops established by Henry VIII at Greenwich; and a French dagger (c. 1600) presented by the City of Paris to Henri IV on his marriage to Marie de' Medici. The **European Armoury III** contains sporting guns, rifles and pistols, including an important collection of Napoleonic era flint-locks, illustrative of the rise of the firearm from the 16th–19th centuries.

First Floor

The white marble **Staircase**, rising grandly to the first floor, has a magnificent balustrade (1719–20) of cast and wrought iron and gilt brass, originally from the stairs leading to Louis XV's *Cabinet de Médailles* in the Palais Mazarin, Paris. One of the finest examples of French metalwork of the period, it was sold as scrap in the mid-19th century, bought by the fourth marquess, and, in 1847, altered to fit Hertford House and installed by Sir Richard Wallace. Hanging on the stairs and **Landing** are important paintings by François Boucher: *A Summer Pastoral* and *An Autumn Pastoral* (1745), with characters from Favart's popular pantomimes. In the first appear the cousins Babette and Lisette, the latter being serenaded by the Little Shepherd who, in the second, feeds her grapes. The more important, superb pair, *The Rising of the Sun* and *The Setting of the Sun*, exhibited at the Paris Salon in 1753, show the sun god Apollo rising from the river Oceana to make his journey across the heavens. In the latter he sinks back below the waves. Madame de Pompadour ordered tapestries from these paintings, made by the Gobelins Manufactory, and displayed them, along with the pictures, at her château at Bellevue.

The **Small Drawing Room** contains fine Canaletto views of Venice, purchased by the third marquess: *Venice: The Bacino di San Marco from the Canale della Giudecca* and *Venice: The Bacino di San Marco from San Giorgio Maggiore* (both c. 1735–44), as well as views by Guardi purchased by the fourth marquess. The **Large** and **Oval Drawing Rooms** were, at the time of the second marquess, magnificent ballrooms where, in 1814, a grand ball was held to celebrate the defeat of Napoleon. Among the objects in the former is a selection of important Sèvres porcelain, including a cup with a portrait of Benjamin Franklin, who had visited Paris in 1776 to gain French support for American independence from Britain. In the Oval Drawing Room, the chimneypiece (c. 1785) is the only one original to the house to survive; the French mantle clock (1775) has bronze figures of night and day reclining either side of the dial; a delicate reading and writing table by Martin Carlin from c. 1783–84, veneered with tulipwood and mounted with plaques of Sèvres porcelain; chairs (1786) by Jean-Baptiste Boulard, which were made for Louis XVI's card room at Fontainebleau; and a roll-top desk (c. 1770) by Jean-Henri Riesener, the leading cabinet maker under Louis XVI and appointed the King's Cabinet Maker in 1774, decorated with marquetry still life panels with books, a globe and papers, one with the seal of the Duc d'Orsay. From this room, bow windows overlook the former courtyard, now the restaurant.

Sir Richard Wallace's **Study** displays more Sèvres, including an ice-cream cooler, part of a service made for Catherine the Great of Russia. Also here is an impressive Boulle wardrobe (c. 1700), with elaborate marquetry and gilt bronze decorations, illustrating scenes from Ovid's *Metamorphoses*. Lady Wallace's **Boudoir** has a number of important pieces: 'fancy' pictures by Greuze (*The Broken Mirror*; 1763) and *Innocence* (a young girl holding a lamb), and by Reynolds (*The Strawberry Girl*); an elaborate writing table and cabinet (c. 1765) for paper files, in imitation oriental lacquer, or green French vernis, with gilded decoration, the cabinet topped by Cupid and Psyche; several small 18th-century French luxury trinkets, such as gold snuff

Jean-Honoré Fragonard: *The Swing* (1767).

boxes with mother of pearl, enamel and porcelain decoration, some set with diamonds and other precious and semi-precious stones; a magnificent gold 55-piece toilet service, including breakfast implements, made in Augsburg in 1757–73; and Antoine-Nicolas Martinière's perpetual calendar, made in 1741–42 for Louis XV, consisting of four gilt-bronze frames containing enamelled copper plaques featuring the months, phases of the moon, days of the week, zodiac signs and Church feast days.

The **West Room** was Lady Wallace's bedroom. Today it displays some of the fourth marquess's exceptional collection of 18th-century French paintings and Louis XVI furniture. Boucher's portrait of Madame de Pompadour shows her in her garden at Bellevue, the statuary group in the background, *Friendship Consoling Love*, a reflection of her now platonic relationship with the king. Also here are Boucher's three canvases *Venus and Vulcan*, *Mars and Venus Surprised by Vulcan* and *The Judgement of Paris*; an elaborate perfume burner (1774–75) by Pierre Gouthière, which was formerly owned by Marie Antoinette; and a delicate worktable (1786–90) by Adam Weisweiler, which belonged to the Empress Josephine. The display continues in the **West Gallery**, where the full extent of the French 18th-century collection becomes apparent. Miniatures are also shown here, including Lucas Horenbout's portrait of Holbein, but the chief exhibits are works by the leading French painters: works by Lancret and Pater; Watteau's well-known *Music Party* (c. 1718), with music-making on a palatial terrace, a countryside vista in the background; his *Harlequin and Columbine* (c. 1716–18), with *commedia dell'arte* characters, including Pierrot and Crispin in the background; and *Gilles and his Family*, the central figure dressed as Harlequin's rival, Mezzetin. One of the Wallace's most famous paintings is Fragonard's *The Swing* (1767), a picture full of artful abandon, flirtation and innuendo, the graceful, provocative girl poised in the air, the action of the swing tossing her delicate slipper in the direction of her lover. The secretaire (1783) by Jean-Henri Riesener was supplied for Marie-Antoinette at the Petit Trianon, Versailles.

On the east side of the house, the **East Drawing Room** was used in the early 19th-century by Isabella, wife of the 3rd Marquess of Hertford. It was here that she would entertain the Prince Regent on his daily visits between 1807 and 1820. The **East Galleries I** is the first of two galleries containing 17th-century Dutch and Flemish pictures, collected mainly by the third marquess, but also by the fourth. The gallery was built in 1871–75 to give much needed extra space. Here are 'low life' genre scenes by Adriaen Brouwer and David Teniers the Younger; Rubens' *modelli* (1628) for two of his proposed series of 24 paintings illustrating the life of Henri IV; Aert van der Neer's *A Skating Scene*; and Jacob van Ruisdael's *Rocky Landscape*. The **East Galleries II** continues the display, with genre scenes, townscapes and Dutch-Italianate landscapes, including Jan Steen's *Celebrating the Birth*, Pieter de Hooch's *A Boy Bringing Bread*, Gerard ter Borch's *A Lady Reading a Letter*, Gabriel Metsu's *The Sleeping Sportsman*, and Jan van der Heyden's *View of the Westerkerk*, Amsterdam. The **East Galleries III** contains mainly landscapes, by Adam Pynacker, Jan Both and Albert Cuyp.

The main showpiece gallery was the **Great Gallery**, added by Sir Richard Wallace. Extending the full length of the back of the house, it was purpose-built for the display of pictures, with top-lighting, as well as for glamorous entertaining. A water-powered lift provided additional access. Important works include Rubens' *The Rainbow Landscape* (c. 1636), a late summer afternoon scene on the artist's country estate. It is the pendant to *Het Steen* in the National Gallery, which had wanted to acquire the painting when it came on the market in 1858 but was outbid by the fourth marquess. Two full-lengths by van Dyck, *Marie de Raet* (1631) and *Philippe de Roy* (1630), were painted shortly before the artist settled in London in 1632. Van Dyck owned Titian's *Perseus and Andromeda*, painted originally for Philip II of Spain, purchased by the third marquess in 1815. Also in the room is a bronze equestrian statuette of Louis XIV, a reduced version of the full-scale work by Desjardins erected in Lyons in 1713 but destroyed at the French Revolution; Poussin's exceptional *Dance to the Music of Time*; Philippe de Champaigne's *Annunciation*, the Holy Spirit in the form of a dove, with rays of divine light illuminating Mary; and Rembrandt's portrait of his teenage son Titus. Probably the best known item in the Wallace Collection is Frans Hals's famous *Laughing Cavalier*. Painted in 1624, the identity of the man, neither a cavalier nor laughing, is unknown. The fourth marquess outbid Baron de Rothschild for the picture, paying six times its auction estimate, which at the time added to the picture's celebrity. The 18th-century portraits were in the collections of the first and second marquesses: Gainsborough's *Mrs Robinson as Perdita* (1781) was commissioned by the Prince of Wales after he had seen the actress perform the role from Shakespeare's *The Winter's Tale* at Drury Lane; she holds the miniature of him he sent to her. Reynolds's *Nelly O'Brien* shows the well-known beauty and courtesan seated with a pet dog in her lap, her face shaded by the brim of her hat. Lawrence's slick portrait *George IV* (1822) was thought by the artist to be his best likeness of the king, and is mentioned in Thackeray's *Vanity Fair*.

WELLINGTON ARCH
(English Heritage)

Apsley Way, Hyde Park
Corner, W1J 7JZ
Tel: 020-7930 2726;
www.english-heritage.org.uk
Open Apr–Oct Wed-Sun 10–5;
Nov–Mar Wed–Sun 10–4
Admission charge (joint
tickets with Apsley House
available)
Tube: Hyde Park Corner
Shop
Map p. 381, 2D

On an island surrounded by the traffic of Hyde Park Corner, approached via an array of confusing pedestrian subways, is the triumphal

Wellington Arch, formerly erected opposite the main entrance to Hyde Park but moved in 1883 to align with Constitution Hill. It now forms part of a processional route from Buckingham Palace to Kensington Palace (the massive gates are occasionally opened to allow horses and ceremonial cars through). Designed by Decimus Burton in 1828, in conjunction with the Hyde Park Corner Screen, it was at first topped with M. Cotes Wyatt's much derided over-sized equestrian statue of Wellington (1838). Described as 'a gigantic triumph of bad taste' (*Punch*) and 'a perfect disgrace' (Queen Victoria), it was in fact liked by Wellington, who was upset at plans to remove it. In 1883 it was finally taken down and replaced with Adrian Jones' magnificently animated *Peace Descending on the Quadriga of War* (1912). The arch has recently been restored and its rooms and viewing platforms are open to the public.

WESLEY'S HOUSE AND MUSEUM OF METHODISM

> 49 City Road, Islington, EC1Y 1AU
> Tel: 020-7253 2262; www.wesleyschapel.org.uk
> Open Mon–Sat 10–4, Sun 12.30–1.45
> Free
> Tube: Old Street
> Shop
> Map p. 383, 1E

John Wesley (1703–91), the founder of Methodism, lived in this Georgian town house on the City Road from 1779 until his death. The tour starts in the basement Kitchen, where the original table can still be seen, and proceeds first into the **Documents Room**, formerly the scullery. Displayed here are Wesley's glasses and spectacles, along with other personal belongings such as his travelling gown, collar and preaching gown, shoes, nightcap and walking stick. A fanciful portrait by Frank C. Salisbury, painted in 1932, taken from the small authentic bust by Enoch Wood, commemorates the union in that year of the Methodist churches. A teapot given to Wesley by Josiah Wedgwood can be seen, along with the chair in which Wesley presided at the first Methodist conference at the Foundry in 1744, and part of the tree from Winchelsea under which he preached his last sermon in the open air on 7th October 1790. Wesley's **Bedroom**, where he died on 2nd March 1791, contains all his original furniture. Only the rope-sprung bed—of the common type at the time, from which derives the expression 'sleep tight'—is a replica. Off one corner is the **Prayer Room**, known as the 'Powerhouse of Methodism', where every morning at 4.30am Wesley awaited his orders from God. His maid had to light the small fire an hour earlier. His **Study** can also be seen, where as well as on spiritual well-being he also concentrated on physical cures. His belief in a healthy lifestyle is demonstrated by his exercise horse, and his interest in alternative therapies by his electric shock machine, used to deaden the nerves of minor aches and pains. An original cockfighter's chair can be seen, given to him by a man who had renounced his participation in the sport. Visiting preachers were quartered in the **Attic**, where the movement was nurtured that provided the poor with spiritual sustenance and that has been credited with helping to prevent an 18th-century Republican revolution in Britain.

Next to the house, with a bronze statue of Wesley in front of it, is **Wesley's Chapel**, 'perfectly neat but not fine', opened on 1st November 1778, retaining its original mahogany pulpit, Communion rail and table. The ceiling is a reconstruction of the original, which was destroyed by fire in 1879. In the crypt is the **Museum of Methodism**, telling the story of the denomination from its foundation to the present day. Paintings include the *Portrait of Peter* (1927) by Herbert Beecroft and the *Holy Triumph of JW in his Dying* (1842) by Marshall Caxton. Wesley is shown in the bedroom here, although it appears considerably larger in order to accommodate the crowd at his bedside. His last words were: 'Best of all, God is with us'. The roots of Trade Unionism in Methodist chapels is examined here, as well as the preaching of Methodism abroad. There is also the warclub of the excessively cruel Chief Thakombau of Fiji, whose conversion was attributed to the impression made by Mary, wife of the preacher James Calvert. She nursed the chief when he became ill and fearlessly pleaded for the lives of 15 women on the island. Beside it is a Priest's Bowl, also from Fiji, once used in cannibal ceremonies, given to the Rev. James Calvert on the conversion of the owner. A small display also celebrates Wesley's brother Charles, who wrote 600 hymns, of which John Wesley is reported to have said 'some of them must have been good'. Charles and John were two of 19 children. While in the area it is also worth crossing the City Road from Wesley's House to **Bunhill Fields**, where their mother Susannah Wesley (d. 1742) is buried, as well as John Bunyan, Daniel Defoe, Isaac Watts and William Blake.

WESTMINSTER ABBEY MUSEUM

East Cloisters, Dean's Yard, Broad Sanctuary, SW1P 3PA
Tel: 020-7222 5152; www.westminster-abbey.org
Open daily 10.30–4
Free
Tube: Westminster
Shop
Map p. 382, 4B

This small museum, situated off the east side of the cloisters, houses some of the abbey's most precious treasures. The chief exhibits are the extraordinary and unique group of effigies, in wood and wax, used in medieval and Tudor funeral ceremonies. They include the earliest known likenesses of English monarchs, and are thus of incomparable significance. The earliest effigies date from the 14th century, when

wooden images—instead of the actual corpse—were used during the funeral proce-
dures: the effigy would have been used for the lying-in-state, would have been placed
on top of the coffin for the journey to the abbey and for the duration of the funeral,
and sometimes marked the place of burial in the abbey prior to the erection of the
monument. The abbey has 21 effigies, which can be divided into three groups:
medieval wooden effigies of monarchs and members of the royal family; later 17th-
century wax figures of royal and noble persons, not used during the funeral ceremonial but placed in the abbey as reminders of the deceased, probably near to the place
of burial; and later wax figures of 'celebrities', tourist attractions which boosted the
meagre incomes of the monument guides. In 1841 the abbey authorities moved the
waxworks, which they had come to see as distasteful clutter, to the upper floor of the
chantry chapel of Abbot John Islip, where they joined the neglected medieval and
Tudor figures, known collectively as the 'Ragged Regiment'. It was not until the early
20th century that interest in them was revived, when the undercroft museum opened.
In 1941 the wax figures were moved to safety to Piccadilly Underground station but
the medieval effigies remained at the abbey—a fateful decision, for in May of that year
the undercroft suffered severe water damage in an air raid. The effigies remained in
this sad situation until 1949, when it was noted that many were in a hopeless condition, their stuffed bodies disintegrating and rotten. Those that survive, entire or partial, have undergone a complete restoration campaign.

Wooden Medieval Effigies

The earliest effigy is that of Edward III, which was used at his funeral in 1377, placed
on his coffin within a magnificent hearse. The body, which would have been clothed
in costly robes provided by the Great Wardrobe, is of carved wood. The head is based
on a death mask and is the earliest known likeness of an English monarch. Anne of
Bohemia's carved wooden head, long and thin, is all that remains of her effigy (queen
of Richard II, she died at the palace of Sheen in 1394). Also head-only is Elizabeth of
York's effigy, which contemporary accounts indicate was incredibly lifelike. Henry
VII's bust, a painted gesso death mask applied over wood, is a powerfully realistic and
skilled likeness (the death mask was the source for Pietro Torrigiano's celebrated terracotta sculpture of the king at the V&A; *see p. 327*) but his stuffed body has not survived. Mary Tudor's effigy was made by her Sergeant Painter Nicholas Lizarde, while
Anne of Denmark's was carved by the skilled sculptor Maximilian Colt, and painted
by the artist John de Critz.

Wax Effigies

After the Restoration in 1660 wax effigies were introduced, wax being a medium which
offered a more startling likeness. The effigies have wax heads and hands, with painted
complexions, wigs of real hair and eyelashes of bristle or canine hair. Their bodies are
of stuffed canvas, clothed in contemporary or near contemporary dress and jewels,
sometimes in garments which had belonged to them. Charles II stands tall and realistic, in his own Garter Robes and monogrammed undergarments. Frances Theresa

Stuart, Duchess of Richmond and Lennox, 'La Belle Stuart', a court beauty who in the 1660s resisted the advances of Charles II, is the best and most compelling waxwork. Commissioned in her will, to be made in wax and to be set up in the abbey in a glass-fronted case, it was made by the professional wax modeller Mrs Goldsmith, who had her own waxworks museum. Installed in the abbey in 1703, the duchess wears her own Coronation robes and has by her side her pet of 40 years, her African parrot, which died a few days after her. If original, it is one of the earliest examples of taxidermy in the country. Catherine, Duchess of Buckingham (d. 1743), a proud stickler for protocol, ordered her effigy before her death and stored it at her house. She wears the robes she wore for the Coronation of Queen Anne in 1704. William III and Mary II's likenesses were not commissioned by the abbey but were pur-

Waxwork effigy of Frances Stuart, famed court beauty and model for the figure of Britannia (1703).

chased, possibly from Mrs Goldsmith, in 1725. Queen Anne, seated and cumbrous, is based on a death mask but—further evidence of the declining effigy tradition—she was not clothed until 1740.

Later Waxworks

Later wax effigies of national figures arrived at the abbey purely as tourist attractions. William Pitt was made by Mrs Patience Wright from a life sitting in 1775 and set up in the abbey after his burial there. Nelson's effigy, however, arrived at the abbey in 1806, despite the fact that he was buried at St Paul's Cathedral. Made by Catherine Andras, Queen Charlotte's official modeller in wax, it is based on a portrait by Hoppner. Nelson wears his own clothes and the shoe buckles he wore at Trafalgar.

Other Exhibits

Among the other exhibits in the museum are a bronze relief portrait of Sir Thomas Lovell by Pietro Torrigiano (c. 1516–20); and stained glass panels (c. 1250–70), almost all that remains of the glass which once adorned Henry III's abbey. There are also two carved alabaster reliefs by Grinling Gibbons and Arnold Quellin from the high altar of James II's Roman Catholic chapel at Whitehall Palace, smartly disman-tled on the accession of the Protestant William and Mary in 1688. Other sculptures from the altarpiece, also by Quellin, now forlorn and much weathered, are in the nearby College Garden (*open Tues–Thur 10–4 in winter; 10–6 in summer*).

WHITECHAPEL ART GALLERY

80–82 Whitechapel High Street, E1 7QX
Tel: 020-7522 7888; www.whitechapel.org
Open Tues–Sun 11–6, also Thur 11–9
Free
Tube: Aldgate East
Café and shop
Map p. 383, 2F

Founded in 1901, the Whitechapel is a leading venue for modern and contemporary art, with a strong programme of temporary exhibitions. Founded in 1901, the gallery has its origins in the exhibitions of paintings organised by Canon Samuel A. Barnett (1844–1913) and his wife Henrietta (1851–1936) in St Jude's National Schools in Whitechapel from 1881. Barnett shared the widespread Victorian belief in the civilising power of culture; the exhibitions were intended as a moral education for the citizens of a deprived East End area, as well as to 'lessen the dead ugliness of their lives'. The Whitechapel's distinguished Arts and Crafts building, with its arched entrance, was designed in 1897 by Charles Harrison Townsend. The narrow site, with exhibition space on two levels, was internally reorganised in 1982 and there is a current plan to extend into the adjacent old public library building.

On its foundation the Whitechapel staged contemporary British art exhibitions (G.F. Watts, the Pre-Raphaelites) as well as Old Master and international shows. From the mid-50s it became an increasingly important venue for avant-garde art, and today the programme's emphasis is very much on modern and contemporary British and interna-tional works, by emerging artists as well as artists who live and work in the East End.

WILLIAM MORRIS GALLERY

Lloyd Park, Forest Road, Walthamstow, E17 4PP
Tel: 020-8527 3782; www.lbwf.gov.uk/wmg
Open Tues–Sat and first Sun of each month 10–1 and 2–5
Free. Wheelchair access to ground floor only
Tube: Walthamstow Central
Shop
Map p. 379, 1E

The William Morris Gallery is dedicated to the great and hugely influential decorative arts pioneer William Morris (1834–96), artist, craftsman, designer and writer as well as typographer and prominent socialist. The museum's collections illustrate Morris' life and works, and that of his associates, contemporaries and Arts and Craft followers.

Morris was born in Walthamstow, less than a mile away at Elm Park. After the death of his father, a wealthy City businessman, the family moved to the museum's building, a substantial Georgian house of the late 1740s, known as The Water House after its ornamental moat in the grounds, where the Morris family would fish, boat and skate. Morris lived here from 1848–56 but today the open fields and countryside which he would have known have been swallowed up by dense terraced housing, a process of suburban development which began in the 1870s with the extension of the railway. In Morris's words, Walthamstow became 'terribly cocknified and choked up by the jerry-builders'. The house was purchased by the newspaper proprietor Edward Lloyd, of *Lloyd's Weekly* and the *Daily Chronicle*, who in 1898 donated it to the people of Walthamstow. The nucleus of the present collections was formed by the Walthamstow Antiquarian Society, and important items were purchased after the closure of Morris & Co in 1940. In 1935 the artist Sir Frank Brangwyn (1867–1956) donated a large collection of his own work, and that of the Pre-Raphaelite painters and his late 19th- and 20th-century contemporaries; and another major donation was made by A.H. Mackmurdo, an architect, designer and founder of the Century Guild, who had introduced Brangwyn to Morris.

The house is set in pleasant, spacious grounds (Lloyd Park) but with rather municipal planting. The old moat survives, and a small aviary houses cockatoos and zebra finches.

Ground Floor

The ground-floor displays begin to the left of the light and airy Entrance Hall, in the former Drawing and Reception Rooms, set up as a museum rather than a home. Exhibits start with Morris's early life, with views of his previous Walthamstow homes, his time at Oxford and his friendship with Edward Burne-Jones. The medieval-style helmet and sword was designed by Morris as a costume prop for the Oxford Union murals, with their Arthurian theme.

There are images of Red House (*see p. 342*), the home of Morris and his wife Jane for five years, completed to designs by Philip Webb in 1859 with interior decoration by Morris, Webb, Rossetti and Burne-Jones. The experience led to the formation in 1861 of the decorative arts firm Morris, Marshall, Faulkner & Company. Items produced by the firm include painted tile panels, for example *The Labours of the Months* (1862) and *Beauty and the Beast* (1863), the latter an overmantel designed by Burne-Jones, Morris and Webb for the Surrey home of the artist Myles Birket Foster. Wallpapers include the original 'Trellis' design, Morris' earliest wallpaper; 'Daisy', block printed by hand (the plant designs taken from Gerard's 1590s *Herbal*), the first to be printed and sold through the company; and the well-known 'Pomegranate'. In

1875 the company became Morris & Co. A photograph shows the company's first shop, which opened in 1877 at 449 Oxford Street. 1870s wallpapers, for example 'Chrysanthemum', were more elaborate in design, echoed in the textile designs, textile printing blocks for which are on show, as well as woven fabrics and photographs of the workshop premises, which in 1881 moved to Merton Abbey.

The portrait of Morris in his thirties was commissioned by his mother from Charles Fairfax Murray. Furniture includes a music cabinet with painted doors by William de Morgan (c. 1865–70) and an oak settle designed by Webb, with gilt gesso reliefs of putti. The 1885 'Woodpecker' tapestry is the only one Morris designed entirely by himself. Burne-Jones stained glass includes *St Cecilia* (1897), and cartoons for *Samuel and Isaiah* (1895) for the Albion Congregational Church, Ashton-under-Lyne, Lancashire.

In 1863 Morris joined the Socialist Democratic Federation, and later founded the Socialist League, which became the Hammersmith Socialist Society. His satchel, used to carry his socialist pamphlets, is on display alongside propagandist texts, the League's device designed by Walter Crane. In 1890 Morris founded the Kelmscott Press near his house, Kelmscott House, Hammersmith. Its most lavish publication, the magnificent 1896 *Works of Chaucer*, is on show. Furniture, pottery and other designs of the rising generation of architects, designers and craftsmen of the Arts and Crafts Movement, influenced by Morris, are exhibited, including work by William de Morgan, Ernest Gimson, Sidney Barnsley and C.F.A. Voysey.

First Floor
Up the broad, carved oak staircase at the rear of the Hall, with its pleasing full-length window overlooking the grounds, are rooms displaying Pre-Raphaelite and other paintings: Ford Madox Brown's study for the head of Chaucer for *Chaucer at the Court of Edward III*; Burne-Jones's *Stella Vespertina* (1880); *The Loving Cup* (1867), a watercolour by Rossetti; Walter Crane's *Love's Sanctuary* (1870); and Arthur Hughes' *Portrait of Mabel and Ruth Orrinsmith*, whose mother had been a decorative painter for Morris, Marshall, Faulkner & Company. Works by Brangwyn include *Old Houses, Taormina*; *Red Dahlias* (c. 1932); *The Swans* (c. 1920); and several etchings. A plain, rectilinear glazed cabinet designed by him contains examples of bold 1930s Brangwynware pottery.

On the other side of the staircase landing are furniture designs by Mackmurdo, including an attractive mirrored overmantel with a gilded wooden framework of recessed mirrored niches for the display of small ceramics. Mackmurdo (1851–1942) was the founder of the Century Guild, which aimed to elevate the status of the applied arts. Another member was Herbert Percy Horne, whose work is also displayed.

2 WILLOW ROAD
(National Trust)

2 Willow Road, Hampstead, NW3 1TH
Tel: 020-7435 6166; Infoline: 01494 755570; www.nationaltrust.org.uk
Open April–Oct Thur–Sat 12–5; March and Nov only Sat 12–5. Tours at 12,
1 and 2pm, self-guided 3–5pm. Also April–Oct on 1st Thur of the month,
tours at 5 and 6pm, self-guided 7–9pm (and not open 12–5)
Admission charge
Tube: Hampstead/ Station: Hampstead Heath
Map p. 379, 2D

2 Willow Road is the middle of three houses designed by the important and uncompromising Modernist architect Ernő Goldfinger, It was where he and his wife Ursula Blackwell, of the Crosse & Blackwell family, lived from 1939. Goldfinger died in 1987 and his wife in 1991, when the house and its contents were bequeathed to the National Trust. An important example of the modern movement, it is especially fortunate that the furniture and contents survive with it, which give a true sense of how the house was lived in.

The entranceway at 2 Willow Road.

Born in Budapest, Hungary in 1902, Goldfinger trained in Paris, where he was introduced to the use of reinforced concrete, and moved to London in 1934. Best known for his monumental, Brutalist high-rise buildings of the 50s and 60s (Alexander Fleming House, Balfron Tower and Trellick Tower, some of London's least-loved landmarks), the Willow Road houses are earlier, built in 1939 to much local opposition. Externally they form a narrow, rectangular block, of concrete with a flat roof, visually unified by horizontal lines. Internally they have large windows with views over Hampstead Heath. The main living area is on the second floor, open-plan with square proportions, vistas through framed spaces and carefully controlled colours and surfaces (smooth polished wooden floors, matt plywood, and textured concrete). The built-in furniture and other interior details, such as the raised open fire, were designed by Goldfinger. Items from his art collection on show include works by Henry Moore and Max Ernst. Goldfinger's designs for the house show spare interiors, but the contents show that the reality of living was less austere.

WIMBLEDON LAWN TENNIS MUSEUM

The All England Lawn Tennis Club, Church Road, SW19 5AE
Tel: 020-8946 6131; www.wimbledon.org
Open daily 10.30–5 (until 8pm during Championships, or close of play if earlier). During Championships open to ticket holders only
Admission charge
Tube: Southfields; Station: Wimbledon (from Waterloo)
Café and shop
Map p. 378, 4D

Originally established as part of the All England Lawn Tennis Club's centenary celebrations in 1977, the museum explores the history and development of tennis from its early antecedents in ancient Greece, via the medieval royal origins of the modern game and genteel disportment on Victorian lawns, to the multi-million dollar professional sport of today. There are reconstructions of the original Wimbledon men's dressing room and of a racquet-maker's shop, and a costume gallery recording the remarkable changes to tennis dress over the past 120 years. Photographic and other memorabilia of stars past and present can be seen, including Björn Borg's racquet. An audio-visual theatre shows highlights of great players in action. The museum can be seen as part of a tour of the All England Tennis Club, which takes you to Court I, the Winter Gardens, the Press Interview Room and the International Box of the world-famous Centre Court.

WIMBLEDON WINDMILL MUSEUM

Windmill Road, Wimbledon Common, London SW19 5NR
Tel: 020 8947 2825; www.wimbledonwindmillmuseum.org.uk
Open April–Oct Sat 2–5, Sun and bank holidays 11–5
Admission charge
Tube: Wimbledon (then bus 93)
Map p. 378, 4C

On the northern edge of Wimbledon common is the old village windmill, formerly one of many, built in 1817 by a local carpenter, Charles March. It is the only hollow-post flour-mill remaining in this country. In the 1860s it was converted into cottages and has undergone several restorations, in the 1890s, 1950s and most recently in 1999, when its sails were restored to working order. Original machinery is on show, and scale models of different types of mill. It was here that Lord Baden-Powell, founder of the international scouting movement, wrote *Scouting for Boys* (1908).

GLOSSARY OF SPECIAL TERMS

Anamorphic An image which appears distorted when viewed from the front, but which comes into line when viewed at a slant

Armillary sphere A globe made of a gradation of hoops, thus forming a sort of skeleton sphere

Architrave Lowest horizontal part of an entablature, coming below the cornice and the frieze, and directly above a window or door aperture; effectively a lintel

Astrolabe Instrument used in astronomy, for calculating the height of stars

Bawley-boat A fishing vessel native to the southeast of England

Boss Decorated block of wood or stone at the point where two or more vault-ribs meet

Breccia Type of sedimentary rock consisting of multiple fragments of geological detritus contained within a finer-grained mother rock

Canopic jar Pottery container with a lid shaped like an animal head, in which the entrails of the dead were placed in ancient Egyptian burials

Cartoon A full-size preparatory drawing for a painting or tapestry

Celadon Oriental porcelain glazed in pale olive-green

Champlevé Enamelling technique used in metalwork, whereby elements of a design are scraped hollow and then filled with powdered enamel before firing

Chasing The process of engraving ornament onto metalwork

Chatelaine Chain for carrying keys or a watch, which fastens to a woman's belt

Coffered Usually of ceilings: a system of inlaid square or rectangular panels let into the ceiling surface

Console Lateral support for a bracket or cornice, or, in the case of a console table, of a tabletop fixed against a wall. Usually shaped like a backwards S, with a scroll top and bottom

Corbel Block built into a wall and supporting the end of an arch or beam

Cove Concave space between the top of the wall and the ceiling

Crazing The random pattern of cracks that appears in the glaze on ceramics

Dado Interior wall surface above the skirting board, reaching to waist or shoulder height

Diaper brickwork Diamond or lozenge-shaped patterns formed by diagonal courses of darker bricks within a lighter brick wall

Diocletian window Half-moon window of three lights, named after a type of semi-circular aperture used in the Baths of Diocletian in Rome

Epistyle The element which sits above the columns: the architrave

Escapement Mechanism which controls the contact in a striking action of a clock or of the hammers of a piano

Exedra Semicircular walled or hedged enclosure in a garden

Flatware Tableware that lies flat—i.e. plates as opposed to bowls—and also cutlery

Flemish bond A system of laying bricks alternating end-on and side-on within each course. The English bond, by contrast, has a course of end-on bricks alternating with a course of side-on bricks

Gesso Gypsum mixed with a stiffening agent, used to prime surfaces for painting and gilding or for modelling

Grisaille Painting in monochrome, ie shades of grey and white

Grotesque Painted or stucco decoration in the style of the ancient Romans (found in the Golden House of Nero, in Rome, which was then underground, hence the name, from the word 'grotto'). The delicate ornamental decoration usually includes patterns of animals, birds, flowers and sphinxes against a light ground

Japanned Lacquered, in an imitation of an oriental style

Jonesian Pertaining to the architecture or theories of Inigo Jones

Knot garden Formal garden originating in Tudor times with a geometric design of interlacing dwarf hedges or shrubs, and beds planted with herbs and aromatic plants

Lustreware Ceramic that has had a metallic overglaze applied, giving it an iridescent sheen

Majolica Fired and glazed decorative earthenware; a type of faïence

Netsuke Miniature figurine of carved ivory, wood or horn used in traditional Japanese garb as a toggle to keep the small box used in lieu of a pocket attached to the sash

Newel Upright post supporting a handrail or banister at the top or bottom of a flight of stairs, or at the point where the stairs turn

Ormolu The name derives from the French *or moulou* (milled gold). Originally a film of gold applied to the surface of furniture mounts, it quickly began to be made of a zinc and copper alloy. The most noted British maker of ormolu finishes was Matthew Boulton

Palladian, Palladianism Style of architecture inspired by the work of Andrea Palladio (1508–80) whose churches and villas in the Veneto, northern Italy, express crisp mathematical forms and a classical purity of line. British exponents are Inigo Jones, Colen Campbell and William Kent. Palladianism had a political angle in that it was a reaction away from the Baroque, which flourished in the Stuart era and by association had overtones of Catholicism

Pallet Projecting part of a clock or watch which transmits movement from the escapement to the pendulum or wheel

Parcel gilt Partially gilded silver or wood

Passementerie Silver or gold braid or lace trimming

Pavonazzo Marble of a dark puce, often mottled, shade

Pendant A decorative element hanging from a roof or vault. In painting, a companion piece to one or more other works conceived by the artist as a related scheme

Peter-boat A small fishing craft

Piastraccia Thread-veined white marble quarried near the town of the same name in Italy

Pier glass Tall mirror filling the space between two windows

Porte-cochère Porch or canopy projecting from a doorway under which a coach can stand while passengers are getting in or alighting

Portland stone Pale-coloured limestone from Dorset, southern England, used for ashlar frontages, and much favoured by Sir Christopher Wren

Predella Rectangular strip of smaller devotional images affixed below the main altarpiece

Quadrant Navigational instrument used for calculating altitude. In shape it forms a quarter circle

Ragstone Coarse stone which is split into flat, many-sided segments and used for wall facing

Repoussé Relief-work in metal that has been achieved by hammering from the back, thus punching out the design

Reredos Screen behind an altar

Rubbed brick A special type of soft brick with a high sand content, easily rubbed into shape after cutting

Rusticated Masonry (especially ashlar cladding) that has been deliberately rough-hewn, with deep grooves between the joints, to give it a massy, monumental look

Samian pottery Fine, ruddy-brown earthenware made across the Roman empire

Sarsenet A type of very fine silk, or in later cases cotton

Scagliola A material originating in northern Italy, made from selenite (a type of gypsum), and used to imitate marble

Sextant Navigational instrument used to measure the angle between two objects and to calculate altitude. In shape it forms a sixth of a circle

Sgraffito Design in low relief, produced by scratching away the surface around the design to reveal colour beneath, the design itself remaining white

State Impression taken from an etching or engraving at a certain stage of its making

Stock brick Term used to describe any brick typical or characteristic of a specific locality, produced in large quantities

Stoneware A type of extremely hard pottery made of a mixture of stone and clay. During firing the stone content vitrifies

Strapwork Type of ornament popular in the 16th and 17th centuries, made up of long, narrow carved or moulded strips which cross, interweave and twine

Tempera A substance variously made from eggs, tree sap or gum, in which pigments are dissolved to create 'paint'. It was widely used before the introduction from the Netherlands of the technique of using oil for this purpose

Term Tapered plinth surmounted by a head and shoulders or head and torso. Similar to a herm, except that herms are topped by a head only

Trebuchet A siege engine used for projecting stones or other missiles

Triforium Aisled arcade above the nave and below the clerestory in a Romanesque or Gothic cathedral

Verdigris Greenish-coloured copper carbonate paint pigment

Vernis Type of imitation oriental lacquer, popular in the 18th century

Wainscot A panelled dado

Window pier The expanse of wall between two tall window apertures

INDEX

Museums and galleries featured in this book are indexed in bold upper case. All artists, architects and craftsmen whose works are mentioned are indexed too. There are also subject references (e.g. Porcelain) which take you to the major collections of work in that field. Prominent figures from history are referenced where they are mentioned in connection with museums, artists or artworks. Major works of art are given in italics. Italicised numbers are picture references. Bold numbers are major references.

A

Abbott, Lemuel, artist *176*, 179
Adam, Robert, architect 13, 174, 268, 329; (Kenwood) 145, 146, 148; (Osterley) 228–32, **230**; (Royal Society of Arts) 256, 258 (Syon) 285–86
Adam, James, architect 145, 146, 230, 256
Adam, John, architect 256
Adam, William, architect 256
Adams, Norman, artist 258
Aelst, Pieter Van, tapestry maker 116
African art 41, 45, 125
Agasse, Jacques-Laurent, artist 128
Aitchison, George, architect 156, 157
Aiton, William Townsend, gardener 50
Albermarle, first Duke of (*see Monck*)
Albert of Saxe-Coburg, Prince 49, 314
ALEXANDER FLEMING LABORATORY MUSEUM 11
Alexander, Daniel Asher, architect 175
Algardi, Alessandro, sculptor 194, 331, 339
ALL HALLOWS UNDERCROFT MUSEUM 11–12
Allan, Sir William, artist 17
Alleyn, Edward 70
Allingham, Helen, artist 51
Alma-Tadema, Sir Lawrence, artist 157, 330
Amati brothers, violin makers 247
Ambassadors, The 206
Ambler, Thomas, architect 336
Amies, Sir Hardy, dress designer 142
Amigoni, Jacopo, artist 143, 231, 260
Andras, Catherine, wax modeller 347
Andre, Carl, artist 289, 303

André, Dietrich Ernst, artist 171
Andreoli, Giorgio, ceramicist 339
Andrews, Michael, artist 296
Angelico, Fra', artist 202
Angerstein, John Julius 199
Anne of Denmark, Queen 179, 346
Anne, Queen 114, 141, 144, 145, 171, 290, 347
Anrep, Boris, mosaicist 200, 292
Antiquities (Assyrian) 37–38; (Egyptian) 34–37, *37*, 62, 234, 271, 321; (Greek) 32, 34, 271; (Roman) 34, 268, 269, 271
Antonello da Messina, artist 204
Appleyard, Fred, artist 246
APSLEY HOUSE 12–17, *13*
Arad, Ron, designer 332
Archer, James, artist 53
Arman, artist 302
Arms and Armour 82, 83, 130, 196, 309, 339
Army Museum (*see National Army Museum*)
Arnolfini Portrait 204
Arp, Jean, artist 301
Artari, Giuseppe, plasterer 228, 328
Arts and Crafts Movement 12, 96, 242–43, 348, 349–50
Arts Council Collection 120
Arup Associates, architects 130
Asloot, Denis van, artist 304
Assyrian art (*see Antiquities*)
Ast, van der, Balthasar, artist 207
Attwood, H. Carlton, sculptor 74
Auerbach, Frank, artist 22, 258, 296
Augenfeld, Felix, architect 90

INDEX BY AREA

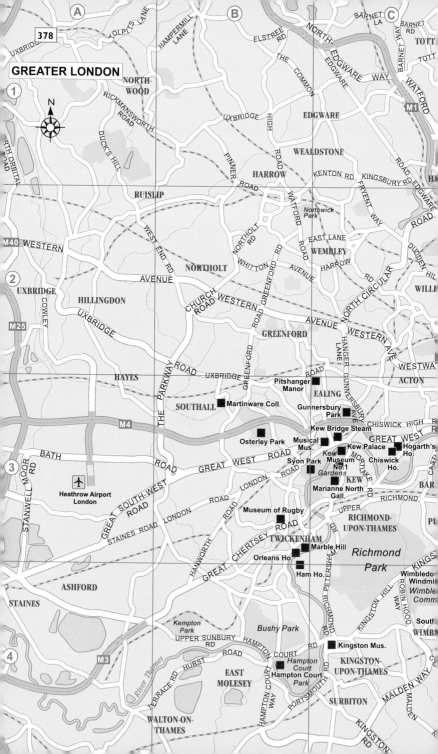